RUSSIAN AZERBAI

Russian Azerbaijan, 1905–1920 describes the rise of national identity among the Azerbaijanis – the Turkic-speaking Muslims of Russia's borderland with Iran – at the opening of the twentieth century. The principal focus is on the period from the Russian Revolution of 1905, when the Azerbaijanis began to articulate their national aspirations, until the establishment of the Soviet Azerbaijani Republic in 1920. The central theme of the book is the emergence of ideas, and then actions, that would create a new collective identity among the Muslims – a sense of nationality.

Azerbaijan was conquered by Russia in the early nineteenth century, and the book analyzes the impact of the conquest on Azerbaijani society, economy, and culture. Russian rule prepared the Azerbaijani community in many ways for the rise of a national movement. Then, from 1905 onward, Azerbaijan was subject to a succession of upheavals and crises that accelerated its political development: three revolutions in Russia; one each in neighboring Persia and Turkey; World War I; and two foreign occupations, Ottoman and British. As Azerbaijani aspirations grew, they found expression in political programs, each reflecting the fluid circumstances of the moment. The high watermark of the national movement came in 1918, with the proclamation of the Azerbaijani Republic.

The period of independence of this small country with its huge wealth of oil, without allies but with unfriendly neighbors, was beset by insecurity and internal dissension. The overthrow of the nationalist government and its replacement by the Soviet regime proved to be amazingly easy. But the native Communists to a degree continued the traditions of the national movement.

SOVIET AND EAST EUROPEAN STUDIES
Editorial Board
JULIAN COOPER   RON HILL   MICHAEL KASER
PAUL LEWIS   ALISTAIR MCAULEY   MARTIN MCCAULEY   FRED SINGLETON

The National Association for Soviet and East European Studies exists for the purpose of promoting study and research on the social sciences as they relate to the Soviet Union and the countries of Eastern Europe. The Monograph Series is intended to promote the publication of works presenting substantial and original research in the economics, politics, sociology, and modern history of the USSR and Eastern Europe.

Titles in print

Rudolf Bićanić *Economic Policy in Socialist Yugoslavia*
Galia Golan *Yom Kippur and After: The Soviet Union and the Middle East Crisis*
Maureen Perrie *The Agrarian Policy of the Russian Socialist-Revolutionary Party from its Origins through the Revolution of 1905–1907*
Paul Vyšný *Neo-Slavism and the Czechs 1898–1914*
Gabriel Gorodetsky *The Precarious Truce: Anglo-Soviet Relations 1924–27*
James Riordan *Sport in Soviet Society: Development of Sport and Physical Education in Russia and the USSR*
Gregory Walker *Soviet Book Publishing Policy*
Felicity Ann O'Dell *Socialisation through Children's Literature: The Soviet Example*
T. H. Rigby *Lenin's Government: Sovnarkom 1917–1922*
Stella Alexander *Church and State in Yugoslavia since 1945*
M. Cave *Computers and Economic Planning: The Soviet Experience*
Jozef M. van Brabant *Socialist Economic Integration: Aspects of Contemporary Economic Problems in Eastern Europe*
R. F. Leslie, ed. *The History of Poland since 1863*
M. R. Myant *Socialism and Democracy in Czechoslovakia 1945–1948*
Blair A. Ruble *Soviet Trade Unions: Their Development in the 1970s*
Angela Stent *From Embargo to Ostpolitik: The Political Economy of West German-Soviet Relations 1955–1980*
William J. Conyngham *The Modernisation of Soviet Industrial Management*
Jean Woodall *The Socialist Corporation and Technocratic Power*
Israel Getzler *Kronstadt 1917–1921: The Fate of a Soviet Democracy*
David A. Dyker *The Process of Investment in the Soviet Union*
S. A. Smith *Red Petrograd: Revolution in the Factories 1917–1918*
Saul Estrin *Self-management: Economic Theory and Yugoslav Practice*
Ray Taras *Ideology in a Socialist State: Poland 1956–83*

RUSSIAN AZERBAIJAN, 1905–1920

THE SHAPING OF NATIONAL IDENTITY IN A MUSLIM COMMUNITY

TADEUSZ SWIETOCHOWSKI

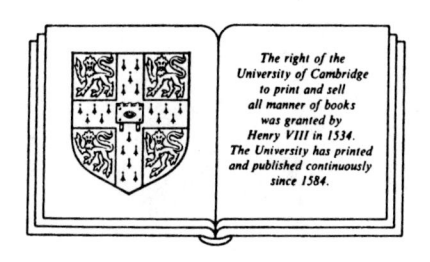

CAMBRIDGE UNIVERSITY PRESS
CAMBRIDGE
LONDON   NEW YORK   NEW ROCHELLE
MELBOURNE   SYDNEY

PUBLISHED BY THE PRESS SYNDICATE OF THE UNIVERSITY OF CAMBRIDGE
The Pitt Building, Trumpington Street, Cambridge, United Kingdom

CAMBRIDGE UNIVERSITY PRESS
The Edinburgh Building, Cambridge CB2 2RU, UK
40 West 20th Street, New York NY 10011-4211, USA
477 Williamstown Road, Port Melbourne, VIC 3207, Australia
Ruiz de Alarcón 13, 28014 Madrid, Spain
Dock House, The Waterfront, Cape Town 8001, South Africa

http://www.cambridge.org

© Cambridge University Press 1985

This book is in copyright. Subject to statutory exception
and to the provisions of relevant collective licensing agreements,
no reproduction of any part may take place without
the written permission of Cambridge University Press.

First published 1985
First paperback edition 2004

A catalogue record for this book is available from the British Library

Library of Congress Cataloguing in Publication data
Swietochowski, Tadeusz, 1934–
Russian Azerbaijan, 1905–1920.
(Soviet and East European studies)
Bibliography: p.
1. Azerbaijan S.S.R. – History.
I. Title.　II. Series.
DK511.A975S94　1985　947'.91　84-12719

ISBN 0 521 26310 7 hardback
ISBN 0 521 52245 5 paperback

Contents

Preface	*page* vii
Maps	xi
1 A century of Russian rule	1
2 The 1905 Revolution and Azerbaijani political awakening	37
3 The era of war and revolutions: ideologies, programs, and political orientations	64
4 Transition to nationhood: in quest of autonomy	84
5 Transition to nationhood: Transcaucasian federalism	105
6 The Azerbaijani nation-state	129
7 The coming of Soviet power	165
Conclusion	191
Abbreviations	195
Notes	197
Bibliography	226
Index	247

Preface

This book deals with Russia's borderland region inhabited by the Azerbaijanis, Turkic-speaking Muslims, a large portion of whom live across the frontier in Iran. The discussion centers on the emergence of ideas and the subsequent efforts aimed at the creation of a new collective identity among the local Muslims – a sense of nationality. Chronologically, this work focuses on the period from the Russian Revolution of 1905, when the Azerbaijanis began to articulate their national aspirations, until the establishment of the Soviet Azerbaijani Republic in 1920. By way of historical background, the discussion extends to major issues of Russian rule in the preceding century.

As opposed to the case of their Armenian and Georgian neighbors, the modern history of the Azerbaijanis, the largest national group in Transcaucasia, has not been a subject of a monograph in any Western language, although some works on the region's history by American scholars discuss in part pre-1920 Azerbaijan. Also, the books on Russia's Muslim community deal in part with the Azerbaijanis, who in some respects led it in the advancement toward modernity.

By contrast, the Soviet historical writing on Azerbaijan is massive. In its various periods, Soviet historiography has exhibited deep differences in the scope and treatment of particular issues, yet generally it has tended to overemphasize some and downgrade other aspects of the Azerbaijanis' past. There has always been an excessive concentration on studies of the working-class movement, which consisted largely of non-native immigrants in the cosmopolitan enclave of Baku. Although Soviet authors stress the existence of a distinct Azerbaijani national identity reaching far back into the past, they give little consideration to the twentieth-century national movement. Even more striking in the Soviet approach to Azerbaijani history is the inclination to obscure the heritage of Islam as well as the significance of the centuries-long links with Persia. Of the indisputable achievements of Soviet historiography are the nonpolitical studies of Azerbaijani economy, culture, and intellectual life, centered more on the nineteenth than twentieth century. These excellent works of scholarship form the building blocks with which, one may wish, Soviet Azerbaijani historians will produce the synthesis of this crucial period of their country's past.

The mass of Soviet publications – books, articles, and collections of documents – account for the largest part of the source material for this book. The primary sources came, however, from depositories outside the Soviet Union, notably from the Public Records Office of Great Britain and the National Archives of the United States. All translations, unless otherwise indicated, are mine.

My research and writing were greatly facilitated by a fellowship from the Woodrow Wilson International Center for Scholars. Moreover, in the frequent seminars at the Wilson Center I was able to discuss various methodological aspects of my work. I take this opportunity to express my thanks to the Wilson Center, its subdivision the Kennan Institute for Advanced Russian Studies, their respective staffs, and the fellows of the 1980–1981 group. Another scholarly body that collectively contributed to the progress in this work was the Columbia University Seminar for Studies in the History and the Culture of the Turks, to which I presented some of the results of my research. I am grateful for comments and remarks made by the members of that seminar. The preparation of the manuscript was made possible with the assistance of my wife, Marie Lukens, who, without sparing her severe criticism, with patience and goodwill participated in every stage of making the text ready for publication. To her I dedicate this book.

A note on transliteration: The Azerbaijani language in the course of the twentieth century has been successively written in three different alphabets: the Arabic, the Latinized script of the early Soviet period, and the Cyrillic-based characters currently in use

Preface

in the Azerbaijani Soviet Republic. Rather than convert all Azerbaijani words into the present-day strongly phonetic orthography and then transliterate them, I have chosen in this book on history to use separate transliteration systems for the Arabic and Cyrillic alphabets. The reader may therefore find the same word transliterated in different ways, though the difference is not beyond recognition. The accompanying table of Azerbaijani Cyrillic characters indicates their Latin-alphabet equivalents. Both transliteration systems are based on E. Allworth, *Nationalities of the Soviet East: Publications and Writing Systems – A Bibliographical Directory and Transliteration Tables for Iranian and Turkic-Language Publications* (New York: Columbia University Press, 1971). The transliteration of Russian, Ottoman, and Persian terms and names is based on the Library of Congress systems.

A more complex problem presented itself in the spelling of Azerbaijani surnames. The innovation of using surnames came to Azerbaijan with Russian rule, and consequently they often assumed Russian endings – as in Väzirov, Taghiyev, Huseynov, and so on. Then, some persons were known under both Russianized and the native-sounding versions of their names. Others, having emigrated to Turkey, had their names Turkicized: Rustambäkov was changed to Rustambeyli, Khasmammädow to Hasmehmetli, Aghayev became famous as Agaoğlu. This book will use only the name under which a given person began his public life in Azerbaijan regardless of any other version of his name, although such a version might be indicated in parentheses. Still, an absolute consistency could not be achieved. For example, Mirza Fath ᶜAli Akhundov, the Azerbaijani best known in the West, will be referred to as Akhundzadä, the form of his name that has been used for a century in publications outside of Russia.

A note on dating: Dates before February 1, 1918 referring to events in Russia or Transcaucasia are according to the Julian calendar, which was thirteen days behind the Gregorian calendar of the West in the twentieth century and twelve days behind in the nineteenth century. All dates after February 1, 1918, are according to the Gregorian calendar.

Azerbaijani Cyrillic characters

Azerbaijani Cyrillic	Latin equivalent	Azerbaijani Cyrillic	Latin equivalent
Aa	a	Өө	ö
Бб	b	Пп	p
Вв	v	Рр	r
Гг	g	Сс	s
Ғғ	gh	Тт	t
Дд	d	Уу	u
Ее	ye*, e†	Үү	ü
Әә	ä	Фф	f
Жж	zh	Хх	kh
Зз	z	һһ	h
Ии	i	Цц	ts
Йй/Јј	y‡	Чч	ch
Кк	k	Ҹҹ	j
Ҝҝ	q	Шш	sh
Лл	l	Ыы	ï
Мм	m	Ээ	ë
Нн	n	Юю	yu
Оо	o	Яя	ya

* initially. † elsewhere. ‡ J replaced Й in 1959.

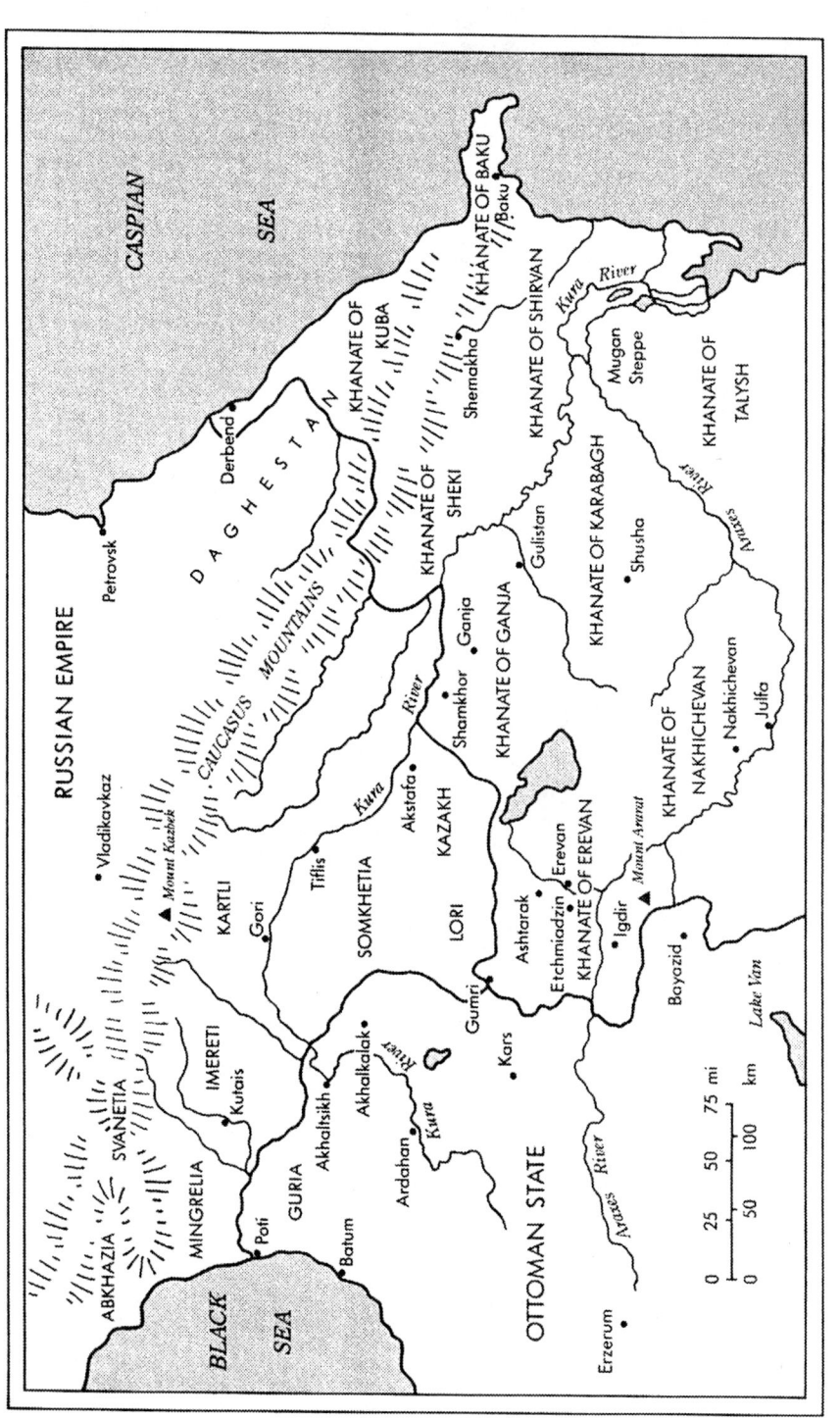

Transcaucasia in the early nineteenth century.

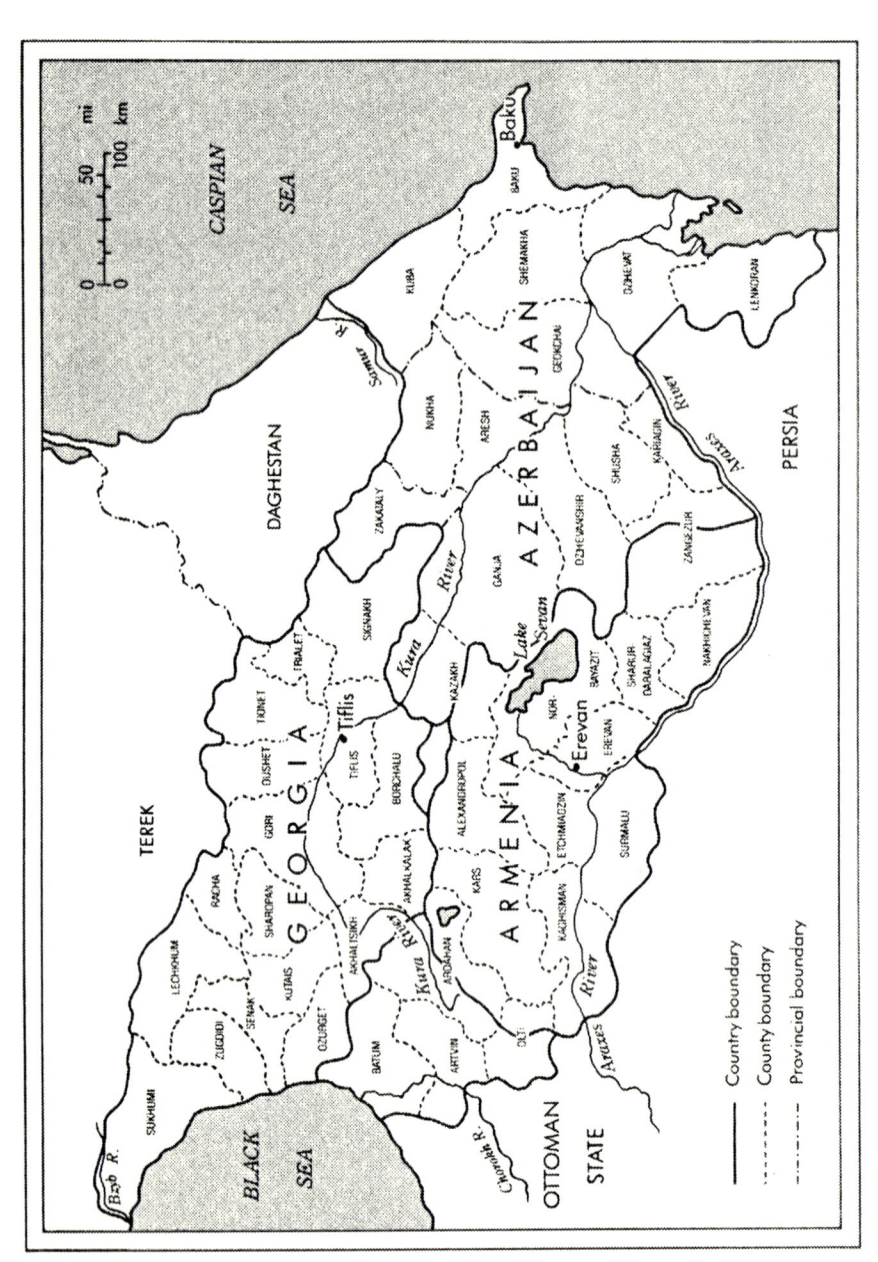

The Transcaucasian republics, June 1919.

Baku and its environs.

1
A century of Russian rule

Azerbaijan is the name for the stretch of land contained by the southern slopes of the Caucasus Mountains on the north, the Caspian Sea on the east, and the Armenian highlands in the west: In the south its natural boundary is less distinct, and Azerbaijan merges here with the Iranian plateau.

From the time of ancient Media and Achaemenid Persia, Azerbaijan was drawn into the orbit of Iran. One theory for the etymology of its name gives a derivation from Atropatenes, a Persian satrap in the time of Alexander the Great. Another, more popular explanation traces its origin to the Persian word *azer*,"fire" – hence *Azerbaijan* "Land of Fire," because of its numerous Zoroastrian temples, their fires fed by the plentiful local sources of oil. Azerbaijan retained its Iranian character even after the conquest of the region by Arabs and conversion to Islam in the mid-seventh century; only some four centuries later, with the influx of the Oghuz Turks under the Seljuk dynasty, did the country acquire a large proportion of Turkic inhabitants. The original population became fused with the immigrant nomads, and the Persian language was gradually supplanted by a Turkic dialect that evolved into a distinct "Azeri" or Azerbaijani language.

After the thirteenth-century Mongol invasions, Azerbaijan became part of the empire of Hulagu and his successors, the Il-Khans, then passed under the rule of the Turkmens who founded the rival Qara Qoyunlu and Aq-Qoyunlu states. Concurrently, in the fifteenth century, there flourished a native Azerbaijani state of Shirvan shahs. In the early years of the next century Azerbaijan became the power base of another native family, the Safavids, who through a vigorous policy of centralization built a new Persian kingdom on the foundation of the Shi'a branch of Islam. The Safavid dynasty lasted for more than two hundred years; its rule ended in 1722, having been undermined by internal strife and the Afghan invasion.[1]

Azerbaijani khanates and the conquest by Russia

In 1747 Nadir Shah, the strong ruler who had established his hold over Persia eleven years earlier, was assassinated in a palace coup, and his empire fell into chaos and anarchy. These circumstances effectively terminated the suzerainty of Persia over Azerbaijan, where local centers of power emerged in the form of indigenous principalities, independent or virtually so, inasmuch as some maintained tenuous links to Persia's weak Zand dynasty.

Thus began a half-century-long period of Azerbaijani independence, albeit in a condition of deep political fragmentation and internal warfare. Most of the principalities were organized as khanates, small replicas of the Persian monarchy, including Karabagh, Sheki, Ganja, Baku, Derbent, Kuba, Nakhichevan Talysh, and Erivan in northern Azerbaijan and Tabriz, Urmi, Ardabil, Khoi, Maku, Maragin, and Karadagh in its southern part.[2] Many of the khanates were subdivided into *mahal*s (regions), territorial units inhabited by members of the same tribe, reflecting the fact that the residue of tribalism was still strong.[3] An outgrowth of the medieval institution of *iqta* (state land grant) was the state ownership of most of the land. Plots were distributed as nonhereditary grants to *bäy*s and *agha*s for services rendered to the ruler, the khan.[4]

Besides the khanates there existed even smaller principalities, sultanates, which usually ended up as dependencies of the former. Some of the khanates expanded at the cost of their neighbors or reduced the latter to the status of clients. In the northern part of Azerbaijan the khanates of Sheki, Karabagh, and Kuba became the most powerful.

Azerbaijan lacked a tradition of unity within an autochthonous, independent statehood, and in the second half of the eighteenth century such statehood could have arisen only through

1. A century of Russian rule

the vigorous expansion of one of the khanates. Soviet Azerbaijani historiography devotes special attention to the wars of the ambitious Fath ᶜAli Khan of Kuba, perceiving in them an attempt at the unification of the country. Fath ᶜAli indeed extended his control over large areas of Azerbaijan, but his aspirations were even higher: He was intent on repeating the feat of the Safavids, who had used Azerbaijan as a base for imposing their power over all Persia.[5] In any case, Fath ᶜAli's schemes came to grief in 1784 when the Russian armies operating against Turkey from the Caucasus Mountains posed a threat to his rear guard. Russia had grown concerned that the expansion of Kuba would create an undesirably strong state in what it saw as its future sphere of influence. Fath ᶜAli found himself forced to relinquish most of his conquests.

The pattern of inconclusive wars continued, the khans making and breaking alliances among themselves as well as with the neighboring powers of Russia and Turkey. Toward the end of the eighteenth century, as the Ottoman state sunk deeper into decline, the shadow that Russia cast over Transcaucasia lengthened ominously.

Russian interest in the region was of long standing and had diverse motivation: the lure of the lucrative trade with Persia and Asiatic Turkey; the desire for local raw materials such as silk, cotton, and copper; the drive for the colonization of sparsely populated lands. But the overriding attraction was the strategic value of the Transcaucasian isthmus.[6] Russia's military involvement here reached back to the time of Peter the Great, whose Persian Expedition of 1722 was aimed at extending the Russian presence in the direction of the Indian Ocean. The Russians had seized a strip of the Caspian coast down to Lenkoran, but their first venture into Azerbaijan ended in 1735 when Nadir Shah rolled back the frontier to the Terek River.[7]

Russia's southward advance resumed, on a more extensive scale, under Catherine II (1763–1796). After the seizure of the Crimea and the Kuban River territory in 1785, most of the Caucasus range fell under Russian administration. By that time Russia had already begun to plan an active role in the politics of the Transcaucasian states. Insecure on his throne, the Georgian king of Kakheti-Kartli, Irakli II, was the first to sign a treaty obtaining Russian protection in 1783.[8] His example was followed by Solomon I of Imeretia and Murtazali, the Daghestani ruler of Tarku. In due course hegemony turned into outright conquest, the latter stage beginning in 1801 when Tsar Alexander I (1800–1825) proclaimed the creation of the Georgian *guberniia* (province) consisting of the lands of the former Kakheti-Kartli kings. The new province also included the sultanates of Kazakh and Shamshadil, the first of the Azerbaijani territories to the incorporated by Russia.[9]

To secure a strategic hold over Georgia the Russian commander of the Caucasus, General P. Tsitsianov, deemed it necessary to extend his control over the Azerbaijani khanates in the direction of the Caspian coast in the east and the Araxes river in the south. Primarily military considerations drove him to carve out for Russia the northern part of Azerbaijan. Technically, Tsitsianov's goal was not incorporation, but rather the imposition of treaties whereby the khanates would accept submission to Russia, a form of vassalage. In some cases, namely Karabagh, Shirvan, and Sheki, this acceptance was affected peacefully. The terms of the resultant treaties guaranteed the khans unrestricted authority in the internal affairs of their states and the right of succession. In return, they agreed to admit Russian garrisons, to pay tribute – in cash or in kind, which included silk, – and, most importantly, to accede to the Pax Russica by surrendering their rights to wage war and conduct foreign policy.[10] Toward those khans who were reluctant to follow suit Tsitsianov applied persuasion by force of arms. In 1804 his troops laid siege to Ganja, where in a memorable show of resistance the local khan, Jävad, was killed in battle. Jävad's realm was incorporated forthwith into Russia as an *uezd* (county) of Elizavetpol, the new Russian name given to Ganja in honor of the Tsar's wife.[11]* Another act of defiance to Tsitsianov's tactics of intimidation was the prolonged fighting in the mountainous area of Jar-Belokan. Tsitsianov, murdered in 1806 upon his arrival in Baku to demand the submission of the khanate, has passed into history as the chief architect of the Russian conquest of Transcaucasia.[12]

An additional complication Russia faced in carrying out this

---

*The name *Elizavetpol* never found acceptance among the Azerbaijanis, who continued to call the town *Ganja*. We will generally use the name *Ganja* here except when context requires the use of the official Russian name.

conquest was the challenge of Persia. The new dynasty founded by the Qajar tribe, which had put an end to the long internal strife in the kingdom, was now poised to contest Russia for sovereignty of what had once been Persia's northern marches. In 1804 an army under Abbas Mirza, the son of the king, Fath ᶜAli Shah, with reinforcements from the khans of Erivan and Nakhichevan, moved against the Russians.[13] Defeated promptly at Etchmiadzin, the Persians withdrew, then reappeared in the spring of 1806, arousing an insurrectionary fever in Karabagh and Sheki, both of which had recently accepted Russian overlordship. The war continued for several years, although at a sluggish pace with the Russians suppressing intermittent uprisings as well as subjugating the khanates of Baku and Kuba (in 1806) and Talysh (in 1809). Only in 1812, after ending the concurrent war with Turkey, did they pursue vigorous fighting against Persia. The brief and successful Russian campaign of 1812 was concluded with the Treaty of Gulistan, signed the same year. The treaty's provisions concerning Azerbaijan ratified the status quo resulting from the Russian military presence, and Fath ᶜAli Shah renounced his sovereignty over the khanates of Karabagh, Baku, Sheki, Shirvan, Kuba, and Derbent. The shah's claims to the northern Azerbaijani khanates were dismissed on the ground that they had been independent long before their occupation by Russia. This amounted to the first and only recognition of Azerbaijani independence, albeit in the past tense.[14]

The Gulistan settlement proved to be merely the end of the first round in the duel of the two powers for the prize of Transcaucasia. Thirteen years later, the conflict flared up anew when Fath ᶜAli Shah sent his army across the Gulistan Treaty border. In May 1826 the Persians occupied Lenkoran, Shemakha, and Nukha and besieged the Russians in Shusha. Abbas Mirza, once again at the head of the troops, entered northern Azerbaijan expecting wide support from a population disgruntled from a quarter-centry of Russian domination. In essence, the Qajars hoped to appear champions of the rights of Azerbaijani khans whom the Russians had driven into exile. They were also counting on the sympathies of those rulers who only nominally retained a tenuous power and felt humiliated as vassals of the tsar.

Indeed, the khan of Talysh immediately started a rebellion against the Russian garrison, and in Karabagh, Shirvan, and

Sheki the population enthusiastically welcomed the returning khans or their descendants.[15] Nonetheless, in the Azerbaijan of that period it was not unusual to find natives fighting on the side of the Russians, driven by the desire for booty or following the mercenary tradition of a people who had for centuries supplied soldiers for the shah's elite forces. There also surfaced a growing current of pro-Russian orientation among some *bäys* and *aghas* who were faced with a choice between subjection to Russia and the ruthlessness of the Qajars.[16]

The Russians, chronically short of manpower in Transcaucasia, were thus able to draw upon local resources to fill the ranks of their militias and auxiliaries. Even though Georgians and Armenians were considered more reliable than Muslims, still in the first Persian war a voluntary "Tatar" cavalry detachment was formed for the defense of Kazakh.* The volunteers remained in the service of the tsar, and by 1810 additional Muslim units were raised. In the second war with Persia, the same Kazakh contingent assisted the Russians in their victory at Shamkochrai. Another "Tatar" squadron distinguished itself in the Battle of Ganja, which turned out to be decisive for the campaign.[17]

After the Persian defeat at Ganja, Tsar Nicholas I (1825–1855) replaced General A.P. Ermolov with the new commander in chief of the Caucasus, I. Paskevich, who brought the war to a victorious end when his forces pushed as far south as Tabriz. With the road to Tehran wide open, Fath 'Ali Shah sued for peace, and on February 10, 1828 the Treaty of Turkmanchai ended the war. As the Russians were facing the prospect of another conflict with Turkey, they tempered somewhat the harshness of their terms. With regard to Azerbaijan, the treaty was largely a restatement of the Gulistan provisions, but the shah was forced additionally to cede to Russia the khanates of Erivan and Nakhichevan and the area of Ordubad.[18]

The Treaty of Turkmanchai, which also opened a greatly weakened Persia to Russian commercial and political influences, closed the period of Russo–Persian rivalry in Transcaucasia. Persia fully acknowledged Russian domination over the region, and

---

*The term *Tatar* was customarily used by Russians to refer to various Turkic-speaking peoples of Russia. As a misnomer with regard to the Azerbaijanis, it will be put hereafter in quotation marks.

1. A century of Russian rule

the third, more distant party to the contest, Turkey, would soon make a similar concession. The war between Russia and Turkey, which had begun within a few months of the Turkmanchai settlement, quickly turned into a series of Ottoman defeats, both on the Balkan and the Caucasus fronts. This time the Russians enlisted the Azerbaijanis on the even larger scale, capitalizing on the antagonism of the Shi^{c}ites toward the Sunni branch of Islam which the Ottoman State symbolized.[19] At the Battle of Erzerum, it was the charge of the Karabagh Regiment that decided the day. The impressive military feats of the Azerbaijanis opened for them careers in the tsarist army, an advantage the Christians of Transcaucasia already enjoyed. In the words of the nineteenth-century traveler and historian Arminius Vambery, the Muslims "adopted the habit of attending the Russian military schools and the Alikhanovs, Taghirovs and Nazirovs became rivals of the Lazarovs, Melikovs and other Armenians."[20]

The war with Turkey, which ended in the Treaty of Adrianople (September 1829), won for Russia the eastern coast of the Black Sea, including Akhaltsik. By pushing its frontier to the southwest, Russia firmly established its strategic control over Transcaucasia.

The treaties of 1828 and 1829 confirmed the fact of the Russian conquest and sanctioned the permanent division of Azerbaijani territory into two parts – the larger, approximately two-thirds, remaining with Persia and the smaller annexed by Russia. Some half-million Azerbaijani-speaking Muslims passed for the first time under the rule of a European power, and henceforth the path of their history would take a different course from that of their ethnic brothers in Persia.[21]

The population of the Russian-held part of Azerbaijan aside from the Azerbaijanis, included several ethnic minority groups: the Lezghians in the northernmost areas, the Persians along the Caspian coast and especially in Talysh, the Kurdish and Turkicmens nomads in the south, and in Karabagh, Armenians, whose number rose dramatically after the Russian conquests as a result of their mass immigration from Persia and Turkey. Following the Turkmanchai peace, Nicholas I decreed the formation of an Armenian *oblast'* (district) comprising the territories of the khanates of Erivan and Nakhichevan, where the concentration of the immigrants was particularly heavy.[22]

The Turkic-speaking Muslims of Russian Azerbaijan, commonly called Shirvanis, differed from those of the Persian part in one essential respect: There was a comparatively large proportion of Sunnis among them. The Russian estimates of the 1830s, although based on incomplete data, show that the ratio of the Shi'ites to Sunnis was almost even, with a slight edge in favor of the latter.[23] While the sectarian distribution did not correspond with the political divisions into khanates, the Sunnis formed a majority in the northern and western areas of the country, subject to religious influences from the mountainous citadel of Sunnism, Daghestan.

The same roughly 50:50 ratio still appears in the statistics of 1848, but figures for the 1860s indicate that the proportion of Sunnis had markedly declined. It stabilized subsequently at the level by which the Shi'ite Twelvers of the Jafarite rite held a clear majority of 2:1 among the population as a whole. The decrease in the proportionate strength of the Sunni element was the result of their emigration to Turkey, a trickle that turned into a torrent after the final suppression of Daghestan by Russia.[24]

The Shi'ite–Sunni split ran deep and it found its reflection in Azerbaijani attitudes toward the nineteenth-century Russian wars. The tsardom was able to make use of the Shi'ites against Turkey not only in 1828 but also in 1853–1855 as well as against the anti-Russian resistance spreading from Daghestan. By contrast, the Sunnis showed signs of restiveness at the time of Russo–Ottoman conflicts, tending to give support – sometimes armed support – to the Daghestanis; finally, many of them demonstrated their disposition by joining the outflow of Muslim emigrants from Russia.

In Daghestan a *ghazavat* (roughly, crusade) against Russia had been under way since the late eighteenth century, but an additional stimulus that reinvigorated the struggle of the mountaineers there was the emergence of the religious–social movement of Muridism, an outgrowth of the Sufi Naqshbandi order. From 1834 on, the *imam* (religious leader) of the Murids was Shamil, an outstanding warlord who waged the *ghazavat* on a hitherto unprecedented scale. In the first years after assuming leadership, he inflicted a series of humiliating defeats upon the Russians and pushed their lines back to where they had been a half-century before.[25]

The echoes of the Daghestani war resounded in a wave of insurgency that swept parts of Azerbaijan in the post-Turkmanchai decade, the last armed challenge to the Russian conquest. As reported by a colonel of the gendarmerie, Viktorov, "in some localities large groups numbering on occasions up to thousands of men could be gathered within two or three days on Shamil's orders."[26] The same report pointed out the effects of the Murids' successes on the attitudes of the population: "Truth and conscience compel me to inform your Excellency that the feelings of fear instilled in the inhabitants by our victorious armies are disappearing as the result of six or seven years of unsuccessful fighting."[27]

Of the four local Azerbaijani uprisings in the 1830s, three broke out in areas with substantial Sunni populations and were directly or otherwise under the influence of the Murids. The descent of the Daghestani warriors into the Jar-Belokan *jamaat*s (agricultural communities) sparked repeated popular revolts in the years 1830–1832.[28] In what became the largest of Azerbaijani insurrections, some twelve thousand inhabitants of Kuba took to arms in 1837 on the call of Shamil, who urged them to express their grievances by fighting the Infidel.[29] Their rebellion was put down with the assistance of the native militia from the predominantly Shi'ite Shirvan. The next year, in Sheki, the entry of the armed bands of the Daghestanis again stirred the population to an uprising, but this subsided as soon as the mountaineers withdrew.[30]

Among the Shi'ites, a major insurrection broke out in the heavily Persian-populated Talysh, where in 1831 the former khan, Mir Hasan, succeeded in arousing many inhabitants to an attack on the Russian garrison. Others natives, however, took the side of the Russians, and in the end Mir Hasan had to retreat across the Persian border.[31]

Uncoordinated and local in scope, these violent outbreaks of disaffection lacked any clear-cut ethnic or social content that might have been a source of sustaining power. Still, they made their impact felt on the increasingly frantic experiments to which the tsardom resorted in its search for a policy to consolidate its hold over Transcaucasia.

The breakup of the khanates and administrative reforms

With the onset of Russian rule there appeared in Azerbaijan the unmistakable features of colonialism. Azerbaijani territory became a military outpost controlling the strategic corridor for the Russian penetration of Persia, a process that progressed apace after the Turkmanchai Treaty of 1828. Azerbaijan was viewed as a potential source of raw materials and as an area suitable for the resettlement of populations from other parts of the Russian Empire. Indeed, the very word *colony* with reference to Transcaucasia gained currency among tsarist officials who had studied the example of French rule in Algeria. The tsar's finance minister, T. E. Kankrin, defined the term and elaborated on its implications for the policy he recommended: "When Transcaucasia is described as a colony," he wrote in a memorandum to Nicholas I in 1827,

the assumption is made that the government would stop short of incorporating this region into the state outright. It is not expected that Transcaucasia would be made into a part of Russia or the Russian nation, insofar as its way of life is concerned; rather, these lands should be left in their position of Asiatic provinces, but hopefully governed more efficiently than in the past.[32]

The aftermath of the conquest saw few and limited modifications in the way the Azerbaijanis had been ruled, and cases of the abolition of khanates, such as Ganja or Baku, were quite exceptional. At first, the tsardom preferred to adopt the indigenous governmental structures to its own needs. The khanates of Talysh, Sheki, Karabagh, Shirvan, and Nakhichevan, the Jar-Belokan *jamaat*s, and the sultanate of Ilusiy were all left intact. In allowing a khan or sultan to retain much of his powers, the Russians' prime consideration was either his loyalty to Russia or his political usefulness to the Russian authorities through his influence over the population. Moreover, the preservation of a khanate's administrative machinery alleviated the strain on the scant supply of Russian officials available and held a promise of financial savings.[33] Only gradually and rather inconsistently did the military government take to disposing of the khans' regimes altogether. General A.P. Ermolov, who in 1816 became the com-

1. A century of Russian rule

mander of the Caucasus, viewed the khanates with suspicion as a disruptive and potentially pro-Persian factor.[34] While paying lip service to the validity of the treaties, he awaited the opportunity to liquidate one khanate after another by resorting to pretexts and subterfuges. He barred the rights of the successor to the khan of Sheki, Ismail, and in 1818 proclaimed his domains a Russian *oblast'*. The next year the khanate of Shirvan was abolished, its ruler Mustafa Khan having been forced to flee to Persia to avoid arrest on conspiracy charges. Similar tactics that Ermolov used against the khan of Karabagh, Mahdi Qulu, produced the same result.[35] The khanate of Talysh, on the other hand, continued its nominal existence until 1844, although it had passed under the military government in 1826 when its ruler had defected to the invading Persians. Likewise, the khanate of Nakhichevan and the sultanate of Ilusiy survived until the same late date. The last of the Muslim principalities in the region, the Daghestani shamkhalate of Tarku, was abolished in 1860.

The removal of a khan did not necessarily amount to a departure from traditional forms of government. During the 1820s in Azerbaijan seven Russian provinces – Baku, Derbent, Sheki, Karabagh, Shirvan, and Talysh – were created, each governed by a *nachal 'nik* (military commander). The new administrative units were in essence khanates without khans. Their boundaries, in most cases, corresponded to those of the former principalities, and their Russian commanders ruled in accordance with local laws and customs. This system of government, known officially as "military–popular" (*voenno–narodnyi*), did not affect the status of native officials at low and intermediate levels so long as they were not objectionable to the Russians. The territorial subdivision into *mahals* and the courts of Shari'a (divinely inspired law of Islam) remained intact, and Persian continued to be the official language of the judiciary and local administration.[36]

Likewise, the perogatives of the supreme authority in the province, the commander, closely resembled those of a khan, although he lacked the power of passing death sentences or ordering the cutting off of ears and noses. "The rights, honor and property of hundreds of thousands of inhabitants depend on a commander's whim," wrote the Senators E. I. Mechnikov and P. I. Kutaisov after their inspection tour of Transcaucasia in 1834. Their report also commented on widespread abuses of power, adding that the commanders "set an example of breaking the law rather than observing it."[37]

This rampant corruption was accompanied by a brutality for which the Russian military government personnel became notorious, and both loomed large among the causes of the unrest in the 1830s. Within the tsarist bureaucracy the unsettled condition of the Russian domains in the Caucasus and beyond fueled a controversy on the definition of a long-range administrative policy. Concerning the question of how to govern these domains, there emerged two schools of thought: One, more pragmatic, favored quasi-autonomous regionalism with implicit accommodation to indigenous traditions and interests; the other, more rigid, emphasized the need for centralization and eventual Russification. With regard to the Muslim parts of Transcaucasia, the first school counseled proceeding at a slow pace in abolishing features of the khanate past, while the second aimed at speedy integration of the region into the Russian state.[38] The echoes of this dispute would henceforth affect every shift in Russia's Transcaucasian policy for decades to come.

In an apparent victory for the integrationists, the 1841 reform of Baron P. V. Hahn dismantled the military government, thereby obliterating all vestiges of the khanates. In its place a uniform civil administration was introduced, and the seven provinces were replaced with *uezds* (counties), their borders drawn without regard to the former khanates' territories. The reform also did away with the residual tribalism of the *mahals*, superseding them with the smallest territorial subdivisions, the *uchasteks*. This act, which in one stroke put an end to the age-old fragmentation of Azerbaijan, at the same time resulted in a massive dismissal of native officials.[39] Furthermore, in the spirit of full integration, there followed an attempt at modifying the socioeconomic structure of the country. Additional ordinances provided for the confiscation of some *tül* holdings – the land grants awarded in the past to *bäy*s and *agha*s – with the view of redistributing them to Russian settlers.[40]

The main effect of Hahn's reforms was not only bureaucratic confusion but also an upsurge in popular disaffection. New outbreaks of insurgency spread in the Caucasus Mountains, and Shamil stepped up his fighting in the years 1841–1842. The minister of war, A. I. Chernishevski, hurriedly dispatched to

1. A century of Russian rule 13

Transcaucasia, advised a more conciliatory approach to the Muslim landholders and urged that the *tüls* be "left as they were."[41] A governmental commission went a step further in its recommendation that "it would be desirable to turn them [*bäys* and *aghas*] into a Muslim upper estate through which the government could exert influence on the inhabitants in accordance with its objectives."[42]

Within less than a year the Hahn reforms were scuttled, and with the pendulum swinging the opposite way yet another reorganization took place that resulted in the establishment of the viceroyalty of the Caucasus. In 1845 all military and civil responsibilities in the region were removed from the authority of the central government departments and vested in the viceroy, who reported directly to the tsar. Count (later Prince) Mikhail S. Vorontsov, a man of vast political and administrative experience, became the first viceroy of the Caucasus.[43]

Vorontsov's main task was to achieve the pacification of the province. His preferred policy was the cooptation of the native elites rather than Russification and integration. Thus in Azerbaijan, where the impoverished *bäys* and *aghas* had seen their aristocratic status eroding, he advocated upgrading their position. On the viceroy's recommendation, Nicholas I issued the December Rescript of 1846, which formally bestowed the hereditary and inalienable rights of the Muslim landholders to the *tül* lands. A centuries-old Azerbaijani institution, legal state ownership of most of the land came to an end with the massive transfer of property titles into private hands. The rescript was intended to raise the *bäys* and *aghas* to the equivalent of the Russian *dvorianie* (gentry), and to provide safeguards for the corporate rights of the Muslim "privileged estate": Their lands could be sold only to other members of the same estate. The benefits received by one social group were thus accompanied by a deterioration in the status of another: In what amounted to a form of serfdom, if a mild one, the tsar imposed on the peasantry specified obligations and dues owed the landlords.[44]

In addition to the provisions of the rescript, the tsardom, acting through the viceroy, took measures to reinforce its newly formed alliance with the Muslim gentry, significantly by providing easy access to civil service careers to "all sons of *bäys* and *aghas* who can present proofs of noble birth."[45] The administrative machinery, after one more reorganization in 1846, was able to absorb the subsequent influx of native officials. This time all Transcaucasia was divided into four *guberniias* – Tiflis, Kutais, Shemakha, and Derbent, – an arrangement that in one stroke created a large number of civil service vacancies.[46] For those of the "privileged estate" who desired to obtain qualifications for the civil service, the viceroyalty extended assistance under the Caucasian Educational Grants.[47] Thus, the 1840s witnessed the rise of an Azerbaijani class of professional bureaucrats possessed of a modicum of European education, a new element in the traditional society.

The retirement of Vorontsov in 1865 signaled the gradual reversal of his accommodative policies. The Russian period of Great Reforms of the 1860s and 1870s, notable elsewhere for disposition toward liberalism, in Transcaucasia represented a transition from quasi-colonial status to organic merger with Russia. Once again on the occasion of a new policy course, the fertile minds of tsarist officials conceived a series of changes in territorial administration: In 1859, after an earthquake destroyed the town of Shemakha, the capital of the *guberniia* was moved to Baku and the province renamed accordingly. The next year, upon the final suppression of Shamil, the Derbent *guberniia* was abolished, and then in 1867 the new Elizavetpol *guberniia* was constructed from parts relinquished by the *guberniias* of Baku, Erivan, and Tiflis. The formation of this province consolidated the bulk of Azerbaijani territory into two *guberniias*, Baku and Elizavetpol, which jointly came to be called Eastern Transcaucasia.[48]

Still, the latest administrative reorganization did not create an ethnically homogeneous entity – nor was it intended to. Large numbers of the "Tatars" remained outside Eastern Transcaucasia, and its two provinces also included sizable groups of Armenians and other minorities. In the Elizavetpol *guberniia* the numbers of "Tatars" and Armenians, concentrated in the Mountainous Karabagh, were 878,000 and 292,000 respectively, according to 1871 figures. In the *uezd*s of this province the proportions of Armenians varied from 21 to 40 percent, thus in some cases nearing half of the population. In the Baku *guberniia* there were 465,000 "Tatars"; first place among the minorities fell to the Russians (77,000), followed by the "Caucasian

1. A century of Russian rule 15

Mountaineers" (63,000), Armenians (52,000), Jews (8,000), and others (137,000). Large numbers of Azerbaijanis found themselves included in provinces with Armenian or Georgian majorities; in the four of five *uezds* of the Erivan *guberniia* the "Tatars" accounted for 32 to 57 percent of the population. In four of the six *uezds* of the Tiflis *guberniia* their proportion was smaller, between 3 and 15 percent.[49]

Typically, there reappeared the familiar correlation between the tsardom's centralization policy and Russification. The same act that established the Elizavetpol *guberniia* did away with the division of the *uezds* into *uchasteks*. The effect was a drastic reduction of native personnel at the lowest level of the bureaucracy, with most of the positions in the territorial administration ending up in the hands of the Russians. This aspect of the changes of the post-Vorontsov period reached its high point under Alexander III (1881–1894). Soon after his accession to the throne, Alexander terminated the special status of Transcaucasia by dispensing with the office of viceroy. When the Grand Duke Mikhail Nicholaevich retired from the viceroyalty in 1882, his successor, Prince A. M. Dondukov, was appointed merely governor-general and commander in chief of the Caucasus. Simultaneously, the tsar restored the authority of central government departments over the local affairs of Transcaucasia.

An important piece of legislation of the Great Reforms era, the Municipal Law of 1870, granted urban communities self-government in the form of a town *duma* ("assembly"), an executive board, and a mayor. The town *duma* was an elective body chosen by taxpayers voting in three separate colleges on the basis of property qualifications. The new municipal authorities were in charge of the economic, education, sanitation, and health affairs of the community, although their fiscal powers remained restricted. The Municipal Law, although intended to give the rising middle classes a share in government at the local level, in Eastern Transcaucasia imposed a strict limit on the representation of the native element. The non-Christian membership of the dumas was set at one-half the total, and this proportion was further reduced to one-third in 1892.[50] Moreover, the governors of the *guberniias* delayed the implementation of the law on such grounds as the "immaturity of the inhabitants," the general backwardness of the country, or shortage of funds; as a result, the first municipal self-government came into being only in 1878, in Baku. It took another nineteen years before municipal reform was instituted in Ganja, Kuba, Nukha, Lenkoran, and Shemakha. The representative organs of rural areas, *zemstvos*, were not introduced in Transcaucasia at all, just as they were omitted in other regions with predominantly non-Russian populations – Poland, Central Asia, and Siberia.

Russification, whose focus so far had been on civil service, assumed a new dimension in the 1880s when the growing Russian community became an even more substantial element in the ethnic composition of the Baku *guberniia*. At first immigrant Russians tended to take up residence solely in the province's capital, but with time the tsarist officials' old vision – of Russians settling in the countryside – began to materialize. By the next decade groups of peasants from Russia were arriving almost weekly, and by 1913, in the Mugan Steppe alone, they established forty-four settlements and held 20,000 *desiatins* of high-quality irrigated land (1 desiatin = c. 2.7 acres).[51] This government-sponsored immigration aggravated the critical problem of land shortage, the more so since the newcomers received larger plots from the pool of land earmarked for distribution than the natives.

The latter viewed the unwelcome influx of Russian peasants as one of the most invidious consequences of the organic merger. In long run, this would be an inexhaustible source of anti-Russian sentiments at the grass roots level.

A reform that went directly against the grain of the native traditions was the introduction in the 1860s and 1870s of the uniform Russian court system and legal procedures in criminal cases. The popular reaction to this was continuous boycott, revealing the depth of the cultural chasm between rulers and ruled. "Not because the Russian judges are bad or unjust," read an Azerbaijani novel.

On the contrary, they are mild and just, but in the manner that our people dislike. A thief is put in jail. There he sits in his clean cell, is given tea, even with sugar in it. But nobody gets anything out of this, least of all the man he stole from. People shrug their shoulders and do justice in their own way. In the afternoon the plaintiffs come to the mosque where wise old men sit in a circle and pass sentence according to the laws of Shariᶜa, the law of Allah: An eye for an eye, a tooth for tooth. Sometimes at night shrouded figures slip through the alleys. A dagger strikes like lightning, a little cry, and justice is done. Blood feuds are running from house to house."[52]

For all the impositions, constraints, and irritants that the Russian policies entailed, it became apparent with time that these policies had also worked for the internal consolidation of Azerbaijan in at least two important respects: The abolition of the khanates helped vitiate divisive local particularisms, and the formation of the two eastern Transcaucasian provinces resulted in a territorial bloc that Azerbaijanis would regard as the core of their homeland. The process of administrative conversion was in turn reinforced by economic and social changes that came, albeit at a slower pace, in the wake of the conquest.

Economic change and Azerbaijani society

As in the case of administrative structure, the initial impact of the Russian conquest on the Azerbaijani economy remained slight, and in some respects retrogressive. Again, it was Kankrin, the Russian minister of finance, who spelled out what were in effect guidelines for Russian economic interests in Transcaucasia: This region was to be, in his words, "a colony producing the raw materials of a southern climate."[53] For a long period that stretched until the mid-nineteenth century, Azerbaijan experienced hardly any benefits from Russian investments. The diplomat and writer A. S. Griboedov, having remarked that no single factory was built there, pointed out another weakness of the local economy brought on by the conquest: "While the bazaars are resplendent with imported goods of all hues, the visitor's eye seeks in vain for home-made products suitable for exchange."[54] A few attempts at the exploitation of Azerbaijan's natural potential for wine and silk manufacture were made by Russian entrepreneurs in the 1830s but met with little success.

Despite open entry to the vast Russian market, the agricultural production in these lands of "southern climate" remained stagnant, the apparent cause of which was the ineffectiveness of the alien government. As in any country of comparable hydrographic conditions, in Azerbaijan the government customarily had been in charge of maintaining irrigation works, and this vital task was neglected by the Russian military authorities. Another branch of Azerbaijan's economy with centuries-old traditions fared no better than agriculture: The extraction of oil hovered at the stationary level of 250,000 *puds* annually (1 *pud* = c. 16 kg), a figure that according to one estimate was less than the region's output in the tenth century.[55] Even such obviously beneficial consequences of the conquest as the termination of internecine wars and invasions produced mixed economic effects on Azerbaijani towns. While some such as Baku, Ganja, Shemakha, and Nukha revived and grew to the size of ten thousand or more inhabitants, others such as Shusha, Kuba, Derbent suffered from a decline in population after 1830.[56]

On the opposite side of the balance sheet were some developments of long-range significance that only the conquest made possible or at least accelerated. The transition to a money economy was stimulated by the requirement that peasants pay their rentals, for lands leased formerly from the khans and now from the Russian treasury, in cash rather than in kind, the practice in the past. The dismantling of the khanates provided impetus to the economic integration of the country, a process further advanced by the replacement in the 1830s of the diverse local currencies by the ruble. Likewise, uniform Russian weights and measures were officially introduced. The elimination of the old customs barriers crisscrossing Azerbaijan proceeded more slowly, surviving until 1846, as the tsarist government kept deriving income from the tolls between the defunct khanates.

Not until mid-century, when Azerbaijan had become sufficiently enmeshed with the Russian market, did the signs of economic revival begin to appear. Soviet historians have painstakingly cataloged instances of structural change and modernized forms of production that could be discerned in the Azerbaijani economy even before the onset on the great oil boom of the 1870s: An increased demand for cotton caused by the American Civil War led to the rise of plantations employing hundreds of workers; specialization and diversification improved the profitability of tobacco growing and viniculture; the expansion of the silk economy made Nukha an international trading center in which a few factories were also built; the copper mines of Kedabek were on the way to becoming major suppliers of the Russian market; the ancient craft of rug weaving, reorganized as a cottage industry, allowed the start of an export trade that made these products of Shirvan, Kuba, Ganja, Karabagh, and Kazakh admired throughout the world.[57]

All this does not materially alter the fact that the Azerbaijani economy was still overwhelmingly agricultural and that agriculture remained primitive. The Agrarian Reform that went into force in the Elizavetpol, Baku, and Erivan *guberniias* only in 1870 – nine years later than in Russia – hardly stands out as a landmark development of social and economic transformations. In Eastern Transcaucasia close to 70 percent of the peasantry had lived on crown lands and were thus exempt in any event from the feudal obligations that the Reform abolished.[58] Under this act peasants were allotted 5 *desiatin*s per adult male, an amount of land so small that one-third of the acreage an average peasant required had to be rented from either the state or local landlords. As for the *bäy*s themselves, the great majority of them owned plots averaging 6.3 *desiatin*s and lived an existence indistinguishable from those of their peasant neighbors, though they continued to exercise their leadership through the village assemblies and elective courts. Only 4 percent of the landlords had estates averaging 1,500 *desiatin*s, from which the pool of privately owned land available for leasing was drawn.[59] Overall, the Azerbaijani countryside remained unshaken in its tradition-bound existence characterized by closely knit village communities and little social stratification or mobility.

The progress of urbanization was slow, and by the end of the nineteenth century 89 percent of the 827,000 inhabitants of the Elizavetpol and 70 percent of the 635,000 inhabitants of the Baku *guberniia*s, respectively, still lived in villages.[60] The lower proportion of rural population in the latter province reflected the special case of the city of Baku, its size swollen by multitudes of immigrants from outside Eastern Transcaucasia. Aside from Baku there were, in the territory of the two *guberniia*s, nine towns (Ganja, Kuba, Salyany, Nukha, Lenkoran, Shusha, Shemakha, Nakhichevan, and Ordubad – all in a preindustrial stage) functioning as centers of administration (Ganja), trade, handicrafts, or small-scale manufacturing. The population statistics of these Azerbaijani towns registered a rate of growth that was far from dynamic, and in one instance (Shemakha) even decline.[61]

Taking Azerbaijan as a whole, the degree of economic and

social change was modest and its pace sluggish; nonetheless, there was a striking exception to this pattern. In the 1870s the extraction and processing of oil suddenly increased at an unprecedented rate. The ripple effects of this growth led to virtually revolutionary transformations, albeit in a geographically limited sphere. It generated employment for tens of thousands of nonagricultural workers; it produced such attributes of economic modernization as labor migrations and the introduction of railroad and steamship transportation; and it brought about the rise of an urban metropolis, Baku. The overall effect of the "oil revolution" was a dichotomy not uncommon for a colonial situation: a generally traditional economy contrasting with one rapidly expanding industry, based on mineral resources rather than manufacturing and geared to the needs of external markets.

After a long period of stagnation, the production of oil began to gain momentum in 1859 when the first kerosene refineries were built in Baku and the surrounding villages. But the real breakthrough came only as the result of a government act, the most consequential one ever issued by the Russian bureaucracy in Azerbaijan. In 1872 the practice of granting oil concessions on crown land was changed into long-term leasing to the highest bidder. The gate was opened wide to investors with substantial capital willing to engage in large-scale, mechanized production. The next year, the first successful drilling replaced the old method of well digging, and a spectacular gusher inaugurated the ascent of Baku to the position of a major world oil-producing center. The prices of privately owned land skyrocketed, and many small kerosene refineries rapidly grew into sizable enterprises.[62] In the long run, the dynamic expansion could be sustained only with large financial outlays not available from local (nor even Russian) sources. The penetration of foreign capital began with the Swedish industrialists the Nobel brothers, who in 1879 founded an oil company in Baku that was soon to become the world's largest. They were followed closely by the Parisian Rothschild family, who formed the Caspian–Black Sea Society for Commerce and Industry; by the 1890s six British-owned companies, in addition to three French, two German, two Belgian, and one Greek, were in operation.[63] The high degree of concentration accounted for the unparalleled advances in volume of oil output, which in 1898 surpassed that of the United States.

The expansion of the oil industry went hand in hand with the urban growth of Baku. At mid-century still a sleepy port on the Apsheron Peninsula, in the 1870s Baku became a typical boom city, with the highest rate of population increase in the Russian Empire: The number of its inhabitants, 14,000 in 1863, rose to 206,000 in 1903, making it the largest city in Transcaucasia.[64] "Below and around the old city a number of new quarters sprang up to shelter the vast influx of people from all parts of the world who have flocked to Baku in the hope of making fortunes," wrote a visitor in 1905, who then described the city as follows:

> Some of the buildings along the quay are large and imposing but everything bespeaks the comfortless vulgarity of the *nouveau riche*. Baku, considering its immense wealth, is one of the worst managed cities in the world. The lighting is inadequate, the wretched horse-tram service pitiable, the sanitary arrangements appalling; vast spaces are left in the middle of the town, drinking water is only supplied by sea water distilled, the few gardens are arid and thin, the dust in ubiquitous – fine and penetrating dust that gets into every nook and cranny.[65]

Baku became a thoroughly multinational urban center in which no single ethnic element was predominant. The three largest groups were the Russians, the Armenians, and the Muslims. The last held a plurality, usually oscillating between 40 and 50 percent, although their statistical designation included the natives of Eastern Transcaucasia as well as the immigrants from northern Persia, Daghestan, and even the Volga region.[66] The Azerbaijanis were for the most part half-workers, half-peasants, of all groups of inhabitants the most closely linked to their village background and the least urbanized. If employed in the oil industry, they worked mainly as unskilled laborers with correspondingly low pay. The better-paid jobs, requiring skills or training, were held by the Russians and Armenians.

This bustling industrial city was hardly a melting pot. Ethnic communities tended to live their separate lives in distinct neighborhoods, and the differences in their economic status perpetuated and accentuated the barriers of culture, religion, and language. Baku had developed in three concentric belts of population. The center, where oil extraction and processing was banned, was inhabited by the well-off: merchants, businessmen, and professionals. Surrounding the city proper were the industrial suburbs, Black City, White City, Zlykh, Akhmadly, and Kish, and the more distant oil field districts with the villages of Sabunchi, Bibi-Eibat, Ramany, Zabrat, and Balakhany. It was here, in the derrick-studded landscape, that the majority of the poorest and least-educated inhabitants, mainly Muslim workers, lived in hastily built shantytowns.[67]

With its multilingual population, large size, and frantic pace of life, Baku was an alien enclave in Eastern Transcaucasia, yet the city irresistibly drew in the enterprising, the ambitious, and the educated from all over the country. Their concentration turned Baku into the virtual capital of Azerbaijan as well as the fountainhead of the rising native industrial bourgeoisie. The oil boom allowed the Azerbaijanis who had previously owned oil wells, kerosene refineries, or land in the Baku area to reap quick fortunes. In the very first stage of the industry's expansion, which lasted until 1872, they still controlled most oil-related enterprises. But even then, as the figures for 1870 indicate, although 88 percent of all wells were "Tatar"-owned, these accounted for only half the total oil output in Baku. As soon as the regulation on bidding for oil leases went into effect, the Azerbaijani capitalists began to lose out to their Armenian, Russian, and Western European competitors. After 1872 the proportion of wells in Azerbaijani hands fell precipitously to 13 percent, and the funds they invested in leases did not exceed 5 percent.[68] Narrow as the margin retained by Azerbaijanis might appear, it was still sufficient for some of their oil men – Taghiyev, Naghiyev, Assadullayev, Mukhtarov, and the Sultanov family – to accumulate great wealth.

Similar situations in which the Azerbaijani Muslims (in contrast to Azerbaijani-born Armenians) controlled only a fraction or no part at all of local industry were generally prevalent in Eastern Transcaucasia, with some notable exceptions. Caspian Sea shipping remained an almost exclusive domain of the "Tatars," who had built up for themselves an unassailable position as middlemen in the trade between Russia and Persia, even in the preindustrial period. Likewise, a few Muslim families controlled most of the silk spinning in Nukha, Karabagh, and Ordubad.[69]

On the whole, the native bourgeoisie, concentrated mainly in Baku, was numerically small, its growth held back by foreign competition. Nor was it politically a very assertive group: Only a quarter of the electorate participated in the elections to the

Baku *duma*, and the assembly's sessions frequently had to be called off for lack of a quorum. On the other hand, the Muslim entrepreneurial class made its influence felt in various aspects of the life of the native community. Symbolic of its involvement outside its strictly business activity was the role of Zeynal ᶜAbdul Taghiyev.

According to legend, Taghiyev's wealth, believed to be the greatest in Transcaucasia, had its origins in a minor earthquake that had brought oil to the surface of his small plot of land. He then multiplied his fortune by investments in kerosene refining, as well as by extensive land and stock market speculations. With time he extended his interests beyond the oil industry: He founded the first cotton mill in Azerbaijan and invested in tobacco and cotton plantations. Although barely literate, he financially supported wide-ranging educational and philanthropic ventures.[70] His generosity often benefitted the endeavors of the intelligentsia, which constituted, along with the bourgeoisie, the Azerbaijani modernizing elite.

The rise of the intelligentsia

A social as much as a cultural phenomenon brought forth by the contact of two civilizations, the European (as represented by Russia) and the traditional Islamic, was the emergence of the native intelligentsia. This group of people shared a set of beliefs, attitudes, and opinions that made it first a channel of transmission of European intellectual values and with time the main agent for change within Azerbaijani society.

The very term *intelligentsia* implies some educational attainment, but in the Azerbaijani case the specific implication was that of European-type education. Conversely, persons trained in the traditional Muslim schools – except those who accepted its commitment to reforms – were not counted among the intelligentsia.

Who were the men that made up the intelligentsia? Initially these were the few Azerbaijanis who by virtue of their occupations were frequently exposed to the Russian environment, for the most part by way of the tsarist military or civil service. Their numbers grew in the Vorontsov era when the doors to government positions were thrown open to the natives. They usually had attended Russian military schools or the "Russo–Tatar" schools that had existed since the 1830s.[71] During the second half of the century, as the civil service was largely purged of the native element, the intelligentsia became dominated by graduates of Russian universities and of the Transcaucasian teacher seminaries in Gori and Tiflis.[72] Indeed, schoolteachers, some of whom took to journalism or other literary pursuits, formed one of its largest professional components by the end of the century.

In a stroke of good fortune the Azerbaijani intelligentsia produced in its early stage a man of brilliance and intellectual accomplishment who in his writings set forth what were to be this group's chief concerns for the future. Mirza Fath ᶜAli Akhundzadä (Akhundov, 1812–1878), a translator in the Chancellery of the viceroy of the Caucasus, gained fame primarily as the author of the first plays in the European style in the Azerbaijani language.[73] "Tatar Molière," as Vorontsov called him, Akhundzadä in the years 1850–1855 wrote a series of comedies satirizing the ills and flaws that he perceived in contemporary Azerbaijani society – all of them, in one way or another, rooted in either ignorance or superstition.[74]

Besides being the pioneer of the theater in the Turkic-speaking world as well as in Persia, Akhundzadä spent several years campaigning for simplification of the Arabic alphabet, a reform he saw as

a medicine with the effect that the letters of this script dating back to the barbarian era would be written jointly,... that the letters would be distinguished one from another by their shape without recourse to the dots. Then, everyone in a short time and without much exertion would be able to read in his native language.[75]

In the writings of his later period – essays, articles, and above all in his philosophical treatise *Three Letters* – Akhundzadä turned to an aggressive social criticism from the standpoint of rationalism and enlightenment in a manner reminiscent of the eighteenth-century French *philosophes*.

Akhundzadä epitomized the contradictions inherent in the uncertain identity of an Azerbaijani of his time: A tsarist official of impeccable loyalty, he described himself as "almost Persian," and his philosophical writings reveal the depth of his preoccupation with all things Persian, both good and bad.[76] Inasmuch as he extolled the pre-Islamic greatness of Persia and castigated the "hungry, naked, and savage" Arabs for having destroyed the kingdom of the Sasanids, he is considered one of the forerunners of modern Iranian nationalism.[77] Nor was he devoid of typically Persian anti-Ottoman sentiments, which were clearly reflected in some of his writings. Still, he has been recognized as a major figure in the movement for the self-assertion of national identity of Turkic peoples by virtue of his role in the literary revival of the native language, a development that, ironically, led to Azerbaijani emancipation from centuries-long Persian cultural domination.[78]

Three interrelated themes in Akhundzada's life were of special relevance for the nineteenth-century intelligentsia. The spread of education was first and foremost, as the aspirations of the Azerbaijani modernizers in this period were still primarily those of an enlightenment movement. Linked to this were secularism and an Azerbaijani literary revival. For Akhundzadä, the son of a Shi'ite clergyman (as his name indicates), secularism was a consequence of his atheistic proclivities, even if these were not entirely consistent. He saw, above all, the grip of religion on all facets of life as an obstacle to learning. "The Persians believe that there are no other people more knowledgeable than themselves, since they have mastered perfectly the study of life after death, that is, theology, and that no other knowledge is worthwhile except for theology."[79] The followers of Akhundzadä are not known to have shared his atheism; in fact, most of them appeared to be genuinely attached to Islam, although they shared his opinion on the great value of learning other than that of theology. An even more compelling reason why secularism became an outstanding characteristic of the intelligentsia was that they saw it as the only practical means for blunting the edges of sectarian strife, and instilling a sense of community into the Muslims of Transcaucasia was otherwise unthinkable. The intelligentsia's perception of this strife, and of the social role of the religious institutions, was graphically expressed by the poet Haji Sayyid 'Azim Shirvani (1833–1888), himself a man of traditional education who came around to the reformist outlook:

>In every province—five or ten towns,
>Fifty thousand *sayyid*s, *akhund*s, and students,

Fifty *darwish*es, fifty cantors,
All their words are pure lies.
Fifty thousand clerics, fifty thousand beggars,
Fifty thousand charlatans and knaves,
All they think of is how to fleece the people,
To leave the people high and dry,
Who, an ignorant lot, do not know what it is all about.
Our Shiʿites scold the Sunnis
Our Sunnis curse the Shiʿites.[80]

The literary revival in the native language stemmed from the need to communicate the ideas of the enlightenment to as wide a public as possible. Akhundzadä, who throughout most of his life composed lyric poetry in Persian, when writing works that carried a message of social importance used a language comprehensible to all his countrymen, which he called *Türki*. The renaissance of a native literature, a by-product of the movement, was thus its first and most tangible accomplishment. The hold of Persian as the chief literary language in Azerbaijan was broken, followed by the rejection of classical Azerbaijani, an artificial, heavily Iranized idiom that had long been in use along with Persian, though in a secondary position.[81]

This process of cultural change was initially supported by the tsarist authorities, who were anxious to neutralize the still-widespread Azerbaijani identification with Persia. In doing so, the Russians resorted to a policy familiar in other parts of the empire, where Lithuanians, for example, were sporadically encouraged to emancipate themselves from Polish cultural influences, as were the Latvians from German and the Finns from Swedish. The case of Akhundzadä, whose plays had been staged in a Russian theater long before they were produced by native performers, was only one instance of the favorable disposition of tsarist officialdom. Akhundzadä's benefactor, Vorontsov, commissioned works on local history from Azerbaijani authors; the Russian magazine *Kavkaz* in the 1840s and 1850s published Azerbaijani poetry; and the tsarist government sponsored the research of Caucasologists that awakened an interest in Azerbaijan's language, folklore, and literature.[82] But Russian support was neither wholehearted nor long-lasting: It was reduced to a reluctant tolerance after the departure of Vorontsov, and was replaced by Russification during the reign of Alexander III.

1. A century of Russian rule

The Azerbaijani literary revival gained momentum in the second generation of the intelligentsia who came of age in the 1870s. By this time the intelligentsia was no longer comprised of scattered individuals but constituted a group of some cohesion. A striking fact about this generation was that it was drawn, to a disproportionately large degree, from the Sunni segment of the population, the obvious explanation for which appears to be the less restrictive influence of their religious establishment: As opposed to the case of the Shi'ites, there are no clergy in the Sunni branch of Islam. Also, the Sunnis were more receptive to the idea of a Turkic revival, given their cultural gravitation toward Turkey, even though it was weaker than that of the Shi'ites toward Persia. Their theologians were trained in Turkey, their primary schools taught Ottoman or classical Azerbaijani, and whatever history a pupil could learn consisted of biographies of the Ottoman sultans. Among the intelligentsia these affinities were reinforced by echoes of the Ottoman constitutional reforms of the recent *Tanzimat* era (1856-1876). Akhundzadä, for all his anti-Ottoman prejudices, in order to promote his alphabet-reform project made a journey to Istanbul, where he expected to find a "better climate" for changes.[83]

Characteristically, the literary revival expressed itself in new media, primarily the modern theater and journalism. Akhundzadä saw the theater as a suitable vehicle for conveying his message to the largely illiterate public through the spoken word, but the novelty appeared too radical for his intended audience. Only toward the end of his life were his plays produced on the native stage, and then due to the efforts of a handful of young intellectuals led by the Baku *gymnasium* teacher Häsan bäy Zärdabi (1832-1907). In the long run these efforts resulted in the rise of the theater, along with its attendant devotees – actors, directors, playwrights, and a loyal public – as an important cultural institution – one, moreover, that enjoyed financial backing from Taghiyev.[84] Following Akhundzadä's dictum that "the purpose of dramatic art is to improve people's morals and to teach a reader or spectator a lesson," the Azerbaijani theater was pervaded by a sense of its didactic mission.[85] Of the playwrights, who vied for the succession to Akhundzadä's mantle, the most accomplished were Näjäf bäy Väzirov (1854-1926) and ʿAbd-ul Rahman Haqvärdiyev (Akhverdov, 1880-1933). Both wrote satirical comedies, but Väzirov also wrote the first Azerbaijani tragedies, the younger Haqvärdiyev following in his footsteps. This innovation, in the view of some scholars, reflected historical conditions: The conflict between change and tradition had reached an intensity that resulted in personal situations of tragic dimensions. The heroes in Väzirov and Haqvärdiyev's tragedies were intellectuals who in the process of striving to reform the old ways were crushed by the hostile, obscurantist environment. The two writers, expressing the sense of isolation experienced by the tiny minority of modernizers, no longer saw ignorance merely as a foible deserving ridicule.[86]

Almost simultaneously with the beginning of theater was that of the Azerbaijani-language press – and as a result of the endeavors of the same *gymnasium* teacher, Zärdabi. In 1875 Zärdabi founded the Baku newspaper *Äkinchi* (Ploughman), an event that would one day be recognized as a milestone in the growth of national awareness of Turkic peoples. This paper, the first Turkic-language publication in Russia, addressed itself primarily to the peasant reader in accordance with Zardabi's *narodnik* ('populist") leanings, a heritage of his student years at the University of Moscow.[87] The *Äkinchi* at once became a subject of controversy among Transcaucasian Muslims.[88] Some Shi'ite 'ulama (scholars) regarded it as insulting to the spirit of Islam to imitate such an Infidel invention as a newspaper. The sensitive issue of language was another point of friction. The *Äkinchi* was written in a simple style, with few Persian and Arabic words for which new terms were being introduced, often coined by Zärdabi himself.[89] Those literati whose preferred language of expression was Persian reacted with hostility to his insistence on using the "unprintable" idiom of common folk. Boycotted by the traditionalists and inaccessible to the mostly illiterate peasantry, the *Äkinchi* inevitably became a forum for the intelligentsia. The circle of its contributors consisted mainly of Sunnis like Zärdabi, whose innuendos that Persia was a backward, fanatical, and inhuman country provoked widespread indignation. An even greater uproar followed an article criticizing the Shi'ite ritual procession of Muharram, whose participants inflict injuries on themselves in commemoration of the martyrdom of the Imam Husain.[90]

The *Äkinchi* failed to enjoy the benevolent attitude tsarist dignitaries had displayed toward the Azerbaijani-language writers

1. A century of Russian rule 29

of the previous generation. Zärdabi was suspect because of his *narodnik* views, and even more so for his pro-Ottoman sympathies; it was in the midst of the war between Russia and Turkey, in 1877, that his newspaper was forced to close down.[91]

The demise of the *Äkinchi* was a blow, albeit not a mortal one, to the Azerbaijani press, and the effort started by Zärdabi was continued by the newspapers *Ziya* (Aurora, 1879–1881) and *Ziya-i Kafkasiyyä* (Aurora of the Caucasus, 1881–1884) and the literary magazine *Käshkül* (Darwish Bowl, 1884–1891). Also published by the Sunnis, these periodicals differed from their predecessor in important respects: They showed no trace of populist tendencies and generally steered clear of controversies, at the price of being comparatively less lively. Moreover, the post-*Äkinchi* press was marked by a pronounced trend away from the Azerbaijani vernacular and toward an increasing Ottomanization of the language. In this sense, the contribution of these three periodicals to the formation of modern literary Azerbaijani was limited. After the closing of the *Käshkül* by government order, no periodical in a Turkic language was allowed until 1904, when the Azerbaijani press was revived with the daily *Sharq-i Rus* (Russian East).[92]

Meanwhile, an issue was taking shape that eclipsed all the other concerns of the intelligentsia: the battle for the future of Muslim schools, the pivotal point in the enlightenment program. Significantly, the battlelines were drawn at their sharpest within the Muslim community, while the Russian role remained secondary.

By Islamic tradition, all learning was in principle religious and education subordinated to theology. The school as an institution throughout the centuries had maintained a sacred character, immune to change, with the effect that it turned into a bastion of militant conservatism. There were two types of Muslim schools, *mäktäb*s and *mädräsä*s, their number in Transcaucasia oscillating between five and seven hundred.[93] *Mäktäb*s were elementary schools installed in mosque compounds where boys were given religious instruction along with lessons in reading, writing, and arithmetic, usually by rote. *Mädräsä*s were institutions of higher education offering preparation for the status of ᶜ*alim* (scholar). At the *mäktäb* level, the quality of instruction varied from school to school, but on the whole its reputation was deplorably low by any modern standard. The Baku newspaper *Kaspiy* went so far as to write that the "*mäktäb*s do not deserve to be called schools." The overall literacy rate remained at the appallingly low level of 4 to 5 percent.[94]

Both the native intelligentsia and tsarist authorities concurred in the desire to see the school system reformed. The government was anxious to exert greater control over Muslim education as well to bring about an increased knowledge of the Russian language. In this latter respect it had the support of the intelligentsia, whose leading representatives, from Akhundzadä to Zärdabi and Shirvani, were all on record as having called for the learning of Russian. They viewed the mastery of that language not only as a means of acquiring modern skills but, more importantly, as a way of overcoming the hermetic insulation of their countrymen from the non-Muslim world, a hope that opened them to accusations of being accomplices in the Russification process. "The Muslims will cease keeping aloof from the Russians under whose protection their lives, dignity, and property are secured," wrote Akhundzadä.

> The spirit of fanaticism that prevails among them will perish forever.... There will appear among the Caucasian Muslims a desire for literacy and an aspiration for learning which will lead them to improve their morals. Until now it was only their religion that prevented the majority of them from learning the Russian language, the knowledge of which, in the opinion of the clergy, makes the salvation of the soul unthinkable.[95]

Despite exhortations in this tone, popular resistance was stubborn, fortified by the belief that the study of Russian would lead to the inevitable Christianization of children. Since any education of a non-Islamic character would meet with an almost total boycott, the only way out of the impasse appeared to be the modernization of the *mäktäb*s. Such a program was the essence of the jadidist movement, which originated among the Volga Tatars and subsequently spread to other Muslim-populated parts of the Russian Empire.[96] Jadidism, its name derived from *usul-i jadid* (new method), aimed at improving the curricula of the *mäktäb*s and their overall approach to teaching. The study of the Qur'an was retained, but memorizing was discouraged; at the same time, science, geography, and modern languages made their entry into the classroom. Also, the teaching of classical literary languages gave way to that of contemporary Turkic, a condition that held little attraction for some Persian-oriented Shiʿites in Azerbaijan. The "new method" found here only partial acceptance, and it met with vociferous opposition from the conservative educators known as qadimists or the followers of the *usul-i qadim* ("old method").[97] Nonetheless, jadidism signified the first Azerbaijani involvement in a process affecting the wider Muslim community outside the confines of Transcaucasia. This involvement was all the more meaningful as some rudiments of nationalism had been infused into jadidism by the endeavors of the Crimean Tatar journalist Ismail bey Gasprinski.[98]

Gasprinski's newspaper, *Tarjuman* (Interpreter), which he published in Bakchisarai from 1883 onward with some funds from Taghiyev, became the unofficial voice of Russian Muslims. Gasprinski assiduously stressed his loyalty to Russia, which he characterized as a generous and civilized nation that would bring progress to the Muslims under its rule. All the same, he was acutely aware of the dangers attendant upon Russification policies, in particular the influence of the Pan-Slavic movement, of which he had first-hand knowledge through his acquaintance with its leading figure, M. N. Katkov. It was largely in response to Pan-Slavism that Gasprinski evolved a defensive program for the unity of the Muslims within the Russian Empire. Inasmuch as these Muslims were overwhelmingly of Turkic stock, his program amounted to launching an ethnocentric movement, which came to be referred to variously as Turkism or Pan-Turkism. The first term connoted its concern with the ethnic identity of the Turkic-speaking peoples, the other its striving for their cooperation and solidarity. Although Gasprinski spoke of one Turkic nation (*qavm*), he stopped short of advocating political action, a prospect that would have been doomed in any case, given the repressive climate of the time. The Turkic unity he preached was to be of a spiritual, linguistic, and cultural nature, and its catchword was his famous slogan: *Dilde, Fikirde, Ishte Birlik* (Unity of Language, Thought, and Work). The first precondition for attaining this goal was to be the creation of a literary idiom understandable to all Turks, from the Balkans to China. Such a common language was indeed formed in the columns of the *Tarjuman*. It was based on the Turkish of Istanbul, that is, Ottoman, though purged of an excess of foreign elements and written using a simplified syntax. The newspaper could be read by the well-educated in most Turkic lands, but for an average reader it was easily intelligible only in the Crimea and Azerbaijan, and less so among the Volga Tatars, while most of the eastern and northern Turks would find it difficult to comprehend without special study. The impact of the *Tarjuman* was apparent in the linguistic Ottomanization of the Azerbaijani press, a tendency that some, including Zärdabi, criticized as leading to artificiality.[99]

At the same time, the growth of Turkism stimulated the Azerbaijanis' search for self-awareness. The most sophisticated of the nineteenth-century newspapers, *Käshkül*, was the first to draw a clear distinction between the notions of a local religious community and nationality, and even ridiculed the common use of one term, *millät*, to denote both. In the form of an imaginary dialog, an author signing himself M. Sultanov portrayed the quandary of a Transcaucasian Muslim as to his identity:

Question: What is your nationality [*millät*]?
Answer: I am a Muslim and also a Turk.
Question: Are you an Ottoman?
Answer: No, I am *bijanli* [a play on words in which the corrupt form of *Azerbaijani* means "soulless"].
Question: Where is the land of the *bijanli*s?
Answer: As far as I can tell, on the other side of the Araxes live the Azeris – on this side the *bijanli*s. Together, it makes Azerbaijani. But separately we are *bijanli*s.
Question: Your language is Turkic so you are a Turk?
Answer: There is no word to describe my position. I am a Turk, but *bijanli*.
Question: Instead of being a *bijanli* Turk, why don't you solve your dilemma by calling yourself an Azerbaijani Turk?[100]

This telling conclusion is the earliest recorded literary statement (if an isolated one) of a nascent national consciousness: Turkishness blended with Azerbaijani identity. It required the third generation of the intelligentsia, the men who launched their public careers in the last decade of the century, to make the first attempts at truly politically inspired activity. This transitional stage involved the acts of individuals more than those of organized groups.

1. A century of Russian rule 33

The first Azerbaijani to take a step beyond the cultural phase of Pan-Turkism was ᶜAli bäy Huseynzadä (1864–1941).[101] While pursuing medical studies in St. Petersburg, Huseynzadä, like Gasprinski before him, became impressed with Pan-Slavism. Thus influenced, in 1889 he traveled to Istanbul to spread the message of one Turkic nation. Because the Ottomans were as yet strangers to the idea of Turkism, immigrants from Russia took it upon themselves to work for their conversion. Such missionary pursuits went against the grain of the official state doctrine, Ottomanism, which proclaimed the unity and equality of all the multiethnic subjects of Turkey. The despotic Sultan Abdulhamid II (1876–1909) was particularly suspicious of any form of nationalism, including Turkic, regarding it as a disruptive force. In Istanbul Huseynzadä addressed his efforts to those disaffected with the regime and became one of the founders of the underground opposition group *Ittihad-i Osmaniyye* (Ottoman Union), out of which the Young Turkish movement was to grow.[102] Even in this select circle he did not find much support for Pan-Turkism, as at that stage the opponents of Adbulhamid were then still committed to Ottomanism. Somewhat more successful were ᶜAli bäy Huseynzadä's efforts in influencing a handful of intellectuals with his writings, which he published under the pseudonym Turan (Land of Turks), after the title of one of his poems. Among those indebted to him were the poet Mehmed Emin and the future prophet of Turkism, Ziya Gökalp, who was to acknowledge ᶜAli bäy as one of his most important teachers.[103] On balance, Huseynzadä had little reason to be satisfied with the reception of his ideas in Turkey under Abdulhamid, and when more promising circumstances suddenly appeared to arise in Russia, he returned hurridly to Baku.

Parallel with rise of Pan-Turkism was the burgeoning of Pan-Islamism, with its call for the unity of Muslims worldwide in response to the encroachments of Europe, a cause that could claim a comparatively broader mass appeal. The two ideologies were not mutually exclusive, as almost all Turkic peoples were Muslims; indeed, Gasprinski never neglected to stress that Islam was a fundamental attribute of the Turkic nation. Many of the leading figures of Pan-Turkism also considered themselves Pan-Islamists, and were usually able to overlook the fact that the two ideologies stemmed from somewhat contradictory premises. The roots of Pan-Turkism lay in the ethnic self-awareness of a particular group of peoples, while Pan-Islamism appealed to the collective consciousness of the ʿ*umma*, the worldwide community of believers in Islam, regardless of linguistic, ethnic, or national distinctions.[104]

Primarily a spontaneous reaction to the pressures of a changing world, Pan-Islamism failed to develop into a uniform doctrine. Even the tsarist secret police, the Okhrana, quick to take interest in Pan-Islamic agitators among the Russian Muslims, conceded the difficulty of defining the nature of the movement and concluded that its followers lacked a clear-cut program or strategy.[105] There was in actuality more than one version of Pan-Islamism, ranging from what served chiefly as a foreign policy instrument for Abdulhamid to a liberal position symbolized by Haji Sayyid Jamal al-Afghani. The latter, a Persian-born itinerant philosopher, was the leading figure of nineteenth-century Islamic modernism. He believed that Islam was compatible with reason and freedom of thought, and encouraged Muslims to adopt Western learning, techniques, and methods (albeit selectively). He exhorted Muslims to rid Islamic culture of dogmatism and superstitiousness and to overcome sectarian divisiveness. At the same time he advised Muslims to treat nationalism as a weapon in their resistance to colonialism, and he believed in eventual unification of all Muslims under one rule, liberal rather than despotic.[106] It was al-Afghani's brand of Pan-Islamism that appealed most to the Azerbaijani intelligentsia, especially as it offered the prospect of Shiʿa–Sunni reconciliation in an ecumenical spirit of modernized Islam.

The most articulate Azerbaijani Pan-Islamist in this generation, the Paris-educated journalist Ahmäd bäy Aghayev (Agaoğlu, 1870–1938), was noted for his youthful contributions to the French press – mainly variations on themes from al-Afghani.[107] Yet his writings of that period displayed a pronounced pro-Persian and anti-Ottoman bias, a curious trait in a man who one day would become a prominent Turkish nationalist. He referred to his countrymen as the *société persané* and spoke harshly of those who had challenged this attitude in the past: "Having completed their studies, they tried to spread among the peasants their nihilist ideas and their non-Asiatic, European ambitions through the newspaper *Äkinchi*. The natives called them 'good for nothing' or 'lost men,' appropriate descriptions considering their dissolute morals and the contempt these individuals showed for their country."[108] In the forthcoming renaissance of Islam, Persia would play a role comparable to that of France in Europe, but "Turkey, which has been making extraordinary efforts to regenerate herself, will not succeed because individualism is dead there."[109]

After his return home in 1895, Aghayev's Pan-Islamism led him to tone down such criticisms in recognition of the truth that it was Turkey, not Persia, that was still the largest independent Islamic state and thus the most likely source of support for Muslims worldwide. With the passage of time he began his tortuous evolution toward Turkism.

A third ideological current, liberalism, had a frame of reference that was more European in character.[110] Its adherents viewed themselves as part of a broadly defined Russian liberal movement committed to the expansion of local self-government and to gradual reforms that would lead to the establishment of a constitutional regime. The hard core of the Azerbaijani liberals was the Muslim representation in the Baku *duma*, made up mainly of merchants and industrialists. They made their voices public through the *Kaspiy*, the only Azerbaijani–owned newspaper (though printed in Russian) in existence at the close of the century. The owner of the *Kaspiy* was Taghiyev, and its editor in chief ᶜAli Mardan-bäy Topchibashev (Topchibashi, 1869–1934),[111] a lawyer with close links to Russian liberals. Under Topchibashev's direction the *Kaspiy* engaged in a series of reformist campaigns for such goals as improvement of the *mäktäbs*, access for the Muslims to positions in the civil service, and alleviation of the peasants' land hunger by reclamation of the Mugan Steppe. With time the newspaper sought to play the role of spokesman for the interests of all Muslims in Russia and, seeking the support of Russian public opinion, invited contributions from Russian writers.[112]

Eclecticism, a characteristic of Azerbaijani political life from its earliest days, was strongly in evidence on the pages of the *Kaspiy*: Beside liberal views, the newspaper also presented Pan-Turkish and even more often Pan-Islamic ideas, especially in a regular column written by Aghayev. But then, among the intelligentsia the ethos of idealism tended to blunt the divisive effect of political distinctions.

Doctrinal flexibility characterized even the Azerbaijani socialists, who had begun their activities at the turn of the century. The first of these were men who had found their way to the Russian Social Democratic Workers Party (RSDWP), in existence in Baku since 1900. Then, in 1904, Azerbaijanis succeeded in forming their own organization under the name Himmät (Endeavor). Its story belongs to the new era starting the next year.

On the eve of the first Russian revolution, the Azerbaijani intelligentsia had produced a core of politically articulate individuals, among whom were germinated the seeds of ideologies that would shape the country's politics for years to come. The growth of these ideologies would be accelerated in a political climate suddenly transformed by the upheaval of 1905, the great watershed date in the history of Azerbaijan.

2

The 1905 Revolution and Azerbaijani political awakening

The onset of the 1905 Revolution

By the turn of the century it seemed that the oil boom had run its course, and in 1898 a prolonged economic depression set in. The resulting unemployment and hardship suffered by the workers turned Baku into a city notorious for labor unrest. The government deemed it expedient to declare in January 1902 a state of emergency under which the police were empowered to bypass established legal procedures in dealing with troublemakers. Nonetheless, the penetration of the working class, at least its non-native segment, by revolutionary organizations progressed apace. Active among the Russians was the RSDWP, the party that in 1903 split into Bolshevik and Menshevik factions.[1] Both wings of the Russian Social Democrats found a formidable rival in the independent labor movement, the Balakhany and Bibi-Eibat Workers Organization. Founded in 1904 by the brothers Lev and Ilya Shchendrikov, this group concentrated on remedying the economic grievances of the local proletariat.[2] The Armenian workers gravitated toward their Social Democratic Hinchak (Bell) Party or toward the more nationalistic Armenian Revolutionary Federation, commonly known as the Dashnaktsutiun.[3]

The accumulated tensions broke out in a spontaneous general strike in July 1903, and then in another one in December 1904. The latter was called by the Shchendrikovs and joined by the RSDWP and the Armenian organizations. This, the largest demonstration of unrest among Baku workers to date, ended in an impressive victory for them: the signing of the first labor contract in Russia.

Soon afterward the Baku proletariat was moved again to action, this time by the news of the massacre of the St. Petersburg workers on "Bloody Sunday," January 9, 1905. The date marked the beginning of the Russian Revolution, which was to shake the tsardom to its very foundations, and the Russian despotism would never recover from the damages it suffered in the years 1905–1907.

Protest strikes and demonstrations against the massacre spread from Baku throughout Transcaucasia on a scale that threw the government off balance.[4] In early February Baku was put under martial law. Then, in a major overhaul of the regional administration Tsar Nicholas II decreed the restoration of the viceroyalty of the Caucasus, entrusting this office to Count I. I. Vorontsov-Dashkov. Like his predecessor sixty years before, Vorontsov-Dashkov was charged with the urgent mission "to establish without delay peace and order in the Caucasus."[5]

The "Tatar–Armenian War"

As Transcaucasia was being seized by the fever of the revolution, the Muslims at first maintained their splendid isolation of indifference toward the turmoil in the world of the Infidel. This least revolutionized part of the local population was shaken out of its passivity only by the outbreak of intercommunal violence. From the Azerbaijani standpoint the upheaval of 1905 started with what became known as the "Tatar–Armenian War."

Antagonism between the two ethnic groups had been simmering for a long time, and it now transcended differences of religion and xenophobic prejudice. "The Armenians have two points in common with the Jews," wrote a Western observer of the nationality problem in the region. "These are their extreme dispersion and their general superiority in education, industry and enterprise over the population among whom they live and this has made them both weak and strong. They have been disliked and feared by their neighbors, and are defenseless against their attack."[6] A large proportion of local Armenians had recently immigrated to Russia's Muslim-populated provinces in the wake of Russia's wars with Persia and Turkey. Throughout the greater part of tsarist rule in Transcaucasia they were on good terms with Russia, regarding that country as their liberator from Muslim overlordship. Under Russia's protective shield the Armenian community had begun modernizing at a pace much faster than the Muslims. Consequently, the Armenians were better prepared to take advantage of the opportunities that arose with the growth of the Azerbaijani economy. In the 1872 auction for oilfield leases in which the "Tatars" were responsible for a meager 5 percent of the successful bids, the share taken by Armenian investors was almost ten times as large. Of the total of 167 oil firms the Azerbaijanis owned 49, mainly small ones, while the wealthy Armenian families, the Mirzoevs, Mailovs, Liazonovs, Aramiants, Tavetosyans, and Mantashyans, controlled 55 large and medium-sized enterprises.[7] By 1900, of the 115 industrial companies operating in the Baku *guberniia*, 29 percent belonged to the Armenians and only 18 percent to the "Tatars."[8] Some industries, such as wine making, fish processing, and tobacco growing, passed entirely into the hands of Armenians who had driven Azerbaijanis out of competition.

Similar disproportions were to be found among the labor force: the Armenians, who accounted for 17.5 percent of all workers in Baku, held 25 percent of the highly skilled jobs, while the Muslims – Azerbaijanis, Lezghians, Persians, and Volga Tatars – formed the overwhelming majority (more than 70 percent) of the low–paid, unskilled workers. Among the Armenians were moreover a large and increasing group of self-employed – 4.83 percent of their total number. They were also the most urbanized of all the peoples of Transcaucasia, 39 percent of them living in cities and towns.[9]

Armenian–Muslim antagonism had grown into a multifaceted problem; in addition to its cultural–religious dimension, it involved such factors as the grievances of the fledgling Azerbaijani bourgeoisie beset by ruinous competition, the conflict of interests between unskilled "Tatar" laborers and Armenian entrepreneurs and merchants, and the animosity of the predominantly rural Muslims toward the largely urbanized Armenians. A contemporary traveler remarked that "the Tatar hatred is directed against the Armenians more than against the Russians. The Armenians are permanent inhabitants, the Russians come as soldiers, officials, temporary employees and leave after a few years. The Tatars are also less afraid of the Armenians than of the Russians."[10]

The difference in social structure of the two communities was paralleled by the degree to which each was politically organized. In contrast to the Azerbaijanis, the Armenians had produced a dynamic nationalist movement spearheaded by the Dashnaktsutiun. This party's avowed objective was the creation of a free and autonomous Armenian state in the Ottoman provinces of eastern Anatolia, and it saw its enemy in Abdulhamidian Turkey, not in Russia. Yet in the 1890s Armenian nationalism found itself on a collision course with the assimilationist drive of the tsardom in a dramatic reversal of Russo–Armenian friendship. As the Armenians bitterly watched their schools closed down on government order and their Gregorian Church pressured to join the Orthodoxy, tsarist officials began to exploit tensions between the Muslims and Armenians. Prince Grigorii Golitsyn, who in 1896 became the governor–general of the Caucasus, made a series of gestures calculated to win over the Muslims. In response to their resentment over the disproportionately strong representation of Armenians in the civil service – allegedly 50 to 90 percent of the positions, he reduced the number of their officials and filled the vacancies with Muslims.[11] In some Russian *gymnasia* the study of the native language was allowed, and in 1904 the long–delayed authorization was granted to publish an Azerbaijani newspaper, the *Sharq-i Rus*. Golitsyn even lent a sympathetic ear to voices asking for an increase in Muslim representation in the municipal *dumas*, though he took no action.[12] In the midst of his rapprochement with the Muslims, in 1903 he carried out the confiscation of the properties of the Gregorian Church. This blow to the symbol of Armenian nationalism brought the community to the brink of rebellion. Armenian terrorists, formerly active in Turkey turned to attempts on the lives of tsarist officials, including Golitsyn, who survived injuries suffered in October 1903 but left the Caucasus shortly thereafter. No successor was appointed for a time, but Golitsyn's policies were carried on with particular zeal by the governor of Baku, Prince V. I. Nakashidze, who soon had to face a situation charged with revolutionary tensions and with few troops at his disposal because of the Russo–Japanese war. Widespread speculation had it that Nakashidze

2. The 1905 Revolution

intended to weaken the antigovernment forces by exploiting the enmity between the Muslims and the rebellious Armenians. In actuality, the measure of the responsibility born by the tsarist authorities for the events that followed has never been fully determined. No incontrovertible proof of official connivance has been discovered, and there was at any rate enough accumulated hostility between the two peoples to set off the explosion without it. It is known, however, that Nakashidze, after a visit to St. Petersburg in January 1905, authorized the issue of large numbers of arms permits to the Muslims.[13]

The first outbreaks of Muslim–Armenian violence occurred in Baku. The immediate cause was the murder of a Muslim by the Dashnakists. On February 6, 1905 thousands of Azerbaijanis, many arriving from nearby villages, attacked the Armenian sections of the city. There followed three days of killing and looting while the police and troops remained conspicuously inactive, as they would be during most of the clashes to come.[14] The horrors of Baku recurred, on a smaller scale, in Erivan on February 20–21, then in May in Nahkichevan and other part of the Erivan *guberniia*, and in early June in Shusha. Another wave of violence swept Baku toward the end of August with an even more destructive fury than in February, and some Armenian–owned oil fields were set on fire. At the end of September the town of Kazakh was burned down in the course of rioting. One of the bloodiest clashes took place in Ganja on November 15–18, and there was another one in Tiflis on November 21. The fighting continued well into the next year, though with lesser intensity.[15] Nor was it contained in the towns: An estimated 128 Armenian and 158 "Tatar" villages were pillaged or destroyed.[16] The estimates of lives lost vary widely, ranging from 3,100 to 10,000.[17] One author who gives a breakdown of the Armenian casualties in various towns notes that "the number of the Tatars killed was still greater, but we have no statistics because the Muhammedans according to some strange custom conceal everything pertaining to the numbers of killed and other such information."[18] Indeed, all the available data suggest that the Muslims, who were usually on the attack, suffered greater losses than the Armenians, though not overwhelmingly so.

The events were reported in the world press, generally with a tone of partiality toward the Armenians, as if echoing the shock of the 1890s massacres in Turkey. In some Armenian quarters exception was proudly taken to the portrayal of the Armenians as merely victims. A publication of the American–Armenian community quoted the following contemporary report from Transcaucasia:

> The view of the Armenians as harmless sheep uncomplainingly stretching their necks to the slaughter is not borne out by the facts.... It is also untrue that the Armenians have always been the chief sufferers. Although in Baku and Nakhichevan this was the case, at Erivan and Etchmiadzin they remained the victors. At Shusha and Baku in September they suffered heavy material losses, but otherwise they fully held their own and paid the Tatars in their own coin.[19]

The blows suffered at the hands of the Dashnakist fighting squads proved a catalyst for the consolidation of Muslim community of Azerbaijan. The "Tatar–Armenian War" generated for the first time solidarity among Muslims in a cause transcending local or sectarian loyalties, and from now on these divisions ceased to be a serious impediment to political action. The symbol of unity was still the green banner of the Prophet, but the religious appeal functioned mainly as a traditional means of mobilizing the Muslim population for an ethnic conflict. Although the slogans sounded "Death to the Infidel," the reference was specifically to the Armenians, excluding Russians, Georgians, and other Christians. The popular element was strongly in evidence in this eruption of what some Russians termed spontaneous nationalism. Throughout the countryside bands of peasants waged guerilla warfare; from their ranks emerged such legendary heroes as Yusuf and Däli ʿAli.[20] The latter temporarily controlled parts of the Elizavetpol *guberniia*, where he fought battles and skirmishes against the Armenians and eventually against government forces as well, as it soon became apparent that the Russian position with regard to the warring communities had drastically changed again.

The pro-Muslim posture of the tsarist authorities did not last beyond the initial period of the fighting; already in May Russian troops were under orders to fire at the "Tatars." This new Russian about-face came with the appointment of Vorontsov-Dashkov as viceroy. A shrewd and experienced politician, Vorontsov-Dashkov cultivated an image of benevolence toward all the peoples of Transcaucasia. All the same, he was a believer in the

2. The 1905 Revolution

"divide and rule" principle, which he was determined to put into practice, although with different partners than had Golitsyn and Nakashidze. The viceroy considered the Armenians a people attached to property, family, and religion and as such natural supporters of law and stability. Upon assuming office, he began at once his persistent work of reviving the old tradition that had made friendship with the Armenians the pillar of Russian rule beyond the Caucasus. For Vorontsov-Dashkov the issue was more than just an expedient in dealing with the revolutionary turmoil, and in his thinking he took a long-range view. Among the top-echelon tsarist officials he belonged to the partisans of a war with Turkey in which he saw the Armenians again playing the part of Russia's advance guard. "Your Majesty is aware," he wrote to Nicholas II, "that throughout the history of our relations with Turkey in the Caucasus area, Russian policy has been based from the time of Peter the Great on benevolence toward the Armenians who have rewarded us with their active aid in the course of wars."[21] His recommendations to the tsar reached beyond the territory of Transcaucasia, as he proposed "to take the initiative in the defense of the Turkish Armenians, especially at this time, so as not to discourage but rather to promote friendly feelings for us among the population of areas which might easily become the theater of our military operations."[22] One of his first moves in office was to ask the tsar to rescind his 1903 decree on Gregorian Church properties. The revocation of this decree in August 1905 paid off immediately in the form of spontaneous public demonstrations of gratitude, in which even Dashnakists joined. At the same time the viceroy applied increasingly stringent measures against the Muslims. In the Tiflis disturbances, he went so far as to distribute arms to the Social Democrat militia to keep the "Tatars" in check.[23] Instances of cooperation between tsarist authorities and the Dashnakists were an open secret, and even the prime minister, P. A. Stolypin, reproached Vorontsov-Dashkov for his leniency toward the Armenian revolutionaries.[24]

In response to the superior organization of the Dashnaktsutiun, various Muslim groups that had been fighting in a hit-or-miss fashion began to coordinate their actions. Yet it took the menacing reality of the Russian–Armenian entente to move the Azerbaijanis to create a clandestine political association, specifically to counteract this danger. Known as the Difai (Defense), the organization was founded in Ganja, in the fall of 1905, on the initiative of some local notables, who thereby started their careers in politics:[25] Shafi Rustambäkov, the brothers Alakpär and Khalil Khasmammädov, Ismail Ziyatkhanov, Näsib Ussubäkov (Yusufbäyli), and Dr. Hasan Aghazadä. From Baku they were joined by Ahmäd Aghayev. The establishment of the Difai signified the rise of Ganja as the center of the national movement in Azerbaijan, a position the town was to hold from then on.

Remarkably, the leaders of the Difai tried to blunt the edge of the intercommunal conflict. Aghayev sternly lectured the crowds in a Ganja mosque that even "wild animals do not devour their own kind" and reminded them that the Muslims and the Armenians had for centuries lived in peace before the coming of the Russians.[26] Similar notes sounded forcefully in a declaration on the "Tatar–Armenian War" that Ziyatkhanov delivered before the State Duma:

> We, the Muslims, were told by the administration: you have been economically enslaved by the Armenians. They are arming themselves and plan to create their state; one day they will do away with you. The Armenians were told that the idea of Pan-Islamism had put down deep roots in all strata of the Muslim community, and one day the Muslims would massacre them. Such was the pattern of the provocation. When the killing started in Baku, the administration tried to find an excuse in the fact that it had not enough troops at hand, and that it could not have foreseen that the clashes would take place. Then, it was said that the clashes had occurred on the ground of national enmity. I declare that there had never been any enmity between us the Muslims and the Armenians on economic grounds alone. We had been living as good neighbors and liked each other.... In the past there had not been any armed clashes and if cases of murder happened, they were single exceptions and had never assumed any large proportions.[27]

In its clandestinely published proclamations the Difai blamed Russia for the recent bloodshed, but also warned the Armenians that violence on their part would be answered in kind. The Difai did in fact resort to acts of individual terror, mainly against tsarist officials – police and military – known to have encouraged Armenians to anti-Muslim excesses. A product of the "Tatar–Armenian War," the Difai, in turning primarily against Russia, broke the long spell of passive acquiescence to tsarist rule in a

2. The 1905 Revolution

country that had seen no organized resistance since the days of Shamil.

The open hand extended to the Armenians above the heads of the angry mobs was more than just a manifestation of the intelligentsia's enlightened humanitarianism, and even more than simply alertness to the scheming of Russian officialdom. Discernible in the Difai's activity was the effect of a perception of the Transcaucasian peoples' unity that had just begun to gain currency among some Azerbaijanis, notably in Ganja. The idea of such a unity had been put forward for the first time in the twentieth century by the Georgian Party of Social Federalists and had found its followers in the obscure Turkic Revolutionary Committee of Social Federalists. After issuing two proclamations in February 1905 under the headline "Peoples of the Caucasus, Unite," calling for the joint struggle of the Muslims, Georgians, and Armenians against Russia, nothing more was heard of the committee. But a marginal group planted the seed of an important idea and the slogans of the unity of the three peoples had reappeared in the tracts of another Ganja organization, Gayret (Perseverance), set up in the summer of 1905 by Rustambäkov, who shortly thereafter became one of the founders of the Difai.[28] There were indications that prominent Difai members maintained contact with their opposite numbers in the Dashnaktsutiun, and both associations cooperated jointly with the liberal wing of the émigré Young Turks, the latter-day Ottoman League of Decentralization.[29] In the two warring communities, the politically organized groups found a common ground in the idea of emancipation from Russia through the unity of the Transcaucasian peoples. When in 1907 the Dashnaktustiun, by far the most powerful party in the region, included in its program a blueprint for the future status of Transcaucasia, the leaders of the Difai may have concluded that its thrust was generally not incompatible with their own aspirations. According to the relevant section of the Dashnakist program, Transcaucasia was to become a component part of the Federal Republic of Russia, but otherwise was to be entirely independent in its internal affairs; its highest authority was to be a democratically elected regional parliament. The territory of Transcaucasia was to be divided into cantons, their borders drawn, wherever possible, on the basis of ethnic composition of the population. Constitutional provisions were to include guarantees of cultural autonomy and the right to use local languages on an equal basis with Russian, the official language.[30]

Azerbaijani liberalism

While forces in Ganja were nurturing a protonational movement aimed at loosening if not serving Azerbaijan's ties to Russia, in Baku programs were being formulated that envisioned the country as an integral part of the Russian state. Azerbaijani liberalism, merely an attitude of mind before 1905, was galvanized to action by the spread of the revolution. The liberal movement still lacked organizational forms, and it continued for some time to be an activity of loosely linked individuals, yet it succeeded in gaining political leadership of the Muslim community. At first the liberals cautiously limited themselves to declarations in the Baku *duma* and articles in the *Kaspiy* demanding equality of rights for Muslims and Christians.[31] Then, after the proclamation of February 18, 1905 convening the State Duma with advisory powers (Bulygin Duma) – an act that seemed to indicate a more accommodating disposition on the part of the tsardom – the liberals took further steps. Petitioning campaigns became their favorite tactic for gaining concessions. Their most comprehensive petition, handed in April to the viceroy and the Russian Prime Minister S. J. Witte, outlined what was in effect the platform of native liberalism at this early stage of the revolution. Bearing signatures that connoted wealth and prestige – including those of Topchibashev, Aghayev, Ziyatkhanov, and Rashid Khan Shirvanski – the document was a register of grievances for which redress was sought, without at any point transcending the established legal order.

Because Transcaucasia by comparison with other parts of the empire was underprivileged in matters of self-government and banking, the liberals called for the introduction of the *zemstvos* and the extension of the facilities of the Nobility Bank and the Peasant Bank to the region. Specific concerns of the Azerbaijani community appeared in requests that were made that the Muslims be given full access to civil service careers, that they be allowed to open a *mädräsä* with a status comparable to that of a Christian theological seminary, and that they be given the opportunity to study the native language in all types of schools. In a section dealing specifically with social problems, the petition also sought a halt to the immigration of Russian settlers and for distribution of Treasury lands as well as portions of large estates under terms of installment purchase.[32]

The response of the government seemed at first to vindicate the moderate line of the liberals' tactics. As a token of good will, Vorontsov-Dashkov tried to make good on the most crucial of all grievances – the exclusion of Transcaucasia from the *zemstvo* system. Only July 16, 1905, he announced a proposal for the reform, to the eager welcome of the educated and propertied classes. A public debate was encouraged that was to be conducted in preparatory conferences at the *uezd* and *guberniia* levels. In the end the chief accomplishment of these gatherings was to reveal the chasm between the ambitions of the elite and the attitudes of the rural masses: They were attended by the intelligentsia and the big landowners, while the peasantry demonstrated its indifferences by staying at home. This lack of peasant interest in the reform, combined with the outbreak of new disturbances in the fall of 1905, gave the viceroy an excuse to shelve the issue of the *zemstvo*s – indefinitely, as it turned out.[33]

Meanwhile, as the crisis of the regime was deepening, Azerbaijani liberals grew bolder and made their venture onto the broader arena of Russia's Muslim politics. As in Transcaucasia, Muslims in other parts of the empire were remarkably slow in joining the tide of the revolution, an attitude Gasprinski's *Tarjuman* explained somewhat apologetically by alluding to their old custom of suffering in silence.[34] Only by the summer of 1905 was there enough support to issue a call for convening a congress of Muslims from all Russia. The strongest backing for this enterprise came from the wealthy Volga Tatar bourgeoisie. These Tatars, the first ethnic group to pass under Russian rule (in the sixteenth century), traditionally held the position of leadership among Russia's Muslims, intellectually as well as economically. They had acquired their wealth as middlemen in Russia's trade with the Muslim East, and their moneyed class consisted largely of merchant families.[35]

The idea of an all-Muslim congress also received endorsement from the potential challengers to the Tatars' position, the Azerbaijanis, of whom the wealthiest were industrialists. Although the Azerbaijanis could not claim an equally long tradition of contact with European civilization, their contributions to Muslim intellectual life were impressive, and the Azerbaijani press – *Äkinchi, Sharq-i Rus,* and especially *Kaspiy* – reflected their ambition to share in the leadership of Russia's Muslim community. Soviet historiography has perceived in the growing rivalry between the Tatars and the Azerbaijanis a manifestation of differences between the commercial and industrial bourgeoisie, respectively, the former committed to the program of Muslim unity, the latter more sensitive to regionalism and ethnic particularism.[36] As the campaign for organizing the congress was led by the liberals, it met with the opposition of conservative–religious elements.

The First All-Russian Muslim Congress convened eventually on August 15, 1905 at Nizhni Novgorod during a commercial fair and included some 15 delegates from the Crimea, northern Caucasus, Transcaucasia, Kazan, Urals, Turkestan, and Siberia. They were for the most part lawyers, teachers, merchants, and landowners, along with a few liberal-minded theologians. Lacking official authorization and seeking not to antagonize the government, the delegates congregated on a pleasure boat. The organizers took precautions to exclude a few left-wing radicals, as their presence might have compromised the whole assembly. The chairman of the congress was Gasprinski, and his deputies Topchibashev and two Tatars, Rashid Ibrahimov and Yusuf Akchurin (Akçuraoğlu), the latter a well-known proponent of political Pan-Turkism.[37] The central issue of the debates was the organizational form the Muslim movement should assume. In the end, the most moderate faction prevailed, and the congress resolved to create, instead of a full-fledged political party, the Rusyanin Musleman Ittifaqi (Union of Russian Muslims), or Ittifaq for short, setting for it the following objectives:

1. The unification of Muslims in Russia within one movement
2. The establishment of a constitutional monarchy based on proportional representation of nationalities
3. The legal equality of the Muslim and Russian populations and abrogation of all laws and administrative practices discriminatory to Muslims

4. The cultural and educational progress of Muslims[38]

Nonpolitical though the congress tried hard to appear, it revealed an unmistakable preference for one of the Russian parties, the Constitutional Democrats (Kadets), which some prominent Muslims had already joined. The Kadet Party, the creation of *zemstvo* leaders, was the hard core of Russian liberalism and had at its head the historian and statesman P. N. Miliukov. Its program called for institution of a parliamentary regime under a constitutional monarchy and for implementation of social and economic reforms, including the expropriation of large estates – subject to compensation.

The question of an electoral alliance with the Kadets was debated and decided in the affirmative at the Second All-Russian Muslim Congress held in St. Petersburg on January 13–23, 1906.[39] The third and most important of the Muslim congresses met on August 16–21, again in Nizhni Novgorod, but this time with official permission. Its chairman was Topchibashev, who skillfully steered the debates through frequently stormy sessions. Over opposition from two sides – such nonpolitical leaders as Gasprinski and the socialists, who rejected the idea of solidarity among classes – the congress resolved to transform the Ittifaq into a political party representing all Muslims in Russia. The platform of the Ittifaq was largely a restatement of that of the Kadets, with additional emphasis on issues relating to Muslim national and religious equality, such as extension of the powers of local self-government and freedom of education in native languages. The fifteen-man central committee of the Ittifaq consisted almost entirely of the Volga and Ural Tatars and included only one Azerbaijani, Topchibashev.[40]

Except for the latter, the Azerbaijani liberals loosened their ties to the all-Russian Muslim movement after the second congress, leaving the field to the Tatars. In a switch confirming that the attraction of their Caucasian particularism was stronger than their commitment to the vision of the organic unity of Russia's Muslims, they concentrated their activities on regional politics. The Azerbaijani liberals acknowledged the specific conditions of their home region, a world unto itself with its mosaic of heterogenous populations. Moreover, the restoration of the viceroyalty had awakened expectations for some tangible improvements along the lines of wider self-government. Following the tsar's manifesto of October 17, 1905 guaranteeing civil liberties and proclaiming the convocation of the State Duma with legislative powers, a group of Baku liberals founded the Muslim Constitutional Party, affiliated to the Baku branch of the Kadets. Some echoes of the slogans circulating in Ganja could be heard in the party's proposals for reorganizing Transcaucasia into an autonomous region with its own legislature, the Seim, and its subdivision into ethnically homogenous administrative units.[41] Even though the Baku liberals were circumspect in their presentation of these views and, unlike the members of the Difai, demonstrated no hostility toward Russia, they came to be accused by none other than the Russian Social Democrats of having in effect accepted the "Caucasus for the Caucasians" battle cry.[42]

As for the idea of all-Russian Muslim unity, it was upheld mainly in the State Duma, where the Azerbaijani deputies took their seats on the benches of the Ittifaq. In the elections to the First Duma, which were completed in Transcaucasia only by the end of May 1906, six Muslim candidates had won seats: Topchibashev, Ziyatkhanov, Alakpär Khasmammädov, M. T. Äliyev, A. Murdakhanov, and the playwright Haqvärdiyev.[43]

The Azerbaijani deputies, who arrived in St. Petersburg after considerable delay, found little opportunity to make their presence felt in the First State Duma before the tsar ordered its dissolution after less than three months of existence (April 27–July 8). Elections to the Second State Duma were decreed at the same time on the basis of modified election laws. In Transcaucasia, the change did not work to the advantage of the Muslims, their elected representation now having been decreased to four deputies from the Eastern Transcaucasian *gubernia*s: Fath ͨAli-Khan Khoiski, Khalil Khasmammädov, Ismail Taghiyev (son of the industrialist), and Zeynal Zeynalov. In addition, the Muslim population of the Erivan *guberniia*, elected the former publisher of the *Sharq-i Rus*, M. A. Shakhtakhtinski. One of the Azerbaijanis in the Duma, Zeynalov, did not sit with the Ittifaq; instead he became the head of the six-man Muslim Labor Group, linked to the Russian Trudoviki (Toilers) parliamentary group. The two Muslim factions differed most deeply on the question of agrarian reforms: Zeynalov called for the distribution of land to the peasants without indemnities; Khan Khoiski, acting as spokesman for the Ittifaq, advocated compulsory redistribution of land, but on the condition of "fair compensation" and in a manner that would not benefit settlers from distant regions of the empire. The question of Russian settlements, by far a more grievous issue for the Azerbaijani public than inequality of land holdings among the natives, figured prominently in the speeches of Shakhtakhtinski and Khasmammädov.[44]

The hopes vested in the Duma as a forum for championing the interests of the Muslims were shattered on July 3, 1907 by the decree dissolving the legislature once again. At the same time Stolypin again altered the election laws, in effect drastically curtailing the number of non-Russian deputies. In the Third Duma, whose largely conservative membership was at last acceptable to the tsardom, the Transcaucasian Muslims were represented by a single delegate, A. Khasmammädov. Now, the revolution having ebbed and the government under Stolypin energetically restoring its hold over Russia, the Ittifaq virtually dissolved and the Azerbaijani liberals became dispersed.

Azerbaijani socialism

To the extent that Azerbaijani liberals were affiliated with the Kadets, the native socialists, as represented by the Himmät (the organization they formed in 1904), were linked to the Russian Social Democratic Workers Party (RSDWP). Both Azerbaijani movements gravitated toward the cause of the Russian Revolution. For the first group its success held the promise of a future under a constitutional monarchy; for the latter, one in a democratic republic. In any event, the liberals as much as the socialists guarded their native identities from their Russian confederates.

The rise of the Himmät on the eve of the revolution was directly related to the fact that the RSDWP's Baku Committee, which included no natives, had disregarded the need for agitation among the Muslims. The first efforts to familiarize Muslims with the ideas of socialism were largely confined to the individual efforts of some Azerbaijani rank-and-file members of the Russian party. In addition, acting independently from the RSDWP, were a handful of young men, mainly from the intelligentsia, who in 1903 formed a debating circle and the next year initiated propaganda activity directed at the Muslim population. Some of the latter, such as M. G. Movsumov, Sultan Mäjid Äfändiyev, and Assadullah Akhundov, were actually RSDWP members, while others, Mammäd Amin Räsulzadä, Mammäd Hasan Hajinski, and Abbas Kazimzadä had no known affiliations outside their small band.[45]

The group assumed the name Himmät after the title of the clandestine newspaper it printed in Azerbaijani. The first issue appeared in October 1904, bearing as its motto on the masthead the Arabic proverb "The joint efforts of men will move mountains."[46] Six editions were published before mid-February 1905, when the police seized the Himmätists' mimeographic equipment – a misfortune that turned out to be of minor consequence now that the outbreak of revolution had created a new environment for political action.

The *Himmät* conducted its agitation in a markedly less doctrinaire manner than its equivalent publications in other languages circulating in Baku, and a Soviet historian has remarked that its articles were written from "non-Marxist positions."[47] In its pages the oppression of the masses was linked primarily to foreign rule. The target of these attacks was not so much the system of capitalism as the tsarist bureaucracy and the Muslim religious establishment, the latter because of its servility to Russian despotism. Some harsh words were addressed to the Europeanized bourgeoisie and intellectuals for abandoning the native language and customs. In its positive aspects the propaganda of the *Himmät* appeared scarcely more revolutionary than the time-honored programs of the intelligentsia. Above all, the call was for the spread of education as the surest way to progress and well-being, including instruction in the native language, and for improvement in the status of women; little regard was given to ideas of social revolution.[48]

Early in 1905 the Himmät group was joined by two capable organizers, themselves members of the RSDWP, though of recent date and no high standing: Mäshadi Äzizbäyoghlï Äzizbäkov (1870–1918), an engineer turned professional revolutionary, and Nariman Näjäfoghlï Narimanov (1870–1925), a man of diverse talents known at first as a writer and educator and recently a medical student in Odessa on a grant from Taghiyev.[49] These two men strengthened the leadership of the Himmät at a time when the numbers of its followers began to grow impressively. The Muslim proletariat proved not to be immune to socialist slogans coming from their coreligionists, the more so because invectives against autocracy and capitalism could be understood as being aimed at the Infidel. As a police report noted, the Himmät "does not include politically conscious workers; however, the mass of Tatars, Lezghians, and Persians listen to the voice of the organization.... It issues tracts. It is headed by energetic individuals who, although lacking in erudition, are possessed of strong revolutionary temperaments that produce an effect on the masses."[50] No longer confining its work to the Baku oil belt, the Himmät branched out to provincial towns and even established cells in Daghestan and Transcaspia. On the first anniversary of the October Manifesto of 1905, which had officially introduced parliamentary system to Russia, the Himmät issued a proclamation attacking the tsardom for having made a mockery of its promise of a freely elected legislature with full powers. In a reference to a notorious example from Ottoman history of royal absolutism suppressing hopes for change, the Himmät stated that "the Manifesto of the Tsar Nicholas turned out to be what the Midhad constitution had become under Sultan Abdulhamid."[51] The Himmät's proclamation was issued in the name of the Muslim Social Democratic *Party* instead of the previously used term *Group*. The high point in the fortunes of the Azerbaijani socialists came at the close of 1906 when the Himmät-backed candidate Zeynalov won election to the Second State Duma.

The Himmät's relationship to the Russian Social Democrats defies any clear-cut definition and has been interpreted in somewhat contradictory ways. Soviet authors emphasize that the Azerbaijani organization, at least after the outbreak of the revolution, became affiliated with the RSDWP. The affiliation was, however, on no higher a level than that of the RSDWP's Baku Committee. In addition, the Baku Committee granted the Himmät autonomous status, an exception to the RSDWP's cardinal principle that party organizations must be formed not on ethnic but on territorial bases. Not only was such a concession unusual, but the fact that it had been granted by a local rather than a central authority made its validity tenuous. The Baku Committee for its part justified its stance by alluding to the "specific character of the work among the Muslims," a formula that conceded that Azerbaijanis could not be reached through more conventional means of agitation.[52]

Neither is much light shed on this relationship by Himmätist proclamations, which were sometimes signed jointly with the RSDWP and the Armenian Social Democratic Workers Party acting together as an electoral bloc. On other occasions these proclamations bore only the signature of the Muslim Social Democratic Group–Himmät, without acknowledging (except in one case), its connection, if any, to the Russians.[53] More revealing was the announcement of the Baku Committee on the occasion of the reunification of the Bolshevik and Menshevik factions, which additionally stated that "the Armenian organization 'Hinchak' definitely has merged with us and has ended its independent existence" and that "the Muslim Social Democratic Group–Himmät once more has confirmed its willingness to work under our guidance."[54] The key word here appears to be *guidance*, and the relationship between the two organizations seems to have been not so much a formal one as an influence exerted by Himmätists who at the same time belonged to the RSDWP. On a higher level the contact was maintained by a member of the Baku Committee, Prokofii A. Dzhaparidze, and, it seems, occasionally also by Stalin, who represented the Caucasian Party Committee. It was Stalin who reportedly unsuccessfully tried in 1906 to pressure the Himmätists into a merger.[55] A deep streak of Muslim–Turkic particularism characterized the Himmät from its inception and throughout its existence, and repeatedly this caused the Azerbaijani organization to resist outright absorption by its Russian opposite number.

For all its personal links with the RSDWP, the Himmät failed to evolve into a centralized and closely knit entity on the Bolshevik pattern. Instead, it continued to operate as a loose association of individuals inclined to radicalism but concerned less with doctrine than with action. The hard core of its leadership were members of the intelligentsia, and for many of them a favorite field of activity was work in the tradition of the enlightenment movement – through educational associations and the press. In 1906 there appeared the first legal socialist publication specifically aimed at Muslims, the bilingual Azerbaijani–Armenian newspaper *Davät-Koch* (Call). Ostensibly an organ of the

2. The 1905 Revolution

shadowy Armenian–Muslim League, *Davät-Koch*, accused the government of fomenting intercommunal strife in order to stave off its own downfall, was suspended by the governor of Baku after putting out sixteen issues.[56] Before the end of the year, the Himmätists revived their press with the weekly *Takammül* (Perfection), whose editors were Räsulzadä and Hajinski. The *Takammül* made little effort to conceal its ideological orientation, although its socialism was tinged with specifically Azerbaijani preoccupations – national oppression, colonialism, mass education, and the political crisis in neighboring Persia. A lively publication that attracted not only leftist contributors, it was closed down by the police in March 1907.[57] The government was now moving to the counteroffensive, and in the Stolypin period the Himmät came face to face with the harsh realities of repression. Some of its leaders (Narimanov, Äfändiyev, and B. M. Sardarov) having been arrested, and others (Räsulzadä, I. M. Abilov, and D. Buniatzadä) having taken refuge in Persia along with hundreds of the rank and file, the weakened party showed little staying power.[58] Subsequently the Himmät lost its following as quickly as it had gained it, and by the end of the year nothing much was left of its existence as an organized force. Still, in December 1909 a handful of Himmätists meeting in Ganja worked out a party program. The document contained no references to the RSDWP, or even to socialism, although it spoke of defending the poor; essentially, it revealed a libertarian tinge in its demands for freedom of speech, press, association, and creed. Its most radical clauses called for free education, an eight-hour working day, and distribution of land to the tillers.[59] The program was intended to serve as a blueprint for the political platform of the Persian *mujtahid* (fighters for faith) movement, but had no practical significance for the Himmät in view of its dispersion.[60] Individually, some of the Himmätists devoted themselves entirely to working within the RSDWP. A notable case was that of Azizbäkov, who in 1911 was elected deputy of the party to the Baku *duma*; others tried to keep alive the flame among their countrymen by means of journalism. An attempt was made to resuscitate the Azerbaijani socialist press with the weekly *Yoldash* (Comrade), which had been closed down in September 1907 after three editions. Likewise, the *Bakï häyatï* published by Buniatzadä in 1911 and the literary satirical magazine *Arï* (Bee) started by him the next year proved ephemeral, unable to survive both the vigilance of the government and the lack of public interest in socialism after the failure of the first Russian Revolution.[61]

Intellectual ferment

Political parties, a novelty in the Azerbaijani experience, proved to be short-lived, unable to withstand the onslaught of the recuperated tsarist regime. While party structures collapsed, the underlying processes shaping the collective consciousness of the Azerbaijanis continued to operate, in some ways gaining momentum even after the revolution in Russia had become a memory.

The upheaval of 1905 brought about the weakening of arbitrary government controls, one of the effects of which was the release of the long-pent-up energies of the intelligentsia. Philanthropic, educational, theatrical, and artistic associations mushroomed, busying themselves with setting up new schools, funding scholarships, and organizing theatrical performances. Symbolic of this cultural revitilization was the staging in 1908 of the first Azerbaijani opera, *Läyla and Mäjnun*, based on the sixteenth-century poem by Fuzuli set to the music of Uzeir Hajibäyli. In the field of education the efforts to promote growth and improvement yielded impressive accomplishments, as the literacy rate more than doubled in 1914. There followed a significant increase in the number of books printed in the native language, and a relaxation of censorship ushered in the golden age of the Azerbaijani press. Between 1905 and 1917 no less than sixty-three newspapers and periodicals were in circulation at one time or another, a remarkable figure given that Azerbaijan's population was still predominantly illiterate.[62] With a few exceptions, these publications appeared in Baku, which became the capital of Muslim journalism in Russia, outdistancing Kazan. Though many of the Azerbaijani newspapers were ephemeral or enjoyed only local circulation, some, representing high intellectual and journalistic standards, found readers far beyond their homeland. Among those were the literary review *Füyuzat* (Abundance) and the dailies *Häyat* (Life) and *Irshad* (Guidance). By far the greatest success story was the immensely popular satirical magazine *Molla*

2. The 1905 Revolution

Näsr al-din, with subscribers even in such faraway lands as India and Afghanistan. The aficionados of the magazine included illiterates who enjoyed its famous cartoons.[63]

In addition to the improved political climate, the Azerbaijani press benefitted from the financial support of wealthy members of the community, some of whom turned into veritable press lords. The ubiquitous Taghiyev owned, besides *Kaspiy*, the *Häyat*, the *Füyuzat*, and later the daily *Täzä Häyat* (New Life). The young aristocratic landowner Isa Ashurbakov financed some Himmätist publications as well as the independent *Irshad* and then the literary journal *Shälälä* (Waterfall), while his father Bashir and after him the oil magnate Murtaza Mukhtarov subsidized the daily *Täräqqi* (Progress). The combination of increased freedom to publish and availability of funds spawned a profusion of journalistic talents. Most were homegrown, but Baku was also attracting writers from outside Azerbaijan, notably from Turkey, Persia, and the Crimea.

Very few Azerbaijani newspapers adhered to a clearcut political line – in this respect even the Himmätist organs were flexible, and conversely, socialists often wrote for the bourgeois dailies. Taken as a whole, the press accurately reflected the intellectual currents at work and, more importantly, functioned as a sounding board for the fundamental dilemmas confronting the intelligentsia. The latter could be reduced to two non-mutually-exclusive issues: the challenge of the revolutionary epoch and the quest for national self-definition. Through newspaper articles the term *milliyätchilik* (nationalism) and the even more precise loan word *nasyonalizm* came into use, and newspapers began addressing their readers not merely as Muslims but also as Caucasian Turks or simply Turks.

The intellectual elite were broadly divided between those for whom the political and social aspects of the revolution were paramount and others who viewed it primarily as an event of national significance. The leading figure among the former was Aghayev, who at this stage of his life identified himself with the left wing of the liberals. After a brief stint as coeditor in chief of the *Häyat* with Topchibashev and Huseynzadä, in February 1906, finding the newspaper too conservative for his liking, he started publication of the *Irshad*.[64] On the masthead of this popular daily appeared an almost Jacobinic-sounding motto, "Liberty, Equality, Justice," and among its contributors were also the Himmätist Narimanov, Äzizbäkov, and Äfändiyev. Aghayev himself could not hold back from attacking the native capitalist class, even though his newspaper received a subsidy from one of its members. The attitude of the *Irshad* toward the revolution was by far more forthcoming than that of most of the somewhat reserved Azerbaijani press. One of its articles predicted that "from the long suffering under the Tsarist oppression energies in the people have been generated which will lead to events overshadowing the French Revolution that had turned the world upside down."[65] The *Irshad*, which encouraged discussions of the crucial issues of the day, carried a revealing debate on the topic "Socialism or Nationalism?" Those who expressed their preference for socialism agreed that for Muslims the road to the future was the same as for the rest of mankind and they should therefore not allow themselves to be diverted by nationalist sentiments. Yet one participant, Harun-bäy Sultanov, gave a telling indication of the use that a Pan-Islamist perceived in the ideology of socialism: It would help to draw the Turks and the Arabs closer together, a union that would bring about the hoped-for revival of the world of Islam.[66]

The majority of views expressed in this debate were clearly in favor of nationalism, though as a theoretical proposition, without qualifying it as Muslim, Turkic, or Azerbaijani. Significantly, Aghayev came around to the same position. In his new press organ, the *Täräqqi*, successor to the *Irshad*, which had been closed down by the government in June 1908, he summarized the conclusion of the debate:

Socialism is such a lofty and magnificent ideal that it is impossible to despise its followers. But we have to consider this ideal as still belonging to the realm of dreams and visions; we believe that not only one, but several centuries, may pass before it becomes a reality. In the meantime nations grow and all of them have to live through the stage called nationalism and that's why we have become its adherents, on the pattern of the English, the French, the Italians, and the Germans.[67]

In a related article Aghayev cited an additional reason for his position: "Nationalism," he wrote, "unites all classes within the society."[68]

One man who believed that with the 1905 Revolution the time had come for Azerbaijanis to define their national identity – and

2. The 1905 Revolution 59

who had no doubt what that identity should be – was Huseynzadä. From 1905 on he exerted a growing if controversial influence over a large contingent of the intelligentsia. Soon after his return from Turkey he began to write for the *Hāyat*, the "Islamic newspaper" whose orientation was Pan-Islamic–religious rather than Turkic–national. Writing in the arts and science column Huseynzadä quietly took to propagating the ideas of Turkism. In an article "What Kind of Learning Do We Need?" he spelled out for the first time what was later to become a famous slogan: "Turkify, Islamicize, Europeanize" (*"Türklashtirmak, Islamlashtirmak, Avrupalashtirmak"*).[69] Subsequently adopted in slightly modified form and popularized by Ziya Gökalp, this slogan became the battle cry of Turkism in the Ottoman State. In Azerbaijan, these three words would one day be symbolized in the tricolor of the independent republic.

Huseynzadä, expounded on the meaning of his slogan – which in essence represented a modernizing program minus secularization – on the pages of the *Füyüzat*. This literary–artistic journal, founded by him in 1906, was distinguished by its intellectual sophistication and breadth of interests, qualities that won it comparison with the renowned Istanbul periodical *Servet-i Fünun* (Treasure of Sciences). "Our publication's concern," wrote ᶜAli bäy Huseynzadä, "is focused on these issues: Turkism, Islam, and European civilization. It follows that our system of thought seeks guidance from Turkic life and from the worship of Islam. It also calls for acquiring the benefits of civilization from contemporary Europe."[70] The *Füyuzat* crusaded for the emancipation of native culture from the double burden of alien influences – the traditional Persian and the more recent Russian. Azerbaijani intellectuals, he argued, should take inspiration from Western thought, following the example of their Ottoman counterparts of the *Tanzimat* era. The group of writers who gathered around the magazine initiated a trend, called at first the *Füyuzat* literature, which, as it grew, later came to be described also as neoromanticism. Its characteristics included an "art for arts sake" aestheticism that sharply contrasted with the populist–enlightenment heritage of the nineteenth century; rich and complex language; and a pronounced consciousness of Turkism.[71]

In Huseynzadä's writings of the period is apparent an apprehension that one day the Azerbaijanis might conceive the idea of a nation of their own, separate from other Turks, and he inveighed against what he perceived as an inclination toward parochialism implicit in the notion of *millät*: "Rise, rise above and step out of the narrow circle of nations [*millät*] and nationalism. Do not allow yourselves to be turned into submissive subjects of particularistic, petty nations."[72] ᶜAli bäy believed that history was moving toward the age of large state organisms, especially those bound together by common religion, language, and culture. He made it sufficiently clear that he envisioned a national destiny for the Transcaucasian Turks in union with the Ottoman State, "the spiritual and political head of the Islamic world."[73]

The *Füyuzat* group, which included non-Azerbaijani Turks- the Ottomans Ahmed Kemal and Abdullah Jevded and the Crimean Tatar Hasan Sabri Ayvazov – took the stand that Turks everywhere should use a single literary language, a modified Ottoman, which would, among other things, benefit the cultural advancement of the Transcaucasian Turks. The Azerbaijani language, rooted in peasant dialects, had failed – so the *Füyuzat* writers argued – to develop the ability to express abstract concepts and complex reasoning. "What we call the native language," wrote Ahmad Kemal, "has for centuries been cut off from contact with progress in politics, philosophy and science and consequently has been arrested in its natural evolution."[74] Contributions to the *Füyuzat* were, for the most part, written in Ottoman, often in a elaborate style with an elitist disregard for the ability of the average Azerbaijani to understand them. After the demise of the *Füyuzat* in December 1907, its linguistic program found continuity in the new literary journals *Yeni Füyuzat*, *Shälälä*, and *Dirilik* (Vitality).

Of all the topics debated in the Transcaucasian press, the question of a literary language became the focus of the longest-lasting and most intense controversy. The real issue looming in the background was that of an Azerbaijani identity. The consciousness of belonging to the Turkic nation (*qavm*) had gained acceptance among the intelligentsia – educated Azerbaijanis had already began to call themselves Turks – but the questions remained: What kind of Turks were they, how should they qualify their Turkishness, and, specifically, should they identify themselves with the Ottomans?

2. The 1905 Revolution

The antecedents of the language controversy are to be found in the origins of the modern Azerbaijani literature and press. Just before 1905 the issue had been revived by the *Sharq-i Rus*, the newspaper whose inaugural issue contained the memorable statement, "We lack a literary language." The author of this statement, Shakhtakhtinski, the first of the twentieth-century *Azärijilar* ("partisans of Azerbaijani"), had appealed for writing in the language spoken by a native population. Admitting that there was no agreed-upon standard of literary Azerbaijani, he nevertheless expressed the hope that it would evolve in the columns of the *Sharq-i Rus*. In the charged atmosphere of the period, this linguistic program was inevitably seen in political terms, and it made the *Sharq-i Rus* the target of accusations that it was serving the Russian aim of dividing the Muslim community. Typical was the following comment by Arminius Vambery:

> Russia has taken the trouble to publish a newspaper in Tiflis, called Shark-Rusi [sic], written in Azerbaijani dialect in which the Turks and Muslims of the Caucasus are represented as having become...an independent nationality, quite distinct from Anglo-Indian and Ottoman coreligionists and speaking in glowing terms of the Tsar's government.[75]

In the years after 1905 opposition to the Ottomanizer was at first motivated by a concern that the public would be alienated by a literature written in an idiom not easily comprehensible to the majority. Understandably, the *Azärijilar* came mostly from populist-leaning circles. In the forefront of their counterattack was the *Molla Näsr al-din*, which enjoyed the largest circulation of any Azerbaijani newspaper (five thousand copies weekly). It had begun publication with a pledge from its editor in chief, Jälal Mammäd Quluzadä, to write in a simple language accessible to everyone. A satirical journal, the *Molla* reveled in demonstrating how the use of Ottoman grammar and expression in Azerbaijani produced comic effects.[76]

The publication of a modest school textbook let loose a storm of controversy when Huseynzadä objected that it had included no specimens of Ottoman literature, but only those in the Azerbaijani vernacular. The reaction of the *Azärijilar* was forceful, and one of them, Omar Faiq Ne'manzadä, wrote angrily: "We do not need to be read by five or ten persons in Istanbul. What we do need is to be read by three or four million of the people of the Caucasus."[77]

The debate assumed a new dimension when after the 1908 Young Turkish revolution, the nationalist-minded writers in Turkey launched their own campaign for purification of the Ottoman language, replete as it was with the Arabic and Persian intrusions. The ripples created by their movement, known as the Yeni Lisan (New Language), had the effect of strengthening the both sides in the Azerbaijani controversy. In 1912, Azerbaijani Ottomanizers began publishing *Shälälä*, written entirely in the reformed Ottoman. *Shälälä*'s declared intention was to "serve the cause of the unification of Turkic peoples on the basis of the Ottoman dialect used by the most advanced of all literatures in the Turkic speaking world."[78]

The *Azärijilar*, for their part, capitalized on the Yeni Lisan's criticism of contemporary Ottoman by contending that "the place where a Turkic language is most Arabized anywhere is Istanbul"[79] – in contrast with Azerbaijani, much of whose vocabulary was drawn from the native vernacular. Even the reformed version of Ottoman, purged of some foreign grammatical forms, still contained, as the *Azärijilar*'s organ *Iqbal* (Future) remarked, no more than 30 percent Turkic words.[80]

As the debate reached its boiling point, the literary critic and historian Färidun bäy Köchärli stepped in with his famous article in the *Molla Näsr al-din*, "The Native Language." The fundamental attribute of every nation (*millät*), he argued, is its language. A nation could lose its wealth, its government, even its territory, and still survive, but should it lose its language not a trace of it would remain. That was the threat hanging over the Caucasian Turks, who had recovered their written language after a long period of domination by Persia, but now were being forced to replace it with Ottoman. "If only this great man [i.e., Huseynzadä] had continued to live quietly in Istanbul, instead of honoring our hapless Caucasia with his arrival. His knowledge and virtues are of little use to us, but he has caused a confusion in our language, indeed he has brought with him a new language."[81] Conceding that the efforts of the Ottomanizers had not been unsuccessful, Köchärli wrote that "in a short period of time the language of the Caucasian Turks became full of Ottoman words and expressions. In our opinion such aping, such

2. The 1905 Revolution

conduct, amounts to national treason."[82] Hyperbolically, the Azerbaijani writer compared the work of the Ottomanizers to the practices of the notorious nineteenth-century Russifier of the Turkic peoples, N. I. Il'minski. This was an aggressive affirmation of Azerbaijani national consciousness, though strictly confined to the domain of language. The date was 1913, and by this time the germination of this consciousness had been stimulated not only by the debates of intellectuals at home, but also by developments across the border, in Persian Azerbaijan, a new center of revolutionary influences.

3

The era of war and revolutions: ideologies, programs, and political orientations

Azerbaijan and the revolutions in Persia and Turkey

The revolutionary period that had ended in Russia proper by mid-1907 extended longer in Azerbaijan, which was rocked by the shock waves of new upheavals. These took place first in Persia, then in Turkey, all in the context of cultures and societies with which the Azerbaijanis identified themselves incomparably closer than with Russia.

From the Azerbaijani perspective there were two meanings to the term *Persia*: One denoted the large, multiethnic kingdom linked to Azerbaijan by the ties of religion, cultural heritage, and, until the nineteenth century, common history. The other meaning was narrower and connoted Persian Azerbaijan, the country of common language and closest ethnic kinship. The bonds between the two parts of the divided land had not dissolved with the Russian conquest; in some respects they grew even stronger with the coming of the industrial age. "Travel back and forth between Azerbaijan and Russia was one of the important factors in the progress of civilization in Azerbaijan," reminisced a prominent native of Tabriz. "Russian commercial and oil wealth attracted the people of Iran. They brought back money, chiefly, but also some knowledge."[1] While the merchants and shipowners from Baku carried on the bulk of the Russian trade with Persian Azerbaijan, Azerbaijani-speaking workers from Persia's Tabriz province regularly migrated north of the Araxes River border. The latter accounted for a large proportion of the

3. The era of war and revolutions

labor force in Eastern Transcaucasia – 15 percent and 12 percent in the *guberniias* of Baku and Elizavetpol, respectively. Like most Muslim laborers, they were predominantly unskilled, and if employed seasonally, as was often the case, they would return home after their work ended. Their mobility is illustrated by the figure of 312,000 entry visas issued by the Russian consulate in Tabriz between 1891 and 1904.[2] During the revolutionary years 1905–1907 the number of immigrants from Persia in the Baku area alone oscillated between 20,000 and 25,000.[3]

The Russian Revolution of 1905 left its impact on events in Persia in two important ways: It temporarily paralyzed the capability of the tsardom for military intervention abroad, and it provided the Persians with an example that encouraged them to initiate their own reforms. Pressures for changes had been mounting for many years under the Qajar regime, whose hallmarks were oppression, corruption and backwardness. At the same time Britain and Russia, competing for economic concessions from Persia, gradually reduced the country to the status of a semicolony, a process that was eventually to lead to the carving out of spheres of influence.[4]

The crisis in Persia came to a head in December 1905, when the Russian Revolution had already passed its peak. A long series of protest strikes, demonstrations, and other disturbances forced the shah, Muzaffar al-din (1896–1907), to grant concessions in response to the popular much as Nicholas II had been forced to do in Russia: On August 5, 1906, he signed a law promulgating a constitution under which the Majlis (Parliament) was to be formed, with elections on the basis of a restricted franchise that mainly benefitted the interests of the clergy and the bazaar merchants. These concessions led to calls for the broadening of reforms, and those who were determined to carry revolution further began to organize. There sprang up the associations known as *anjumans*, a term describing both people's councils and political clubs, as well as organizations of the republican-minded *fedayin* (self-sacrificers) and of the militantly Islamic *mujtahid*, all of which grew particularly strong in Persian Azerbaijan.[5]

This economically most advanced of Persia's provinces was from the start the stronghold of the constitutionalist movement. As the author of a contemporary account of the Persian Revolution noted:

All competent observers seem to agree that the deputies from Azerbaijan, and especially from Tabriz, constituted the salt of the Assembly. Their arrival at the capital on February 7, 1907, was hailed with enthusiasm.... From their arrival, moreover, dated the growing strength and boldness of the Assembly, its determination to make its power felt and its voice heard, its refusal to be ignored or suppressed.[6]

A major reason Tabriz assumed this role was its proximity to revolutionized Russia, Russian Azerbaijan in particular. The channels of communication between the two Azerbaijans, each in the grip of turmoil, were many. In Baku, the mass of the immigrant laborers quickly became exposed to the propaganda of the *Himmät*, and here in 1906, on the initiative of Narimanov, the first organization of Persian workers was set up under the name Ijtimai Amiyyun (Social Democracy). It soon branched out to Tabriz, where the first labor union was also formed.[7] In the same year Narimanov founded in Tiflis a committee to supply the Tabriz revolutionaries with contraband arms and ammunition and revolutionary literature.[8]

The fate of the Persian Revolution was not the concern of the socialists alone, and support was forthcoming from other quarters and in different forms. According to the Soviet Azerbaijani scholar Mammäd Jäfär, the literary output in Russian Azerbaijan that dealt with the events in Persia would fill more than ten volumes.[9] Intellectual contacts were extensive. The Baku newspapers *Häyat* and *Irshad*, which circulated in the Tabriz province, were instrumental there in stirring interest in the Russian reforms. Once the upheaval in Persia was under way, the Baku press, which had reacted to the Russian revolution with bewildered reserve, seemed to be more aroused by what was happening over the Araxes border. Some articles in the *Irshad* read as if they were addressed to readers in Persia, where they were considered "incendiary and much in demand."[10] For those who did not read Azerbaijani, a Persian-language edition of the *Irshad* was issued by the Persian writer Sadeq Mamalek. Ahgayev himself wrote contributions to Persian newspapers, which on the pattern of the Baku press began to mushroom as the revolution progressed.[11]

Of all publications from Transcaucasia, the most widely read in Persia was *Molla Näsr al-din*. Because of the ban imposed on the *Molla* by the viceroy of Persian Azerbaijan, its circulation there was clandestine until the restriction was lifted at the demand of the Azerbaijani deputies to the Majlis. Aside from fueling revolutionary sentiments through its commentaries and cartoons, the journal exerted a formative influence on the emerging literary–satirical journals in Persia. Indebtedness to the *Molla*, sometimes to the point of outright imitation, was evident in the Tabriz magazine *Azerbaijan*, the Resht *Nasim-i Shimal* (Northern Breeze), and the Tehran *Sur-i Israfil* (Trumpet of Israfil), notably in the latter's column "Charand-Parand," written by Mirza Akbar Khan Dakhhoda.[12] The publisher of *Nasim-i Shimal*, Sayyid Ashraf Gilani, translated into Persian the poems of the bard of this age of revolution, the leading *Molla* writer, Mirza Alakpär Sabir.[13] Sabir's diatribes against despotism and attacks on the rich and powerful were recited at political meetings – and by the soldiers at the front line once the Persian Revolution had developed into a violent conflict.

This new turn came about on June 23, 1908, when the successor to the deceased Muzaffer al-din, Muhammad ᶜAli, staged a counterrevolutionary coup. Troops under the Russian commander of the Persian Cossack Brigade, Colonel Liakhov, bombarded and dispersed the Majlis, after which followed the formal reinstitution of the absolutist regime. Yet the coup's main effect was to trigger civil war, as some provincial centers, foremost among them Tabriz, refused to acquiesce in the shah's seizure of power. The Tabriz constitutionalists immediately took over control of the city and organized a militia. Its commander was Saᶜtar Khan, an illiterate horse trader whom the European press soon began to call "the Azerbaijani Pugachov" – alluding to the eighteenth-century Russian peasant rebel leader. The folklore of both Azerbaijans, starting with the poetry of Sabir, elevated Sattar Khan to the stature of a legendary hero.[14]

It was in this phase of the Persian crisis that the involvement of the Russian Azerbaijanis became most active. Mammad Jafar, discussing the intelligentsia's view of the turmoil in Persia, arrived at the conclusion that it was seen as "on the one hand a revolution of the Iranian people for their liberation from the oppression by the despotic regime of the Shah, and on the other as aiming at freedom for Southern Azerbaijan, at emancipating it from Persian rule, and at creating an independent Azerbaijan, which would eventually bring about the abolition of the Turkmanchai frontier."[15] At the same time there occurred, in Tabriz, the first outburst of "Pan-Azarbaijani" sentiment, fed by notions of solidarity and unity of the partitioned land. Spontaneous and without a definite program, "Pan-Azarbaijanism" was to resurface periodically at various junctures of history, a constant if subdued feature of Azerbaijani politics. "Pan-Azarbaijanism" fitted well the spreading consciousness of Turkism. Tabriz was subject to influences not only from Russia but also from Turkey, and these grew in strength with the Young Turks' ascent to power in Istanbul in the summer of 1908. The Tabriz insurgents, encouraged by the success of the revolution in Turkey, issued a declaration, separatist and pro-Ottoman in tone, warning that unless a satisfactory settlement was reached with the Tehran government, "the Sultan would be as good as the Shah."[16] The age-old Shi'ite antagonism toward the Ottomans was clearly losing its intensity, a process that the English historian E. G. Browne ascribed to the effects of al-Afghani's teachings.[17] The new regime in Istanbul, for its part, was sympathetic to the idea of a Turkic state in northern Persia, but the Young Turks' attention was absorbed with a host of more pressing contingencies. The support they gave the Azerbaijani rebels did not exceed token military incursions along the Persian frontier. Nonetheless, the perceived link between the Young Turks and Sattar Khan alarmed Russian officials, who feared the rise of an independent socialist republic in the Tabriz province.[18]

The Russian officials' fear of such a government stemmed from the presence of political emigrants from Transcaucasia in Tabriz. As the new phase in the Persian Revolution coincided with the mounting wave of Stolypin's repressive measures, revolutionaries poured southward across the border. Their number included Georgian Mensheviks, Russian Bolsheviks, and a contingent of battle-hardened Dashnakists, but the majority were Azerbaijanis, mainly Himmätists.[19] The role of the latter was acknowledged in the official Russian press by such comments as that in the St. Petersburg *Novoe Vremiia* (New Times): "Tatar semi-intellectuals from the Caucasus, forgetting that they are Russian subjects, involve themselves eagerly in the Tabriz disturbances and send there their volunteers."[20]

In October the forces of the shah laid siege to Tabriz, whose story would one day be depicted in a literary record of the events,

3. The era of war and revolutions

the famous novel *Dumanli Tabriz* (The Fog of Tabriz) by the Himmätist writer M. S. Ordubadi. Despite growing starvation, which in the end reduced the populace to eating grass, the defenders, their resolve stiffened by the Transcaucasians, successfully resisted their ineffectual adversaries until the intervention of the Russian army in April 1909. After the fall of the city the surviving Transcaucasian revolutionaries dispersed and made their way home.[21]

The suppression of Tabriz did little to save the throne of Muhammad Ali. As his troops were bogged down in Persian Azerbaijan, a rebel force that included a component of volunteers from Transcaucasia marched from the Caspian province of Gilan and advanced on Tehran. After the capital city fell into the hands of the insurgents, Muhammad Ali was deposed on July 16, 1909 and the constitution restored under the regency of Asad ul-Mulk.

In the second constitutional period, one of the émigré Himmätists, Räsulzadä, rose to political prominence throughout Persia – unlike his comrades, whose activities had been limited to Tabriz and Gilan provinces. Räsulzadä, who one day was to become the standard-bearer of Azerbaijani nationalism, at this stage of his political life identified himself with the national cause of Persia – exemplifying how nebulous could be the distinction at the time between the two national loyalties.[22] Like most educated Azerbaijanis as proficient in Persian as his native language, Räsulzadä in August 1909 founded the Tehran daily *Iran-i nou* (New Iran). In the words of Browne, this was "the greatest, the most important and the best known of all Persian newspapers, and the first to appear in the large size usual in Europe. It...introduced to Persia the journalistic methods of Europe and became a model for other papers."[23] *Iran-i nou* was renowned for its radical militancy, and in particular for Räsulzadä's articles, signed under the pen name Nush (Sting), attacking the ineptitude of the new government of Vali Khan Sepahdar. In October 1911, *Iran-i nou* became the organ of the Democratic Party of Iran, remaining in the hands of Räsulzadä until May 1912, when the Russian legation demanded his deportation. He left hastily for Istanbul – where soon hundreds of Persian refugees followed him – after military intervention by Russia later in 1912 brought the revolutionary epoch in Persia to a brutal close.

In contrast to the recent revolutions in Russia and Persia, the overthrow of the despotic regime of Abdulhamid in Turkey by military coup was swift and permanent. On July 24, 1908 the constitutional regime was restored, and the dominant force became the Young Turkish Committee of Union and Progress (CUP).[24] The crisis in Turkey involved no volunteers from abroad, no prolonged battles, no mass exoduses – yet in the long run the Young Turkish revolution, hailed with hope by Sabir, produced deep and enduring consequences for the Azerbaijanis. Under the new liberal regime in Istanbul, the Ottoman apostles of Turkism found a field for unrestricted activity. This included pursuit of their concern for their ethnic cousins abroad, and the Ottoman public at last became aware of the fact that more Turks lived in Russia than in Turkey itself. Intellectuals took the lead in these endeavors, and in December 1908 the first association devoted to promoting Turkism, the cultural–scholarly *Türk Derneghi* (Turkic Society), was born.[25] Russian Turks were invited to participate in this work, and soon their representatives were taking up residence in the Ottoman capital. The Azerbaijani contingent was particularly strong. In the same manner that the Himmätists had been finding their way to revolutionary Persia to continue their struggle, the cream of the Azerbaijani intellectual elite were emigrating to CUP-governed Turkey, now the land of promise for their ideological inclinations and literary ambitions. Their number included such well-known figures as Aghayev, Huseynzadä, Ussubäkov, the poet Mammäd Hadi, the journalist Karabäy Karabäkov, and, after his expulsion from Persia, Räsulzadä.

Pan-Turkism, previously an amorphous cultural movement, now coalesced in Turkey into organizational forms in a variety of clubs and associations, enjoying the support of the press and, increasingly, of the government. Pan-Turkism also began to assume political coloration. The sociologist Ziya Gökalp became the leading thinker of the movement and preached a national Turkish revival in the Ottoman State. This call went hand in hand with his vision of Turan, the mythical homeland of Turks and cradle of their history. "Oghuz Khan, a figure obscure and vague for the scholar, / is familiar and clearly known to my heart. / In my blood he lives in all his greatness

3. The era of war and revolutions

and glory. / He is the delight of my heart. / The fatherland of Turks is neither Turkey nor Turkestan: / it is the great land eternal, it is Turan," wrote Gökalp in one of his poems.[26] The peoples inhabiting Turan, the extreme Pan-Turkists claimed, would one day be united under the leadership of Turkey, bound together by ties of language and religion as well as by the benefits of modern European civilization.

Whereas Turan was a far-off ideal, the crowning achievement of the Pan-Turkish movement, for the short term Gökalp proposed a more realistic alternative:

> Today the Turks for whom cultural unification would be easy are the Oghuz Turks, that is Turkmens, for the Turkmens of Azerbaijan, Iran and Khwarezm like the Turks of Turkey belong to the Oghuz strain. Therefore, our immediate ideal for Turkism must be Oghuz or Turkmen unity. What would be the purpose of this unity? A political union? For the present, no! We can not pass judgement on what will happen in the future, but for the present our goal is only cultural unity of the Oghuz peoples.[27]

Thus was added to the program of Pan-Turkism a new strain, Oghuzianism, which singled out the Azerbaijanis as the closest relatives of the Ottoman Turks and made them the object of their special attention.

The immigrants from Azerbaijan played a highly visible role in Pan-Turkish activities in Istanbul, some of them even assuming political or governmental positions. Huseynzadä, together with Gasprinski and Akchuraoghlu, were invited to join the Supreme Council of the CUP, and Aghayev was appointed inspector of the Istanbul school district. Aghayev, always a prolific writer, also became one of the leading contributors to the theoretical journal of Pan-Turkism, *Türk Yurdu* (Turkic Homeland) which was established in 1911 by Akchuraoghlu.[28] Ahmäd bäy had by now completed his long political evolution from his pro-Persian position regarding Pan-Turkism. Echoing the theories of his teacher from his Paris days, Ernest Renan, he defined *nationality (qavmiyyet)* as the sum total of attributes falling into three categories: first and foremost language; then religion, morals, and customs; and finally, common history, land, and fate.[29] Aghayev's writings on Pan-Turkism and the Turkic nation in the *Türk Yurdu* bore the imprint of his particular Azerbaijani perspective, especially with regard to the Shi ͨa–Sunni split. "Religious strife makes us forget that we are Turks," he wrote, "and sectarian differences often drive us not to take the side of the Turks, but to go against our own kind."[30] Anticlericalism, the most consistent trait in Aghayev's intellectual makeup, again surfaced in his condemnation of the role of religion in holding back the growth of Turkism:

> How could a national consciousness have taken root among a people who are constantly preoccupied with religious quarrels, who have always lived under a foreign influence?.... When in Persia there appeared the teachings of Bab, the Azerbaijani Turks, more than anybody else, sacrificed themselves for the new faith, despite the fact that the founders of Babism were Persians. Likewise, today the same Turks are fighting for a Persian freedom and constitution.[31]

Addressing himself to the Ottomans, he reminded them of their ingrained misconception of nationality as the function of religion: "Even today in Istanbul we call our brothers, the Azerbaijani Turks, Persians, although they speak a language which is only slightly different from the dialect spoken in Istanbul."[32]

Aghayev and Huseynzadä had by this time linked their political fortunes with the cause of Turkey, whereas other Azerbaijani émigrés chose to return home. Some later were to disclose a characteristically Azerbaijani feeling of superiority regarding the accomplishments of contemporary Ottoman civilization, and there was in this feeling a trace of appreciation for Russia. Yet for all their reservations, Azerbaijani intellectuals in general became committed to the ideas of Turkism, which after 1908 had grown into the dominant current in Azerbaijani political thinking, a fact amply reflected in the Baku press of the period. Even the conservatives, suspicious of any form of nationalism and inclined to share the Shi'ite prejudice against Turkey, were swept up by the surge of Islamic solidarity with the Ottomans, who had suffered from European aggression in the Tripolitanian and Balkan wars. An astute observer of the Transcaucasian scene, Vorontsov-Dashkov, reporting to the tsar in 1913, gave this evaluation of the political attitudes of the local Muslims:

> I must note that should we ever have to deal with a separatist movement among any of the peoples of the Caucasus...this could occur only among the Muslim population owing to its numerical superiority over the other ethnic groups, and the possibility of an outburst of religious fanaticism fed by the proximity of the Caucasus to the Muslim states.[33]

3. The era of war and revolutions

The Rise of the Musavat Party

At the same time that many prominent Azerbaijanis were seeking a forum for their activities in revolutionary Turkey, some lesser-known men who stayed behind in Baku were laying the foundation of what was to evolve into the largest Azerbaijani political organization, one, moreover, that was nationalist in character. A handful of former Himmätists, led by Karbalai Mikailzadä and Abbas Kazimzadä, all of whom shared a disillusionment with the Russian Revolution but felt affected by the worldwide national stirrings among Islamic peoples, organized themselves in 1912 into a clandestine association under the name Musavat (Equality).[34] The name, according to one of the founding members, signified the association's desire to achieve for Muslims equality of rights with Russians while striving at the same time for the freedom of the whole Islamic world.[35] The Musavat's first act was to issue a manifesto that – for all the radical past of its authors – ignored social (and for that matter nationalist) issues. Still couched in terms of ʿumma consciousness, the document appealed to Pan-Islamic rather than Pan-Turkic sentiments. Recalling that the "noble people of Islam had once reached with one hand to Peking...and with the other built at the far end of Europe the Alhambra palace," the manifesto deplored the present-day decline of Islamic power.

With a view to restoring the fortunes of Islam, the Musavat put forward the following program of political action:

1. Unification of all Muslim peoples regardless of nationality or sectarian affiliation
2. Restoration of the lost independence of Muslim countries
3. Moral and material assistance to Muslim peoples struggling for the preservation or restoration of their independence
4. Aid in developing the defensive and offensive strength of Muslim peoples
5. Abolition of all barriers obstructing the spread of these ideas
6. Establishment of contacts with parties striving for the progress and unity of Muslims
7. Establishment, when necessary, of contacts and an exchange of views with foreign parties concerned with the well-being of mankind
8. Intensification of all forms of the struggle for the progress of the Muslims and the development of their commercial, industrial, and economic life[36]

The program of the Musavat, notable for its generalities and formulations, clearly intended to accommodate the interests of a broad spectrum of the public. At this early stage of the Musavat's existence, the only clues to its political orientation was its program's emphasis on "Muslim progress," implying a desire not to attract conservative elements, and its reference to the development of "commercial, industrial, and economic life, which seemed to be addressed to the native middle classes. Indeed, the Musavat was to draw a large part of its following from among the intelligentsia, students, merchants, and entrepreneurs, and its natural base of support became Baku. For reasons of security, its members were organized into three-man cells that spread out throughout Transcaucasia and even reached some towns in Persian Azerbaijan. Yet for a long while the Musavat, which soon began to call itself a "party," did not appear to be very active. Its Baku chapter even issued a warning to members to avoid open criticism of the government for fear of reprisals. Guidelines for the present were confined to maintaining strict secrecy and selectively increasing membership.[37]

The dearth of evidence concerning the Musavat's early activity was one day to prompt the Soviet historian Ia. Ratgauzer to express doubt whether the party had in fact existed before 1917, a view his colleagues emphatically rejected.[38] After 1912 the Musavat from time to time, though admittedly not often, made its existence known by issuing proclamations, as in connection with the First Balkan War of 1912. Addressing itself to "Our coreligionists," the party condemned Russia for having engineered the aggression against "the Ottoman Caliphate, the heart of the Islamic world." "Our only hope," the proclamation stated, "and the road to salvation lie in the independent existence and progress of Turkey."[39] The First Balkan War, besides increasing pro-Ottoman sentiment among Azerbaijanis, signaled their split with Russian liberals, who had fully supported the attack on Turkey.

In 1913, the Musavat acquired a leader of political experience and intellectual accomplishment in the person of Räsulzadä. One of those Azerbaijani émigré who chose not to stay in Turkey indefinitely, he took advantage of the tsarist amnesty on the three hundredth anniversary of the Romanov dynasty to return home. Soon after joining the Musavat Party he became its guiding spirit and began exercising the unchallenged authority he was to enjoy

3. The era of war and revolutions

for many years to come. During his exile in Istanbul he had drawn close to the *Türk Yurdu* group, but he always retained a special admiration for al-Afghani, whose writings on the relationship between Islam and nationality were a formative influence on him. Upon his return to Baku, Räsulzadä resumed his career as a journalist, and wrote on topics that touched upon political theory. With two articles, "Language as a Social Factor" and "The Yeni Lisan Group and Their Turkish," he joined the language debate on the page of the *Shälälä*. Arguing that language is a major unifying force for any community, he in effect rejected the positions of both the *Azärijilar* and the Ottomanizers. He criticized the program of the former on the grounds that encouraging a separate literary Azerbaijani ran counter to the idea of Turkic peoples' unity – yet he declined endorse the Ottomanizers. In his view, which echoed the opinions of the Yeni Lisan movement that sought to purify the Ottoman language, Ottoman, with its admixture of foreign words could hardly be called a Turkic language. Räsulzadä's alternative was a new, purified Turkish, still in the process of formation among the younger generation of writers in Turkey.[40]

In another article published by the *Dirilik*, Räsulzadä discussed the relationship between the terms ^c*umma* and *millät*, insisting that there was a clear distinction to be made between the two concepts. ^ɔ*Umma*, he argued, carried an exclusively religious meaning and expressed the collective consciousness of Muslims worldwide, whereas *millät* referred to a community based on common language, culture, and history as well as religion, the last being only one of its elements.[41] In its proper sense, then, *millät* could not be taken to denote a religious group; its connotation was primarily secular, and its attributes were clearly those of a nationality. A secular definition of nationalism was later to underlie the ideology of Musavatism, but Räsulzadä stopped short of defining the nationality of his compatriots – that would have to wait until global war and revolution had created new circumstances for the national self-expression of the peoples of the Russian state.

World War and Azerbaijan

The entry of Russia into the war against Austria-Hungary and Germany in July–August 1914 was greeted in general with manifestations of support throughout the empire, including Transcaucasia. The Muslim deputies to the State Duma expressed their unshakable commitment to the war effort, and the Baku press printed countless declarations in the spirit of Russian patriotism. Taghiyev offered to underwrite the military hospital, and together with other Baku industrialists and merchants he financed the formation of volunteer units to fight on the German front.[42]

The Muslims of Transcaucasia, like their coreligionists elsewhere in Russia, were exempt from the draft, though some served in the tsar's army as volunteers and career soldiers. Among the latter were about two hundred Azerbaijani commissioned officers, including generals such as Samäd bäy Makhmändiarov, ᶜAli Agha Shikhlinski, and Huseyn Khan Nakhichevanski.[43] The last was in command of the "Savage Division," which was the largest Muslim unit to fight in the war on Russia's side and whose elite cavalry regiments consisted entirely of Daghestani and Azerbaijani volunteers.

Patriotism and loyalty to the Russian state remained simple matters so long as the war was being waged against Germany and Austria-Hungary. However, barely three months after the fighting started, Turkey had joined the hostilities with an attack on Russian naval bases in the Black Sea. Writing in the Istanbul press, Aghayev, now an influential Ottoman journalist, rationalized that Turkey had no choice: As Russian defeats at the hands of Germany could be expected to grow heavier, the Allies would eventually demand that Turkey open the Straits in their bid to save Russia.[44]

The Ottoman State entered the war proclaiming it a *jihad* ("holy war") and calling on Muslims all over the world to support its cause. The circular that the CUP sent to its local branches was more specific than the *fetva* (Islamic legal ruling) on the *jihad* concerning the war aims of Turkey; it reflected both the Pan-Islamic and Turanian aspirations of the Young Turkish leadership.

The national ideal of our people and our land drives us toward destroying the Muscovite foe and toward achieving in this manner the natural frontiers of the state in which our brothers in race will be included and united.... Religious considerations drive us toward liberating the Islamic world from the domination be the Infidel.[45]

3. The era of war and revolutions

In terms of war strategy these ideological premises lay behind the two main offensive objectives of the Ottomans: the attack on Egypt in pursuit of the Pan-Islamic goal and the thrust to the Caucasus as a stepping stone to the creation of Turan. The head of the ruling Ottoman triumvirate, Vice-Generalissimo Enver Pasha, gave priority to the second goal, as he rightly perceived the limited appeal of Pan-Islamism outside Turkey.

Although Turkey entered the war with hesitations – indeed, many CUP leaders were plagued with misgivings – some political groundwork in the Caucasus region had been laid in advance of the Ottoman invasion. Secret contacts established with Georgian separatists, represented by the German-backed Committee for Independent Georgia, resulted in formation of the Georgian Legion attached to the Ottoman army and an Ottoman commitment to recognize a future independent Georgian state.[46] As part of their plans to restructure Transcaucasia, the Young Turks also approached the Ottoman Dashnakists, their political allies since 1908. During the Dashnaktsutiun congress held in Erzerum in August 1914, the CUP representatives, Ömer Naji Bahaeddin Shakir, and Hilmi bey, had proposed to Dashnakist leaders the creation of an autonomous Armenian state consisting of certain Armenian-populated parts of Turkey and areas to be taken by force from Russia. In return, the Armenians were to organize an uprising behind the Russian lines. The Ottoman Dashnakists were ready to pledge full loyalty to Turkey but would not accept the idea of an anti-Russian revolt. They therefore turned down the CUP's offer, possibly together with a good chance to avert the tragic fate in store for the Armenians in Turkey.[47]

Potentially the largest reservoirs of support for the Ottoman advance on the Caucasus were the Muslim populations across the Russian frontier. Of these, the Georgian Ajars were the most eager to rise up against Russia, but the Ottomans also hoped for revolts in Daghestan and Azerbaijan upon entry of their troops. Contacts with Azerbaijanis were maintained through émigrés in Istanbul, but significantly the Ottoman government made no pronouncement on the future status of Azerbaijan during the first phase of the war. Rather, options were kept open for the time when the Turanian empire should have been assembled, which included the absorption by Turkey of the Azerbaijanis on the lines of Oghuzianism. Meanwhile, at the outbreak of the war, a modest Ottoman expeditionary corps of three understrength reserve divisions was assigned to a grandiose operation aimed at Russian Azerbaijan. Its commander, Halil bey, the young uncle of Enver, was under orders to march into northern Persia and to attack Baku from the south, with the ultimate goal of clearing the Caspian coast of the Russians and trapping their main force in the west, in the vicinity of the Ottoman border.[48]

The hostilities on the Caucasus front began in early November with the penetration of the Ottomans into the area of Batum, where the local Muslim Lazes and Ajars welcomed them by rising against the Russians.[49] Simultaneously the Ninth and Tenth Ottoman Army Corps fought a successful battle at Köprüköy, on the Ottoman side of the frontier. Sufficiently encouraged by these initial results to order a major offensive, Enver Pasha personally took command of the Third Army, which consisted of eleven of the forty divisions available in Turkey. His immediate objective was to defeat the Russian forces in their main base of operations between Kars and Sarikamish, after which the conquest of Transcaucasia would not present excessive difficulties. The fighting started on December 22. After an exhausting march through snow-covered mountain tracks, the Ninth Corps engaged the Russians at the railhead of Sarikamish, while the Tenth Corps cut the rail communications between Sarikamish and Kars. Simultaneously, at the northern front, the Russians were forced to abandon Ardahan. At this moment panic seized the Russian civilian authorities, who hastily readied for evacuation. Even the Russian field commander in the Caucasus, General Myshlaevski, prepared to withdraw his armies from Transcaucasia, and the tsar's government appealed to its Western allies to launch a diversionary attack in order to relieve the Caucasus front, a request that planted the seed of the Gallipoli operation. The threatening situation was resolved in the Russian's favor partly because of the battle fatigue of the Ottomans, partly because of the energetic action taken by the Russian chief of staff, General N. Iudenich. The Russian counterattack at Sarikamish destroyed the Ninth Corps by mid-January. Decimated as much by cold, disease, and hunger as by fighting, the Ottoman Third Army lost 85 percent of its original component of 90,000.[50] The Battle of Sarikamish was decisive in setting the future course of the war on the Caucasus front. In the spring of 1915 the Russian forces with the help of Armenian irregulars entered Turkish Armenia, where fear of Armenian disloyalty led the Ottoman government to order deportations and killings. In addition, the Ottomans wished to remove the ethnic barrier between the Turkic peoples of Russia and Turkey. Armenian estimates of lives lost reached 1 million.[51] In the same year General Liakhov meted out revenge on the Ajars and Lazes for the support they had given the Ottomans: Of the population of 52,000 in the Chorokha Valley, only 7,000 were left alive.[52]

After a long lull in the fighting, in February 1916 the Russians captured the fortress of Erzerum and two month later the port of Trebizond. Just as the Ottomans were preparing for a counteroffensive, a well-timed Russian blow wiped out the reconstructed Third Army. In July the Russians reached their farthest point of advance in Anatolia, Erzincan. On their southern wing they were making preparations for a thrust toward Mosul to achieve a linkup with the British, who were converging toward the same point from central Mesopotamia.

In the very days when the outcome of the Battle of Sarikamish had hung in the balance, the Ottomans had carried out their Turanian-inspired foray into Persian Azerbaijan. As Halil's force was at the last moment reassigned to fill the thinned-out ranks of the Third Army, a detachment of only 3,000, largely auxiliary Kurdish cavalry, could be dispatched to Tabriz.[53] Accompanying them were political refugees who had left Persia after the collapse of the revolution and were now seeking to return with Ottoman help.[54] Seizing an undefended Tabriz in early January 1915, the Ottomans stood at the doorstep of Russian Azerbaijan. A prominent Young Turk, Ömer Naji, reputedly the moving spirit of Turkey's Caucasus policy, was named the CUP inspector general for Azerbaijan and East Caucasus.[55] His nomination signified Ottoman intentions to treat the two Azerbaijans as a single entity and hinted at their possible unification under Ottoman auspices. Ömer Naji began at once to enlist the Persian Azerbaijani Shahseven tribesmen for the march on Baku, but by the end of January he had to abandon Tabriz hastily. The Ottomans had succeeded in taking the city only because of the temporary withdrawal of Russian troops for the defense of Kars and Sarikamish, but once the Battle of Sarikamish ended, a Russian army corps quickly reoccupied the Tabriz province.

Still, the Ottomans made repeated inroads into this area of strategical importance for their eastward expansion.[56] In the spring of 1915, Halil, who at last had at his disposal his expeditionary force, moved from Mosul toward Tabriz, but was stopped by the Russians at Khoi and forced to retreat to Anatolia when a large Armenian uprising broke out at his rear in the area of Van. On two other occasions the undefatigable Ömer Naji tried to carry the flame of the anti-Russian insurgency to Persian Azerbaijan. In the fall of 1915 he briefly seized Sudjubulak, a feat he repeated again the next spring, shortly before his death.[57] In no instance, however, did these Ottoman incursions create a new strategic threat to Baku.

As the Russo–Ottoman conflict was getting under way, Azerbaijani attitudes became more complex, and inevitably they were affected by the changing fortunes of the war. The Ottomans for their part attempted to contact the Muslims of Transcaucasia through their agents, who were directed by the Special Organization (Teshkilat-i Mahsusa) in charge of propaganda and subversion behind enemy lines. In 1914 and 1915 some acts of sabotage occurred, anti-Russian leaflets were circulating, and the government regarded it as necessary to close down a few Azerbaijani newspapers.[58] During the tense days of December 1914, as Enver Pasha's offensive was at its high point, the representatives of the Armenian, Georgian, and Muslim communities met in Tiflis to discuss the Armenian proposal for raising native militia to fight the Ottoman invader. The Azerbaijani spokesmen, declaring loyalty to Russia, avoided making any commitments.[59]

At this point of the war, the first project on record for an independent state of Transcaucasian Muslims was conceived in the circles of former Difai members. Their emissary, Aslan Khan Khoiski, the nephew of Fath ʿAli Khan Khoiski, secretly crossed the lines and arrived at Enver Pasha's Erzerum headquarters in February 1915. The purpose of this visit was to obtain Ottoman endorsement for the formation of a republic that would include the *guberniia*s of the Baku, Elizavetpol, and Erivan, as well as Daghestan and Terek.[60]

3. The era of war and revolutions

The project was a clear indication of the Azerbaijanis' preference for independent statehood rather than union with Turkey. The latter alternative, Aslan Khan indicated, would be even less acceptable than remaining under Russian sovereignty. He also asked German officials for guarantees for the status of the future republic.[61]

The timing of Aslan Khan's mission was fortuitous, for Enver Pasha had just suffered the Sarikamish disaster, and so gave his approval to the project. In return the Azerbaijani emissary promised that the Muslims of Transcaucasia and Daghestan would launch an uprising as soon as Ottoman forces could lend it support from Persian Azerbaijan. Aslan Khan mentioned a figure of hundreds of thousands insurgents ready to fight, an assertion that caused his interlocutors to doubt his seriousness or sense of responsibility or both.[62] In any case, the subsequent course of the war was most inauspicious for carrying out these insurrectionary designs.

The ruthless revenge taken by the Russian military on the Lazes and Ajars in the spring of 1915 was intended as a warning to the other Muslim populations of Transcaucasia. All the more remarkable, in this light, was the defiant speech delivered in the State Duma by the Baku deputy Muhammad Jafarov, who passionately condemned the government for the repressions of the Muslims:

> In Transcaucasia this policy has found its expression in open incitement against non-Russian nationalities in provinces either immediately affected by military operations or situated in the rear of the Caucasus Front. There, behind the roar of the battle, horrible things have been perpetrated on the utterly helpless, peaceful Muslim population. Its lives and property are in jeopardy. The extortion, robbery, and murder of Muslims have become a matter of everyday occurrence. Wholesale expulsions of the male population, violation of the unprotected women left behind, ruined and devastated villages, an impoverished, hungry, terror-stricken and unprovided-for population – this is the situation of the Muslims in the region. We are in possession of facts and official data confirming every word that I have said, but we find it impossible to give them publicity here. In due course we shall speak about them again. For the present we shall only remark that the local and central authorities have been placed in possession of the facts, but nevertheless, nothing has changed in the position of the Muslims.[63]

In choosing to speak so, Jafarov may have sensed that the long-overdue retirement of the seventy-eight-year old Vorontsov-

Dashkov was imminent. In September 1915 the viceroy, known for his anti-Muslim bias and blamed in particular for the massacre of the Ajars, was replaced by the Grand Duke Nicholas Nicholaevich, whose appointment heralded a new Russian approach to dealing with the Transcaucasian Muslims. On his way to Tiflis the grand duke stopped over in Baku, where he invited Muslim notables to apprise him of the needs of their community. In another conciliatory gesture, Räsulzadä, despite his record of revolutionary activities, was granted permission to publish an Azerbaijani-language daily, *Achiq Söz* (Open Word). First issued in October 1915, it called itself a "Turkic newspaper," the description purporting to put an end to the still prevalent confusion of terms – Tatars, Transcaucasian Muslims, Caucasians, and so on. The new terminology met with no objections from the authorities, as the term *Turkic (Tiurski)* had already gained currency in some Russian publications. The first number of the *Achiq Söz* contained an editorial by Räsulzadä expressing cryptically what he would later claim to be a statement of Azerbaijani national aspirations. The editorial voiced the hope that the global conflict would end "with a peace which would secure the independence of oppressed countries, or else the peace would be of short duration. Only nations united in their strivings for statehood will achieve independence, since only they could have confidence in themselves and their ideals, derived from unity and perseverance."[64] Räsulzadä also replied, in the article "Our Needs," to the grand duke's benevolent inquiry to the Muslim community. The leader of the Musavat, still an underground organization, was surprisingly moderate in listing the concessions that he expected from the tsarist government, such as creation of primary schools with the native language used for instruction, granting autonomy for Muslim religious administration, and establishment of a Muslim teachers' seminary. Such moderation went hand in hand with the *Achiq Söz*'s support for Russia's war effort and was consistent with its official stance of Russian patriotism.

The improvement in relations between the tsardom and the Azerbaijani community coincided with the fortuitous recovery of oil prices – an especially welcome event for Baku oil producers – after a steep decline at the beginning of the war because of the threat to the Black Sea shipping lanes. In fact, in the view of many Azerbaijanis the evolution of the world conflict still held the promise of political advantages for their country. A literary vignette offers a plausible insight into the way of thinking of some of the native elite:

"Yes," said a fat man with brilliant eyes and a long moustache, "everything will indeed be different after the war." This was Fath ᶜAli Khan of Khoi, a lawyer by profession. We knew that he was always thinking about the People and their Cause. "Yes," he added fervently, "and as everything will be so different we need not beg for anyone's favors. Whoever wins this war will come out of it weak and covered with wounds, and we, who will be neither weakened nor wounded, will be in a position to demand, not to beg. We are an Islamic, a Shiᶜite country, and we expect the same from the House of Romanov as from the House of Osman. Independence is everything that concerns us! And the weaker the great powers are after the war, the nearer is freedom for us. This freedom will come from us, from our unspent strength, from our money and our oil. For do not forget: the world needs us more than we need the world."[65]

Yet on the Caucasus front, instead of a desirable stalemate, the scales were tipping heavily in favor of one side. The year 1916 began with a series of impressive Russian victories, and the inhabitants of Baku soon grew accustomed to the sight of long columns of Ottoman prisoners of war marching through the city on their way to the detention camp on the offshore island of Nargin. In a remarkable psychological about-face that might well be explained by the Shiᶜite tradition of *taqiya* (right to dissimulation and apostasy), Azerbaijani religious leaders found it politic to hold thanksgiving prayers on the occasion of the Russian entry into Erzerum. In the same spirit of loyalty to Russia, the *Kaspiy* condemned the 1916 revolt of the Central Asian Muslims as "a dark spot which weakens the struggle against the external enemy."[66] During this later phase of the war the Azerbaijani national movement was kept barely alive only through the efforts of the émigrés residing in Turkey. Huseynzadä and Aghayev, active in the Committee for the Defense of the Rights of the Muslim Turco–Tatars in Russia, were among the signatories of memoranda and appeals calling for the Central Powers to stand up for the rights of the Russian Muslims whenever the peace treaties were to be negotiated.[67] The Azerbaijanis at home were sinking deeper into their complacent apathy, from which they were to be awakened suddenly by the outbreak of a new revolution in Russia.

4

Transition to nationhood: in quest of autonomy

The February revolution

Under the strain of the war the tsarist empire reached the stage of collapse. On February 23, 1917 hunger riots broke out in Petrograd. When the rioters gained the support of striking workers, the garrison of the capital mutinied, and the Petrograd Soviet of Workers and Soldiers Deputies began its meetings. The State Duma refused to defer to the tsar's authority any longer, and its Provisional Committee formally requested his abdication. After some hesitation, Nicholas II acquiesced, thus ending the three-century-long reign of the Romanov dynasty, and indeed monarchy in Russia. Supreme authority passed into the hands of the Provisional Government that was to remain in office until the democratically elected Constituent Assemby should convene at a future date.

One of the first acts of the new regime was to repeal all legislation restricting the rights of Russian citizens on the basis of religion or national origin.[1] The Provisional Government also acted promptly to overhaul the administration of the ethnically non-Russian regions with a view toward giving a larger share of local power to representatives of the native populations. In Transcaucasia the Grand Duke Nicholas Nicholaevich was forced to resign his post despite his declaration of loyalty to the revolutionary regime. On March 9, civilian authority over the provinces beyond the Caucasus Mountains and the occupied territory of Turkey was transferred to the newly created Special Committee for Transcaucasia, known under the acronym Ozakom. The committee, which was to act as a "collective viceroy," consisted of deputies representing the national groups of the region in the State Duma. The chairman of the Ozakom was a Russian Kadet, V. A. Kharlamov, and its other members were A. I. Chkhenkeli, a Georgian Menshevik; Prince K. Abashidze, a Georgian Social Federalist; M. I. Papadjanian, an Armenian Kadet, and M. Y. Jafarov, an Azerbaijani with no party affiliation, subsequently a Musavatist.[2]

The Ozakom was from the very start a target of criticism on the grounds that it failed adequately to represent Transcaucasian nationalities and to win the confidence of the masses because it refused to take a stand on the agrarian question. Moreover, the proliferation of political organizations eager to exercise power challenged and soon eclipsed the authority of the Ozakom. In Eastern Transcaucasia these organizations fell into two categories. One was the soviets, largely Russian in their ethnic makeup and dominated by the parties of the left, the Social Democrats and the Social Revolutionaries (SRs), the latter a peasant-oriented group that carried on the radical traditions of Russian populism. By far the most influential of the soviets was that of Baku, whose chairman was Stepan Shaumian. A Bolshevik intellectual of powerful personal appeal, Shaumian had won election to his post before his return from exile, even though at the time (early April) there had been only nine Bolsheviks among the fifty-two members of this soviet.[3] The second category of organizations was the network of purely native Muslim national councils and diverse other organizations. These were grouped together under the umbrella of the Council of Muslim Public Associations, a coordinating body that was headed by Topchibashev and whose Executive Committee was under the leadership of M. H. Hajinski.[4] Of the "public associations," the most successful in attracting popular support were emergent political parties, each standing for one of the ideological currents that were to shape Azerbaijani politics: nationalism, socialism, and Pan-Islamism. Nationalism at this juncture still meant, broadly, Turkism, with only a trace of Azerbaijani identity, and the main proponents of this ideology were two groups whose power bases were respectively Baku and Ganja. The Musavat, active in the former city, was in the process of transforming itself from a clandestine cadre into a mass party. It gained its supporters among the Baku intelligentsia, the lower middle classes, and to no small degree those of the native proletariat who appreciated the leftist credentials of the party's founders. Yet there is no evidence that during the first weeks of its legal existence the Musavat concerned itself with much more than the purely organizational problems of rapid growth. The Musavatist leaders apparently lacked a program of action until they came to find an inspiration from the politicians of Azerbaijan's second city.

Within a few days of the fall of the monarchy there sprang up in Ganja the Turkic Party of Decentralization (Türk Adäm -i Märkaziyyät Firqäsï).[5] Its very name was reminiscent of the Ottoman League of Decentralization with whose members the Difai had contacts dating back to 1906.[6] Just as the Ottoman group had advocated sweeping administrative reforms in Turkey, so did the Ganja party call for the restructuring of the Russian state into a federation of autonomous units that would assure the free development of its component nationalities. The direct forerunner of the Adäm-i Märkaziyyät was the Difai, and the familiar names of Rustambäkov, Dr. Aghazadä, and the brothers Khasmammädov reappeared among its leaders. Likewise, their disposition toward federalism reached back to the 1905 Revolution, but this time the idea of the Transcaucasian union gave way to a more ambitious design concerning all Russia.

The Adäm-i Märkaziyyät, commonly known as the Federalists, enjoyed a following among the largely rural and small-town population of Ganja province, while its leadership included some large local landowners. This latter fact had no adverse effect on its popularity, which stemmed from the Federalists' vigorous advocacy of Turkism. The party's founder and moving spirit was Ussubäkov, the son-in-law of Gasprinski and a well-known promoter of Turkism who after 1908 had emigrated to Turkey and lived there for some time.[7]

Also generally inclined toward nationalism was the Independent Democratic Group. A small band of politicians with no claims to a mass following, it included highly respected and influential men, some of whom had gained their political experience in the State Duma and the Ittifaq of the 1905 period. The spokesmen for the Independents were Topchibashev and Khan Khoiski.

Azerbaijani socialism was represented by the Himmät. Unlike the Musavat, this party lacked the advantage of a continuous

4. Transition: in quest of autonomy

existence that would have provided a foundation for rapid growth after February 1917. Those Himmätist veterans of 1905 who had remained committed to socialism had become members of the RSDWP, and it was in this capacity that several of them met to debate whether they should try to revive the Himmät at all or instead call on Muslim workers to join the ranks of the Russian Social Democrats. After much soul searching, acknowledging that it was unlikely many Azerbaijanis would join a Russian organization, they eventually opted for a separate native identity. On March 3, the party resumed its activity, "taking into account the psychology of the Muslim masses as well as the fact that the Himmät had its own history."[8] The Himmätists might even have felt their hand forced by the existence in Baku of a socialist association of immigrants from Persia, the Ädalät (Justice). Founded in 1916 by a group that included Asadullah Gafarzadä, Bahram Aghazadä, and Agha Baba Yusifzadä, the Ädalät saw itself as the successor to the former Ijtima-i Amiyyun of the 1905 period.[9] Another organization of Muslim workers in Baku, the Birlik (Union), representing the Volga Tatars, was in the formative stage. The Ädalät and the Birlik both looked to their Azerbaijani comrades for guidance and assistance, and in the future both would more or less affiliate themselves with the Himmät.

The head of the new Himmät's provisional committee was Narimanov and its other members Äzizbäkov, Buniatzadä, M. N. Israfilbäkov, and H. N. Sultanov. The latter two were new faces in this company, with no past in the old Himmät but with close ties to the Bolshevik wing of the RSDWP.[10] Himmätists were admitted to the Executive Committee of the Council of Muslim Public Associations, but when they found themselves outnumbered by the nonsocialist majority they proposed that the council limit its work to cultural affairs and demanded two-thirds of the seats on the commission that was to reorganize the council. When outvoted on these questions, they abruptly withdrew from the Executive Committee in July.[11]

The reborn Himmät, though far more Marxist in its character than ten years previously, failed to recapture its following. It faced a formidable contender for the allegiance of the masses in the Musavat, the party that attracted a large segment of native workers in Baku. Furthermore, the Himmät, having so far managed to steer clear of the Bolshevik–Menshevik strife, could no longer escape the consequences of polarization within the RSDWP. The Transcaucasian branch of the RSDWP, after a brief reunification, split again, this time irrevocably, in June 1917. The Azerbaijani socialists were forced to take sides, with the result that the Himmät broke up in a manner paralleling the alignment among their Russian comrades: The Baku Himmätists, following Narimanov, declared themselves pro-Bolshevik, whereas the provincial chapters tended to side with the Mensheviks, dominant in the rest of the region, notably in Georgia. In Tiflis I. M. Abilov, S. Aghamalioghlï, A. Pepinov, and A. H. Garayev formed the nucleus of the Himmät's Menshevik wing and began publishing its two newspapers, *Al Bayraq* (Red Ranner) and *Gäläjäk* (Future).[12]

The division among the Himmätists was neither as deep-seated nor as permanent as was the case with the RSDWP. As if in tacit recognition of the fact that the quarrel was not of their making, the two factions maintained contact with one another. As late as December 1917 they were still jointly represented at the meeting of the Muslim Socialist Congress of the Caucasus, and in the course of the next three years the party was twice reunited. During most of this period, the Bolshevik Himmät went through the motions of carrying on the routine of political work, showing limited vitality, even though its leaders were often simultaneously active in the Russian party. Unlike the Menshevik Himmätists, they refrained from running for elections to representative bodies and as a group were absent in the Baku Soviet.

Those at the opposite end of the political spectrum, the religious–conservative elements, at first assumed a wait-and-see attitude before establishing a unified organization in September 1917, when the Baku group Rusyada Muslumanliq (Muslims in Russia) and the Ganja Ittihad-i Islam (Union of Islam) merged as one party under the composite title Rusyada Musulmanliq–Ittihad.[13] Its ideological pronouncements accepted the Shari'a as the supreme source of guidance for political action. Fundamentally Pan-Islamist, the Ittihad rejected the idea of Turkism or any other form of nationalism, which it considered a force disruptive to the ᶜ*umma*, and displayed particular hostility to the notion of Azerbaijanism. Likewise, it opposed tendencies toward separation from Russia and called for the unification of all Russian Muslims within one organization that would champion their religious identity. As a matter of practical policy, the Ittihad came out in favor of a democratic and decentralized Russian republic under which Muslims would attain "freedom from European capitalism and imperialism."[14] This formula, in which the word *European* was the key, indicated a proclivity to combine Islamic conservatism with some traits of social radicalism, a blend that occasionally found the Ittihad taking positions close to those of the far left. The Ittihadists were not particularly adept at the polls, but their influence among the population was stronger than it appeared from their representation in elective bodies. It was the only party with an appeal to the hard core of the Azerbaijani peasantry, even though its leaders were for the most part professional men and town dwellers. Two of the most prominent Ittihadists once had ties to the Himmät of the 1905 period: the millionaire Isa Ashurbäkov, who had given financial support to socialist causes, and Karabäkov, the driving force of the Ittihad, who had also established close links with the Young Turks but who during the war gained the reputation of being an ardent tsarist loyalist.[15] Karabäkov incurred the intense dislike of the Musavatists, and he reciprocated by vilifying them as godless opportunists. Quite apart from this personal issue, the antagonism between the two groups, one symbolizing commitment to change and the other attachment to tradition, was so deep that it emerged as a major feature of Azerbaijani domestic politics, in a pattern typical for a society in transition.

Autonomy – what kind?

The first attempt to define Azerbaijani aspirations under the conditions of the new revolutionary upheaval was made at the meetings of the Muslim Congress of the Caucasus in Baku on April 15–20. Notably, this event included the participation of delegates from Daghestan, whose presence was meant to affirm the historic ties of the Transcaucasian Muslims with their co-religionists to the north. The meeting resulted in a triumph for the Adämi-i Märkaziyyät, which swayed the majority of participants – particularly the Musavatists – in favor of its program. The final resolution included the statement that "the interests of the Muslim nationalities would be best served by a form of Russia's governmental structure based on a democratic republic organized on territorial–federative principles."[16] The congress heard even more outspoken demands for an autonomous status for Azerbaijan, but gave them no endorsement. Indeed, on the motion of Taghiyev the very name *Azerbaijan* was stricken from the final resolution. This circumspection resulted partly from an unwillingness to antagonize the Provisional Government and partly from the need to consult with other Muslim groups in Russia on a common line of conduct. The congress also called for state support for native schools, establishment of a university with the native language as a medium of instruction, and the appointment of new members of the Ozakom so that the Muslim population would be represented more equitably.[17] On the central issue under debate, territorial autonomy, the majority encountered opposition from two extremes: from the socialists on the left, who insisted on maintaining solidarity with revolutionary Russia, and from the conservatives on the right, who argued along the lines of their Pan-Islamic views. As for the centrist groups, the common stand taken by the Adäm-i Märkaziyyät and the Musavat started the process of their gradual fusion into one party. Having embraced the autonomist program of the Ganja Federalists, the Musavat became its vociferous advocate in the forum of the all-Russian Muslim movement.

In the spring of 1917 the differences that had begun to divide the leaders of the Russian Muslims during the 1905 Revolution reappeared with an intensity unknown before. The fundamental question remained the same: unity of the Muslim community within Russia versus the recognition of ethnic and regional particularisms. The period 1905–1907 had ended with the apparent victory of the proponents of organic unity – in this case, the Tatar liberals. The spread of Pan-Islamism and Pan-Turkism seemed to have reinforced the unitarian current. Yet the process of differentiation among Russian Muslims was progressing apace, and the awareness of local interests kept asserting itself. Politically, the chasm between Muslim leaders and the Kadet party had grown wider because the latter advocated conquest of the Turkish straits as a chief war aim of Russia. As the Muslim liberals took to denouncing their Russian opposite numbers, they found themselves under pressure from Muslim socialists. These were now by far more numerous than in 1905, and they usually took as their models the Russian SRs and the Mensheviks.

4. Transition: in quest of autonomy

Against this backdrop of changes within Russia's Muslim community there emerged two schools of thought on the fundamental issue of unity versus diversity, each with a different proposal for the political organization of the Muslims in the unfolding Russian revolution. Representatives of ethnic groups that formed compact masses within particular regions such as Transcaucasia, Turkestan, Kirghizia, Bashkiria, and the Crimea generally favored territorial autonomy. They envisioned the Muslim-populated territories of the future as self-governing in all matters except those of vital concern for the whole Russian state. The Tatars, widely dispersed in various parts of Russia, were the most articulate champions of the opposing viewpoint. In no position to claim the right to an autonomous territory, they stood for cultural autonomy with in the framework of a centralized body that would represent the interests of all the Muslims of Russia vis-à-vis the government on the highest level. Calling as they did for Muslim unity, the Tatars, in their insistence on organizational centralism, also defended the status of their bourgeoisie and intelligentsia as the leaders of Islam in Russia.[18]

The two camps clashed head-on at the All-Russian Muslim Congress that opened in Moscow on May 1, 1917. The occasion offered a spectacle of unusual tactical alliances among political factions of the Muslim community. The socialists, in their loyalty to the cause of the Russian Revolution, came out against territorial autonomy, sharing to that extent the stance of the Tatar bourgeoisie. In their view such a solution would increase the power of landlords and capitalists, classes holding back social progress, whereas a centralized Russian republic would secure the well-being and cultural rights of the Muslim masses.[19] The Ossetinian Menshevik Ahmad Tsalikov warned that the fragmentation of the Muslim community would serve imperialist schemes to "divide and rule."[20] The Pan-Islamists for their part fought a rearguard battle to slow down the breakup of the ᶜumma into national entities built on secular foundations.

The key speaker for the bloc of territorial autonomists was Räsulzadä, who urged for a solution in terms of nationality rather than religion and reminded the Pan-Islamists that certain peoples had come to feel that they were "Turks first and Muslims second." A program of autonomy limited to creating a single all-Russian organization, would fail to render justice to the growing national self-awareness of Turkic peoples and their aspirations:

> The question that has to be asked is: What is a nation? I believe that the outstanding characteristic of a nation consists of the bonds of the language and history, of the bonds of customs and tradition. It is said sometimes that Islam is the embodiment of a nation because when a Turco-Tatar is asked to what nationality he belongs, his answer is: I am a Muslim. But this is an erroneous view.... There is no Christian nationality, and likewise there is no Islamic one. In this great Muslim house there must exist separate dwellings for Turks, Persians, and Arabs.[21]

Räsulzadä carried his argument a significant step beyond Pan-Turkism by emphasizing that various Turkic-speaking groups had already developed identities distinct from one another even though they all formed one nation: "The Volga Tatars have today their own literature, their own poets. Turkestan has its own rich literature. The literature of the Kirghiz has also begun to flourish. None of these peoples would agree to renounce their literatures and their spoken dialects."[22] He conceded that an All-Russian Muslim Council could be useful, but mainly for coordinating the religious life and cultural development of autonomous territories.

Passions ran high at the congress – some delegates walked out after Räsulzadä's speech – but the vote on the resolution concerning the form of autonomy resulted in an impressive victory for his theses, a confirmation of the strength of centrifugal forces among the Russian Muslims. By a majority of 446 to 271 the congress endorsed the call for transforming Russia into a "democratic republic based on national–territorial–federal foundations," although it also adopted two provisions that took into consideration the minority platform: (1) Muslim peoples not inhabiting a clearly defined territory should be granted the benefits of cultural autonomy; (2) a central Muslim administration should be established with authority over the cultural and religious affairs of all Muslims of Russia.[23] In addition, the congress created the All-Russian Muslim Council, the Shura, and called on the Provisional Government to allow the formation of Muslim military units under Muslim commanders.[24]

Encouraged by the results of the Moscow meeting, the Mu-

4. Transition: in quest of autonomy

savatists now moved toward a speedy merger with the Adäm-i Märkaziyyät. By the end of May the two groups agreed to unite as the Turkic Party of Federalists–Musavat (Türk Adäm-i Märkaziyyät–Musavat Firqäsï), the title reflecting the hybrid character of the new organization. The basis of the fusion was the declaration defining the party as "democratic, based on the laboring masses" and its aims as the "defense of the economic and class interests of the masses, as well as the national–cultural aspirations of Turkic and other Muslim peoples in Russia."[25] The declaration contained an outline for administrative reorganization of Turkic-populated regions, stressing that these should remain "parts of an indivisible Russia," but it left in abeyance the thorniest issue for both sides – agrarian reform. For the time being, the question was disposed of in a deliberately vague formula: There should be a maximum limit set on land holdings, and surplus acreage should be transferred to the peasants in accordance with regulations to be determined by the particular conditions of agriculture in each locality. The merger of the two parties was formally initiated on June 20 with the formation of a joint Central Committee consisting of four Musavatists from Baku – Rasulzadä, Hajinski, Rafibäkov, and Väkilov – and four members of the Adäm-i Märkaziyyät – Ussubäkov, Rustambäkov, Dr. Aghazadä, and M. M. Akhundov.[26]

The new party, which continued to be called by the short name Musavat, at one stroke became the largest political force in Azerbaijan, dominant among the Muslims in Baku as well as the provinces. Its two constituent groups chose to ignore their differences in the belief that these were secondary to what they held in common – their commitment to federalism and, more important, the secular nationalism underlying it, the very essence of the ideology known as Musavatism. A nation, as an official party statement would later define it, was "the community of language, religion, tradition, culture, literature, history, and law. The community of religion in itself does not constitute a nation, contrary to the mistaken assumption of some of our contemporaries. From the standpoint of the above attributes the Turks are a nation."[27]

Nonetheless, differences persisted, and the effect of the unification was that the two groups became the wings of the party: the left, or Baku, and the right, or Ganja. The existence of this distinction was a major cause of the political zigzagging that would become a stock-in-trade of the Musavat, and it would lead to situations when the Baku and Ganja Musavatists followed divergent political courses. At the same time, the heterogeneous character of the party gave rise to a remarkable tactical flexibility that allowed it to cooperate with successive diverse partners.

The October Revolution and Baku politics

By the end of August the steadily deteriorating domestic situation of war-weary Russia took a dramatic turn for the worse with General L.G. Kornilov's attempt to overthrow the Provisional Government. Even though Kornilov's march on Petrograd at the head of a few army units ended in failure, its shock waves undermined the very foundations of the liberal–democratic Kerenski regime. Above all, the "Kornilov affair" contributed to a spectacular upsurge in Bolshevik strength throughout Russia. The Bolsheviks, whose party since July had been facing the prospect of delegalization, suddenly saw their fortunes brighter than ever in the wake of the mobilization of revolutionary forces for the defense of republican Russia.[28]

For the Muslims, particularly in Transcaucasia, Kornilov's venture – which, had it succeeded, would have put an end to their autonomist aspirations – in its failure became a source of acute embarrassment, for at a time when Muslim leaders were demanding from the government the right to form national military units, the all-Muslim Savage Division had joined Kornilov's march on Petrograd.

In Baku, the Executive Committee of the Council of Muslim Public Associations hastened to issue a statement condemning the counterrevolutionary attempt and fully supporting the Provisional Government.[29] Even more vehement was the reaction of the Musavat: The party organized protest meetings in the Muslim sections of Baku, and its conference of September 1 recommended that its Central Committee take all measures necessary to defend the revolution, including a "call to members" to take up arms should the need arise.[30]

Such declarations fell short of dispelling the mistrust of the non-native left. The Musavatists were denied seats in the Bureau

4. Transition: in quest of autonomy

for the Struggle against the Counterrevolution that was set up for the emergency of the "Kornilov days."[31] Despite this and similar slights, the Musavat adopted an activist posture in tune with the general upsurge of radicalism. It endorsed the program of the Russian socialist parties with respect to workers' rights and gave full backing to the general strike that broke out in Baku at the end of September. Simultaneously, the Musavat was stepping up its criticism of the city soviet as insufficiently democratic – as it included no representation of the largest segment of the working class, the Muslims.[32] By attacking the Soviet, which was under the control of the SRs and Mensheviks, the Musavatists drew closer to the Bolsheviks, who for their own reasons were also demanding changes in its composition. The Bolshevik campaign rode the wave of post–general strike militancy among the Baku workers and achieved some degree of success. On October 13 the soviet's new Executive Committee was elected, again under Shaumian, but now dominated by the Bolsheviks in alliance with the faction of Mensheviks–Internationalists. Two days later the soviet accepted the proposal for broadening itself by admitting additional deputies from factories and military units, a step that further increased Bolshevik influence. The elections to the soviet that took place on October 22 were a disappointment for the Bolsheviks, however, whereas the Musavat made an impressive show of strength. The Azerbaijanni party won pluralities in all but one of Baku's industrial districts, a telling testimony of support from Muslim workers, among whom no other organization gained any appreciable number of votes. The results of these elections, embarrassing for the non-native left, were not published, and we have only the unofficial figures following:[33]

Musavatists	8,147
SRs	6,305
Dashnakists	5,289
Bolsheviks	3,883
Mensheviks	687

The victory of the Musavat was likely to upset the overall balance of power in Baku, and in the end the election results were deemed invalid on the grounds of alleged irregularities. Though the Musavatists might have felt themselves cheated of their electoral success through the collusion if not instigation of the Bolsheviks, they continued to show the latter their sympathies. There were issues of greater importance at stake than the elections to the soviet, which in any case the Azerbaijanis expected to win again.

After the failure of the last Russian offensive on the Austrian front in June 1917, Musavatist support for the war, never enthusiastic, entirely disappeared. During the summer the Azerbaijanis began criticizing the Provisional Government for its conduct of the war and publicly defended the Bolsheviks against accusations of defeatism and treason. By September the Musavatist press was printing that Russia was no longer capable of continuing the struggle and that this truth ought to be publicly acknowledged. Not unlike the Bolsheviks, the Musavatists viewed the war as the chief obstacle in the path to their goal, except that what they aimed for was not a socialist society but national autonomy. "The Musavatist criticism of the Provisional Government assumed some peculiar forms," reminisced a Russian observer of contemporary events.

In the editorials of the party's official publication we read that the government was inept in converting magnificent promises into reality, that its policy continued to be dominated by the spirit of Miliukov, that it failed to disavow the annexationists in the issue of the Dardanelles, and that it had at its head an incompetent person, a dreamer, a braggard, and abnormal man who was acting as a lackey of the Kadets and capitalists.[34]

Another reason for the Musavatists' animosity toward the Provisional Government was even more fundamental, and hinged on the question of the nationality policy. This was the question on which the post-tsarist regime was, as a matter of principle, reluctant to take a stand. The Provisional Government saw itself as the trustee of the state's integrity until the Constituent Assembly should have assumed its powers. Meanwhile, no effort was to be spared to keep the territory of Russia intact, and no legislation should be passed diminishing the sovereignty of the state. All the same, despite this frequently restated official position, allowances had to be made in response to special circumstances. Poland, which from 1915 had been under German and Austrian occupation, received recognition of its independence from Russia within several days of the overthrow of the monarchy. Also, the Provisional Government quickly restored the

4. Transition: in quest of autonomy

autonomous status of Finland, a country that was of limited economic significance to Russia and that had never been fully incorporated into Russia's state structure. These two cases stood in sharp contrast to the government's refusal to take even preparatory steps toward the future autonomy of the Ukraine. Other inconsistencies were obvious in official policy toward minorities. The acceptance of national councils – the Muslim Shura or its Ukrainian equivalent, the Rada – as organs of self-government led to the shift of local power away from the Provisional Government, as its authority was declining while that of the national councils was growing. Similarly, the government caved in to pressures for creation of military units on a national basis. In general, however, the successor regime to the tsardom clung stubbornly to the status quo ante in Russia's nationality problem, a dangerous exercise in inflexibility during a revolutionary period.[35]

Unlike the moderates of the ruling coalition, Lenin had for long appreciated the significance of the nationality question. He saw nationalist and separatist movements as useful means for undermining the established order, but was in principle against them. In his view, nationalism was a passing phase in history, a product of the rise of capitalist economy, and socialists should thus strive for the unification of the proletariat of all countries. Still, the grievances of oppressed nationalities were a fact of inherent revolutionary potential, and before 1917 Lenin had gradually worked out his rather involved theory of national self-determination.

In its simplest terms, this theory can be summarized as follows: self-determination meant only the right of secession from Russia, not any intermediate form of federal relationship. The non-Russian peoples would have to make a choice between independent existence as small, economically weak states or assimilation into a democratic Russia. Faced with such an alternative, most minorities would opt against secession. They should therefore be given a right that, in their own interest, they should decline to exercise. Issuing a call for national self-determination, Lenin at the same time in effect disapproved it.[36]

Before February 1917, the Bolsheviks had not widely shared Lenin's views on the nationality question, and some considered them inconsistent and self-contradictory. These views received substantial Bolshevik support only at the April 1917 All-Russian

Bolshevik Conference, which launched the slogan "National Self-Determination for All, Including the Freedom of Secession." The leaders of the Musavat took this slogan at face value and perceived it as an encouragement for autonomist solutions, even though the Bolsheviks in the same breath were spelling out their reservations. The April conference had also drawn the distinction between the right to secession and the advisability of secession by a given nationality at any particular moment: It would be up to the party of the proletariat to decide on individual questions of secession in consideration of the overall interests of the struggle for socialism.[37]

With regard to the specific situation of the Caucasus, the Bolsheviks were slow to make their position clear, and did so only several months later at their regional convention on October 7. The resolution on the nationality question included the following recommendations:

1. Autonomy should be granted the Caucasus, along with the creation of a regional, democratically elected Seim.
2. New administrative units should be created that are organized on economic bases and extensive self-government instituted. These new units, wherever possible, should also correspond to the national makeup of the population.
3. The Provisional Government should recognize the right of national self-determination, including the right of secession. "At the same time," the resolution read, "the convention does not recommend either secession or the creation of federal states by the nationalities of the Caucasus." Instead, the Bolsheviks called for the "unity of democracy in the Caucasus above the national distinctions" in the interest of the working class movement.
4. Recognizing the need for education in native languages, the Bolsheviks opposed attempts to attempts to place schools under the control of separate national organs of power: "All education should be concentrated in the hands of the Caucasian Seim and the territorial self-government."[38]

Although the tenor of this statement again clearly failed to meet the Musavatists' expectations, they may have sensed enough ambiguity in the statement on the not-to-be-exercised right of self-determination to sustain their pro-Bolshevik disposition. The leaders of the Musavat could interpret this ambiguity as a sign of the Bolsheviks' weakness or as the Bolsheviks' attempt to keep open their options for compromise. Since the Bolsheviks had only a limited following in Baku and an even smaller one in the

4. Transition: in quest of autonomy

rest of Transcaucasia, they would have to grant concessions in return for support in their maneuvering. The possibility of a Bolshevik seizure of power did not, as subsequent events were to prove, unduly disturb the Musavat. To maintain their rule over the region the Bolsheviks would have to depend on the Azerbaijanis. Beyond these calculations loomed what was probably the most deeply seated cause for Musavatist confidence: Increasingly there were indications that in the months to come tottering Russia would have less say in Transcaucasia while the voice of Turkey would grow stronger. Pro-Ottoman sympathies within the ranks of the Musavat were rapidly surfacing in the fall of 1917, and the antiwar campaign was one of their manifestations.

One day after the Bolshevik coup in Petrograd, on October 26, there met in Baku as scheduled the first congress of the unified Musavat. The meeting's main reaction to the overthrow of the Kerenski regime was to press forcefully the issue of autonomy. The program the Azerbaijani party adopted at this juncture outlined its vision of the future in the following terms:

1. The governmental structure of the Russian state should be based on a federation of republics established on the principle of national–territorial autonomy.
2. The constitution of the state, besides guranteeing political liberties such as freedom of speech, press, conscience, assembly, association, and strike, should contain the following assurances: inviolability of the system of federal republics, uniform application of labor laws, and solution of the agrarian question in accordance with conditions prevailing in the autonomous units.
3. Each nationality possessed of a defined territory, – that is, constituting a majority in a given area of the Russian state – should be granted the right of autonomy. In the opinion of the Party, such Turkic lands as Azerbaijan, Turkestan, Kirghizia, and Bashkiria should obtain territorial autonomy. The Volga and Crimean Tatars and other Turkic peoples inhabiting Russia should be granted national autonomy. The Party takes upon itself the obligation to assist by all means those non-Turkic co-religionists who may strive for their autonomy.
4. Nationalities not inhabiting defined territories should be granted the right of national and cultural autonomy.
5. The legislative process within both territorial and national–autonomous units should belong exclusively to their representative bodies.
6. The autonomous units represented in organs of the state should

have the right to act jointly in pursuit of their common goals and requests.[39]

Other parts of the program dealt with the nature of the relations between the autonomous republics and the central government, the latter's authority to be restricted to matters of common concern for the state as a whole, such as defense, foreign policy, currency, the administration of railways, and the postal service. In performing these functions the central government would be subject to control by an assembly consisting of representatives of all the autonomous republics, which in turn would be entirely self-governing in their internal affairs. Legislative powers, territorial administration, and the justice and educational systems within each republic would be the exclusive domain of its elective bodies and the executive organs that issued from them.[40]

In this grandiose blueprint for restructuring the Russian state, one point was of particular relevance to the ongoing dispute within the Musavat. The Baku "old guard," which had favored the outright expropriation of landed estates, reached a compromise with the former members of the Adäm-i Märkaziyyät by accepting the formula that agrarian reform be carried out in accordance with local circumstances. Impilicit here was the recognition of the position of the party's right wing that the government should purchase rather than seize the land for distribution among the peasants.

Granting this momentous concession to the Ganja landlords did little to prevent the Baku Musavatists from taking further steps in their rapprochement with the Bolsheviks. The party congress had refrained from issuing statements on the most recent developments in Petrograd and instead left to its Central Committee, whose chairman was Räsulzadä, decisions on dealing with the situation as it unfolded. In fact, the first proclamation of the new regime on the nationality question sounded encouraging. The Declaration of the Rights of the Peoples of Russia issued on November 2, 1917 by the Council of People's Commissars (Sovnarkom) over the signatures of Lenin and Stalin (then commissar for nationalities affairs) spoke of the equality of those peoples as well as of their right of "secession and the formation of independent states."[41]

Soon after the promulgation of this statement of general principles, in early December 1917, Sovnarkom issued a manifesto

4. Transition: in quest of autonomy

addressed to the "Toiling Muslims of Russia and the Orient" and appealing to their religious and national feelings and resentment of European colonialism:

> Muslims of Russia, Kirghiz and Sarts of Siberia and Turkestan, Turks and Tatars of Transcaucasia, Chechens and Caucasian Mountaineers – all you whose mosques and prayer houses have been destroyed, whose beliefs and customs have been trampled underfoot by the Tsars and oppressors of Russia: from now on your beliefs and customs, your national and cultural institutions, are free and inviolable. Organize your national life freely. This is your right. Know that your rights, like the rights of all the peoples of Russia, are now under the protection of the Revolution and its organs, the Soviets of Workers, Soldiers, and Peasants. Support this Revolution; it is your government. Muslims of the Orient, Persians and Turks, Arabs and Hindus – all you whose lives, property, fatherlands, and liberties have been the objects of speculation by the predatory robbers of Europe, whose lands have been seized by the spoilers who started the present war: Our banners carry the liberation of all the oppressed peoples of the world.[42]

This proclamation also bore the signatures of Lenin and Stalin, two Bolshevik leaders already known for their interest in the Orient. The former had frequently voiced his belief that peoples under colonial rule would be a crucial factor for the victory of the worldwide revolution; the latter, a Georgian by birth, had the reputation of being more familiar with and more sympathetic to the non-European nationalities of Russia than most other Bolshevik leaders. These early steps of Lenin's government left their impact on the Musavatists' behavior in Baku politics.

The news of the overthrow of the Kerenski government reached Baku the following day, October 26, provoking an immediate crisis within the city soviet. Its moderate factions, the SRs, Dashnakists, and Mensheviks, anxious to stave off a Bolshevik takeover of the city, voted for the creation of a local Committee of Public Safety to exercise special emergency powers and to function as the supreme authority in Baku.[43]

In a countermove, Baku Bolsheviks hastily convened a conference of the recently broadened soviet. More receptive to their influence and to Shaumian's eloquence, the meeting voted to support Lenin's Sovnarkom, to endorse his slogan "All Powers to the Soviets," and to order the Committee of Public Safety to disband. Yet even the broadened soviet proved less than manageable for the Bolsheviks when it met on November 2 to debate the practical issues of the transfer of power. By now, the long-brewing split of the SR Party into separate organizations had finally materialized, a process that the most recent events speeded up. The Right SRs disapproved of the Bolshevik coup, while the Left SRs gave their full backing to the new revolutionary government. Together with the Dashnakists and Mensheviks, the Right SRs demonstrated their opposition by walking out of the soviet. The remainder of this body, now under control of the Bolsheviks and their Left SR allies, proclaimed itself legitimate and elected a new Executive Committee, again with Shaumian at its head.[44]

In the midst of this crisis, the Musavat first indicated its tacit support for the Bolsheviks by refusing to join the Committee of Public Safety. Then, on November 7, the party's Baku Council approved the overthrow of the Provisional Government, blaming it for prolonging the war and failing to fulfill the expectations of Russia's national minorities. Concerning the situation in Baku, the Musavatists presented a set of proposals and statements that would indirectly result in an increase in their share of power:

1. The government ought to be purely democratic and consist of the representatives of the revolutionary democracy regardless of nationality or party affiliation, in accordance with the real strength of each party.
2. The liquidation of the conflict that has arisen within the Baku democracy as a means of crushing Bolshevism is a most harmful step for the goals and tasks of the whole democracy.
3. To recognize as inexpedient the tactics of a part of the democracy aimed at the isolation of the Bolsheviks and the walkout of this part of the democracy from the Soviet of Workers and Soldiers Deputies.
4. To arrange for the immediate elections of a new soviet on the basis of a general, equal, direct, and proportional suffrage.
5. The Musavat Party, finding the peaceful solution of the conflict essential, calls the whole democracy to join in the tactics of conciliation and, recognizing the action of the Committee of Public Safety as harmful to the policy of conciliation, delcares that it cannot possibly participate in the said Committee.[45]

In addition to the valuable support of the Musavat the Bolsheviks gained endorsements from other Baku groups, among them the Caspian merchant fleet, the labor unions, and the city garrison. The soviet became generally accepted as the center of political

4. Transition: in quest of autonomy

authority in Baku. Its only potential contender was the city *duma*, which continued to function under the chairmanship of Khan Khoiski. In the days of the October power struggle the elections to the *duma* were held with the participation of voters only from the city proper and to the exclusion of the industrial districts, which were still not formally incorporated into the municipal administration. No clear majority emerged, but the Bolsheviks captured a plurality of 16 percent. Other groups did not run separately but rather on joint slates, such as the Muslim National Parties (which gathered 25 percent of the vote), the Socialist Bloc (Mensheviks and SRs – 24 percent), and Armenian National Parties (20 percent).[46] Unlike the soviet, the Baku *duma* represented both the "revolutionary democracy" and the bourgeoisie, a circumstance that did not make for its effective operation. For their part the moderate parties, badly split among themselves over mounting municipal problems, were unable or unwilling to stop the Bolsheviks from playing the crucial role in the *duma* as well.

Of the many contingencies with which the city government had to grapple, the most urgent and politically explosive was the growing shortage of food. The situation deteriorated further with the outbreak of an anti-Bolshevik rebellion in Daghestan, an event that cut off Baku from its regular supplier of grain, the northern Caucasus. While the Baku Soviet was dispatching a military expedition against the Ter-Daghestani regime in Vladykavkaz, the Musavat was hailing the Daghestani Mountaineers as allies in the struggle for autonomy. The regional conference of Muslim organizations that met in Baku on December 9–12 expressed its solidarity with the Daghestanis by calling for a joint national assembly of Transcaucasian Turks and Caucasian Mountaineers.[47] In Baku, anger among non-Muslims at the Daghestanis spilled over onto local Azerbaijanis, and squads of soldiers took to requisitioning food from Muslim households. The Muslims in turn reacted in a mass demonstration of protest on December 12. Thousands of men, some wielding arms, held a meeting denouncing robberies, violence, house searches, and all other kinds of discriminatory treatment. When a deputation of prominent Muslims met with the soviet's committee in charge of public order, they heard from Dzhaparidze what would become a monotonously repetitious argument: "Political leadership had not ignored the Muslims – it was simply that they were culturally more backward than the rest of the population and revolutionary groups had no influence over them."[48] This was an acknowledgment of the mutual impenetrability of the two worlds, the revolutionary milieu and the Muslim community. The Bolsheviks were, in effect, writing off the latter as an active force in promoting the revolution.

Amid signs of strain in the Musavatist–Bolshevik relationship the elections to the Baku Soviet took place on December 12–13, this time on the basis of a modified electoral procedure and redrawn district boundaries. The results were sorely disappointing for the Musavatists: they obtained twenty-one seats, far behind the Bolsheviks' fifty-one. Ahead of them were also the Dashnakists with forty-one, the Left SRs with thirty-eight, and the Right SRs with twenty-three.[49] Although the Azerbaijanis were again deprived of an electoral victory, their reaction was equivocal. In the meeting of the Baku Soviet Räsulzadä declared: "The Musavat Party is not opposed in principle to the transfer of power to the soviets, yet because of the fact that the Baku Soviet has not been democratically elected, the Musavat Party refuses to recognize the power of the said soviet and shall not enter its Executive Committee."[50] It was becoming increasingly clear that the Bolsheviks, having seized the reins of power in Petrograd, lacked any inclination to institute reforms that would grant autonomy to Azerbaijan. Instead, they constantly reiterated the theme of consolidation of the revolutionary democracy around Lenin's Sovnarkom; all they had to say on autonomy was that it could not mean a rule by nationalists.[51] In a move suggesting that his regime intended to tighten rather than relax the grip of centralized power, Lenin on December 18 appointed Shaumian special commissar for the Caucasus, and Dzhaparidze became his replacement as the chairman of the Baku Soviet. By this time the Musavatists, especially those of Ganja, were shifting the focus of their activities from Baku to the wider field of Transcaucasian politics, as the region began drifting away from Russia in its state of disintegration.

5

Transition to nationhood: Transcaucasian federalism

Transcaucasia on the road to secession

The reaction of the rest of Transcaucasia to the Bolshevik coup contrasted sharply with the predominant attitude in Baku. In Tiflis, the Menshevik-dominated Regional Center of the Soviets, the actual locus of power beyond the Caucasus, lost no time in denouncing the Bolsheviks as helping the cause of the counterrevolution, no matter whether they were to succeed or were to be crushed by military force.[1] A Committee of Public Safety was formed in the Georgian capital, and it proved more effective in controlling the local situation than its equivalent in Baku.

The fact that, outside Baku, the Sovnarkom had not been recognized anywhere in Transcaucasia led to touchy political and constitutional problems that would plague the regional leaders for months to come. Although, as far as the major non-Muslim parties were concerned, the central government of Russia no longer existed, they were unwilling to loosen their ties to Russia. The Georgian Mensheviks were at this stage still sincerely opposed to nationalism. Led by such men of revolutionary fame as Noi Zhordania, Irakli Tsereteli, and Nicholas Chkheidze, they formed the hard core of Menshevism in Russia and saw their future in the context of all-Russian politics. The Dashnakists retained their commitment to a pro-Russian orientation, which was strengthened by the circumstance that the Russian armies had already driven the Ottomans out of parts of historic Armenia. Elimination of the Russian presence south of the Caucasus Mountains would have spelled a dramatic reversal for the prospect of Armenian national aspirations.

Despite their loyalty to Russia, the Mensheviks, Dashnakists, and Right SRs in rejecting Sovnarkom's legitimacy implied that Transcaucasian politicians would have to step in and assume responsibility for administration of the region. They hoped that such an action, bordering as it did on separatism, would be only a temporary measure in effect until a lawful government of Russia should have emerged from the elections to the Constituent Assembly. For the moment, a convocation of political and social organizations in Tiflis resolved on November 11 to establish an interim government for the region under the title Transcaucasian Commissariat, or Zakavkom.[2] In this manner Transcaucasia joined the rush to create regional centers of power that was taking place throughout Russia — in some cases in negative reaction to the Bolshevik coup, in others in positive reaction to their November 2 Declaration of the Rights of the Peoples of Russia. The Zakavkom in no sense acknowledged the legitimacy of these Bolshevik acts; rather, it assumed its duties in the name of a democratic Russia.

The new Transcaucasian government, unlike its predecessor the now-defunct Ozakom, was primarily the organ of the regional non-Bolshevik left. Its eleven members were elected from major national groups and their respective parties, the politically most experienced Georgian Mensheviks holding the strategic posts: E. P. Gegechkori served as chairman as well as commissar for external affairs, while his party comerade A. I. Chkhenkeli was in charge of internal affairs. A Georgian Social Federalist, Sh. Alekseev-Mekhtiev, became commissar for justice. Of the three Armenians, Kh. Karikjian (in charge of finance) and H. Ohanjanian (public welfare) were Dashnakists, while G. Ter-Ghazanian (supplies) represented the Armenian Social Democrats. The Russian SRs D. Donskoi and A. V. Neruchev were in charge of military affairs and agriculture, respectively. Of the three Azerbaijanis on the Zakavkom, none belonged to the Baku wing of the Musavat that had sided with the Bolsheviks, but A. Khasmammädov from Ganja, a member of the party's Central Committee, served as commissar for state control. Khudad Malik-Aslanov, in charge of transportation, and a member of the former Ozakom, Jafarov, now commissar for commerce and industry, were independents with close links to the Musavat.[3]

In its inaugural proclamation of November 18, the Zakavkom

5. Transition: Transcaucasion federalism

stated, with overtones of regret: "The peoples of Transcaucasia who have marched hand in hand with Russia and linked their fate with hers find themselves at this crucial moment of history left to their own resources for the first time. They are in a position where they have to take with their own forces measures to avert the approaching economic and social disaster."[4]

The Zakavkom declared that it intended to retain its powers only until the Constituent Assembly shall have convened, but should its convocation prove impossible "in view of Russia's situation," it would then subordinate itself to the caucus of the deputies elected to that Assembly from Transcaucasia and the Caucasus front. Although its authority was temporary, the Zakavkom promised not only to work for the alleviation of such current problems as the threat of hunger, collapse of finances, and dislocation of transport, but also to launch fundamental reforms, including the introduction of *zemstvos*, the confiscation of large landed estates, and institution of measures aimed at "equitable solution of the nationality question" – an impressive set of tasks, hardly any of which would be tackled during the Zakavkom's tenure.[5]

Within two weeks of the Zakavkom's formation, on November 26–28, elections to the Constituent Assembly were held throughout Transcaucasia. A total of 2,455,274 votes cast was distributed among the major parties as follows:[6]

Mensheviks	661,934
Musavat	615,816
Dashnaktsutiun	558,400
Muslim Socialist Bloc	159,770
SRs	117,522
Bolsheviks	95,581
Himmät	84,748
Ittihad	66,504

Under the formula of allocating one seat for every 60,000 votes, the Georgian Mensheviks secured eleven seats in the Assembly, the Musavat ten, the Dashnaktsutiun nine, the Muslim Socialist Bloc two, and the Bolsheviks, SR's, Himmät, and Ittihad, one seat each. The results of the elections were especially revealing of the respective strengths of two parties: the Bolsheviks, who with less than 4 percent of the total vote in Transcaucasia could not claim popular support anywhere except in Baku proper, where they came out first with 22,276 votes out of 111,050; and the Musavat, which although second in voting power in the region, did not enjoy in the Muslim community the nearly monopolistic position of the Dashnaktsutiun among the Armenians or of the Mensheviks among the Georgians.[7] The Azerbaijanis displayed an unexpectedly high degree of political differentiation, their strongest party polling no more than 63 percent of the votes. A good Muslim vote showing was made by the Muslim Socialist Bloc, a group that had emerged in the fall of 1917 as the native equivalent of the Russian SRs. Led by Aslan bäy Safikiurdski and Ibrahim Haidarov, the Bloc was, not unlike its Russian prototype, a somewhat loosely knit association that sought its support among the peasantry. The Ittihad, although placing fourth among the Muslim parties (8 percent of the Muslim vote), proved its ability to enlist the peasants' backing in some districts and scored a spectacular victory of 77 percent in the Baku *uezd*.[8] The general inference to be drawn from the voting results was that the Azerbaijani electorate had given less than overwhelming but still solid endorsement to the Musavatist program of territorial autonomy. It was also apparent that the prospect of loosening their ties to Russia had a stronger attraction for Azerbaijanis than for Georgians and Armenians.

The deputies who had won the first democratic elections in Russia did not have a chance to begin their legislative work. The Constituent Assembly, whose SR majority was unfriendly to the Bolsheviks, could not expect the toleration of the Sovnarkom. When the Assembly refused to subordinate itself to the soviets, Lenin ordered it forcibly dispersed after its first meeting on January 5, 1918, thereby ending prospects for the establishment of parliamentary democracy in Russia.

Predictably, Baku and the rest of Transcaucasia again reacted in different ways to the new political crisis. The Baku Soviet on January 23 voted in favor of the Bolshevik motion approving the Sovnarkom's action.[9] The Musavat, having at first condemned the dispersal of the Assembly, in the end gave hesitant support to the Bolsheviks, as it seemed that once in power they were coming around to a more sympathetic view of federalism. Facing the potential rapid disintegration of the Russian state,

5. Transition: Transcaucasion federalism

Lenin now began to see federation of national republics as a means of stopping and reversing the process.[10] This was one of the last instances of a common stand taken by two uneasy allies. Soon afterward the Musavatists and the Bolsheviks would part ways for good on the question of the Transcaucasian parliament.

In the eyes of the Georgian Mensheviks, the dispersal of the Constituent Assembly was an act severing the last tenuous link between Transcaucasia and Russia under the rule of their Bolshevik rivals. At their urging the deputies from Transcaucasia met in Tiflis to settle the issue of supreme authority over the region as stipulated in the Zakavkom's November declaration. Historically, the call for a regional representative body had been associated with the idea of the Transcaucasian peoples' union and sounded echoes of the 1905 slogan "Caucasus for the Caucasians." The earliest advocates of such a legislature, the Georgian Social Federalists, had suggested it be named the *Seim*, a term reminiscent of the parliament of Poland, a country that once had a distinct status within the Russian Empire. Demands for formation of the Seim had arisen at various times after 1905 and from such diverse groups as the Georgian émigrés in Turkey and Germany and the Transcaucasian Bolsheviks in the last days of the Kerenski regime. Yet in February 1918 these same Bolsheviks were the most vehement in agitating against the creation of the Seim, which they now saw as a step toward cutting Transcaucasia loose from the new Soviet Russia. The protest campaign they launched in Tiflis was so frenzied that local authorities ordered their newspapers closed down. Some lives were even lost in a bloody clash between demonstrators against separatism and the Menshevik militia.[11]

The Menshevik proposal to establish the Seim also met with the opposition of the Dashnakists and the SRs, and the Transcaucasian parliament might have never materialized had it not been for the backing of the Musavatists. Additional support came from the Himmät–Mensheviks, who generally accepted the guidance of their Georgian comrades. The Azerbaijani Mensheviks disregarded Narimanov's denunciation of the Constituent Assembly as the "Duma in disguise" and his pleading for recognition of the legitimacy of the Sovnarkom.[12] A majority, by two votes, turned out to be in favor of creating the Seim, and its inaugural meeting took place in Tiflis on February 10, 1918.

The membership of the Seim was determined, on the basis of the November elections, by lowering the minimum votes to one-third the number that had been required for a seat in the Constituent Assembly. On the basis of this formula, the larger parties tripled the number of their deputies and minor ones obtained representation that the voters had previously denied them. This distribution of seats brought to the Seim thirty-three Georgian Mensheviks, a thirty-man Musavatist delegation that included a few members of the Muslim Independent Group, twenty-seven Dashnakists, seven representatives of the Muslim Socialist Bloc, five SRs, four Himmät–Mensheviks, and three Ittihadists. Two Georgian parties, the National Democrats and Social Federalists, as well as the Transcaucasian branch of the Kadets, all of which had polled less than the minimum number of votes in November, each now received a seat in the Seim.[13]

From its inception the Seim confronted a cluster of interwoven dilemmas: How should they define the status of Transcaucasia vis-à-vis Russia? What was Russia at this moment when Transcaucasia chose to boycott the Sovnarkom and the democratic Russian republic no longer existed? Concomitant were the questions of the Transcaucasian parliament's jurisdiction: Since the most pressing of all tasks was clearly termination of hostilities on the Caucasus front, in what capacity should the Seim enter the negotiations? Should it constitute itself as a sovereign body – an act that would amount to legal separation from Russia?

Of all the groups in the Seim only the minuscule party of Georgian Social Federalists drew bold conclusions from its appraisal of political realities: The formation of the Seim, they contended, marked a stage in the disintegration of Russia, a process that would result in the rise of independent national states, among them the federal republic of Transcaucasia.[14] By comparison, the declarations of other parties were replete with ambiguities, reservations, and contradictions, their disagreements over issues of peace and sovereignty auguring no good for the effectivness of the Seim.

The spokesman for the Georgian Mensheviks, Zhordania, seemed less concerned with Transcaucasian independence than with breaking away from the Russia of the Bolsheviks. He blamed the Bolsheviks for capitulating to Germany in the peace talks

5. Transition: Transcaucasion federalism

then under way in Brest-Litovsk. Transcaucasia would negotiate its own peace with Tukey, but not a humiliating one. Zhordania proposed that the Seim undertake the task of organizing the Transcaucasian republic, which he envisioned as a system of small cantons corresponding to the checkered pattern of ethnic distribution.[15]

To the Armenians, the Georgian views seemed to lean too much toward separatism. The Dashnakist parliamentary faction consisted mainly of deputies from outside Baku who maintained their loyalty to the Russian democracy of the future. Speaking for the Dashnaktsutiun, H. Kachaznuni called for concluding a peace that would assure autonomy for Turkish Armenia, for imposing a federal structure on Transcaucasia based on nationally homogeneous provinces rather than cantons, and for forming a regional government made up of truly socialist elements. This last point, suggestive of ethnic animosity implied exclusion of the Musavat from participation in a future Transcaucasian government.[16]

There was no unanimity among Muslim deputies on the nature of their relationship to Russia. The Musavatist leader from Ganja, Dr. Aghazadä, denounced traditional Russian centralism as outdated and bankrupt. The wave of the future was national self-determination and this goal was to be attained through a program of territorial autonomy. Without mentioning secession, the Musavat's declaration recognized the authority of the Seim as sovereign, comparable to that of the Constituent Assembly. The Seim should concern itself above all with a speedy conclusion of the peace, the *"conditio sine qua non* for solving the agrarian as well as other social and national problems."[17]

The controversy surrounding the issue "Autonomy, but what kind?" continued to divide Muslim politicians. The Ittihadist Yaqub Mir Mäkhtiyev made it clear that his group was as opposed as ever to any form of separation from the Russian state: Russia, when organized as a democratic republic, would grant its ethnic and religious minorities the right to establish councils in charge of schools, theaters, museums, and universities. In view of the current crisis engulfing Russia, the Pan-Islamists agreed for the moment that the Seim should be recognized as the Supreme if temporary organ of power in Transcaucasia.[18]

The Baku "March Days"

As 1917 neared its end, the basic fact underlying the condition of Transcaucasia concerned not developments in Tiflis or Baku politics but rather an elemental process under way in eastern Turkey: the crumbling of the Russian Caucasus front. As masses of revolutionized soldiers continued boarding homebound trains, the Russian command at the front accepted the idea that empty trenches could be filled with new units raised locally on a nationality basis. In practice this expedient proved to be of limited military value, but inevitably it produced far-reaching political reverberations. The Armenians, who had the most reason to fear the Ottoman invasion, were the first to form a national corps, whose commander in December 1917 became the famed general Ozanian Andranik. By this time a Georgian corps had also been organized under General I. Z. Odeshelidze. Transcaucasian Christians received encouragement in this undertaking from British, French, and American consular and military representatives, whose main concern was that Ottoman armies hitherto engaged against Russia might be relieved for operations against the British in Mesopotamia.[19] Understandably, Allied plans for reviving operations on the Caucasus front made no provision for using Muslim troops to fight the Ottomans. Yet just as the Armenians dreaded the prospect of Ottomans marching into Transcaucasia, the Azerbaijanis became apprehensive when they saw the Armenians arming themselves amid growing intercommunal tensions.

In 1917 Azerbaijani leaders began claiming that the most harmful by-product of Russian rule was the tsarist policy of exempting Muslims from the draft. From the first weeks after the overthrow of the monarchy the Russian Muslims had been petitioning for the right to form their own units, with the aim of redressing the disadvantage with regard to their militarily trained Christian neighbors. Kerenski's cabinet delayed its assent until the end of September, and even then held off the supply of equipment. In Transcaucasia Muslim military units began forming only after the fall of the Provisional Government. Like their Armenian and Georgian counterparts, they were organized under the auspices of national councils. The nucleus of the Muslim National Corps was the "Tatar" cavalry regiment of the Sav-

5. Transition: Transcaucasion federalism

age Division transferred from Petrograd. General Shikhlinski assumed overall command, and the officers came from the ranks of the disintegrating Russian army, with Muslims given preference. Moreover, in the fall of 1917, training native officers began in the cadet school in Baku.[20] Azerbaijanis still lacked sufficient arms, and both the Caucasus front command and the Baku Soviet refused to provide them, the soviet insisting that armed forces be organized on a class rather than ethnic basis, by recruiting reliable workers.[21] In the end, war-weary Russian soldiers, many under the sway of the Bolsheviks, became the chief source of weapons for the Azerbaijanis. Instances of Azerbaijanis disarming troops, sometimes with the threat or actual use of violence, further exacerbated the strain between the Musavat and the Bolsheviks. In January 1918 the rush to seize arms from the Russians led to a large-scale clash, the "Shamkhor Massacre." The Azerbaijanis, who in this case acted with the approval of the Tiflis authorities, anxious to prevent arms from passing eventually into Bolshevik hands, intercepted a troop train at the Shamkor station on the Tiflis–Baku rail line. When the soldiers refused to surrender their equipment the Azerbaijanis attacked, and close to a thousand lost their lives in the fighting. This tragic incident, which the Azerbaijanis regarded as their baptism under fire, gained them vast quantities of war materiel while provoking shock and fury among the Baku Bolsheviks.[22]

With more arms now in their possession, the Azerbaijanis launched a largely spontaneous drive to take the control of the countryside, the effort only sporadically coordinated by the Ganja National Council, the most influential center of Muslim power in the provinces.[23] In the Mugan Steppe, the pent-up hostility of native Azerbaijanis toward settlers from Russia erupted in violence, and the Russians naturally turned for help to the Baku Soviet. In early March soldiers of the Savage Division disarmed the pro-Bolshevik garrison in Lenkoran, and Azerbaijani irregulars seized the Bolsheviks' munitions deport in Shemakha. Simultaneously, the Daghestani Lezghians under Imam Najm ul-din Gotsinski drove the Bolsheviks out of Petrovsk, severing Baku's land communications with Russia. Meanwhile, bloody skirmishes between Muslims and Armenians were breaking out continuously, the most serious of them in Erivan, Ardahan, Ganja, and Karabagh.[24]

It was under such circumstances that the Bolsheviks' new tactical alliance, this time with the Dashnakists, was taking shape. Although Shaumian kept thundering against all and any nationalists, he singled out those Muslims "who dream of making Baku into the capital of Azerbaijan."[25] The name *Azerbaijan* in his mouth had the ring of a term of derision. Bolshevik mistrust extended even to the Baku Himmät: Strapped for funds and discouraged from growing, the organization marked its existence by publication of a newspaper of small circulation.

By contrast, Bolshevik criticism of the Dashnakists seemed moderate, and the Armenians reciprocated. The Russian Kadet A. Baikov in his memoirs of the revolutionary period in Baku made the following comment on the nature of Armenian–Bolshevik relations:

> Throughout the Russian revolution the Armenians displayed an attachment to Russia, seeing in her their only protection from physical annihilation. It was their instinct of self-preservation that dictated to the Armenians their nonresistance to Bolshevism and their occasional collaboration with the Bolsheviks. The Armenians often would say: We go only with Russia, be it even Bolshevik, rather than with anyone whoever against Russia. Or, putting it in other terms: The Bolsheviks are still Russians, therefore better than Turks.[26]

The Dashnaktsutiun made attempts to contact the Sovnarkom, and in local Transcaucasian politics deals were in the making between Shaumian and prominent Dashnakists in whom, a historian of Armenia has remarked, "the Russian orientation outweighed aversion to communism."[27] The Dashnakist–Bolshevik understanding was more workable in Baku than in other parts of Transcaucasia, where Armenian politicians preferred to remain on good terms with the Mensheviks.

By late winter 1918 the Muslims in Baku were growing concerned over the presence there of Armenian troops. As opposed to the situation in the countryside, Azerbaijani forces in the city were at a disadvantage with regard to the well-armed Dashnakists. Ironically, the Armenian units were supposed to depart for the front but were unable to do so because railway communications had been disrupted by Muslim bands. Conferences of local Muslim and Armenian national councils on the evacuation of the Dashnakist forces ended fruitlessly, as the Baku Musavatists had no control over those who had stopped the railroad traffic.

5. Transition: Transcaucasion federalism

As fearful Muslim inhabitants began leaving the city on a scale that threatened to affect its population balance, the Bolsheviks in the soviet did nothing to calm the situation.[28] Whereas in the past they refrained from calling for civil war lest it degenerate into a new "Tatar–Armenian" massacre likely to sweep them away, now they perceived that a clash between the two nationalisms could work to their advantage. At this juncture, the Azerbaijanis, though potentially more dangerous to the Bolsheviks, were still militarily weak in Baku; at the same time, even a Dashnakist victory could not result in the Armenian minority's permanent rule. Shaumian's speeches began to include references to the unavoidability of the violent struggle. "The Baku Soviet should become the main center and bastion of the civil war in Transcaucasia," he said on March 15.[29] He singled out the "Muslim nationalist *bäy* and khan parties" along with the Zakavkom as the chief enemies of the revolution. The Bolsheviks also drew encouragement from dissention in the Seim and from the exacerbation of national rivalries. They were readying themselves for the civil war, the outcome of which would make them the uncontested masters of Baku and in the long run of all Transcaucasia. With this prospect in mind Shaumian requested and obtained additional war material from the Sovnarkom, although Lenin pointedly advised him to temper decisiveness with prudence. Apparently fearing that his gifted disciple might act impetuously, he reminded Shaumian that "so far we have been saved only by the contraditions, struggles and conflicts among the imperialists. Be able to take an advantage of these conflicts. For the moment we have to learn diplomacy."[30]

Shaumian was confident that in the event of a showdown with the Azerbaijanis the Baku Dashnakists would not present a threat to the Bolsheviks but would rather constitute a source of support, and so he chose firmness over diplomacy. By mid-March the soviet initiated moves designed to break the blockade of Baku. The soviet's forces, dispatched to Lenkoran, Shemakha, and the Mugan Steppe, wrested these areas from the Muslim guerrillas.

Within the city, the aggressive posture of the soviet increased tensions among the Muslims. The incident that set off the explosion occurred on March 24 when the soviet ordered the disarming of the men of the Savage Division on board the ship *Evelina* in Baku harbor.[31] The Muslims reacted spontaneously, raising barricades during the night, and the next day they held protest meetings in the Baku mosques. At this point Shaumian was still agreeable to Narimanov's last-minute call for mediation. The Azerbaijani Bolshevik pleaded for resolving the crisis peacefully, as he feared the "political war" would too easily degenerate into an intercommunal massacre.[32] A deputation of Azerbaijani politicians visited Dzhaparidze, but the talks broke off abruptly after on the soviet's soldiers were fired upon. Hearing the news, Dzhaparidze telephoned Narimanov: "We accepted your proposals, but what can we do if the Muslims start a political war?"[33] Later on, Shaumian would admit: "We exploited the opportunity of the first armed assult on our cavalry unit and began an attack on the whole front."[34]

The crucial question the outcome of the confrontation between some ten thousand Azerbaijanis and six thousand Baku Soviet troops was the attitude of the Dashnakists with their four thousand or more well-armed men. The Armenians had at first declared their neutrality, and so the Muslims entered battle in the belief that they would not have to fight the Dashnakists, only to see the latter join the soviet's forces on March 31.[35] Overwhelmed by such a powerful combination, the Azerbaijanis sued for a cease-fire the next day. The soviet's Committee of the Revolutionary Defense, which had just castigated "the criminal schemes of the counterrevolutionaries grouped around the *bäys'* Musavat Party," now delivered to the Azerbaijanis an ultimatum with surprisingly moderate terms:

1. The unequivocal recognition of the authority of the Baku Soviet and complete subordination to its orders
2. The withdrawal of the Savage Division and other Muslim units, to be accompanied by the withdrawal of the Armenian forces
3. The reopening of the Baku–Tiflis and Baku–Petrovsk railroad lines[36]

In their first armed confrontation with Bolshevik centralism the Azerbaijanis had suffered a loss, although the penalty was not exorbitant. The truly tragic turn of events came after acceptance of the ultimatum, when the Dashnakist allies of the Bolsheviks took to looting, burning, and killing in the Muslim sections of the city. Narimanov now saw the realization of his dire forebodings. His description of this second phase of the conflict not only gave vent to his bitterness toward the Dash-

5. Transition: Transcaucasion federalism

nakists but also suggested his feelings about the Bolshevik–Dashnakist alliance against the Muslims:

> Even if a Muslim happened to be a Bolshevik, no quarter was given. The Dashnakists would say: We do not recognize any Bolsheviks; once you are a Muslim that is enough. They killed whom they pleased, they stripped and emptied houses.... Under the banner of Bolshevism the Dashnakists committed all kinds of atrocities against the Muslims. Not only men, but even pregnant women were not spared.[37]

The fighting did not subside until the night of April 2, with a loss of lives estimated by Shaumian to be three thousand.[38] Muslim survivors by the thousands were fleeing the city in panic. Their national council and political organizations disbanded, their leaders sought refuge in Ganja or Tiflis.

The Baku crisis added to the strains within the Seim. The Zakavkom's commissar for the interior, Ramishvili, reported that the Bolsheviks had started an offensive in Transcaucasia, but announced no countermeasures. Moreover, the Menshevik parliamentary faction condemned both the Bolsheviks' conduct and the "attacks on Baku from outside," a reference to the activities of the Azerbaijani guerillas.[39] This apparent evenhandedness was intended to facilitate the mission of Ramishvili to Baku to mediate an end to the "fratricidal struggle." Predictably, the Bolsheviks rejected the effort at mediation. The reply of the Committee of the Revolutionary Defense was typical in considering the nationality question strictly from the standpoint of class warfare only: "Any peace delegation would serve no purpose. There has not been any fratricidal struggle in Baku. There was and is continuing beyond the limits of Baku a civil war against counterrevolutionary *bäy*s and khans."[40]

The Georgians' handling of the crisis provoked indignation among the Azerbaijani deputies. Räsulzadä and Safikiurdski threatened that their respective groups would withdraw from the Seim unless the Transcaucasian government made an effort to dislodge the Bolsheviks from Baku. In the end, the Zakavkom assembled a mixed Georgian–Azerbaijani force and sent it eastward along the Tiflis–Baku rail line while the Daghestani regiment of Imam Gotsinski moved on the city from the north. Poorly coordinated and undertaken with inferior strength, the operation was easily repelled by the Baku Soviet's troops, whose successful counterattacks extended the soviet's power over a large portion of the Baku *guberniia* by the end of April.

"The results of the fighting are splendid for us," reported Shaumian to the Sovnarkom on April 13. After describing the course of events, he concluded, with exultation: "Our Bolshevik influence was already strong in Baku and now we are masters of the situation in the full sense of the word."[41] In his enthusiasm, Shaumian might not have remembered that in 1905 he himself had accused the tsardom of reaping in benefits of the Muslim–Armenian massacres. It is doubtful that to him, as opposed to the Azerbaijanis, any similarity suggested itself.

As soon as the danger around Baku had passed, the Committee of the Revolutionary Defense reminded the Dashnakists that the terms of the ultimatum applied to them as well. The Armenian National Council was ordered to merge its troops with the Soviet's forces and to cease conducting searches, making arrests, and collecting taxes.[42] The Dashnakists went through the motions of compliance, and the soviet refrained from strict enforcement of its demands, as the Bolsheviks were loathe to antagonize another ethnic community – one, moreover, whose support was crucial for their hold on power. They were determined, however, to eliminate quickly the remaining strongholds of their traditional rivals and opponents. The bourgeois press was ordered to close down, along with a Menshevik newspaper. Another decree dissolved the city *duma*, which was in any event an ineffectual alternative to the soviet's monopoly of power.[43] Then, on April 25, a new executive body with authority over the city and the outlying areas of the *guberniia* came into being under the name Baku Sovnarkom, a local replica of Lenin's government. Although the Bolsheviks were still a minority in the Soviet, they gained nine of the twelve posts in the Baku Sovnarkom, the balance falling to their Left SR allies. The list of the commissars included, among others, the familiar names of Shaumian (chairman and commissar of foreign affairs) and Dzhaparidze (internal affairs), as well as Narimanov (social welfare) and a representative of the Muslim Left SR organization Äkinchi, Mir Hasan Väzirov.[44] Only now did Azerbaijanis gain positions of responsibility in their soviet-run native city. Their appointment was in line party with the Bolsheviks' efforts to conciliate the Muslim population after the slaughter, partly with the their need to counterbalance the Armenians. The Muslim Socialist Bureau, made up of the Himmätists and members of the Ädalät and Äkinchi, was recognized as the sole voice of the Baku Muslims. The Baku Sovnarkom tried to accommodate the bureau's demands concerning Muslims' welfare and security – up to the point of stirring up resentment among the Armenians.[45] Still the embittered mass of Muslims showed little responsiveness to the Bolshevik gestures. After the "March Days" Azerbaijani leaders spoke no longer of autonomy but rather of separation and placed their hopes no longer in the Russian Revolution but in support from Turkey.

The Transcaucasian Federation

The new regional government of Transcaucasia found itself at first confronted and soon overwhelmed by the issues of war and peace. The Zakavkom was the highest political authority in the proximity of the Caucasus front and as such was forced to take a stand on the proposal for a temporary cease-fire that the front commander, General Przhevalski, had received from his Ottoman opposite number, Vehib Pasha. With the endorsement of the Transcaucasian Commissariat, the Russian and Ottoman commands signed an armistice agreement in Erzincan on December 5, 1917. The demarcation line was drawn along the position held by the Russian army, and the agreement was conditional upon the Ottomans refraining from a transfer of their troops to the Mesopotamian front.[46]

The Erzincan armistice marked the entry of Turkey as a new factor in the equation of Transcaucasian politics. The Ottomans viewed the disintegration of Russia as on opportunity to recover not only territories lost since 1914, but possibly also those that Russia had wrested from Turkey during the nineteenth century. In addition, their thinking was increasingly colored by the resurgence of Turanism. The vision of the conquest of Turkic lands in Russia once again captivated the mind of Enver Pasha, the more so because he desired compensation for the "accursed deserts of Arabia" that Turkey was now in process of losing. The Committee of Union and Progress created a special Caucasian Department under Hasan Rusheni, who in March 1918 embarked on a secret mission to Baku, where he assembled a network of agents and established contacts with pro-Ottoman elements in Azerbaijan, the northern Caucasus, and Turkestan.[47] On the level of public activities, Istanbul intellectuals, including Azerbaijani expatriates, were galvanized to renewed efforts. While Ziya Gökalp wrote on the necessity for an expansionist policy, Aghayev stimulated public interest through articles on the Turkic character of the national movements among the Russian Muslims, and Huseynzadä delivered lectures on his native Transcaucasia, which he called the "land of the Turks." He saw its future in terms of one of three alternatives: a federation of the Caucasus, separate Muslim and Georgian states, or the union of the Turkic parts of the region with Turkey in the form of a viceroyalty (*hidiviyet*).[48]

For the present, Ottoman diplomacy chose to pursue a strategy of maneuvering Transcaucasia into a declaration of independence. A relatively weak state such as would emerge, with a large proportion of Muslim inhabitants, would be an incomparably more manageable neighbor than any Russia. On January 14, 1918, Vehib Pasha put out feelers to the Zakavkom starting negotiations for a formal peace with an independent Transcaucasia. The Zakavkom, reluctant to assume the prerogatives of a sovereign body separate from Russia, asked for a delay of three weeks to consult other non-Bolshevik governments.[49] Likewise, the Transcaucasian leaders declined the invitation of Vehib Pasha to send delegates to the Brest-Litovsk peace conference between Russia and the Central Powers, even through the latter, the Ottoman general affirmed, would do their best to secure recognition of the government of Transcaucasia.[50]

Finding the Zakavkom evasive or undecided, the Ottomans began to apply pressure. Vehib Pasha, after issuing protest notes concerning the massacre of Muslim civilians by Armenian bands behind the front line, on February 12 ordered his troops to advance – in violation of the cease-fire agreement. Georgian and Armenian units offered only token resistence, and the Ottomans entered Erzincan and Erzerum, moving in the direction of Van, Ispir, Kars, and Batum.[51] Nonetheless, on February 23 Vehib Pasha replied favorably to the Zakavkom's inquiry about negotiating a permanent peace. By this time the Georgian Mensheviks had already begun to weigh the possibility of an independent

5. Transition: Transcaucasion federalism

Transcaucasia. One of the essential points they pondered was whether the Muslims would be loyal citizens of the prospective state, ready to defend it, if need be, even against the Ottomans. Such questions, repeatedly voiced in the Seim, were not answered publicly but rather at the caucus of the representatives of all parliamentary groups called by the Musavat on March 1. In a statement that provided an unusually revealing insight into the thinking of the Azerbaijani political leadership, Ussubäkov declared that the Muslims could not be counted upon to fight against Turkey. The Transcaucasian state was hardly the ideal of the Musavatists. Now that the disintegration of the Russian army had created in Tabriz a situation resembling that in Baku or Ganja, Pan-Azerbaijani sentiments were again on the ascendance. The Musavatists had set their sights on what would amount to a Greater Azerbaijan consisting of the Persian part of the country as well as Daghestan. Upon entering the Seim they reluctantly accepted the present dividing line between the two Azerbaijans with the hope of erasing it some day. Significantly, Ussubäkov expressed no enthusiasm for the alternative of union with Turkey – since Transcaucasia, owing to a hundred years of Russian rule, was more advanced than Turkey. "Turkey, however," said Ussubäkov, "recognizes that fact and has let us know that she would be accommodating."[52]

The Muslim position had a dampening effect on the Georgians' view of independence, but the Seim could no longer escape the legal implications of the approaching peace talks. The solution it adopted was another exercise in evasiveness, bordering on self-contradiction: Without declaring Transcaucasia an independent state, the Seim pronounced itself competent to conclude a peace with a foreign power.[53] In its guidelines for the negotiations with the Ottomans the Seim asserted that the peace with Turkey was to be permanent and the 1914 international boundaries reestablished; moreover, the Transcaucasian delegation was to try to secure the right of self-determination for eastern Anatolia, particularly for Turkish Armenia within the Ottoman state.[54]

The peace delegation was selected not as a team of diplomats, but as an assemblage of politicians representing the parliamentary factions of the three Transcaucasian nationalities. Its head was the Georgian Akaki Chkhenkeli. The Azerbaijani component of the delegation included two Musavatists, Hajinski from Baku and Khasmammädov from Ganja, and one representative each from other parties: Haidarov (Muslim Socialist Bloc), Mir Yaqub Mäkhtiyev (Ittihad), and Alakpär Shaikh-ul-Islamzadä (Himmät–Menshevik). This large company departed by sea for Trebizond, where negotiations with the Ottomans were to begin on March 12.[55]

No sooner had the Transcaucasian side in the Trabizond parley assembled then it learned that its hand had been weakened by a major diplomatic development: On March 2 the Zakavkom had received a note from the Soviet deputy commissar for foreign affairs, L. M. Karakhan, that the Treaty of Brest-Litovsk to be signed the following day stipulated the cession by Russia to Turkey of Batum, Kars, and Ardahan as well as the territories occupied since 1914.[56] It became clear that refusal of the Zakavkom to attend the Brest-Litovsk conference meant a stiffer price to pay in Trebizond. Several days later, on March 10, Vehib Pasha requested that Transcaucasia evacuate all the territories in question. The Seim reacted in a stormy debate that disclosed the true extent of division among the Transcaucasian nationalities. While the Armenians and Georgians clamored for rejection of Ottoman demands, the Azerbaijanis advised concession – all the easier for them as Turkey coveted no part of their land. Khan Khoiski urged restraint pending the outcome of the Trebizond talks. He reminded the Seim that Turkey had on many occasions encouraged Transcaucasia to declare independence and that the Zakavkom had declined to send its representatives to Brest-Litovsk. "Therefore, when the government of Turkey is now asking us, considering us as a part of the Russian Republic, to fulfill the terms accepted by Russia, one could not deny the logic of such a standpoint."[57] From this moment, the Azerbaijanis, including the Ittihad, became the most outspoken advocates of Transcaucasian independence. The evolution of the Pan-Islamists' position was characteristic: Although they continued their opposition to nationalism, they came to view secession from Russia as a stepping-stone to eventual union with Turkey rather than as move toward Azerbaijani statehood. It was the Ittihadist Mäkhtiyev who, speaking for all the Muslim deputies, on March 25 told the Seim that they would not support further peace

5. Transition: Transcaucasion federalism

negotiations unless Transcaucasia decided to become an independent republic.[58]

As the Seim was immersing itself in acrimonious quarrels, in Trebizond the Ottomans were unshakable in their insistence that the peace be based on the provisions of the Brest-Litovsk settlement. Within the Transcaucasian delegation a rift developed when its Muslim members began recommending acceptance of Ottoman terms.[59] Khasmammädov, however, wished to make a significant exception to the areas to be ceded to Turkey. Perhaps because his concern for the interests of the Azerbaijani oil industry was stronger than his pro-Ottoman sentiment, he proposed that Transcaucasia retain Batum, the terminal of the oil pipeline from Baku.[60] Nonetheless, the same delegate warned his Georgian and Armenian colleagues that should a stalemate in the negotiations lead to a renewal of hostilities, the Muslims would refuse to fight their Ottoman coreligionsits.[61]

In fact, military operations continued throughout the duration of the Trebizond parley, with the Ottoman forces advancing steadily. Behind the front line, Muslim guerrillas, particularly aggressive after the Baku "March Days," harrassed the rear of the Transcaucasian army's Armenian and Georgian units. When on April 10 Chkhenkeli finally accepted the Brest-Litovsk Treaty as the basis for further negotiations, most of the areas claimed by the Ottomans had already passed into their hands, with the major exception of Batum. Yet Transcaucasia reacted unpredictably when Vehib Pasha presented an ultimatum to evacuate the city. The conclave of regional leaders decided to reject the ultimatum, their resolve backed by Rustambäkov, another prominent Musavatist, who argued for the need for Transcaucasia – and Azerbaijan – to retain this Black Sea port.[62] On April 13, the Seim met in an atmosphere of anti-Ottoman frenzy. The key speaker was Tsereteli, famed for his oratory in the 1917 Petrograd Soviet. Branding the Brest-Litovsk Treaty the death warrant for the Russian Revolution, he expressed his confidence that the Transcaucasian army would successfully resist the Ottomans "if we were not betrayed in the rear."[63] Rustambäkov, speaking on behalf of the Musavat, changed his earlier stand and now declined to support the war, but volunteered his good offices for the peaceful solution of the conflict.[64] His offer did little to mitigate the bitter recriminations heaped upon the Musavatists by Georgian and Armenian orators. The non-Muslim majority voted to declare war on Turkey, and the Mensheviks, in a resurgence of their loyalty to Russia, issued a mainfesto to the Russian proletariat. "Transcaucasia," read the manifesto, "has rejected the Brest-Litovsk Treaty because to comply with it would mean the separation from Russia."[65] The next day the Trebizond delegation was recalled to Tiflis by the Seim, provoking indignant protests among its Azerbaijani members. Hajinski termed the decision to break off the peace talks in order to start a war "a scandal unequaled in the history of international relations."[66] He withdrew in anger from the delegation, saying that he had a mandate from his party "to go to Istanbul to take the final steps toward the conclusion of peace which is indispensable for us."[67]

The war between Transcaucasia and Turkey lasted only eight days. The Ottomans easily took Batum, but were stopped at the fortress of Kars, which was defended by the Armenians. On April 22 Vehib Pasha proposed resuming the peace talks, and the Seim eagerly agreed.

Transcaucasia entered the second round of the peace parley as a fully sovereign state. After recent outpourings of loyalty to Russia, this was a dramatic turn of events, but not an improbable one in the unreal world of Transcaucasian politics. The Seim accepted its new legal status the same day it agreed to parley, April 22 – more as a diplomatic expedient than as the fulfillment of a long-cherished idea. The back-bench Menshevik deputies perfunctorily condemned Russia, sunk in choas and anarchy, for deserting Transcaucasia in its hour of need. The present situation called for a new political orientation toward the independence of the region.[68] The most revealing explanation of the shift in the Georgian position came not from a Menshevik but an SR, I. Lordkipanidze, who saw "some guarantees of our existence" in the fact that now "not only Turkey, but also its allies will participate in the peace negotiations" – a hint at the hopes of playing the Germans off against the Ottomans. "In the final analysis there is still another consideration: If the Central Powers badly need the Baku – Batum railway it would be better for us to be defeated as an independent state, because no one knows how circumstances may yet change."[69]

5. Transition: Transcaucasion federalism 125

Once the Georgians joined the Azerbaijanis on the independence issue, the Armenians had no choice but to go along, and an overwhelming majority voted for the motion that "the Seim resolves to proclaim Transcaucasia an independent, democratic, federative republic."[70] There was no display of enthusiasm on the benches of the non-Muslims.

A long-time proponent of independence, Chkhenkeli undertook the task of forming the government of the new Transcaucasian Federation. He immediately ordered the evacuation of Kars and then presented to the Seim his cabinet. The makeup of the ministry reflected the increased weight in the affairs of Transcaucasia of the Azerbaijanis, who received five of the thirteen portfolios: transportation – Malik Aslanov; education – Ussubäkov; commerce and industry – Hajinski; and state control – Haidarov. Four Georgians held the strategic positions of foreign affairs – Chkhenkeli; interior – Ramishvili; war – Georgadze, and agriculture – Khomeriki. Of the four Armenians only Khatisian was appointed to a key position, that of finance minister, while Saakian, Khachaznuni, and Erzikian became the ministers of supplies, social welfare, and labor, respectively.[71] The main tasks of the government, outlined by Chkhenkeli in his address to the Seim, were (1) drafting a constitution, (2) delineating the frontiers of the republic, (3) ending the state of war, (4) suppressing the forces of anarchy and counterrevolution, and (5) instituting land reform.[72] In practice, securing a peace would absorb all the efforts of the government. Speaking for the Musavat, Rasulzadä greeted the cabinet cordially, but in his speech he reminded them of two issues missing from the prime minister's list: the union of Transcaucasia with Daghestan and the liberation of Baku from the rule of foreign agents.[73]

Peace talks resumed on May 11 in Batum, now under Ottoman occupation. Again the Transcaucasian delegation was inordinately large, consisting of forty-five delegates, although only six delegates had voting rights, among them Hajinski and Räsulzadä. The conference admitted as participants the representatives of the North Caucasus Mountaineers Republic, which had proclaimed its independence the same day that peace talks had resumed. The new state stretched nominally from the Black Sea to the Caspian coast and included Daghestan, which was the perennial candidate for merger with Azerbaijan but that at this point chose a separate way.[74] Of greater significance was the presence in Batum of a German delegation, with observer status, led by General Otto von Lossov, the military attaché to Turkey. The chief Ottoman delegate, the justice minister, Halil bey, set the tone for the talks in his declaration that since "blood had been shed" between the two states after the date of the Brest-Litovsk settlement, its provisions could no longer serve as the basis for negotiations.[75] In his draft of a treaty on peace and friendship, Halil presented Turkey's new territorial claims, which included the Akhalkalak and Akhaltsik *uezd*s of the Tiflis *guberniia*; the Surmalu, Aleksandropol, and most of the Etchmiadzin *uezd*s of the Erivan *guberniia*; and the Kars–Aleksandropol–Julfa railroad. In addition, Transcaucasia was to allow to Ottomans to use its railways for military operations against the British in Persia.[76] Chkhenkeli in his counterproposals insisted on upholding the Brest-Litovsk terms. He also attempted to involve Germany, Austria-Hungary, and Bulgaria in the negotiation process. Halil bey rejected both points. To add weight to his demands, the Ottoman forces subsequently penetrated deep into Armenian territory.[77]

With the peace talks effectively deadlocked, the Batum Conference assumed a new character: It became a hub of behind-the-scenes maneuvering and intrigues that ultimately would decide the fate of Transcaucasia. Deputations from the Muslim parts of Georgia and the North Caucasus were petitioning the Ottomans for incorporation into Turkey. Noticing how widespread this desire was, von Lossov remarked: "The nimbus of Turkey among the uneducated Muslim masses is rising every day since the fall of Batum and Kars, which Turkish propaganda depicts as great victories."[78] The Azerbaijani members of the Transcaucasian delegation again broke the common front by declaring themselves in favor of Halil bey's draft. In their eyes the cession of some Armenian-populated territories would offer the advantage of increasing the Azerbaijani plurality in Transcaucasia. Moreover, Hajinski and Räsulzadä, it was generally believed, were in secret contact with the Ottoman delegation, just as their Georgian and Armenian colleagues sought counsel and support from the representatives of Germany.[79] The non-Muslims were well aware of the strain that had developped in German–Ottoman relations and saw it as a ray of hope. The

5. Transition: Transcaucasion federalism

Germans, looking askance at Ottoman expansion eastward at a time when the Mesopotamian and Palestinian fronts were tottering, preferred a settlement along the lines drawn at Brest-Litovsk and wished to avoid a clash between Turkey and Soviet Russia, which might easily involve Germany. The Berlin government was also mindful of its own interests in Transcaucasia and North Caucasus and hoped to secure more influence in these strategically and economically important regions. Germany sought to acquire raw materials, particularly oil, and was negotiating to this effect with the Moscow Sovnarkom.[80] In Batum, von Lossov, who personally wanted to see the North Caucasus joined to the Reich, showed himself sympathetic to the sufferings of the Armenian population, and even more so to the quandaries of Georgian politicians. As the Batum Conference had so far failed to produce results, on May 19 he offered to serve as mediator.[81] The Armenian and Georgian delegates welcomed this proposal, but Hajinski and Räsulzadä raised objections, which subsequently made the two Azerbaijanis the targets of their colleagues' accusations that they were more concerned with the interests of Turkey than of Transcaucasia.[82] In any case the Ottomans declined von Lossov's offer, upon which the German team left Batum on the ship *Minna Horn*. Before his departure, the German general wrote Chkhenkeli that according to reliable information Transcaucasia was in a state of disintegration and that he was leaving in order to obtain instructions from his government. On the following day, May 26, the Ottomans issued another ultimatum with a deadline of seventy-two hours.[83] The Ottomans' intransigence as well as their hostility toward Armenia made it obvious that the Transcaucasian Federation had not long to live in its present form. The Azerbaijanis in Batum, as if trying to salvage some of the protection of federalism for an uncertain future, sounded out the Georgians about the alternative of a dual state cut loose from the doomed Armenia. The Georgians, however, made it clear that they wanted a republic of their own, a decision they had already reached in their secret dealings with von Lossov's delegation.[84] It had been agreed that in order to outmaneuver the Ottomans, Georgia would place herself under German protection. In fact, a military mission led by Colonel Kress von Kressenstein was already in Tiflis busily establishing a German presence. The *Minna Horn*, arriving in the port of

Poti, waited there to receive the plenipotentiaries of independent Georgia for signature of the pact with Germany.[85]

There remained still the formality of administering the coup de grace to the Transcaucasian Federation, a task Tsereteli performed brilliantly in the Seim on May 26. The distinguished Menshevik stated that "it is impossible to speak of the unity of Transcaucasia as this unity has not existed in reality. And since it does not exist, the truth must be said openly."[86] His oratory bristled with denounciations of those Muslims who had assisted the invading enemy in their desire for union with Turkey. Tsereteli further blamed the Musavatists for duplicity in their failure to disavow this treacherous conduct, although he admitted that "the best of them would say: Such acts do not have our support."[87] He concluded that Georgia, left to itself and faced with mortal danger, had to assume responsibility for its own fate.

The declaration of Georgia's withdrawal from the federation was followed by the Seim's resolution to dissolve the Transcaucasian Republic. The death knell of month-old union sounded for each of its component nationalities the end of the transition toward separate existence as independent republics.

6
The Azerbaijani nation-state

The Ottoman tutelage

Upon the dissolution of the Transcaucasian Federation the Muslim representation in the defunct Seim constituted itself into the Azerbaijani National Council and on May 28, 1918 proclaimed that a new nation was born. The proclamation, which was to be referred to later on as the National Charter, read as follows:

1. Azerbaijan is a fully sovereign state; it consists of the southern and eastern parts of Transcaucasia under the authority of the Azerbaijani people.
2. It is resolved that the form of government of the independent Azerbaijani state is a democratic republic.
3. The Azerbaijani Democratic Republic is determined to establish friendly relations with all, especially with the neighboring nations and states.
4. The Azerbaijani Democratic Republic guarantees to all its citizens within its borders full civil and political rights, regardless of ethnic origin, religion, class, profession, or sex.
5. The Azerbaijani Democratic Republic encourages the free development of all nationalities inhabiting its territory.
6. Until the Azerbaijani Constituent Assembly is convened, the supreme authority over Azerbaijan is vested in a universally elected National Council and the provisional government responsible to this Council.[1]

So far only a geographical reference, *Azerbaijan* now became the name of a state, and some 2 million people, called variously Tatars, Transcaucasian Muslims, and Caucasian Turks, officially became Azerbaijanis. The very use of this name by a state with no clearly defined borders would soon bring objections from

Persia.² There were suspicions in Tehran that the Azerbaijani Republic served as a device of Turkey for detaching the Tabriz province from Persia, the more so because the Ottomans had again occupied this province during June 1918. Consequently, the Azerbaijani government, to allay Persian fears, in its documents for circulation abroad would accommodatingly use the term *Caucasian Azerbaijan*.

After the proclamation of independence, the next step in organizing the world's first Muslim republic was the choice of a prime minister. This fell upon Khan Khoiski, who formed his cabinet the same day, May 28. He began his work by notifying foreign governments of the establishment of the Azerbaijani Republic, with a temporary capital at Ganja.³

Meanwhile, in Batum, the Transcaucasian delegation split up and each of the successor states negotiated its own conditions of peace. On June 4, all three signed their separate treaties of "peace and friendship" with Turkey. Unlike the case of Armenia, reduced to barely four thousand square miles of its territory, or Georgia, forced to relinquish two of her districts, there was some substance to the term *friendship* describing the Azerbaijani–Ottoman settlement. Azerbaijan not only retained all its territory but under Article IV of the treaty received the promise of Ottoman military assistance for restoration of security and order, an obvious reference to suppression of the Armenian bands active in Mountainous Karabagh and the recovery of Baku.⁴ Yet ironically, the treaty stopped short of recognizing Azerbaijan as an independent state. The Ottomans clearly regarded Eastern Transcaucasia as a part of the Turanian empire-in-the-making, which was also to include the North Caucasus, northern Persia, and Turkestan. The chief instrument of Enver Pasha's Pan-Turanian policy in Transcaucasia was a motley Ottoman–Azerbaijani–Daghestani force, the "Army of Islam." Its commander was Enver's half-brother, Nuri Pasha, who had arrived in Ganja to set up his headquarters at the end of May. The Army of Islam was built around the Ottoman Fifth Infantry Division and included General Shikhlinski's Muslim National Corps, elements of the Savage Division, and bands of irregulars. Altogether, under Nuri's command were sixteen to eighteen thousand men, of whom the Ottomans accounted for one-third, with the balance made up mostly of militiamen lacking military training.⁵ Osten-

6. The Azerbaijani nation-state 131

sibly, this was an entirely irregular force remaining outside Ottoman jurisdiction, as the Istanbul government wished to avoid complications with Soviet Russia – and even more with Germany – for breaking the provisions of the Brest-Litovsk Treaty.

Nuri Pasha's instructions were to start military operations for liberating the Muslims from Bolshevik rule "in accordance with the request of the independent Islamic government of Azerbaijan" by June 2 – that is, even before the signing of the Azerbaijani–Ottoman pact.[6] The population greeted the Ottoman soldiers warmly and feelings of Muslim solidarity were riding high, but relations between the Ottoman commanders and Azerbaijani leaders soon proved to be less than cordial. Those Musavatists who had cautioned against uncritical admiration of the Ottoman State began to see their reservations vindicated. The Ottoman military failed to show consideration for the sensibilities of the young Azerbaijani administration, and local officials began registering complaints on these grounds. Nuri Pasha himself did not hesitate to interfere with the politics of the friendly country. He let it be known that his sympathies lay with the conservative and Pan-Islamist elements rather than with the leftists or Musavatists, who might be suspected of being in an "Azerbaijan-first" frame of mind. Neither did he show much regard for the National Council, inasmuch as this body owed its existence to the Russian Revolution. A political crisis arose in mid-June when Nuri Pasha expressed his disapproval of the Khan Khoiski cabinet, which included ministers objectionable to him. When a distressed delegation from the National Council sought his audience, he referred them to his adviser, Ahmäd bäy Aghayev. Now a ranking Ottoman official and one of the architects of the Pan-Turanian program, Ahmäd bäy warned the Azerbaijanis that the cabinet lacked popular support – that it might even witness a revolt and that in such a case the Ottomans would not defend it. He recommended dissolution of the National Council and appointment of a new government by Nuri Pasha, although in the end he agreed to allow the National Council to form a cabinet on condition that it forthwith suspend its activity as a governing body.[7]

In protest against Ottoman meddling the deputies of the Muslim Socialist Bloc and the Himmät withdrew from the National Council. Amid bitter remarks about the "Ottoman brothers who came to disperse us" and the "men around His Excellency the Pasha," the rump legislature agreed with the opinion of its speaker, Räsulzadä, that "unless we find some legal way out there will be the danger of the black reactionaries taking over power."[8] On June 17 a compromise went into effect. Khan Khoiski presented his second cabinet, which included six members of the previous one with the addition of a new six. From the first cabinet of nine men three names were dropped: Haidarov of the Muslim Socialist Bloc and Shaikh-ul-Islamzadä, both of whom were considered too far to the left, and the Musavatist Jafarov, viewed as an Azerbaijani nationalist unfriendly to Turkey.[9] The same day the National Council transferred its prerogatives to the government, which thereupon assumed legislative powers pending the convocation of the Azerbaijani Constituent Assembly at an unspecified future date.

The period that followed, later to be described as the "June reaction," was notable for a series of unpopular moves resulting from Ottoman pressures: The implementation of the Zakavkom's land reform decree was suspended until its approval by the Azerbaijani Constituent Assembly, the labor unions were suppressed, and the socialists' activities were banned. Generally, the policies applied under Ottoman military rule were perceived as eroding the democratic achievements of the Russian Revolution.[10] Ottoman authorities removed from Azerbaijan a few political figures, among them Räsulzadä, by inviting them for a prolonged visit to Turkey. In Tabriz, the occupiers resorted to even harsher measures: They deported to Kars the radical leader of the Democratic Party of Azerbaijan, Shaikh Muhammad Khiabani, an erstwhile companion of Sattar Khan.[11] The Democratic Party was disbanded, leaving as the only legal political organization the pro-Ottoman Union of Islam, the local namesake and rough equivalent of the Ittihad from north of the Araxes River.

The ripple effects of Ottoman interference would in the long run reinforce the trend toward Azerbaijanism within the republic's ruling elite: Azerbaijan's relations with Turkey would henceforth be tainted with resentment and distrust, while Pan-Turkism would be reduced to a purely cultural doctrine.[12] Indeed, one of the few Ottoman steps sincerely welcomed by the Azerbaijanis was the importation of teachers to help in the Turkification of the educational system, an action that the aroused some protest among the Turkish public on the ground that the teachers were sorely needed at home.

Despite the clouds hanging over their friendship, the Azerbaijanis drew close to the Ottomans in the face of a threat from their common adversary. On June 10, the Baku Sovnarkom launched its long-contemplated offensive on Ganja. Its immediate goal was to stamp out that "hotbed of the Muslim counterrevolution" and to forestall an Ottoman attack, but Shaumian also had hopes of extending the soviet's power into Georgia and Armenia, where he expected peasant uprisings.[13] The chief accomplishment of the Baku Sovnarkom's move turned out to be reducing the friction between its Muslim enemies. The thirteen-thousand-man-strong First Caucasian Corps of the Red Army based in Baku, its ranks filled with Armenians, achieved some initial success and by mid-June reached the halfway point between Ganja and Baku. The advance of the Reds was stopped by the Army of Islam in the four-day battle fought at Geokchai between June 27 and July 1. Subsequently, the Muslims launched a counteroffensive.[14] Pursuing the Baku Soviet troops, Nuri Pasha's forces reached the outskirts of Baku by the end of July.

The Ottomans and Azerbaijanis, in their effort to dislodge Bolshevik rule in Baku, came into conflict with the ambitions of Germany. In the summer of 1918 the focus of German interest in Transcaucasia was shifting away from Georgia and toward Baku and its highly coveted oil reserves. Active German involvement in the struggle for Baku began under the prodding of Moscow's ambassador to Berlin, Adolf Ioffe. As the Army of Islam marched toward the Apsheron Peninsula, Ioffe protested to the Germans over the violation of the Treaty of Brest-Litovsk and insisted that they intervene to halt the Ottomans.[15] The Berlin government, shrugging off responsibility for the actions of the "bands" operating in the plains of Azerbaijan, was nevertheless willing to take advantage of circumstances and so proposed using its influence to prevent the Ottomans from entering Baku if Soviet Russia in return would supply Germany with oil shipments. This suggestion, which Lenin eagerly endorsed, reflected the community of Soviet and German interests in the issue of Baku. At Lenin's request, on July 8 Stalin informed Shaumian from his headquarters in Tsaritsyn of the proposed deal, adding: "It is possible that we will have to give in to the Germans in the Georgian question, but we will make such a concession only under the condition that the Germans recognize that they must not interfere in the problem of Armenia and Azerbaijan."[16]

The rapid advance of the Army of Islam to the gates of Baku put to the test the German–Soviet compact. Not only was the flow of oil to Germany likely to be delayed, but the German general staff feared even more serious consequences. On August 4 General Ludendorff threatened Enver Pasha with withdrawal of German officers from the Ottoman high command unless the operation was called off. "I could not tolerate," he wrote, "the danger of a new war with Russia provoked by the Turkish authorities in blatant contradiction to the terms of the treaty."[17] The Germans subsequently learned with relief that the Fifth Division's attack on Baku had been repelled and that fighting had subsided as the Ottomans rested while awaiting reinforcements.

German–Soviet talks continued and on August 27 resulted in the signing of a supplementary treaty to the Brest-Litovsk settlement. Part IV of the agreement, dealing with the Caucasus, contained the following provisions: (1) Russia would agree to German recognition of an independent Georgia; (2) Germany would give no assistance to the military operations of any third power outside the territory of Georgia and the Brest-Litovsk boundaries of Turkey; (3) Germany would take measures to prevent any third power from crossing the boundary line of the *uezd*s of Shemakha and Baku. (4) Russia would deliver to Germany either one-quarter the oil extracted at Baku or a specified monthly quota.[18]

The Soviet–German agreement, if it had been capable of enforcement, would both have jeopardized Enver's Pan-Turanian design and precluded the existence of a viable Azerbaijan. Räsulzadä, still on his sojourn in Istanbul, delivered a memorandum to the embassies of the Central Powers on September 12 protesting German recognition of Russian sovereignty over "the natural capital of Azerbaijan and its political, cultural, and economic center."[19] This act – asserted the memorandum – was contrary to the right of national self-determination proclaimed by the Russian government and accepted by the Central Powers.

6. The Azerbaijani nation-state

Räsulzadä might have taken heart from the fact that at that moment the fall of Baku was a foregone conclusion.

The fall of Baku

Since the formation of the Baku Sovnarkom in April 1918, the city and its environs had lived under the rule of the Commune – a name harking back to the example of Paris in 1871 and connoting dictatorship of the proletariat on a local scale but in union with the whole of Soviet Russia. A series of radical reforms had been hastily enacted under the aegis of the Commune, including reorganization of the courts and the schools and expropriation of the banks, merchant marine, and fisheries. The most momentous measure of all, nationalization of the oil industry, was not undertaken until June 2.[20] In this case the overriding concern was to maintain continuity of oil shipments to Russia, a matter that was of vital importance to the survival of Lenin's regime and that commanded the particular attention of the Baku government. With the establishment of the local Sovnarkom, oil deliveries, which had lagged for many months, surged impressively.[21] For all its zeal in carrying out socialist reforms this Sovnarkom was probably the most tolerant of the Bolshevik governments at the time, and the Baku Cheka (secret police) made few arrests on political grounds. One reason for this moderation was the inherently weak position of the Bolsheviks in Baku. A minority within the Soviet, they were supported only by the Left SRs and acquiesced to by the Right SRs, Dashnakists, and Mensheviks. Moreover, the makeup of the Baku Soviet was hardly representative of the majority of the population, and only to a negligible degree of its largest group, the Muslims. "The fateful failure of the Commune, indeed its tragedy," wrote a Soviet historian

was its inability to win over the native masses. Despite Shaumian's and particularly Dzhaparidze's efforts to present their party as the champion of the Muslim poor, the Azerbaijanis remained passive and sullen. On the other hand, many Bolsheviks persisted in their contempt for the Muslims, whom they regarded as immature from the revolutionary viewpoint and culturally inferior.[22]

The Baku Soviet leaders' simplistic approach to these masses was to incite class warfare within the Muslim community. In late 1917 and early 1918 there had occurred some incidents of land seizure by peasants, but the signs of incipient revolutionary violence were dissipated in the surge of national strife of the "March Days."[23] Once in power, the Bolsheviks, concerned about Muslim hostility, made some efforts to gain a following among the peasantry, such as appointing their Himmätist comrades commissars for outlying areas of the city: Äzizbäkov for the Baku *guberniia*, Äfändiyev for the Baku *uezd*, Israfilbäkov for the *uezd*s of Lenkoran and Jevat, and Yusufzadä for the *uezd* of Kuba.[24] The commissars began whipping up support for the Baku regime and set up village soviets, forty in all; but these, in the words of Äfändiyev, were "still very weak and did not sufficiently know what to do."[25] A Congress of Peasant Soviets of the Baku *uezd* met on May 26–30, but it represented a district where there were no large estates to be distributed to the peasantry. "Our situation is different," said Shaumian in his speech to the congress: "In our *uezd* the prime asset is the oil-bearing land, and this should be made into state-owned property."[26] The significance of the occasion was mainly symbolic, and it was used to merge the Executive Committee of the Peasant Soviets with that of the Baku Soviet. Another act of similar nature was the decree issued on June 19 by the Baku Sovnarkom over the signature of Väzirov on "Socialization of Land in Transcaucasia and the Daghestani Oblast'."[27] The document provided for the immediate transfer of large landowners' properties to the as-yet-nonexistent Soviet Land Committees, which were to distribute the land to the toiling peasants. A historian of the Baku Commune, commenting on the ineffectiveness of this decree, wrote:

> Unlike those of central Russia, the Azerbaijani peasants had not seized land on a large scale and the land reform proclaimed by the Baku Sovnarkom was gratuitous and meaningless. The Leninist *smychka* [union] of peasants and workers was never realized in the Baku province, and the Commune was seriously weakened, first by its failure to attract the poor peasantry, and finally, by the defection from the Bolsheviks of their constituents, the workers.[28]

The credibility of Bolshevik policy toward the Muslim masses was further strained by the fact that the Dashnakists wielded powerful influence in the Baku Soviet, and even more so in its

6. The Azerbaijani nation-state

armed forces, which were 70 percent Armenian and under the command of an Armenian officer, Colonel Z. Avetisian. During the June offensive on Ganja, Armenian soldiers let loose their hostility toward Muslims in incidents of looting and violence, with the effect of undermining any pro-Bolshevik sympathies that might have germinated among the peasantry.[29]

The defeat of the Red Army at Geokchai and Nuri Pasha's subsequent counteroffensive brought to a head the long-simmering political crisis in Baku, a city increasingly suffering from hunger and ill prepared for defense. With Russia unable to provide any meaningful aid to the Commune, those in Baku who were neither Bolsheviks nor Muslims began to agitate for inviting the British Expeditionary Force under General Lionel Dunsterville. This force had been stationed since February 1918 in northern Persia, where it kept watch on Ottoman movements and was also involved in some fighting with the Persian nationalist leader of the Gilan Province, Mirza Kuchuk Khan. In late June Dunsterville occupied the Caspian port of Enzeli, which had been held by the Bolshevik Soldiers' Soviet, and from there he was preparing for a move on Baku.[30]

The possibility of bolstering the defenses of the city with British troops had been contemplated for some time in Baku, but it met with the growing opposition of the Bolsheviks.[31] Rather than let British imperialism gain a foothold in Baku, Shaumian preferred to see the city fall – in all likelihood temporarily – into the hands of the second-rate power of Turkey, terrifying as that prospect might be for the local Armenians. The Baku Sovnarkom agreed, however, to accept the services of Colonel Lazar Bicherakhov, a tsarist Cossack officer who had fought with the British against Kuchuk Khan. Bicherakhov joined the battle on July 7 with fifteen hundred men and assumed command of the right wing of the Baku defense line.[32] As the situation around the city was growing more hopeless, Bicherakhov at the end of July withdrew his detachment from the front and headed north to Petrovsk. Just previously, on July 25, a meeting of the broadened Baku Soviet – its majority made up of Dashnakists, Right SRs, and Mensheviks – had overruled Shaumian and voted to call for the help of the British. The Baku Sovnarkom, refusing to go along, resigned en masse.[33] The next day the Commune was succeeded by the "Dictatorship of the Tsentrokaspiy [Caspian fleet] and the Presidium of the Executive Committee of the Soviet." The new government, consisting of the Right SRs from the Executive Committee of the Tsentrokaspiy, gained the full support of the Dashnakists and proclaimed its loyalty to a democratic Russia as opposed to Lenin's regime.[34] The Dictatorship immediately issued an invitation to Dunsterville, with whom unofficial contacts had already been established by the Armenian National Council. The British landed in Baku between August 9 and 17 with a force of three battalions, a battery of field artillery and some armored cars.[35] This was less by far than had been expected in Baku – and even weaker than the Red Army force that had withdrawn from the fighting on August 19 and had attempted to sail to Astrakhan before being intercepted and disarmed by the Dictatorship.

The relations between the Dictators and the British were marred from the start by mutual distrust and recriminations. The new rulers of Baku were disappointed with the meager aid they received, while the British laid all the blame on the lack of discipline and demoralization of the local soldiers. Convinced that nothing could be done to save Baku, Dunsterville was ready to evacuate his men by September 1, but the Dictatorship threatened to open fire on any British ship leaving port. Reluctantly, the British general concluded that he had no choice but to hold on until the final attack on Baku.[36] After a lull in the battle, the Ottoman troops, now under the direct orders of the Eastern Army group commander, Halil Pasha (formerly bey), and reinforced by the arrival of the Thirty-sixth division, had been pressing hard since August 26.* At this point, the Ottoman operation although still in contradiction of official German policy, received no more opposition from the German military. In the Germans' opinion, British intervention had created an entirely new situation: It was not so much Soviet Russia but rather Britain that might now revive the eastern front. Anxious speedily to eliminate the British output in Baku, Hindenburg went so far as to order two German brigades to Transcaucasia, not only to assist the Ottomans but also to seize the Baku oil fields.[37] The Ottomans declined to accept this assistance.

---

* Halil, the uncle of Enver, became pasha and was hailed as an Ottoman war hero after his victory over the British at Kut al-Amarna.

6. The Azerbaijani nation-state

The decisive assault on the city began on the morning of September 15. By the end of the day ships loaded with the "Dunsterforce" men were departing from the harbor. Following suit, the members of the Dictatorship and tens of thousands of Armenians fled to Enzeli or to Bolshevik-held Astrakhan. The Ottoman forces refrained from entering Baku until September 16, a delay that gave local Muslims, Azerbaijani irregulars, and Ottoman marauders a free hand in the city's Armenian sections. The revenge for the "March Days" was ferocious, and conservative estimates set the number of Armenian lives lost at some nine to ten thousand, a figure higher than the total of Azerbaijani fatalities in all previous outbreaks of intercommunal violence.[38]

Another, though indirect, consequence of the fall of Baku was the fate that befell a group of twenty-six Baku Soviet commissars, among them Shaumian, Dzhaparidze, Äzizbäkov, Väzirov, Korganov, and Fioletov. Having been jailed by the Dictatorship, the commissars gained release just before the Ottoman entry and left the city on the ship *Turkmen*. Instead of sailing as intended for Astrakhan, the *Turkmen* headed for Krasnovodsk on the eastern coast of the Caspian where the group was arrested by the British-supported local SRs, taken out into the desert, and shot in a mass execution that was to become the most widely publicized case of martrydom for the Bolshevik revolution.[39]

British tutelage and the consolidation of the republic

The triumphal parade of Ottoman troops through the streets of Baku marked the high point of the drive for Turan. By the end of the summer of 1918 the armies of Enver Pasha held in their grip not only northern but also southern Azerbaijan, the occupation of this Persian province having been accomplished at the same time as the successful siege of Baku. Further extending the scope of the Ottoman conquests, the Fifteenth Division was sent along the Caspian shore to Daghestan, which it occupied in October.[40]

As the Istanbul newspapers were eagerly filling their pages with reports of the successes on the Caucasus front, the overall military situation of Turkey was deteriorating catastrophically: The British forces in Palestine and then in Syria kept rolling relentlessly forward; the allies were advancing in the Balkans, and most ominous of all, the Germans continued to retreat in France. These hard facts began to show their impact on the Ottoman attitude toward Azerbaijan. In a gesture that was generally understood as a step from acquiescence toward recognition of the Azerbaijani regime, Räsulzadä, Safikiurdski and Khasmammädov were officially received by Sultan Mehmed VI at the Aya Sofya mosque on September 6.[41] Formal recognition of Azerbaijan as well as Armenia by Turkey was in fact agreed upon in the German–Ottoman protocol signed on September 23, during the visit of the Grand Vizier Talaat Pasha in Berlin. The Germans withdrew their previous objections and even undertook to secure Soviet consent to recognize the two Transcaucasian republics.[42] When the Ottomans took Baku they proclaimed to have done so on behalf of the Azerbaijani government, and Nuri Pasha forthwith invited Khan Khoiski to transfer his offices from Ganja to the recovered capital of the country. The Ottoman general was now careful to avoid any appearance of interfering in Azerbaijani affairs, and he routinely referred all matters other than the military ones to the local authorities. "Nuri hides behind the government of Azerbaijan, and the latter behind him," remarked a disgruntled German officer.[43]

As the Young Turkish leaders were still speaking of setting up independent and friendly nations – if no longer of new Ottoman provinces – in the zone between Turkey and Russia, the Ottoman State itself was on the verge of total collapse. On September 30 Bulgaria surrendered to the Allies, making continuation of the war by Turkey impossible. The CUP government fell on October 9, and the new cabinet of Ahmed Izzet Pasha signed an armistice with the Allies in Mudros by the end of the month. Two provisions of the agreement dealt with Transcaucasia; Article 11 required the evacuation by the Ottomans of the entire region, and Article 15 stipulated that the Allies would take over the control of the Transcaucasian railways and occupy Baku. No mention of the Transcaucasian republics was made in the text of the armistice agreement.[44]

In Baku, in a last-minute effort to salvage something for the future of the cause of Turan, Nuri Pasha authorized his soldiers

6. The Azerbaijani nation-state   141

to join the Azerbaijani army. Willing Ottoman officers and enlisted men would be eligible for promotion, and their contract with the Azerbaijanis would be signed for a minimum of one year. Hundreds availed themselves of the opportunity to continue their military careers, although the transfers could be made only on an individual basis. When Nuri Pasha attempted to put whole detachments under Azerbaijani command, General W. M. Thomson, who had succeeded Dunsterville in the British North Persian Force, took a firm stand: All Ottoman units must leave Baku in one week and Transcaucasia within a month.[45] The Azerbaijani representatives Ussubäkov, Rafibäkov, and Aghayev who paid Thomson a visit in his headquarters in Enzeli, heard few encouraging words. The British commander refused to recognize the Azerbaijani government, which in his view had been created by Ottoman intrigues and could not claim to represent the will of the people. Concerning the future, his statement to the Azerbaijani delegation seemed to indicate that Britain was guided more by expediency than by any long-range policy considerations concerning Transcaucasian Muslims: Baku had to be evacuated not only by the Ottomans but also by Azerbaijani forces; the city and its industrial outskirts were to be occupied by the British, with Thomson acting as governor-general of Baku and another British officer as head of the police. On the other hand, Thomson agreed to leave the rest of the country under Azerbaijani administration; although withholding formal recognition, the Allies would maintain contact with the Azerbaijani government. The final decision on national self-determination would be made at the future peace conference, where the Azerbaijanis would be allowed to present their views.[46] Thomson additionally declared that the forces assigned to the occupation of Baku were to include the White Russian contingent under Bicherakhov, although no armed Armenians would be admitted to the city.

The landing of some two thousand Indian Army troops on November 17 was greeted enthusiastically by the Russian community of Baku. Upon his arrival, Thomson ordered that the green, red, and blue Azerbaijani flag with crescent and star be removed from the pier. In his first proclamation he did not so much as mention the name of Azerbaijan, but praised Russia, reaffirming Britain's friendship for and support of that country:

"The Allies cannot return to their homes without restoring order in Russia and placing her in a position to again take her proper place among the nations of the world."[47] As Thomson now seemed to be contradicting what he had promised in Enzeli, Azerbaijani statesmen were overtaken by gloom and a sense of helplessness. Some of them, including Ahmäd bäy Aghayev, hastily entered into negotiations with the Russian National Council, the Kadet-dominated, self-styled representative of the "one and indivisible" non-Bolshevik Russia. In tune with the trend of his thinking over many years, Aghayev voiced the opinion that Azerbaijan was not capable of surviving as an independent entity and had to lean either on fraternal Turkey or on the great Russian nation. Since Turkey was in a state of collapse, there remained no alternative but reconciliation with the Russians, whose culture, in any case, he said, was higher than that of the Ottomans.[48]

Khan Khoiski's cabinet proved to be less despondent than Aghayev, hardly a popular figure among some Musavatists after the June governmental crisis, and declined to follow his advice. Before long the Azerbaijanis were finding out that their prospects were not nearly as inauspicious as had appeared from General Thomson's initial moves. His prime concern – indeed, the only political task he was charged with – was to establish order and maintain peace in Eastern Transcaucasia. For this reason alone he was unwilling to give a blank check to the Baku Kadets, who had the backing of only a small fraction of the local population. Within a week of his arrival he had to remind them bluntly that at the moment Russia simply did not exist and that the future status of Transcaucasia was to be resolved by the peace conference. Nor would he agree with their contention that Azerbaijan was no more than a figment of the imagination of a few hundred political adventurists; the Khan Khoiski government, he pointed out, remained the only effective civilian authority in the country. The British developed a high regard for the Azerbaijani prime minister, and an official report termed him as "one of the ablest men in Baku" and "also one of the few men who loyally helped Thomson."[49]

Soon after snubbing the Russians over Azerbaijan, Thomson found himself taking the side of the Muslims in their quarrel with the Armenians. The issue at point was Mountainous Karabagh, the western part of the Elizavetpol *guberniia*, whose pop-

6. The Azerbaijani nation-state   143

ulation consisted of Azerbaijanis and Armenians in a ratio of 3:2.[50] A strategic corridor, Karabagh formed a link or a barrier (depending on who controlled it) between the Muslims of Eastern Transcaucasia and Turkey. After the withdrawal of the Ottomans, General Andranik made an attempt to establish Armenian authority over this disputed territory, but on December 1 Thomson asked him to cease his military operations. Andranik complied, and the British general resolved in mid-January 1919 to put Karabagh, together with the Zangezur *uezd*, also claimed by the Armenians, under provisional Azerbaijani administration. In what the angered Armenians considered heaping insult upon injury, Thomson approved the nomination of Khosrow Sultanov, a reputed Armenophobe, as governor of the two areas.[51] Reacting to bitter Armenian criticism, Thomson remarked: "The fact is that in Azerbaijan some Armenians are much disappointed that the British occupation is not an opportunity for revenge. They are reluctant to accept it that [the] peace conference is going to decide and not military forces."[52]

Historians of the British involvement in the Russian Civil War observe in Thomson's gestures toward the Azerbaijanis a rather typical disposition among the military with an India Army background.[53] To this group of officers Russia always appeared the main enemy, and so they regarded the rise of independent borderland states as a welcome development. The Muslim part of Transcaucasia, with its abundant natural and population resources, seemed potentially the most viable of these states as well as the most politically reliable. Unlike Armenia and Georgia, it lacked religious ties with Russia, and being predominantly Shi^cite it was regarded as likely to stay aloof from Turkey.[54] Such considerations accounted for the favorable disposition of the British military toward Azerbaijan, a factor that left its imprint on the character of the new occupation. To be sure, the foreign forces made their presence felt. The British, who sent to Transcaucasia two divisions, the largest contingent of their troops engaged in Russia, maintained a garrison in Baku, where they imposed martial law. They controlled the railways, the most important of which was the Baku–Batum line over which oil exports, this time for British needs, again began to flow. The profits the British derived from purchasing and reselling Baku oil would one day become the subject of controversy: Whereas the Soviets would blame Britain of virtual robbery through underpayment, the British would contend that the overall cost of the occupation had been higher than the value of oil bought from Azerbaijan and that the resale profits had been adversely affected by the decline in world prices.[55]

British involvement during this period also extended into some branches of the civilian administration. The British supervised the currency issue by the Azerbaijani State Bank with a view toward limiting inflation; they reorganized the food-rationing system, which greatly improved the food supply situation; they set up a Labor Control Office to mediate labor disputes in the oil fields and railways.[56] In the course of settling these disputes the British sometimes resorted to arresting and deporting Russian Bolśhevik activists. They also completed the restoration of private ownership of the oil and shipping industries nationalized under the Commune. The Azerbaijani War Ministry was ordered to move to Ganja; and British officers occasionally intervened in the routine business of local authorities.[57] On the other hand, the British, whose long-range aims in Transcaucasia – except for the preferences of some military men – were anything but clear to themselves, refrained from tampering with the political process of the Azerbaijani state, in which respect they differed sharply from the Ottomans.[58] Indirectly, the British presence affected Azerbaijani politics in two important ways: It provided a sense of security against outside threats, and it stimulated the growth of national institutions along democratic–liberal lines. General Thomson officially acknowledged the formation of the new, parliamentary cabinet of Khan Khoiski with the statement that Britain would support it as the only legal authority in Azerbaijan.[59]

Azerbaijani leaders showed their political acumen in playing up to the democratic sensitivities of the British. The day before Thomson landed in Baku, the reconvened National Council passed a law concerning elections to the Constituent Assembly that provided for direct elections, proportional representation, and universal suffrage – thereby making Azerbaijan the first Muslim country ever to enfranchise women.[60] No date was set for the voting, and the elections were destined never to be held, yet the National Council proceeded at once to reconstitute itself as an interim, broader-based legislature. Assuming, significantly,

6. The Azerbaijani nation-state

the name of Parliament, the body enlarged itself by coopting new members and representatives of national minorities.

The Azerbaijani Parliament was to consist of 120 deputies, of whom 96 – the difference arising from the boycott by many Armenian deputies – had agreed to join by the time of its festive inaugural session on December 7, 1918. In the assembly hall the Musavatists sat in the center, the Ittihadists on the right, and the Himmät–Mensheviks and the Muslim Socialist Bloc on the left. Initially, there were 11 parliamentary groups; later some would amalgamate, the relative strength of each varying as deputies changed party allegiance. In December 1918 the Musavat was represented by 38 deputies, the Ittihad by 11, the socialists by 12, the Ahrar (Liberal) Party by 10, the independents by 9, the Dashnaktsutiun by 7, other Armenians by 4, and other national minorities by 5.[61]

The socialist parliamentary group included the members of the Muslim Socialist Bloc and the Social Democratic Workers Party–Himmät (Menshevik). The newly formed Ahrar Party was a close ally and almost a replica of the Musavat, but it had a stronger following among the peasantry and attracted mainly Sunnis, a testimony to the irrepressible vitality of the Muslim sectarianism.[62]

Although the largest political force, the Musavat held less than half the seats in Parliament, unlike the situation in the National Council where it had commanded an absolute majority. The formation of a government now was possible only with the participation of other parties, and so coalition cabinets inevitably ending in a governmental crisis became a feature of Azerbaijani politics. As a foreign observer noted, a "large number of ministerial portfolios were devised to accommodate various parties."[63] There were altogether five cabinets in less than two years, between May 28, 1918 and the end of independence on April 28, 1920. Each of them but the last was put together without the participation of the Ittihad, the party that retained the status of a quasi-permanent opposition. The first three were headed by Khan Khoiski (May 28, 1918, June 17, 1918, April 5, 1919) and two others by Ussubäkov (April 5, 1919, December 29, 1919).[64] The instability of the executive had the redeeming merit of enhancing the role of Parliament, which now became the focus of Azerbaijani political life. The number of plenary sessions (105) and of legislative proposals (203) give a measure of the pace of parliamentary activity.[65] The office of the president of Parliament, held by Topchibashev, was recognized as that of the head of state.

At the opening of Parliament Räsulzadä delivered an address that in effect outlined the updated program of the Musavat. With the onset of the era of democracy, the party was still to be guided by the principles of nationalism and federalism – yet nationalism now defined as recognition of the truth that the Azerbaijanis, although part of the larger family of Turkic peoples, constituted a nation of their own. Quite apart from the fact that open manifestations of Pan-Turkism would now be bad politics, the Musavat had indeed reached the stage where it preferred to forsake the shibboleths of Turkic unity in exchange for the idea of the Azerbaijani nation-state. There remained the fundamental concern for external security – hence the continuing commitment of the party to federalism. Räsulzadä hoped for the eventual establishment of a viable world order by the League of Nations, but for the present he advocated close regional ties with other Transcaucasian republics and Daghestan.[66] Regarding the internal problems of Azerbaijan, the Musavat would be inspired by radicalism. The meaning of this third principle was broad: It called for the defense of the political achievements of the democratic revolution, including freedom of speech, press, and association; the securing of the cultural and political rights of national minorities; and the promotion of the interests of workers and peasants. As for the agrarian reform question, the Musavat recommended that (1) all landed estates, whether privately owned or previously belonging to the Russian state, be distributed to the peasants at no cost; (2) peasants be permitted to acquire title to these lands; (3) a maximum amount of privately owned land be set by law; (4) those who had invested capital and labor in their lands subject to distribution be compensated from a special fund raised through property taxes.[67]

As it turned out, it was easier to draw guidelines for such social reform than to pass the appropriate legislation, let alone implement it. Within the Musavat, division on the agrarian question between the left and right wings of the party ran as deep as ever. The right-wing Musavatists delayed submitting the land reform legislation to Parliament for a whole year after Räsulzadä's ad-

6. The Azerbaijani nation-state

dress. Not until December 1919 did the left wing push through the party's second congress a somewhat modified version of a draft law, which subsequently reached Parliament's Agrarian Committee. There, after a perfunctory debate, a decision was postponed again, as were many other difficult problems, until the convocation of the Azerbaijani constituent assembly.[68] The structure of land ownership in Azerbaijan, under which the Treasury held approximately 30 percent of all arable land, the peasants 50 percent, and large proprietors some 20 percent, remained basically unchanged under the independent republic. Failure to resolve this social issue left Azerbaijan vulnerable to dangers from within and without. The peasants in some areas, especially in Ganja province, whose hopes had been stirred by the slogans of the Russian Revolution were again becoming restless. There was a recurrence of land seizures, and in some instances the government had to send in troops to protect landlords. Inevitably, the Bolsheviks directed their propaganda at pockets of discontent in the countryside, and social grievances were invoked to argue for the sovietization of Azerbaijan.[69]

Aside from the agrarian problem, the tasks facing the small group of Azerbaijani leaders with little or no administrative experience were staggering. Azerbaijan after 1918 was a typical textbook example of a postcolonial country ill prepared for the trials of independent existence. The expedients its leaders resorted to were equally typical, beginning with attempts to adapt as much preindependence governmental machinery as feasible. Territorial administration was reorganized on the *guberniia* level by breaking up two provinces into four: Baku, Ganja, Karabagh, and Zakataly.[70] The *uezds*, however, retained their previous form. The old judicial system, the Chambers of Treasury and of Commerce, and the Fiscal Inspectorates all continued to function. The key difficulty in building the new state lay not in revamping institutional structures but in finding qualified personnel to man them. As the Azerbaijani intelligentsia was able to fill only part of the positions in the government bureaucracy, crash programs were instituted to train candidates for all kinds of jobs down to the level of railwaymen and telegraph operators. Moreover, as some foreign observers noted, the weakness of the native cadres was not only in their numbers: "The moral stamina of the officials of the new republics has not been equal to the occasion. In Azerbaijan certain governmental privileges are bought and sold on the local exchange."[71] At the middle and lower levels, Russian civil servants kept their posts; they were even allowed to conduct official business in Russian, although all state employees were given a two-year deadline for learning Azerbaijani.[72]

Now that the intelligentsia were running the country, the old dream of education in the native language began to materialize. It was in this field that the new regime concentrated its special effort, which enjoyed a measure of success that reversed the long trend of Russification. Teaching of Azerbaijani became obligatory in schools at every level, and the history of Turkic peoples replaced that of Russia. In many primary schools instruction in all subjects was given in the native language, but lack of personnel slowed down the Turkification of secondary education. A special board was in charge of preparing textbooks, largely through translation, and continuing recruitment in Turkey partly alleviated the shortage of teachers. Simultaneously, newly opened teachers' seminaries were training Azerbaijanis, and the government sponsored over a hundred young men to study in Turkey and Europe.[73] In the second year of independence, higher education became for the first time available in Azerbaijan with the opening of Baku University on September 1, 1919.[74] Among the far-reaching educational reforms, a project for Latinization of the alphabet was under consideration.[75]

A dearth of trained manpower no less than of equipment was the main impediment to building the Azerbaijani army, a matter of obvious urgency given the precarious condition of Transcaucasia. The work of transforming the militias of the preindependence Muslim National Corps into a regular, combat-worthy force had started in earnest only after the arrival of the Ottomans, who had helped in the training of Azerbaijani officers and specialists. Under the parliamentary regime, the Ministry of War passed into the hands of Sämäd bäy Mäkhmandiarov, a soldier of distinguished record and formerly a general of artillery in the Russian army. His principal assistants were General Shikhlinski and General Suleyman Sulkiewicz, the latter a Lithuanian Tatar who had run the German-installed administration of the Crimea and who after the war made his way to Azerbaijan, where he became chief of staff.[76] A part of the officer corps consisted of those Turks who had stayed behind after the November 1918 evacuation or had been Russian prisoners of war. Among the remainder were numerous Russians and some Georgians, and they rather than the Turks set the tone for the Azerbaijani military establishment. Commenting on the high proportion of former tsarist officers in the Azerbaijani army, Narimanov remarked that they supervised drills with whips in hands. "The organizational structure, regulations, etc. are copied from the Russian model under Nicholas II."[77]

Combining former guerillas, new draftees, and a sprinkling of Azerbaijanis who had seen military service under the tsardom, the Azerbaijani army reached a strength of some thirty thousand men.[78] Their fighting quality was unproven except in small-scale operations against the Russian settlers in the Mugan Steppe or the Armenian insurgents in Karabagh, and General Mäkhmandiarov kept warning that it would take a long time and much trial and error to forge an effective army. Future plans included expanding the armed forces to fifty thousand, with additional equipment to be purchased from Italy. The young republic footed a heavy bill for its military establishment: the estimated expenditures for 1919 amounted to 140 million rubles, or 13 percent of the state budget – a large sum to spend in a disrupted economy.[79]

Even though Azerbaijan on the whole fared better economically than her closest neighbors and foreign visitors found an aura of luxury in Baku by comparison with the austerity of Tiflis or the poverty of Erivan, the republic was beset by a structural economic crisis that marred the period of independence. The country's economy had grown as an appendage of Russia's, and it suffered heavily when the Russian Civil War severed Azerbaijan's links with its traditional markets and sources of supply. In 1919 Azerbaijan was cut off again from her granary, the northern slopes of the Caucasus seized by the Russian White forces. At the same time, with export outlets closed, the production of industrial crops – cotton, silk, and tobacco – declined sharply. By far the most serious problem was the plight of the oil industry: Its exports under the independent republic fell precipitously to some 30 percent of the immediately preceding years' average.[80] Whatever quantities of oil could be sold went to buyers in Transcaucasia and northern Persia or via Batum to the British forces and their allies. In a review of Azerbaijan's economic condition, an official government publication made the following comment on the significance of exports to Russia: "Regardless of the amount of oil that Europe may buy from us, the Azerbaijani finances will not be restored to normal as long as the Russian markets remain closed to us."[81]

Despite the low volume of exports, a predicament compounded by the postwar drop in world prices, the government was resolved to prevent drastic cuts in oil production, as high unemployment would be politically explosive. The owners of the oil industry were thus granted subsidies to cover wages and operating expenses, with the result that by early 1920 an entire year's production of crude was filling every storage tank available and the government contemplated pumping the oil into the sea.[82] The cost of these subsidies, together with those of maintaining the army, bureaucracy, and educational system, were covered by heavy deficit financing. Estimated government expenditures for 1919 amounted to 1,085 million rubles and revenue to only 665 million. A part of the budgetary gap, 250 million rubles, was covered by a new currency issue, with consequent inflationary pressures.[83] Unemployment, though partly under control, rose nonetheless, and by May 1919 there were some ten thousand idle workers in the Baku area. The discontent of the city's proletariat erupted in strikes, and some resurgence of the Bolsheviks' popularity became noticeable, especially among the non-native workers. Yet difficult as circumstances appeared, some Azerbaijanis found reason for cautious optimism. Its oil wealth alone assured the country a sound economic foundation for an independent existence. Western European interest in Baku's oil products increased in the second half of 1919 when the pipeline to Batum was put into operation, and possibilities existed of obtaining credits that would see the republic through this initial period.[84] One day, it was hoped, with the end of civil war in Russia, bright prospects would emerge for a free, prosperous Azerbaijan. Such prospects, however, depended on the answers to two questions: Who would win the struggle in Russia? and even more important, What would be the attitude of the victor toward an Azerbaijan that had cut itself loose from Russia?

6. The Azerbaijani nation-state

Diplomacy in quest for survival

Grievious though the domestic problems of the Azerbaijanis were, the ultimate fate of their republic depended on developments in the outside world, and the period of independence was marked by the obvious primacy of foreign affairs. Azerbaijan continued to live in the shadow of the Russian giant, which, even if temporarily paralyzed by its civil war, remained the overwhelming concern of the Baku regime. The harsh reality facing Azerbaijan was that while the Russian Civil War precluded its economic recovery, the continuation of this conflict made possible the very existence of the independent republic. Conversely, a speedy and decisive victory of either side in Russia would in all likelihood spell the end of the Azerbaijani state. This realization raised for the Azerbaijanis the question: Which of the two sides in the Russian struggle was a lesser threat?

Of all the governments that mushroomed in 1918 throughout the former Russian Empire, that of Azerbaijan was among the least anti-Bolshevik, a remarkable distinction given the fresh memories of the "March Days" and Soviet Russia's open claims to Baku in the summer of that year. The Azerbaijanis were eager to find reassurance in Moscow's repeated proclamations of the right to national self-determination. Such statements were all the easier to take at their face value when the main forces of the Red Army operated in geographically distant regions. As early as in its Ganja days, the Khan Khoiski government instructed its representative in Tiflis that "it is our desire to live in perpetual friendship with Russia in general and with the Soviet regime in particular."[85] Only days after the cabinet installed itself in Baku, Azerbaijani officials conducted talks with the delegate of the Moscow Food Supply Committee I. P. Orlov, who was asked to transmit to the People's Commissariat for Foreign Affairs a proposal to establish regular diplomatic relations with a view toward facilitating commercial exchange. These early contacts ended with the arrival of the British, who imposed an embargo on oil shipments to Soviet Russia. Azerbaijani authorities were nevertheless lax in suppressing the illicit trade with Astrakhan that was being conducted on a growing scale in the Caspian Sea. As the British General T. Bridges noted in his report on the significance of the Baku oil for the civil war in Russia:

"There is a very large amount of oil products stored at Baku and waiting for transport to their natural markets in Russia via Astrakhan, and one of the chief grievances of the Azerbaijani is that he has not been allowed to trade with the Bolshevists. This, and also the fact that Baku will probably turn Bolshevists again, seem sufficient reasons for [the White Army's General] Denikin to occupy the place at once on the grounds of military necessity."[86]

During most of 1919, of the two sides in Russia, it was the Volunteer Army ("White" Army) of South Russia under General A. I. Denikin that gave the Azerbaijanis a greater sense of immediate threat. The conservative military, fighting for a "one and indivisible" Russia, were least likely to respect the sovereignty of secessionist states. Also, Denikin's forces represented a danger closer to home. In the early winter, an ominous conflict (though inconclusive due to British mediation) broke out between the volunteers and Georgia over control of the Black Sea coastal areas of Tuapse, Sochi, and Sukhumi.[87] Following this conflict Denikin began his invasion of the North Caucasus Mountaineers Republic. The Azerbaijanis became alarmed: Anticipating that Baku's oil might be the next objective of the Whites, Khan Khoiski appealed to the British for protection.[88]

The attitude of the British was at first reassuring to the Baku government: Although they were committed to the support of Denikin, they had no intention of helping him seize Baku. In any case, the British insisted that the Volunteers concentrate themselves on fighting the Reds and not be distracted by quarrels with small republics on their rear. In January 1919 Thomson drew a demarcation line, running along the main range of the Caucasus Mountains and the northern frontier of Daghestan, that the Volunteers were not to cross. In addition, responding to the urging of Khan Khoiski's cabinet, he imposed curbs on the activities of Denikin's political and military agencies in Azerbaijan and undertook a series of quick moves intended to warn Denikin against making attempts to take over Azerbaijan from within. On March 1 the British disarmed the Russian Caspian Fleet anchored in Baku and ordered General Przhevalski, who was recruiting men for the Whites, to quit at once Azerbaijani territory. Bicherakhov's detachment was disbanded, and the

6. The Azerbaijani nation-state 153

colonel himself, who had already set up a shadow Caspian Government, was invited to England, ostensibly to receive a decoration.[89]

All these measures fell short of deterring Denikin's forces from crossing Thomson's demarcation line in the spring of 1919 in order to occupy the northern part of Daghestan, including Petrovsk. As the advance of the Whites continued, the Azerbaijani government delivered a protest note to Thomson stating that it would be "compelled to come to the aid of the Mountaineers with all the means at its disposal."[90] A wave of solidarity with the neighboring Muslim peoples swept the country, crossing political divisions. An all-party parliamentary committee coordinated efforts to assist the Daghestanis, which included sending armed volunteers and emergency subsidies.

The perception of a common danger soon inspired joint efforts to bolster regional security. On June 16 Azerbaijan and Georgia signed a mutual defense pact. The two republics invited Armenia to join in, but the Erivan government declined, as it was unwilling to be a party of any anti-Russian alignment.[91]

Again the British tried to calm down the situation, this time by accommodating Denikin: The drawing of a new demarcation line on June 11, running south of Petrovsk, acknowledged his conquests in Daghestan. Still, Denikin, who in the summer was reaching the peak of his strength, was less disposed than ever to comply with British-imposed restrictions. The resistance of the Daghestanis, aided by Azerbaijani volunteers and Ottoman expatriates, only provoked him to occupy the rest of their country, down to the frontiers of Azerbaijan and Georgia. Once more the British acquiesced, and on August 4 drew a third line along these frontiers.[92] Only now did Denikin call a temporary halt to operations in Transcaucasia in order to channel all his efforts into his fateful offensive against the Reds in the north. In his instructions to General N. N. Baratov, his official representative in the region, he wrote that although Transcaucasia was to be considered an integral part of Russia, the local administration could be tolerated for the time being.[93]

As Azerbaijan was bracing itself for Denikin's invasion, its diplomats were waging an uphill struggle for recognition and support from the powers assembled at Versailles. The delegation to the Paris Peace Conference was headed by the highest officeholder in the republic, Topchibashev, in whose company were the deputies to Parliament Hajinski, Mäkhtiyev, Muharramov, and Aghayev and the editor of the official government newspaper *Azärbaijan*, Jäyhun bäy Hajibäyli.[94] En route, they were delayed three months in Istanbul awaiting entry permits to France. Another slight was the arrest by the British of Aghayev – who ironically was carrying letters of recommendation from Thomson – and his deportation to Malta along with a group of the CUP members with whom he had remained in close contact. The Azerbaijanis reached Paris only at the end of April 1919, too late to lay necessary groundwork and lobby for their cause. Unlike their neighbors, they lacked support comparable to the Armenophile movement in the West or the Georgian Mensheviks' connections with international socialism.

The Azerbaijanis sought, usually without success, interviews with Allied officials, and only with difficulty obtained an audience with President Wilson. In a distinctly cool reception he offered them little encouragement. His remarks summarized the guiding principle of Allied policy toward the states that had seceded from Russia: The Peace Conference had no intention of splitting the world into small pieces and so the question of Azerbaijan could not expect solution before that of Russia. On a more positive note, he advised the Azerbaijanis to think in terms of a confederation of Transcaucasian peoples, which possibly might receive protection from one of the Great Powers as a mandate of the League of Nations.[95] Topchibashev in his subsequent report to Baku wrote that "the leading political idea of the Allies was the desire, which must be beyond doubt, to decide the issue of Russia as a whole and for the solution of the all-Russian problem to make use of such men residing in Paris as Sazonov, L'vov, Maklakov and others."[96] The influence wielded by these White Russian émigré politicians in Versailles clearly disturbed the Azerbaijanis, and they tried to counteract it by writing countless memoranda, often jointly with other states that had been parts of Russia, full of detailed explanations of their need for independence and international recognition thereof.

The Transcaucasian problem and its "obscure, complex and dangerous implications" for the Allied statesmen first surfaced at Versailles in the form of the claims and counterclaims of the various governments involved.[97] Territorial demands were especially extravagant, and those who presented them showed little

6. The Azerbaijani nation-state 155

concern for the hard facts of geography, ethnic distribution, economy, or international politics. The Armenians asked to be rewarded for their wartime support of the Allied cause by the creation of a large state. The frontiers of this projected Greater Armenia stretched as far west as the Mediterranean port of Iskenderum and included seven provinces of eastern Anatolia, the Erivan *guberniia*, the southern parts of the Tiflis *guberniia*, as well as the Zangezur, Shusha, Dzhevanshir, Kazakh, and part of the Ganja *uezds* of the Elizavetpol *guberniia*.[98] These frontiers were based primarily on historic and strategic premises; within their state the Armenians would constitute a minority of the population. By virtue of its territorial ambitions, Armenia acted both as a Transcaucasian and as an extraregional entity with far-reaching interests.

The claims of Persia on Azerbaijani territory went even further: The Tehran government requested the restoration of the "cities and provinces wrested from Persia after the Russian wars," which included all of the Azerbaijani republic and a part of Daghestan.[99] As a nonbelligerent during the world war, Persia was refused admission to the conference, and the memorandum of her chief delegate, ᶜAli Qulu Khan, was greeted with ridicule by Western diplomats. Writing to Baku, Topchibashev remarked that the Persian delegation itself did not expect its demands to find satisfaction in Versailles, and added a note on what was, in his view, the real meaning of Persian intentions: "They keep telling us that we should unite with them; they want it very much and talk about our intelligentsia, which does not exist among them."[100]

Nor did the Azerbaijani government distinguish itself by the modesty of its claims. The memorandum submitted by Topchbashev proposed the incorporation into the republic of a large portion of the Erivan *guberniia* as well as the more distant areas of Kars and Batum on the grounds of their religious affinity and economic links with Azerbaijan.[101] These demands aimed at establishing a unified state of all the Muslims of Transcaucasia regardless of geographic contiguity, with its capital in Baku. In its nonterritorial items the Azerbaijani memorandum showed more restraint, requesting that:

1. The Peace Conference approve the separation of Caucasian Azerbaijan from the late Russian Empire. Azerbaijan shall be a fully inde-

pendent state under the name of the Democratic Republic of Azerbaijan within the frontiers shown on the attached map.

2. The representatives of the delegation of the Republic of Azerbaijan shall be admitted to the work of the Peace Conference and its Commissions.

3. The Republic of Azerbaijan shall be admitted to membership in the League of Nations under whose high protection the republic wishes to be placed.[102]

The powers in Versailles were in no hurry to have their hands tied vis-à-vis the Russia of the future by the recognition of separatist governments. The Allied Supreme Council was willing, however, to consider the more urgent question of replacing Britain as the temporary guardian of Transcaucasia. Whatever British greed for the wealth of Baku might have been, whatever the profits from the resale of oil, they were not enough to compel Britain to forego its priorities, which lay elsewhere: There was a shortage of troops to garrison restive Egypt and India, Britain was suffering from a financial crisis, and parliamentary opposition to Britain's intervention in the Russian Civil War was mounting. "The British interests were not sufficiently strong to warrant more than a brief continuance of this thankless responsibility,"[103] read a Foreign Office memorandum. Lloyd George's government had decided as early as February 1919 – that is, barely three months after Thomson's landing in Baku – to evacuate Transcaucasia as soon as possible. At the beginning of April the Supreme Council proposed that Transcaucasia be placed under the occupation of Italy, which agreed to accept the mandate over the region. Thomson, who had told his superiors that the British withdrawal was "an act of perfidy" perpetrated on the newly born republics, officially informed the Baku government on May 10 of the council's decision.[104] The Azerbaijanis reacted by protesting both the pullout of the British and their replacement by the Italians, a prospect that seemed to hold little appeal for the local regimes. "In none of the Provinces of Transcaucasia is the Italian occupation looked on seriously," remarked General Bridges.[105] Other reports mentioned that "the Italians were considered incapable of handling the situation" and that they lacked "prestige, financial resources and experience."[106] In any event, the involvement of Italy proved to be purely exploratory in character. An extraordinary mission under the Prince of Savoy visited Baku on May 16, and in their footsteps came a

6. The Azerbaijani nation-state

group of military experts headed by Colonel M. Gabba. The Italian visitors acquainted themselves with the condition of Azerbaijan and promised assistance for its defense needs. Colonel Gabba, much impressed by Azerbaijan's economic potential, inquired of the Baku ministers about the possibilites of immigration for Italian labor.[107] Italy's interest in Transcaucasia, however, failed to survive the change of cabinet in Rome. The new prime minister, Francesco Nitti, canceled the plan of an Italian mandate over territory that Russia, he foresaw, would again claim as her own. Meanwhile, the British proceeded with their evacuation and most of their troops had departed Transcaucasia by the end of August, leaving behind a small garrison in Batum and a diplomatic mission under the High Commissioner Oliver Wardrop.

As no Western power was now willing to provide protection, the Azerbaijanis, in search of security, attempted to strengthen cooperation with equally weak neighboring states. Their relations with Persia, after a start that boded ill, underwent a dramatic improvement, a proof of the vitality of the ties between the two countries. Diplomatic links had in fact been established soon after Persia presented her territorial claims at Versailles. The Azerbaijani vice-minister of foreign affairs, Adil Ziyatkhanov, took up residence in Tehran as the republic's representative, and from Persia a diplomatic mission under Sayyid Zia al-din Tabatabai traveled to Baku to negotiate agreements on tariffs, postal service, and commerce.[108] An additional aspect of Tabatabai's mission was the talks on the desirability of unification of the Azerbaijani Republic with Persia in some form of a confederation. The project held for both sides the prospect of fulfillment of their boldest ambitions: Persia would recover the territories lost to Russia, and Baku would achieve union with Tabriz.

It was the signing of the Anglo–Persian Treaty of August 9, 1919, an act that virtually turned the Qajar kingdom into a British protectorate, that gave the Baku government its strongest stimulus for seeking unification. While many Persians opposed the treaty out of patriotism, the Azerbaijanis, concerned about the survival of their state, saw in it a chance for a roundabout way of slipping back under the British shield. In Paris on November 1, 1919 Topchibashev submitted to the Persians proposals for a pact effecting economic and political union, including a common foreign policy.[109] Details were to be ironed out by the two governments and the union subject to the approval of their parliaments. For the Baku regime the most essential element of these proposals was the stipulation that Azerbaijan receive assistance from Britain in the same form as it was to be provided to Persia. By the same token, the Azerbaijanis hinted that they were disinterested in joining a weak and backward Persia without the benefit of her link to Britain. This back-door attempt at regaining British protection miscarried when the Majlis refused to ratify the Anglo–Persian Treaty. It was doubtful, in any case, if Britain would have been prepared to extend her obligations to the Azerbaijani republic even had the latter been united with Persia.[110] This setback caused no harm to the growth of contacts between the republic and its southern neighbor, however, and the process culminated in the signing of a treaty of friendship and commerce in March 1920.[111] The rapprochement of Baku and Tehran and the desperately pro-British orientation of the Musavatist regime, however, produced inimical repercussions in Tabriz, where the spreading anticolonialist and separatist movement led by Khiabani was severely antagonized. This movement, opposed to British domination over Persia as well as to the central government in Tehran, additionally developed hostility to the Azerbaijani republic. Not surprisingly, Khiabani and his followers found sympathy from the far left opposition to the Musavatist regime, the Himmät and Ädalät, where the notions of revolutionary Pan-Azerbaijani solidarity resurfaced.[112]

In the end the most solid achievement of Azerbaijani diplomacy remained the mutual defense pact with Georgia. The two republics gained a sense of having improved somewhat their position vis-à-vis Russia, but more importantly, the pact established a harmonious atmosphere between Baku and Tiflis, especially as Azerbaijan now renounced its claims to the Muslim parts of western Transcaucasia. Azerbaijan, which had borne a major share of the responsibility for the breakup of the Transcaucasian Federation, now became an active proponent of regional cooperation. The main forum for drawing together the three neighboring states was the series of Transcaucasian conferences held at the government level. Despite an essential community of interests, the conditions for resurrecting the union with Georgia and Armenia were hardly propitious. Armenia,

6. The Azerbaijani nation-state 159

instead of attending the first Transcaucasian conference in November 1918, attacked Georgian territory in a dispute over the Borchalu *uezd*, and the fighting was stopped only by British intervention.[113] The second of the conferences began on April 25, 1919, to the accompaniment of bloody clashes between Armenians and Azerbaijanis in Karabagh and Nakhichevan. The latter area, a Muslim-populated part of the Erivan *guberniia*, was deemed unrelinquishable by the Armenians. Once again the British had to put out the fire: Fearing that Azerbaijani irregulars and Ottoman volunteers in Nakhichevan might establish a strategic link with Turkey, Thomson, in a reversal of his pro-Muslim stand, ordered the area placed under Armenian administration.[114] Meanwhile the Transcaucasian conference dragged on, ending with Armenia's refusal to join Georgia and Azerbaijan in an anti-Denikin alliance.

During October and November of 1919 a dramatic turn in the Russian Civil War took place as the Volunteer Army bit off more than it could chew in its drive on Moscow. Having reached as far as Tula, the Whites met with a vigorous conteroffensive that forced them into a disorderly headlong retreat southward. Denikin's defeat was no cause for rejoicing in the Transcaucasian republics, as it was obvious that they would face a more formidable enemy in the victory-drunk Bolsheviks. At this juncture, the fate of Transcaucasia again came to the attention of the statesmen in Versailles. They believed that should the Bolsheviks be allowed to break through the Caucasus Mountains, the road to Persia, Turkey, and the rest of the Middle East would lie open for the spread of the revolution. In the Western European press and in the diplomatic rumor mills, hints were bruited about concerning the dispatch of Western military aid, perhaps even troops, to bolster the defenses of the Caucasus.[115] In fact, in January 1920 high-ranking Allied commanders were discussing the defense needs of Azerbaijan and Georgia with their delegations in Paris. The only tangible outcome of these talks was the de facto recognition of these two republics by the Supreme Council on January 12 and of Armenia on January 19; de jure recognition was to follow when the peace treaty with Turkey was signed. Soon afterward, Azerbaijan was recognized by Japan and by Denikin, his cause by then practically lost.[116]

All these gestures could hardly offset the fact that in the same winter of 1920, the British government had begun a definite reappraisal of its Russian policy. Rather than continue to support the secessionist regimes, thereby prolonging the unpopular and costly involvement in the Russian Civil War, London now considered moves toward coming to terms with Moscow.[117]

The vague promises of military assistance (though not troops) for Transcaucasia were not withdrawn at once but made conditional on the three republics' settling their differences, for the Allied leaders feared that arms delivered to Transcaucasia might find use in internecine warfare.[118] The Armenians and Georgians in fact continued to argue the issue of their frontiers at the international conferences in London and San Remo. A large-scale conflict broke out in Karabagh between the Azerbaijanis and Armenians, where the latter started an uprising on March 22, 1920 in response to growing apprehension of hostile encirclement by Soviet Russia, a prospective successor to the Azerbaijani Republic, and Turkey – a power whose weight was again making itself felt in Transcaucasia.[119]

The Azerbaijani Republic and Turkey

A special chapter in Azerbaijan's foreign and domestic affairs was its postwar relations with Turkey – whatever Turkey might mean at that time. The Ottoman State, subject in part to foreign occupation, was split between the Allied-backed regime of Sultan Mehmed VI and the resistance movement, whose leader became in the summer of 1919 the war hero Mustafa Kemal Pasha. Baku's official contacts were with the sultan's regime in Istanbul, but the facts of geography drew the Azerbaijanis into an uneasy and complex relationship with the insurgents, who began to call themselves Turks rather than Ottomans and whose base was eastern and central Anatolia.[120] An additional dimension of diversity was the split within the bloc of antiimperialist forces in Turkey between the Kemal-led Nationalists and the loyalists of the former CUP regime. The Young Turks, anxious for restoration of their power, were the rivals of Kemal, and he prudently kept them from gaining control of his movement. At his insistence the participants in the September 1919 Nationalist Congress in Sivaş took an oath renouncing the CUP and its policies.

6. The Azerbaijani nation-state 161

The rift between the two groups, while subdued in Anatolia, was more pronounced in Transcaucasia.[121] The Turkish factor in Azerbaijan did not vanish with the withdrawal of the Ottoman troops after the Mudros armistice. Former Ottoman military personnel and schoolteachers who had entered Azerbaijani service were the most visible sign of the Turkish presence. Among the native population, Turkey's prestige enjoyed a resurgance when Kemal entered upon his war of liberation against the Allies. Although Turkish influence in Azerbaijan always remained strong, it was at first tilted toward the Young Turks. In the last days of World War I, Enver Pasha sought to use Baku as a base from which to launch his campaign to reconquer Turkey but failed even to reach the Azerbaijani capital.[122] The same intention had motivated Nuri Pasha in his attempt to transfer Ottoman forces to Azerbaijani jurisdiction in the aftermath of the armistice. The Young Turks saw possible advantages accruing from cooperation with Soviet Russia in the struggle against Western imperialism, and Kemal held the same view. In the Erzerum meeting of the Association for the Defense of the Rights of the Eastern Provinces (July– August 1919), Kemal exhorted the Turks to draw inspiration from the heroic battles of the Russian people against foreign intervention.[123] In private he said repeatedly that Soviet Russia should be enlisted for the assistance of Turkey, although there could be no question of adopting Bolshevism as the ideology of the Nationalist movement. Both Kemalists and the Young Turks sought contacts with the Bolsheviks, and one of the most suitable venues for this purpose seemed to be Azerbaijan. The first prominent Turk to appear in Azerbaijan after the war was the familiar figure of Nuri, who escaped British detention in Batum early in 1919, joined the fighting against Denikin in Daghestan, and after the fall of the Mountaineers Republic moved to Baku. Here, under his aegis, the semiofficial Representation of the People of Turkey was set up in September 1919.[124] The Representation's task was to solicit support for the Turkish struggle, including financial aid from the Baku regime. The Azerbaijani cabinet split over the issue and finally equivocated for fear of alidenating the British.[125] More promising proved to be the Turks' contacts with the Bolshevik underground facilitated by the Baku Himmätists. The chief Turkish negotiator was not Nuri but rather Fuat Sabit, a man closer to Kemal. In October Sabit reported to Kâzim Pasha

Karabekir, commander of the Fifteenth Army Corps in eastern Anatolia: "I asked them," wrote Sabit,

"how could they give us any aid if there is no social or economic basis for Bolshevism in our country; if the traditions and culture of our people have been contrary to the introduction of a social revolution. They answered me that they were willing to give us aid in every way, but since at the present time there exists no other possibility, they could supply only financial means. Whatever amounts are needed will be provided at once.[126]

Another channel of communications between Turkey and the Bolsheviks was opened through the efforts of Halil Pasha. After the war the former commander of the Ottoman Eastern Army Group found himself under arrest on the sultan's order but escaped to offer his services to the Nationalists. Kemal was not averse to making use of the experience and prestige of this prominent Young Turk – who was, at that, a relative of Enver. As he also may have preferred to keep him out of Anatolia, Kemal sent Halil on a secret mission to Transcaucasia to arrange for military assistance from Soviet Russia.[127] By December 1919 Halil had made his way to Azerbaijan, where he established contacts with members of the Bolshevik Regional Committee, while maintaining contact with the Baku government. Halil's immediate concern was to secure the strategic corridor linking Anatolia with Azerbaijan, and to this end he joined forces with the volunteers resisting Armenian rule over Nakhichevan.[128] The participation of Turks in the Nakhichevan fighting inspired speculation in Western newspapers about a secret compact between Azerbaijan and the Kemalists for taking concerted action against Armenia. In Paris, Topchibashev emphatically denied these rumors – apparently in good faith, as the alleged deal would jeopardize the Allied support that he was strenuously seeking for Azerbaijan.[129]

The Turks, both those in Transcaucasia and those in Anatolia, showed little consideration for the delicate diplomatic position of the Azerbaijani government. Kemal himself is on record as having predicted that the weak Transcaucasian republics would sooner or later return to Russian rule, an opinion widely shared in Turkey.[130] Together with Karabekir, he outlined the general aims of a Turkish grand strategy with respect to Transcaucasia: The interests of Turkey's struggle for independence required

6. The Azerbaijani nation-state 163

the suppression of Armenia, the neutrality of Georgia, and the inclusion of Azerbaijan into the Soviet system. In this manner Azerbaijan would serve as a bridge through which Soviet aid would flow to an embattled Anatolia. Conversely, an Azerbaijan governed by a Western-oriented elite was in the eyes of Turkish Nationalist leaders an instrument of British policy and a barrier separating Turkey from a friendly Russia. Kemal reacted to Allied recognition of the Transcaucasan republics with obvious concern. In a circular to his military chiefs he wrote that the imperialists were plotting to separate the Turks from the Bolsheviks by upholding the independence of Armenia, Georgia, and Azerbaijan. "Should this plan succeed and the nations of the Caucasus are made into a solid wall blockading our country, the outcome for Turkey would certainly be the destruction of her resistance down to its very foundation." Consequently, Kemal's recommendations were

to start official and unofficial mobilization on the eastern front, to concentrate our forces for the breaking of the Caucasian barrier, to contact the new governments of the Caucasus, particularly those of Islamic Azerbaijan and Daghestan, in order to determine their standpoint with regard to the schemes of the Entente powers. Should the Caucasian nations decide to act as a barrier against us, we will agree with the Bolsheviks on a coordinated offensive against them.[131]

This Turkish attitude signified the abrupt reversal of a political tradition that in the past had allowed the Azerbaijanis to see in Turkey the natural supporter of their strivings for emancipation from Russia. As for Pan-Islamism and Pan-Turkism in Turkey's foreign policy, Kemal rejected these two programs outright, unlike the Young Turks, who upheld them even after 1918. In Kemal's view, Pan-Islamism and Pan-Turkism not only were incompatible with Turkey's need for friendship with Russia but, more importantly, conflicted with his "Turkey-first" brand of nationalism. All the same, the Turkish war of liberation gained a large and growing number of sympathizers in Azerbaijan. They came from a broad spectrum of the public, including, remarkably, the Pan-Islamists, who believed that the Young Turks would eventually replace the Nationalists; the leftists, who perceived in events in Turkey the beginning of a worldwide antiimperialist upheaval; and those of diverse political persuasions who were generally opposed to a narrow Azerbaijani nationalism. Responding to popular sentiments, the second cabinet of Ussubäkov, as a token of good will in December 1919 granted a subsidy to Kemal.[132] This gesture did little to alter the disposition of the Turks, nor did it stop a variety of Turkish residents in Azerbaijan from undertaking activities that in effect undermined the Azerbaijan Republic. Nuri, whom even Halil described as acting childlishly, combined his enthusiasm for the Bolsheviks with an intense dislike of the Musavat that dated back to the June 1918 crisis.[133] At that time his close relationship with the Ittihad, the group that provided Nuri and thus the Young Turks with their political followinng in Azerbaijan, had also begun. In the midst of the malaise spreading throughout the friendless and endangered country, the Turkish general epitomized the coalition of right and left pitted against Azerbaijani statehood.

7
The coming of Soviet power

Azerbaijani Communists and Russian Bolsheviks

Within a few days of the opening of Parliament the Himmät's new platform was outlined in a declaration written by Shaikh-ul-Islamzadä and printed in the official government newspaper. Its two main points were (1) recognition of the fact that the newly created republics had won independence as a consequence of the principle of self-determination and (2) recognition of the necessity for socialist participation in the democratic governments of the emerging states.[1]

The advent of the parliamentary regime revived the languishing Azerbaijani socialist movement. By early 1919 the membership of the Himmät in Baku alone reached some three hundred, two-thirds of them workers.[2] In March the party healed its split by admitting the remnants of the pro-Bolshevik faction. The Himmät was also infused with young blood, a seemingly healthy development except for the fact that some of these men in their twenties were Bolshevik-oriented. The same was true of the former pillar of the "Tiflis Center," Garayev, who together with other youthful radicals – Mirza Davud Huseynov, Mir Fattah Musävi, and Ashum Äliyev – took seats in the party's central committee side by side with the old-guard Mensheviks Abilov, Aghamalioghlï, and Pepinov. Garayev and Musävi, who were also appointed deputies to Parliament, soon began to act as spokesmen for the Bolsheviks.

Bolshevik influence, which had reached its nadir in the summer of 1918, regained some ground in the first year of Azerbaijani independence. The liberal atmosphere encouraged by the presence of the British permitted the resumption of Bolshevik activities, albeit in semilegal forms. In November 1918 the surviving members of the party, now renamed the All-Russian Communist Party (Bolsheviks) – RCP(B) – organized a provisional bureau, later the Baku Committee, whose moving spirit after March 1919 was Anastas I. Mikoyan.[3] The Bolsheviks' first move was to infiltrate the Baku Workers Conference, a permanent body made up of delegates from oil fields and factories. On May 6 the conference launched a citywide strike in order to win primarily economic concessions, in particular collective bargaining. The strike, however, collapsed within two days after the Bolsheviks injected political demands by calling for "All Power to the Soviets in Azerbaijan" as well as support for Soviet Russia. The Azerbaijanis were the first to return to work, and the Himmät withdrew its backing of the strike.[4]

For the Bolsheviks, a key lesson of this setback was their need to establish a channel of communication with the natives. This would entail exerting effective control over the far left Muslim organizations, including the Himmät, the Äkinchi, and the Ädalät. In the case of the Himmät, the task proved less than simple, given the party's traditions, its largely Menshevik leadership, and the distrust among the rank and file for all things Russian. Commenting on the scant appeal the Russian Bolsheviks held for the Azerbaijanis, Mikoyan wrote to Moscow in May 1919: "An acute lack of intelligent, committed, and energetic Muslim activists in our party makes it possible for the nationalistically tainted Right wing of the Muslim socialists to hold a part of the Muslim workers under their sway."[5] In the same report, he remarked that even those who might desire soviet-type government "are fearful that this would be a foreign, Russian rule, and that they themselves would have no access to power."[6]

Rather than seek an outright takeover of the Himmät, the Bolsheviks chose to bring about its breakup by fomenting internal dissention. A special resolution of the Baku Committee of July 15, 1919 recommended efforts to "speed up the split within the Himmät party, to detach organizationally its Communist wing, and then to subsidize it."[7] As Mikoyan recollects, Garayev and Huseynov, because of their "softness of character," were reluctant to follow these recommendations.[8] Eventually, in what appeared at first to be a rebellion of radical youths against the moderate leadership, the Left–Himmätist group led by these two men and Musävi broke away in late July. Once again, Russian pressure had opened a crack in the Azerbaijani socialist movement.

The men formerly linked with the Tiflis Center, now regarded as rightists, retained the name Social Democratic Workers Party–Himmät. Remaining aloof from the Bolsheviks and committed to the parliamentary system, they stated their position in a declaration delivered to Parliament by Pepinov: "While championing the interests of the workers, we are not defending the Bolsheviks. The government has no reason to fear that we in the Parliament would not give equal support against dangers from either the Left or the Right."[9] As an expression of his readiness to share responsibility for upholding the republic, Pepinov in December 1919 joined Ussubäkov's as cabinet minister of labor.

The Left–Himmät, which after the split called itself the Azerbaijani Communist Party–Himmät, sought to win power for the soviets in Azerbaijan. In accordance with the recommendations of the Baku Committee of the RCP(B), it absorbed the Marxist-oriented core of the Äkinchi, whose leader was Ruhullah Akhundov.[10] The third Muslim socialist organization, the Ädalät, was left intact. The Baku Committee held this Persian group in low regard, as it demonstrated little class consciousness and was organizationally weak.[11] Some of its cells were united with the Himmät, and a Himmätist, Buniatzadä, also served as the chairman of the Ädalät's Central Committee.[12]

While the native Communists increased their strength by regrouping their forces, they did not relish the prospect of their eventual dissolution and absorption by the Russian party. Throughout the second half of 1919 a bitter controversy raged in the Communist underworld of Transcaucasia, ostensibly over the name the Communist organization in Azerbaijan was to assume. The Tiflis-based Kraikom (Regional Committee), the highest Bolshevik authority south of the Caucasus Mountains, felt that the party should be merely a territorial branch of the RCP(B). The Himmätists for their part wished to remain an autonomous structure under a name reflecting their traditions and national identity. Consequently, they proposed as alternatives the titles Muslim Communist Party–Himmät, Turkic Communist Party–Himmät, and Azerbaijan Communist Party–Himmät.[13] The real issue, of course, was that of Russian centralism versus Azerbaijani particularism, now intensified by the Azerbaijanis' experience of statehood. Behind the dispute over the party's name loomed the fundamental question: Would Azerbaijan upon sovietization become a mere province of Russia, or would it win a measure of autonomy within the Soviet system?

The Baku Himmätists gained support among their comrades who had taken refuge in Russia following the debacle of the Commune. They congregated for the most part in Astrakhan, where there resided Narimanov, Sultanov, Äfändiyev, and Musabäkov, the cream of the Bolshevik faction of the party in the years 1917–18. Here they organized a local bureau of the Himmät and resumed publication of a newspaper under the same name. They also established extensive secret contacts with Baku.[14]

A few of these Azerbaijani refugees eventually moved to Moscow, where they assumed positions in government agencies that gave them some voice in shaping Soviet policies concerning Muslims. Äfändiyev became commissar for affairs of Transcaucasian Muslims; Shakhbazi became an official in the same commissariat, Israfilbäkov an official in the Near Eastern Section of the Commissariat for Foreign Affairs, and Särdarov deputy chairman of the Bureau of the Muslim Communist Organizations.[15] By far the highest position was held by Narimanov, who after his arrival in Moscow in June 1919 was first made the head of the Near Eastern Section in the Commissariat for Foreign Affairs and then deputy commissar of the Commissariat for Nationality Affairs. Narimanov advocated carrying the revolution to the Muslim East, not excluding the lands outside the former Russian Empire. "Let the Soviet power be brought to all states and nationalities professing Islam: in ten years they will achieve what they were unable to accomplish in a century," he wrote in a letter.[16] The natural base for this undertaking, he contended, was Azerbaijan. In his memoranda, reports, and lectures Narimanov called for the sovietization of his homeland with the assistance of Russia. Yet he cautioned that Azerbaijani workers "are not as revolutionary as the Russian, Armenian, or other proletariat. The reason for this is the chauvinist attitude of some Mensheviks of the

7. The coming of Soviet power

Himmät party, as well as widespread ignorance and inertia. National and religious prejudices also play their role."[17]

Narimanov believed that Russia should proclaim an independent Soviet Azerbaijan – an idea some Baku Bolsheviks had considered after the May strike but the Transcaucasian Party Conference had rejected.[18]

The Moscow-based Himmätists used their influence to bring the case of Azerbaijan and its native Communists before the Politburo of the RCP(B) on July 19, 1919. At this point in the Russian Civil War, the Denikin's offensive was in full swing and Moscow had already acknowledged the independence of formerly Russian Poland, Finland, and Estonia. The Politburo, acting jointly with the Organizational Bureau of the Central Committee, adopted a resolution bearing the ponderous title "On Recognizing the Himmät Party as the Autonomous Communist Party with the Rights of an Oblast' Committee and on Recognizing Azerbaijan as an Independent Soviet Republic."[19] The language of the resolution was strikingly cautious to the point of ambivalence:

It is recognized that the Central Committee in principle has no objections to the proposals of the Himmät Party, it being understood that the definitive solution of the issue will be submitted for the approval of the Transcaucasian Committee of the RCP(B). Comrade Stalin will be informed about its decision, which will be binding if no objections are raised by him. The same applies to the recognition of an independent Azerbaijan.[20]

Much extolled by Azerbaijani historians as the triumph of a correct nationality policy, the whole of this statement is in fact flawed by contradictions and replete with caveats. The party of the independent country would be merely autonomous; moreover, its status would be no higher than that of a district organization. Clearly, the meaning of Azerbaijani independence was to be autonomy on the pattern of the Soviet Ukraine or Byelorussia, an important concession in itself. Still, the willingness to tolerate the existence of an autonomous Himmät ran contrary to the principle of centralism, which precluded federalism in the structure of the party. Most contradictory of all, the final decision on the question of Azerbaijan, that distant and little-known land, was relegated to the Kraikom, which had always been stubbornly opposed to the Himmätists' aspirations.

In stormy meetings in Tiflis the Azerbaijanis fought for their cause. Invoking the equivocal resolution of the Politburo, they argued that their party's right to autonomous status followed logically from the fact of Soviet Azerbaijan's independence. In addition, they alluded to tactical considerations: If Azerbaijani Communists openly were to become functionaries of a Russian organization, their following among Muslim workers would decline drastically. Already the Himmätists were being branded as foreign agents working for the restoration of Russian rule.[21]

All these arguments, presented by Huseynov and Sultanov, who had become members of the Kraikom, were rejected on the ground that concessions granted the Azerbaijanis would have to be extended to other nationalities as well. Also, the party bureaucrats in Tiflis were loath to see the affairs of Baku slipping from their jurisdiction. The Himmätists for their part were unwilling to desist, despite accusations of nationalist deviation and separatism. A spirit of rebellion was brewing in their ranks. Instead of preparing for merger with the RCP(B), they put forward an alternative that smacked of the heresy spread by the Tatar Communist Sultan Galiev: separate Communist parties for Muslims and all others.[22] The Himmät would consist exclusively of Azerbaijanis, the Ädalät would retain its status as an organization for immigrants from Persia, and the Baku chapter of the RCP(B) would admit all other nationalities.[23] In every respect the Ädalät supported the position of the Himmätists, an indication not only of Muslim solidarity but also of the organizational affinity of the two groups at both the leadership and the grass roots levels. In late October the Himmät and Ädalät both refused to participate in a Bolshevik caucus in charge of planning an armed uprising.[24] Similarly, the next month the Muslim organizations boycotted a conference called by the Baku Committee to discuss unification with the CPR(B). This was the high point in the Azerbaijani Communists' effort to assert the national identity of their party.

For the Baku Bolsheviks, the dispute was taking a troublesome turn. They soon confronted the Muslim Communist leaders with a fait accompli by absorbing one after another the cells of the Himmät and Ädalät. The haste with which this was accomplished was necessary, so the explanation went, in view of the appalling

7. The coming of Soviet power

state of these groups' organizational work, especially the Ädalät's, whose cells held no meetings and even lacked membership lists.[25] By late 1919 the idea of retaining an independent Persian Communist Party in Azerbaijan was abandoned, possibly because of the Ädalät's steadfast support for the Himmät. All the same the Baku Committee favored granting a concession to the Azerbaijanis on the issue of the party's name – even as the RCP(B) was swallowing up Himmätist cells.

Moreover, the Baku Bolsheviks were anxious to win freedom from the Kraikom's control. To arrange for a high-level intervention Mikoyan and Akhundov were dispatched to Moscow.[26] Impetus for an early decision on the question of the Azerbaijani Communists also came from S. M. Kirov, the Bolshevik leader in command of southern Russia. Kirov complained early in 1920 that within the Kraikom "our orthodox – or more appropriately, old – men, comrades Nazaratian, Makharadze, and others, are incapable of sharing our views on the Himmät and the Armenian Communist party."[27] Only in January 1920, as Soviet Russia began laying the diplomatic groundwork for the conquest of Azerbaijan, did the final word come from Moscow. According to the resolution of the Eighth All-Russian Conference of the RCP(B) of December 2–9, 1919, all national organizations on Soviet territory were to dissolve and to join the Communist Party at the level of its territorial subdivisions.[28] With regard to still-unsovietized Azerbaijan, the imposed solution amounted to a compromise in favor of the Baku Committee's positon: There was to be one Communist organization for all nationalities inhabiting Azerbaijan, and all references to its Muslim or Turkic character were to be dropped, as was the name *Himmät*. The party would be called *Azerbaijani*, a term carrying both territorial and national connotations. More gratifying to the Himmätists was the fact that their members made up the largest number of delegates appointed to the constituent congress. The Himmät's representation from Baku would equal that of the RCP(B) – that is, thirty men each – with another sixty delegates coming from the Communist organizations in provinces that were mostly Himmätist. The Ädalät gained thirty votes as well. Thus, a solid majority of Muslims controlled the congress that opened in Baku on February 11, 1920.[29] Two days later, the formation of the Azerbaijani Communist Party (Bolsheviks) – AzCP(B) – was proclaimed. Reflecting the strength of the native element, the forty-three-man Central Committee consisted predominantly of Azerbaijanis, with Huseynov as chairman. The congress concluded with a manifesto calling for the overthrow of "the rule of *bäys*, khans, capitalists, and nationalists."[30]

Their long quarrel now settled, the Communists stepped up preparations for the seizure of power. Beginning in the summer of 1919, aid from Astrakhan was used to finance publication of an impressive array of newspapers in Azerbaijani. Although frequently suppressed by the government, these papers quickly reappeared with new mastheads and in many cases under the same editor, Garayev.[31]

In their propaganda, the Communists continued their intensified campaign against the Musavatist regime and put forward alternatives for the cloudy future of Azerbaijan: the question of land reform would find a radical, long-overdue solution with sovietization; an Azerbaijan ruled by the soviets would enjoy friendly relations with Russia, the indispensable market for the country's products; and the resumption of oil exports would at once terminate the country's economic difficulties. Soviet power would not, however, mean the loss of national independence – quite the contrary: "What they call independence is of benefit to only 5% of the nation, the capitalists, big landowners, and some others; what we call independence will be enjoyed by 95%."[32] Only then would the Azerbaijani people become truly sovereign, as opposed to their situation under the present rulers, who were nothing more than the puppets of the British, who in turn were far away and little concerned about the fate of Azerbaijan. "English imperialism cannot and never will give independence to our country. If England had sincerely wished to make other peoples independent, why, one could ask, did she destroy the independence of the Turkish State, and why is she now trying to strangle the people of Turkey?"[33] The Communists were quick to capitalize on echoes of the national liberation struggle in Turkey by appealing to the Pan-Islamic and Pan-Turkish sentiments still alive among the masses.

The Azerbaijani Communists undoubtedly experienced an upsurge in poplularity. Party membership reached four thousand by late April 1920, an increase of one thousand since the

7. The coming of Soviet power

beginning of the year.[34] This growth was concentrated in Baku and its vicinity. In the provinces the inhabitants remained little affected and party activities often lagged. As reported from Karabagh to the Central Committee of the AzCP(B) "In the Shusha *uezd* of Karabagh our effort is weak inasmuch as we lack good, experienced comrades familiar with the conditions."[35] The deficiencies of the cadres increased in March 1920, after the government, attempting to contain the Communists, began arresting and deporting aliens. The Kraikom radioed the following alarmist message to Moscow:

> The functioning of legal organizations and institutions has become greatly restricted. The work among the Muslims suffers from it; the Muslim party activists, in the main youthful, are without experience and ability for work. We categorically demand that the Central Committee send here Comrades Musabäkov, Äfändiyev, and Shakhbazov. Narimanov should depart as the Red Army approaches. Otherwise, future work is impossible.[36]

Twilight of independence

The essential weakness of the native Communists was of little comfort to the leadership of the republic, then sinking into disunity and dejection. The crisis of the regime spread from the centerpiece of independent Azerbaijan, the Musavat Party, which suffered from the deepening division between its left and right wings. As the clouds on the political horizon grew thicker, the left gained ascendancy. Led by Räsulzadä and Hajinski and strengthened by the defection of Ussubäkov from the right, the left persuaded the Musavat's Second Party Congress, meeting on December 9–12, 1919, to endorse its land reform program. More importantly, the leftists insisted upon reshuffling the government so as to facilitate relations with Russia.

At the end of December 1919 Ussubäkov presented his second cabinet, a broad coalition of the left-wing Musavatists, independents, Himmät–Mensheviks, the Socialist Bloc, and the Ittihad. The list of his ministers included Ussubäkov as prime minister, Khan Khoiski (foreign affairs), Hajinski (interior), Hamid bäy Shakhtakhtinski (education), Makhmändiarov (war), Pepinov (labor), Rashid Kaplanov (finance), and Khudad As-

Ianov (commerce).³⁷ The inclusion of the Ittihad was a signal development. As an opposition party, it had undergone a curious evolution from the far right to the left end of the political spectrum. The Ittihad came to consider itself the group closest to the Bolsheviks and reportedly contemplated merger with them early in 1920.³⁸ For almost a year now the Ittihad had affirmed its acceptance for "all principles of socialism as long as these do not contradict the fundamental tenets of the religion."³⁹ The party's newspaper contained articles on the compatibility of socialism and Islam, the faith "that not only is the spiritual message, but also an institutional form for the social and political life of the Muslims."⁴⁰ Such rapprochement was consonant with the Ittihadists' hostility toward nationalism. They appreciated the Communist movement as a supranational force and believed that the support Communism offered the Muslim world in the struggle against Western imperialism compensated for its secular bias.

Within a few days of its formation, the new government was facing a series of developments that tested its cohesion. On January 2, 1920 a note from the Soviet commissar for foreign affairs, Grigori Chicherin, was the opening salvo in a war of nerves against the Azerbaijani republic. In what sounded more like an appeal to the local proletariat than a diplomatic communication – the note was reprinted and widely publicized by the Communist press in Baku – Chicherin demanded that the Baku regime enter at once into negotiations with Soviet Russia

> for the conclusion of a military agreement between the commands of both countries for the purpose of accelerating the defeat of the White Guard armies in the South of Russia.... Denikin is an enemy not only of Russian peasants and workers but also of peasants and workers of Azerbaijan and Georgia.... We are turning, before it is too late, to the Azerbaijani people with a call to begin a struggle against Denikin. Social and political interests of its toiling classes, if properly understood, should make Azerbaijan agree to our proposals.⁴¹

The Azerbaijani government immediately convened the Committee of State Defense, which resolved to "ascertain the position of the British with regard to the current situation and to use their influence in the interest of the Republic."⁴² It was in reaction to this Soviet pressure that the Allied Supreme Council granted recognition to Azerbaijan and that the discussions on military aid to Transcaucasia began in Paris.

7. The coming of Soviet power

There followed an upsurge of optimism among the Azerbaijani leaders, and Foreign Minister Khan Khoiski, believing his hand strengthened by the Allies' reaction, declared that Azerbaijan was unwilling, as a matter of principle, to intervene in the internal affairs of Russia – that is, to take sides in the civil war. His government, stated Khoiski, was nevertheless eager to normalize relations with Moscow.[43]

A second note from Chicherin of January 23 showed that the Soviet side was not deterred by Western recognition. The people's commissar denounced Azerbaijan for failing to join the common struggle against Denikin and repeated the proposal for a military alliance. He reminded Khan Khoiski of the Sovnarkom's principle of respect for the rights of the laboring masses to national self-determination and of the numerous instances in which this principle had been consitently observed by the Soviet government.[44]

In his note to Chicherin of February 1 Khan Khoiski disputed the latter's accusations and insisted upon Soviet "unconditional recognition of the independence and sovereignty of the Azerbaijani Republic" before further negotiations. He also cited the precedents of Soviet recognition of Poland, Finland, and Estonia.[45]

Chicherin's reply of February 20, took into account the advice of the Central Committee of the AzCP(B) that "the recognition of the Azerbaijani Republic is useless and offers no advantages."[46] The Soviet commissar skirted the issue of recognition and, with reference to Estonia, explained that Soviet Russia's diplomatic relations had with that country been established only after prolonged and complex negotiations. The Azerbaijanis' latest reply, wrote Chicherin, was tantamount to a rejection of Soviet proposals.[47]

As the Soviet diplomatic offensive mounted and no further support from the West appeared forthcoming, strains began to surface in the Azerbaijani cabinet. Among its members, the most outspoken proponent of the "placate-Russia" school of thought was M. H. Hajinski, minister of the interior. Amid growing tensions he offered the hope that Azerbaijan could buy its survival through extensive concessions to Moscow. As a first step he recommended legalization of AzCP(B) activities, a gesture the Communists neither needed nor particularly desired.

Hajinski's chief opponent was Khan Khoiski, who in January 1920 proposed to a conclave of Musavatist notables a plan for coping with internal dangers, beginning with the replacement of Hajinski as minister of the interior by a reliable Musavatist. Should such a move provoke the resignations of socialists and Ittihadists, Khoiski reasoned, so much the better: A new cabinet would emerge through the cooptation of trusted and determined men. This new government should be provided with broad powers, including the authority to dissolve Parliament and decree early elections to the Azerbaijani Constituent Assembly.[48]

Khan Khoiski's attempt at stiffening the resolve of the leadership of the state brought about mixed results. Hajinski was dismissed from the Ministry of the Interior and replaced by the tougher-minded Rustambäkov, who began to harass and disrupt the work of the Communist Party. In order to forestall the resignation of the socialist ministers Hajinski was kept in the cabinet as the new minister of commerce and industry. In this capacity he continued to propagate his views, but now with an economic rationale. The Bolsheviks, he argued, would be more likely to tolerate an independent Azerbaijan if its friendly government stood ready to supply Russia with raw materials, especially oil, on favorable terms. At the conference of the Musavat leaders in mid-March, Hajinski's reasoning swayed a majority of participants, including Räsulzadä, who openly took the side of the Russian-oriented faction.[49] Khan Khoiski and some others who maintained that the only way to deter the Russians was to build up strong defenses on the northern frontier were overruled. The Azerbaijani ruling elite realistically and prudently began preparing for the inevitable.

As the Red Army drove relentlessly southward and prospects of help from the Western powers were all but vanishing, the Azerbaijani situation justified little optimism. Those who lacked faith in the effectiveness and, indeed, sensibility of armed resistance correctly observed that the disarray in the military establishment was no less pervasive than in the civilian departments. The deputy minister of war, Shikhlinski, was cooperating with the Communist underground, while many officers who had served in the tsarist army were disinclined to fight Russia in any guise. General Makhmändiarov shocked Parliament by stating that the entire Azerbaijani army could not stand up to a single

Russian battalion.[50] He openly expressed the generally held but unspoken view that Western recognition of Azerbaijan was worthless so long as Russia withheld her recognition. The high command avoided taking any defensive measures against the Red Army. The Turkish officers, for their part impatiently awaited the change of regime in Baku, as a Soviet Azerbaijan would then bring Lenin's Russia closer to Kemal's Turkey.

With such sentiments prevailing among a large part of the officer corps, demoralization spread rapidly throughout the ranks. Communist infiltration of the army went unchecked, and some units were soon honeycombed with party cells. As military discipline broke down, desertions rose to alarming proportions. The Azerbaijani army ceased altogether to be a factor in Baku's strategy vis-à-vis Moscow on March 23, when a large Armenian uprising supported by the Erivan government broke out in Karabagh and the Azerbaijani high command promptly committed virtually the entire army against the insurgents.[51] Meanwhile, in late March and early April the Red Eleventh Army was consolidating its occupation of the North Caucasus and Daghestan. Moscow had already decided to carry the momentum of this conquest in Transcaucasia. On March 17 Lenin had issued a directive to the head of the North Caucasus Revkom (Revolutionary Committee), Grigorii Ordzhonikidze, stating that

> it is extremely, extremely important for us to take Baku. Exert all efforts in this direction, but at the same time do not fail to show yourself doubly diplomatic in your announcements and make as sure as possible that firm local soviet authority has been prepared. The same applies to Georgia, but in this case I advise even greater circumspection. Settle the matter of troop transfers with the Commander in Chief.[52]

To coordinate the military and political aspects of the invasion, a special organ, the Kavbiuro (Caucasus Bureau), was established on April 8, with Ordzhonikidze as chairman, Kirov as his deputy, and two Georgian Communists, Budu Mdivani and Aleksandr Stopani, as members. A historian of this formative period of the Soviet Union has remarked that the creation of the high-powered Kavbiuro indicated Moscow's lack of belief in the ability of the local Communists to seize power on their own. Accordingly, the role of the Regional Committee and of Transcaucasian Communist organizations was downgraded to carrying out "such actions as . . . necessary to lend the conquest an appearance of an internal revolution."⁵³

As the seventy-thousand-strong Eleventh Army moved toward the unprotected Azerbaijani frontier, the republic found itself engulfed in the last of its political crises. At the end of March, the deputies of the socialist parliamentary group withdrew their support for the Ussubäkov cabinet in protest over the arrests of Communists. This was the last action undertaken by the Social Democratic Himmät, a party that had already been reduced to a handful of politicians and was now in the final throes of disintegration. One by one, within the space of a few weeks, the Menshevik–Himmätists – with the exception of Shaikh-ul-Islamzadä, who resided in Paris – joined the Communist Party, thus ending once and for all the split among the Azerbaijani Marxists.

Ussubäkov's government, which had also lost the backing of the Ittihad, resigned on April 1, unable to cope with contingencies within and without the country. Its fall presented Hajinski with the opportunity to form a new cabinet. His grand design was to put together another left-of-center coalition, this time including Communists. Indeed, he regarded their participation as the cornerstone of his ministry, therefore making it acceptable to Russia.⁵⁴ With the backing of Halil Pasha, who considered Hajinski a friend of Turkey, an enemy of Britain, and a man able to deal amicably with the Communists, Hajinski began to solicit Communist support in prolonged and inconclusive talks.⁵⁵ Meanwhile, Ussubäkov's cabinet carried on as a caretaker government amid reports of a heavy concentration of Red troops on the coastal strip across the frontier. On April 15 an alarmed Khan Khoiski, in the last of his notes to Chicherin, demanded an explanation of these moves and repeated Azerbaijan's readiness to negotiate. No reply was forthcoming.⁵⁶

In these frantic spring days, the Baku Kemalist Turks, anxious to influence events to the benefit of the Ankara government, entered the fray. In early April they held a meeting to coordinate the efforts of their various groups. Some of the participants had already been working closely with the Azerbaijani Communists and had organized the Turkish Communist Party in Baku in March.⁵⁷ The coordinating conclave, with Halil Pasha and Fuad Sabit in attendance, adopted a resolution establishing

7. The coming of Soviet power

guidelines for Turkish policy regarding the Azerbaijani crisis. Its three main points were:

1. Overthrow of the present, pro-British Azerbaijani government as soon as possible and its replacement by one capable of cooperating with the Bolsheviks.
2. Formation of a committee to expedite the change in government, with subsections in charge of propaganda, publications, and military operations, the last to include Bolsheviks.
3. No occupation of Baku by the Red Army unless the Turkish Communist Party requested it. In the opinion of the Committee, shared by the Turkish and Azerbaijani Communist parties, invasion of Azerbaijan should be avoided.[58]

The Turkish Communists transmitted this resolution to Karabekir Pasha, who used it to draft instructions for the Turkish military mission to Moscow. To his recommendations dated April 8 Karabekir added that Turkey should pressure the Baku government to accept the "aims and principles" of the Bolsheviks and to join the "group of the Soviet states."[59] Anticipating success in this undertaking, the Turks saw no necessity for Soviet military action in Azerbaijan. In fact, Karabekir echoed the concern of many Turkish and Azerbaijani Communists who possibly hoped to use the pasha in a roundabout way to reinforce their own arguments against the entry of the Red Army with the Russians. Karabekir's recommendations, with some modifications, were incorporated into the letter that Mustafa Kemal sent to Lenin on April 28 but that did not reach Moscow until June.[60] By that time the good offices of the Ankara regime had become superfluous, as the Soviets had already taken over Azerbaijan.

In yet one more attempt to soften the impact of the forthcoming invasion, a deputation of the AzCP(B) under E. A. Kvantaliani called on the headquarters of the Eleventh Army in Petrovsk, where they sought and received assurances that the Red troops would refrain from crossing into Azerbaijan for at least twenty four hours after the start of the coup the party was planning at that very moment.[61]

Of the Turks in Baku, Halil Pasha played the most active role. He tried to convince the Azerbaijanis that they had no reason to fear the entry of the Red forces, which, he argued, were only marching in transit on their way to Karabagh, Armenia, and then to Anatolia where they would join the Turkish war of liberation. Halil was even able to offer proof of Russian good intentions: He, Halil, was soon to assume command of the Eleventh Army. Meanwhile, the Ittihad in street demonstrations against the government charged that the pro-Western leaders of the Musavat had blocked the Red Army from rushing to the aid of Turkey.[62] In expectation of assuming his new command, Halil left Baku on April 26 for Daghestan. Here the Eleventh Army commander, Levandovski, informed him that Moscow had said nothing about his apppointment, whereupon Halil headed for the Russian capital for further discussions.[63]

The Azerbaijani Communists finally made their position clear to the premier-designate: They would not accept any portfolios, but if Hajinski behaved properly toward them, they would not oppose his cabinet in the near future. In effect, the Communists told Hajinski not to disturb them so that they could prepare his downfall at their leisure. In desperation, he begged for admission to the Communist Party, and to alleviate his fears for his personal safety the Communists gave him a meaningless membership card.[64] On April 22, Hajinski told the stunned Parliament of the failure of his mission. In the panic and confusion that followed, many high officials packed up and boarded trains for Tiflis. Others, such as Rustambäkov, clung to the notion of a dictatorship of the Musavat – or more precisely, of its right wing – a doomed prospect without the backing of the army.[65] Still others arranged for a government delegation to meet with Ordzhonikidze with an offer of oil deliveries and economic cooperation. These trade talks continued until news arrived from Baku of the fall of the republic.

The Commmunist seizure of power

The leaders of the AzCP(B) decided that the situation was ripe for proceeding with their plan for a coup, which they fixed for April 27. Three days before, on April 24, poorly armed Communist fighting squads began mobilizing in anticipation of the signal for action. On April 25 all party committees were put under the orders of combat commands with the warning that anyone found guilty of insubordination would be punished by death.[66]

7. The coming of Soviet power

Shortly after midnight on the fateful twenty-seventh of April, telephones rang in Baku with reports that four armored trains had crossed the border at Yalama station and that General Shikhlinski had failed to carry out his orders to blow up the railway bridges. The news must have surprised the Azerbaijani Communists, for the Russians had disregarded the twenty-four-hour waiting period.[67] In the morning, while the Red Army trains, now well on their way to Baku, were crushing the token resistance of the Azerbaijanis, the Central Committee of the AzCP(B) issued a proclamation. It announced the overthrow of the "treacherous, criminal, counterrevolutionary" government of the Musavat Party and declared that the only lawful authority was now the Provisional Azerbaijani Military–Revolutionary Committee (Azrevkom) consisting of Narimanov, Huseynov, Musabäkov, Buniatzadä, Alimov, and Garayev.[68]

The Azrevkom was nonetheless concerned about maintaining an appearance of legality in the takeover. At noon, as Parliament met in an emergency session, Sultanov delivered an ultimatum demanding that the body surrender all its powers within twelve hours. The ultimatum (as the Parliament's reply made clear) also contained various assurances, some of a face-saving nature and others intended to guarantee the safety of the overthrown regime's personnel.

While the deputies deliberated, the Communist sailors of the Caspian flotilla turned the guns of their warships toward the Parliament building. Equally menacing was the posture of the Parliamentary Guard Regiment, which consisted of Turks.[69] At the beginning of the emergency session the war minister, Makhmändiarov, declared that armed resistance was unthinkable. Some deputies called for transfer of the government to Ganja, whence it could direct a war of defense, but they were in a distinct minority. The Ittihad and the socialists expressed their joyful acceptance of Soviet power.[70] The Ahrar, as a party of the people, saw no reason to oppose the Communists, who stood for the same interests of the masses. Speaking on behalf of the Musavat, Räsulzadä voiced reservations. He warned that

even if supposedly the commander of the entering army is a Turk, the army is still Russian, it is an invading force; its goal is to establish the frontier along the 1914 line. Having come here under the pretext of marching to Anatolia, it will not willingly leave our country. There is no need for surrender to the Bolsheviks by accepting unconditionally the ultimatum in order to reach an understanding with Red Russia.[71]

Räsulzadä's preference was for "a government of radical deputies, provided with extraordinary powers, who would secure the cooperation of struggling Turkey and revolutionary Russia." In the end, he declared that since all the other parties were unwilling to defend the independence of the republic, and since the Musavat could not shoulder this task alone, his party accepted no responsability for whatever happened.[72] He then joined in the task of drafting Parliament's reply to the Azrevkom.

As the reply was being prepared, the Menshevik–Himmätist Aghamalioghlï seized upon the dire threat of the invasion to harangue the deputies into submission:

Let no one dare to gamble with any resistance, let no one risk bringing destruction upon the city and shedding innocent blood! And for whose sake? Because of the change of government now under way, which will bring to power, instead of Ussubäkov, Khoiski, and other defenders of parasites and idlers, such men as Narimanov, Mirza Davud [Huseynov], and others who defend the interests of the workers and peasants.[73]

At 11:00 P.M. on April 27, 1920, Parliament voted, with one deputy opposing and one abstaining, that it had accepted the following conditions to communicate to the Communists:

1. Full independence of Azerbaijan under Soviet power will be maintained.
2. The government formed by the Communist Party of Azerbaijan will have provisional authority.
3. The final system of government in Azerbaijan will be determined without any outside pressure, by the supreme legislative organ of Azerbaijan, the Soviet of Azerbaijani Workers, Peasants, and Soldiers.
4. All functionaries of the governmental agencies will retain their posts and only persons holding positions of responsibility will be replaced.
5. The newly formed provisional Communist government guarantees the life and property of the members of the present government and parliament.
6. It will take measures to prevent the entry of the Red Army under battle conditions.
7. The new government will resist, using strong measures and all the means at its disposal, all outside forces, from whatever quarter, aiming at the suppression of Azerbaijani independence.[74]

With this act of abdication the experiment in Azerbaijani inde-

7. The coming of Soviet power

pendent statehood officially came to an end, one hour before the deadline set by the Bolshevik ultimatum.

The takeover was almost bloodless, and outside Parliament few people were aware of the drama played out within its walls. The population's only present concern was the imminent entry of Red troops into Baku. "By the evening of April 27 a strange atmosphere of tension hung over the city," wrote a correspondent of a Communist newspaper.

Streets were full of people. They gathered in small groups, whispered one to another. The news that the Red Army was on its way, that it had already taken the Khachmas station, rapidly spread throughout the city. The disturbed philistines kept repeating: If we could only avoid armed clashes. They went to bed full of anxiety. ... The city fell asleep not knowing what the transition to the new regime would be like, and how would this new regime would act. The evening newspapers which came out under the next day's date, April 28, kept silent about what was afoot. These were their last editions.

April 28, 1920: This day brought brisk liveliness to all corners of the city. In the streets there began to appear scenes typical of the revolutionary seizure of power. An armored vehicle rumbled noisily on the pavement. Trucks rushed around filled with workers clutching rifles in their calloused hands. On Sadova Street by the Naberezhnaia, students were registering to join the fighting squads. Trucks distributed weapons in the working class districts. ... The Baku population, having visualized bloody clashes, felt relieved because of the instantaneous transition to the new regime. Some welcomed it sincerely, others with fear in their hearts.[75]

On the same day the Azrevkom sent a telegram to Lenin officially announcing that the "Musavatist" government had been overthrown and requesting that Soviet Russia provide fraternal assistance as the new Soviet power in Azerbaijan was "unable to hold off with its own forces the pressure of internal and external counterrevolution."[76] By this time the streets of Baku were swarming with men in Red Army uniforms; Levandowski had already set up his headquarters in the city, having arrived there ahead of his troops. April 28 also marked the formation of the Azerbaijani Sovnarkom with an all-native membership consisting mostly of ex-Himmätists. The chairman and commissar for foreign affairs was Narimanov; other commissars were H. N. Sultanov (internal affairs), J. Ildirim (military and naval affairs), A. H. Garayev (labor and justice), H. M. Musabäkov (agriculture, commerce, and industry), M. D. Huseynov (finance), J. Väzirov (postal and telegraph services), and A. Älimov (health).[77] This was a moment of triumphant fullfillment for the most radical segment of the Azerbaijani intelligentsia, although they could have few illusions that the ultimate power rested with Ordhzonikidze's Kavbiuro.

Lenin, in acknowledging the change of regime in Baku, assessed the event primarily in terms of Russia's economic needs, finding in it solace for reverses that the Bolsheviks had suffered elsewhere: "Yesterday brought us two pieces of news, one of them quite grievious," he said at a public meeting.

The Polish government had decided to abandon its recent policy of maneuvering in the question of negotiating with us and began hostilities on a broad front. Poland has already taken Zhitomir and is moving on to Kiev. . . . On the other hand, we received yesterday news from Baku which indicates that our industry has taken a turn for the better. We all know that our industry has come to a standstill for the lack of fuel, but now the news comes that the Baku proletariat has taken the power in its hands and overthrew the Azerbaijani government. This means that we now have such an economic base that can put life back into our industry.[78]

Two weeks before the coup, Lenin had already appointed an official to take charge of the Baku oil, A. P. Serebrovski, who immediately upon the entry of the Red troops began to organize shipments to Russia.[79]

The aftermath of the conquest

In the emerging governmental structure of Soviet Azerbaijan the supreme executive as well as the legislative organ was the Azrevkom. Ironically, sovietization turned out to mean an absence of soviets, which by definition were elective bodies. The only exception was in Baku, where there were sufficient numbers of reliable voters. Otherwise, the territorial administration passed into the hands of hundreds of *revkoms* (revolutionary committees), each appointed from above: on the *uezd* level by the Commissariat for Internal Affairs and in townships and villages by their *uezd* equivalents. Because in many parts of the country not enough Communists could be found to constitute a *revkom*, typically a chairman would be sent in from Baku and members

7. The coming of Soviet power

recruited from among the local population, even those with non-Communist affiliations in the past.[80]

Political parties, with the obvious exception of the AzCP(B), were disbanded, not always on the Azrevkom's order. Following the coup, the Ittihad issued a statement to the effect that the party had seen the fullfillment of its goals with the April 27 revolution and therefore advised its members to join the ranks of the Communists.[81] In a similar manner, the Menshevik–Himmät, whose leaders had for some time declared themselves Bolsheviks in everything but name, dissolved itself. Within a year Aghamalioghlï would become commissar for agriculture, the first of his many posts in the Soviet government. Abilov was appointed Azerbaijani ambassador to Ankara, and two other prominent Mensheviks, Jämalbäkov and Saniyev, entered the service of the Cheka. Of the socialist bloc leaders who had supported the Bolshevik takeover, Safikiurdski and Riza Karasharov were rewarded with positions in the Baku Soviet. In the case of the Musavat, its left wing attempted to avert dissolution of the party by reorganization under its aegis. A conference of left-wing Musavatists on April 28 endorsed cooperation with the Azrevkom with the reservation that the Bolsheviks "observe the obligations given and signed by them."[82] Among the leaders of the left-wing Musavat, Räsulzadä was the beneficiary of a special consideration, probably on account of his Himmätist past and personal links with the Bolsheviks. Later in the year he was invited by his long-time acquaintance from 1905, Stalin, to Moscow, where he reportedly was offered a high government post in Azerbaijan. In 1922 he succeeded in escaping from Russia to begin the life of an itinerant national leader in exile.[83] Like many others, Räsulzadä made use of the hospitality extended by Kemalist Turkey, the country that in the end became the favorite haven for Azerbaijani political refugees.

Some prominent figures of the old regime fared less well. Selective arrests and the first executions started on the morrow of April 27 and reached a crescendo of bloody reprisals a few weeks later in the wake of spreading resistance to the Communist rule. Among the fatalities were Ussubäkov, General Sulkiewicz, Ziyatkhanov, Rafibäkov, Khan Khoiski, and Aghazadä, the last two assassinated in their exile in Tiflis.[84]

The Bolshevik intention was to carry forward the impetus that had gained for them the prize of Azerbaijan, and their next moves branched out in two directions. The first was westward, aiming at the conquest of the remainder of Transcaucasia. Ordzhonikidze believed that a few short weeks would be enough to overrun Georgia and Armenia. The main force of the Eleventh Army raced across the plains of Azerbaijan and in early May deployed on her western borders. The expectation was that in each of the neighboring republics the drama that had unfolded in Baku, a classic scenario for the seizure of power, would be reenacted: a Communist revolt synchronized with the entry of the Red troops. Yet the Communist underground in both Georgia and Armenia proved to be weaker than in Baku and the local regimes possessed of a stronger will to survive.[85] A small uprising that broke out in Tiflis on May 2 was put down by the government at once. In some towns of Armenia, May Day demonstrations led to chaotic fighting against the Dashnakist government forces, with the result that the local Communist organizations were almost totally destroyed.[86] The Eleventh Army was hardly more fortunate: As its advance elements crossed the Georgian frontier they met with vigorous counterattacks. It became obvious that the invasion would be a long, drawn-out, costly affair, an unwelcome prospect for Soviet Russia at a time when it had its hands full with the Polish war. On May 5 Lenin cabled Ordzhonikidze ordering him to stop the hostilities, and two days later Russia and Georgia hastily signed a peace treaty in which Moscow unconditionally recognized the independence of Georgia.[87]

The other direction of the Bolshevik drive was the southward penetration of Persia, the propects of which were enhanced by the spread of revolutionary movements in Persian Azerbaijan and Gilan. Khiabani's Democratic Party, after months of preparation, staged a revolt in Tabriz against the Tehran government on April 15, 1920, virtually on the eve of the fall of Baku. The rebels proclaimed an autonomous republic under the name *Azadistan* ("Land of Freedom") rather than *Azerbaijan*, to distance themselves from the Baku "Musavatist" regime.[88] The program of the Tabriz revolt indicated a friendly disposition toward Soviet Russia, hostility to British imperialism, and, somewhat contradictorily, a tendency toward separatism as well as the desire to speak for the interests of all Persia. The main points of this program were:

1. Elimination of the predatory presence of foreign powers in Persia
2. Expulsion from Persian Azerbaijan of the officials appointed by the Tehran government
3. Faithful implementation of the constitution
4. Struggle for democracy against the Great Powers and their Persian allies
5. Establishment of diplomatic and trade relations with Soviet Russia.[89]

The political aims of Khiabani's movement – whose followers, largely merchants and artisans, called themselves liberals – have been the subject of diverse interpretations.[90] Soviet Azerbaijani historians add one specific trait to desciptions of Khiabani, presenting him as an apostle of the Azerbaijani national liberation struggle, a man whose significance for both parts of the country is comparable to that of Sattar Khan.[91] In fact, Khiabani, who had no use for Pan-Azerbaijani solidarity with the imperialist-backed Musavatists, viewed the Bolshevik coup in Baku positively, regarding it as the victory of the former Himmätists. Soon, however, he began to have second thoughts as evidence accumulated indicating that the last word in Baku belonged to the Russians and that they were moreover pursuing a policy of expansion. On May 18 the Red forces raided the port of Enzeli, where they established a base of operations in support of the Soviet-type local regime of Mirza Kuchuk Khan in Gilan.[92] Khiabani, now increasingly suspicious of Soviet Russia, reacted as an indignant Persian patriot, at the same time continuing his rebellion against Tehran. Declaring that foreigners, be they Russian or British, had no right to intervene in the internal affairs of Persia, he warned that should the Bolsheviks attempt to annex any part of Persian territory, the Persian Azerbaijanis would fight against them to the last man.[93] Such a contingency did not occur, but Khiabani's Azadistan soon became a haven for insurgents opposing Soviet power north of the Araxes.

Within a month of the seizure of Baku, the Soviet thrust beyond Azerbaijan had lost its momentum. This realization contributed to the restiveness of the Azerbaijanis as they recovered from the demoralizing shock of the swift conquest. Opposition was neither unified nor to any large degree organized, although there emerged two centers of anti-Soviet political activity: the Committee for the Salvation of Azerbaijan established by the refugees in Tiflis and the clandestine association of young Musavatists.[94] The mainspring of the challenge to Communist rule consisted of the spontaneous reactions of the population, disaffected as they were by massive food requisitions, the harsh arbitrariness of the Soviet government, as well as its militant secularism. The spirit of discontent also spread to the Azerbaijani troops, which had been hardly noted for their deep attachment to the old regime. Specific grievances among the military stemmed from attempts to remodel the Azerbaijani army on the Red Russian pattern, a process that involved the dismissal of officers and breaking up of units. The decision to replace the commander of the Ganja garrison, Colonel Mirza Qajar, and his staff by Red Army officers set off the first and most violent of the Azerbaijani uprisings.[95] Thus, belatedly, opened the true Battle of Azerbaijan.

The Ganja garrison, eighteen hundred strong, mutinied on the night of May 28 and proceeded to seize the Muslim part of the town.[96] Heavy fighting centered around the railroad station, where the Azerbaijanis attempted to dislodge the Russians keeping open the rail line for reinforcements. When large Red Army forces hastily arrived by rail, Ganja was surrounded and cut off from the countryside. On May 29 the Russians launched a series of attacks, only to be repelled with heavy losses, but in the end the Russians' superior artillery carried the day. Some one thousand mutineers perished; others managed to escape to the mountains, where a number of armed groups were already gathering.[97] The retribution that followed was massive and ruthless. Sultanov, arriving from Baku to supervise the suppression of the uprising, ordered several hundred summary executions. Outside Ganja, an extensive purge of the army claimed among its victims six generals, six colonels, three majors, and seven captains. Most of the latter were among the group of seventy-nine men shot on the island of Nargin the day after the Ganja mutiny broke out.[98]

A special order issued by the Eleventh Army command conveys a sense of alarm in its guidelines for dealing with the expected spread of insurgency: The Red forces were to concentrate into large units, no smaller than brigade strength, and occupy

7. The coming of Soviet power

points suitable for prolonged defence. Wire communications were to be backed up by cavalry detachments maintaining contact among strongholds. The order foresaw the possibility that the "disturbances rooted in national and religious prejudices [may] assume a massive character,"[99] in which case the army units were to withdraw to Baku as a base for counteroffensives. For the present, commanders in the field were ordered to take steps to disarm the population: Persons who hid their weapons or attempted resistance were to be executed on the spot; those who handed in their arms voluntarily were to be given substantial cash rewards – up to 3000 rubles for a rifle, from 1 to 5 rubles for a cartridge.[100]

In retrospect, these precautionary measures seem excessive given the character of the anti-Soviet uprisings and their scope. The insurgency did in fact spread over some parts of the country, but never exceeded the Ganja fighting in intensity. Only after that strategically vital town had been thoroughly pacified and the Russian forces deployed for combat elsewhere did a major uprising begin in Karabagh. At its head stood Nuri Pasha, now like many other Pan-Islamists disillusioned with the Bolsheviks. The insurgents seized Shusha, where an Azerbaijani infantry regiment passed over to their side, but soon came face to face with a Red Army cavalry division supported by an air squadron. Although the Reds were threatened by another uprising in Zakataly, they easily retook Shusha on June 15. Nuri's force disintegrated soon afterward, its remnants retreating across the Persian frontier to the area held by Khiabani.[101]

In Zakataly, the direct cause of the revolt was the order of the local *revkom* to disarming the inhabitants, but the movement also exhibited the characteristics of a religiously inspired uprising. A *molla* (cleric), Hafiz Äfandiyev, assumed leadership and brought under his command a thousand villagers and a regular Azerbaijani army batallion.[102] After ten days of fighting the rebels dispersed, some taking refuge in the mountains of the neutral zone between Georgia and Azerbaijan.

While harsh repressive measures blunted the edge of the insurgency, its effectiveness suffered further from the weaknesses inherent in spontaneous rural rebellions. In their limited scope, lack of coordination, and short duration, the Azerbaijani anti-Soviet uprisings resembled nothing so much as the insurrectionary movements in the traditional society of the first half of the nineteenth century. Just as a hundred years before, these widely scattered revolts were put down quickly, separately, one after another. Even though the Russians could no longer exploit Sunni–Shi'a antagonism, they occasionally sent against the insurgents detachments of native workers, thereby introducing an element of civil war, this time of city versus countryside.[103]

Still, the insurgency continued, albeit haltingly. A new wave of unrest began in September 1920, the same month delegates from thirty-eight countries met in Baku for the First Congress of the Peoples of the East. This festive occasion, intended to celebrate the triumph of the Communist revolution in Azerbaijan and to herald its further advance in Asia, was followed by a series of Muslim uprisings against Soviet rule. Of these, the most extensive broke out in Daghestan, where it threatened to cut off Eleventh Army communications with Russia. In this traditional stronghold of Muslim resistance fighting continued well into the spring of 1921 in the name of defense of the Shari'a. The struggle made its impact felt on Azerbaijan in various ways, but most notably by example and encouragement.[104] The Daghestani guerilla leaders, Imam Gotsinski, Said-bey, and Ali Khanov, found those who, primarily out of religious impulse, emulated them in Azerbaijan. In the Kuba *uezd* Hafiz Äfändiyev raised a group of five thousand fighters; in Karabulak a guerilla force led by Jammad bäy was active, in Karadanli another one under Khan Shirvanski. In November 1920 a large band led by a certain Namaz seized mountain passes in the Dzegam River valley, tying up Red Army forces for weeks. At the end of the year the southern coastal area of Lenkoran was the scene of a major revolt that could be put down only by a complex military operation involving combined attacks by sea and land.[105]

All-but-final blows were dealt to Azerbaijani armed resistance, which smoldered until 1924, by the Soviet conquests of Armenia on December 2, 1920 and of Georgia on March 18, 1921. With the fall of these two independent republics, the Communists consolidated their hold over Azerbaijan, confirming once again the indivisibility of the fate of the Transcaucasian peoples in the face of their giant neighbor.

Conclusion

In 1905 *Azerbaijan* was still merely a geographical term describing a stretch of land partitioned between Russia and Persia. The only articulated group identity of its inhabitants was that of being Muslim, and their collective consciousness expressed itself primarily in terms of the universalistic *'umma*. The period between this date and the Soviet conquest of Baku in 1920 witnessed the rise of the independent republic, which purported to be the embodiment of the Azerbaijani nation. These fifteen years would seem to be an astonishingly short time for a transformation of such magnitude – were it not for two basic facts of history.

First, Azerbaijani society had been in many ways prepared for this transformation by the preceding century of Russian rule. The main effect of this rule was to integrate Azerbaijan by ending the political fragmentation of the khanate period and by unifying the country's economy. A cultural and social by-product of the contact with Russia was the rise of the intelligentsia, a group that subsequently sought to assume leadership of the emerging community. The role of the intelligentsia represented the native effort at integration. This was pursued by healing Sunni–Shi'a antagonism and promoting education and modern forms of communication in the new literary language. Also, the secular-minded intelligentsia was that part of society first affected by the waning of *'umma* consciousness, which it sought to replace with the ethnocentric ideas of the Turkic *qavm* and Azerbaijani *millät*.

Second, from 1905 on, Azerbaijan was subject to a succession of upheavals and crises that immensely accelerated its political development: three revolutions in Russia, one each in neighboring Persia and Turkey, a world war, and two foreign occupations, one Ottoman and one British.

The era of stability and gradual changes reaching back many decades into the nineteenth century had come to an end. The intelligentsia, stimulated by the turbulent currents of history, began to claim the role of spokesman for Azerbaijani aspirations. In some respects, this was a process resembling the rise of movements for national emancipation among other peoples of Russia, but it possessed distinct qualities stemming from the Islamic context. In the universalistic tradition of Islam the very idea of a nation as a group identity was a novelty. This was an idea that had come to Azerbaijan in the wake of the impact of Europe, largely through the intermediation of Russia, and it was not inherently anti-Russian. In fact, Azerbaijani attitudes toward Russia were always ambivalent. Already Akhundzadä expressed the typical dilemma: on the one hand a deep attachment to the native cultural heritage, on the other an appreciation for Russia as a vehicle of much needed change. In various forms and degrees this attitude would reappear in the thinking of most Azerbaijani intellectuals, including the twentieth-century nationalists. Then, such intellectual considerations were in harmony with the interests of the Azerbaijani economy, which since the onset of the oil boom had expanded in direct proportion to the needs of the Russian market.

Other factors than the impact of Europe and Russia that shaped incipient national consciousness in Azerbaijan were a sense of unity with the world of Islam, of ethnic affinity with the Ottomans, and of identity with the Persian Azerbaijanis. All the same, Azerbaijani leaders possessed a strong awareness of native particularism that kept them from being subordinated to broader-based movements, whether All-Russian Muslim unity, Pan-Turkism, or Transcaucasian federalism. As Azerbaijani aspirations grew they found expression in political programs, each reflecting the fluid circumstances of the moment. Such programs were invariably linked to orientations toward an outside power that conceivably could further Azerbaijani interests. Thus, the program-minimum of the nascent national movement, autonomy within the Russian state, was also an orientation toward the cause of revolution in Russia. When the revolution in Russia either failed, as in 1907, or offered no prospects for help in attaining

Conclusion

autonomy, as in 1918, the Azerbaijanis would shift their hopes to Turkey. Pan-Turkism as an ideology contributed greatly to the growth of national consciousness, and the Azerbaijanis increasingly became aware of their Turkishness, but the Ottoman orientation did not sit well with their ambition to run the affairs of their country by themselves. Out of the failures of the Russian revolutionary and Ottoman orientations there emerged, almost by default, the program of independent Azerbaijani statehood. This had been foreshadowed by the intermediate stage of Transcaucasian federalism, a program destroyed by national animosities and outside pressures.

The period of the Azerbaijani Democratic Republic was the high water mark in the evolution of the national movement, but still not the fulfillment of its program-maximum, a distinction reserved for the little-articulated idea of uniting the two parts of Azerbaijan. Even the program of the Azerbaijani nation-state was linked to a foreign orientation of a most improbable character: an orientation toward Great Britain, a distant power with a fleeting interest in Transcaucasia. Not surprisingly, the period of full independence that followed the British military withdrawal turned out to be the twilight of the republic, marked by a desperate search for means of survival and by internal dissention.

Azerbaijani political development suffered from the existence of a chasm separating the Europeanized elite and the tradition-bound masses, even though the elite was possessed of flexibility, moderation, open-mindedness, and political sophistication. While the intelligentsia experienced an evolution that took it in quick succession from Pan-Islamism to Turkism to Azerbaijanism, the masses remained on the level of *'umma* consciousness with its typical indifference to secular power, foreign or native. The idea of an Azerbaijani nation-state did not take root among the majority of the population; the very term *nationalism* was either not understood by them or, worse, it rang with the sound of a term of abuse, a fact the Communists exploited in their propaganda against the Azerbaijani Republic. This might help explain why the overthrow of the republic was amazingly easy. Even those who subsequently rebelled against Soviet rule did not fight for the restoration of the fallen regime.

The native Communists who inherited power from the republic shared the general outlook of the intelligentsia rather than that of the masses; indeed, they were part of the national movement's socially radical wing. For all the hostility they expressed toward counterrevolutionary bourgeois nationalism, they recognized the validity of the state as a form of national existence. At the same time they cherished no illusions regarding the possibility of any Azerbaijani state remaining independent. "For Soviet Russia, the union with Georgia and Armenia is not a matter of particular importance – but Baku – that is the very life of Soviet Russia," Narimanov warned his old-time acquaintance Ussubäkov.[1]

Under the circumstances, the Hämmätists strove to strike the best deal attainable, which could mean no more than some form of autonomy. But then, in all truth, independent statehood had not been the consistently pursued goal of the national movement. Rather, it had set its sights on the more realistic prospect of autonomy, the program outlined in great detail by the Musavat in the fall of 1917. To achieve national autonomy, the Himmätists put up a struggle in the councils of the Russian party, where they displayed remarkable tenacity and unity. The Russian Communists, for whom the very reference to an autonomous Azerbaijan had been anathema as late as 1918, came around to recognize the claims of their Azerbaijani comrades. In fact, what seemed at first a concession to the nationalist sentiments of local leftists heralded the long-range Soviet policy toward Russia's Muslims. This policy amounted to the continuation, and indeed, acceleration of the development of distinct national identities among the Muslims, a course of action intended to wean them away from the Islamic past of their traditional societies.

Abbreviations

The following abbreviations are used in the notes and the bibliography:

A.I.S.	Azärbayjan Injä Sanaati
A.J.	Asiatic Journal
A.K.A.K	Akty sobrannye Kavkazskuiu Arkheograficheskuiu Kommissieiu
A.N.Az.S.S.R.	Akademiia Nauk Azerbaidzhanskoi Sotsialisticheskoi Sovetskoi Respubliki
A.N.Az.S.S.R., Iztvestiia, Ser.Ob.N.	Seriia Obshestvennykh Nauk
A.N.Az.S.S.R.,Izvestiia, S.Ist.Fil.Pr.	Seriia Istorii, Filosofii i Prava
A.N.Az.S.S.R., Ser. Lit. Iaz. Issk.	Seriia Literatury, Iazyka i Isskustva
A.N.S.S.S.R.	Akademiia Nauk Soiuza Sotsialisticheskikh Sovetskikh Respublik
A.R.	Asiatic Review
A.T.	Azeri Türk
A.Y.B.	Azerbaycan Yurt Bilgisi
Az.G.U., Uchenye Zapiski	Azerbaidzhanskii Gosudarstvennyi Universitet, Uchenye Zapiski
I.J.M.E.S.	International Journal of Middle Eastern Studies
J.A.	Journal Asiatique
J.R.A.S.	Royal Asiatic Society, Journal
K.P.Az., Ts.K.	Kommunisticheskaia Partiia Azerbaidzhana, Tsentral'nyi Komitet
M.E.J.	Middle East Journal

Abbreviations

M.I.	Mir Islama
M.N.P., Zhurnal	Ministerstvo Narodnogo Prosveshcheniia, Zhurnal
M.S.O.S.	Seminar fur der Orientalische Sprächen, Mitteilungen
R.M.M.	Revue du Monde Musulmane
S.M.O.M.P.K.	Sbornik Materialov dlia Opisaniia Mestnostei i Plemen Kavkaza
T.A.	Türk Amacı
T.K.	Türk Kültürü
T.M.	Türkiyat Mecmuası
T.T.K., Belleten	Türk Tarih Kurumu, Belleten
T.Y.	Türk Yurdu
W.I.	Welt des Islams
Z.D.M.G.	Deutsche Morgenlandische Gesellschaft, Zeitschrift

Notes

Chapter 1. A century of Russian rule

1. On Azerbaijan before the mid-eighteenth century, see A.N.Az.S.S.R., *Istoriia Azerbaidzhana* (Baku, 1958), vol. 1; V. Bartol'd, *Mesto prikaspiiskikh oblastei v istorii musul'manskogo mira* (Baku, 1925); A.K. Alizade, *Sotsial'no-ekonomicheskaia i politicheskaia istoriia Azerbaidzhana XII–XIV vv* (Baku, 1956); D. Ibragimov, *Feodal'nye gosudarstva na territorii Azerbaidzhana XVveka* (Baku, 1952); F. Sümer, Azerbaycanın türkleşmesi tarihine umumi bir bakış, *T.T.K., Belleten* 21 (1957), 429–47; P.B. Golden, "The Turkic Peoples and Caucasia," in R. G. Suny(ed.), *Transcaucasia: Nationalism and Social Change* (Ann Arbor, University of Michigan, 1983), pp. 45–68.
2. On the khanates, see G. Leviatov, *Ocherki po istorii Azerbaidzhana XVIII veka* (Baku, 1948); G. Abdullaev, *Azerbaidzhan v XVIII veke i vzaimootnosheniia s Rossiei* (Baku, 1965), pp. 86–111; I. P. Petrushevski, *Ocherki po istorii feodal'nykh otnoshenii v Azerbaidzhane i Armenii v XVI – nachale XIX veka* (Leningrad, 1949).
3. On the government of the khanates, see Abdullaev, *Vzaimootnosheniia*, pp. 105–11; A. Mil'man, *Politicheskii stroi Azerbaidzhana v XIX – nachale XX vekov* (Baku, 1966), pp. 39–49.
4. On the land tenure in the khanate period, see Petrushevski, *Ocherki*, pp. 184–207; idem, "Persidskie ofitsial'nye dokumenty kak istochnik dlia istorii feodal'nykh otnoshenii v Azerbaidzhane i Armenii," *Problemy istochnikovedeniia* 3 (1940), pp. 5–44; I. M. Gasanov, *Chasnovladetel'cheskie krest'iane v Azerbaidzhane pervoi poloviny XIX veka* (Baku, 1957). For a collection of documentary sources, see A.N.S.S.S.R., Gruzinskii Filial, *Ukazy kubinskikh khanov* (Tbilisi, 1937).
5. Abdullaev, *Vzaimootnosheniia*, pp. 182–281; idem, *Iz istorii Severo-Vostochnogo Azerbaidzhana v 60–80 gg. XVIII veka* (Baku, 1958), pp. 36–136; I. Gadzhinski, "Zhizn' Fet-Ali-Khana Kubinskogo," *Sbornik gazety Kavkaz* (Tiflis), (1847), 213–33.

6. On Russia's expansion into the Caucasus, see A. V. Fadeev, *Rossiia i Kavkaz v pervoi tretii XIX veka* (Moscow, 1958); N. A. Smirnov, *Politika Rossii na Kavkaze v XIV–XIX vekakh* (Moscow, 1958); J. F. Baddeley, *The Russian Conquest of the Caucasus* (London, 1908); P. Butkov, *Materialy dlia novoi istorii Kavkaza* (St. Petersburg, 1869); F. Kazemzadeh, "Russian Penetration of the Caucasus," in T. Hunczak (ed.) *Russian Imperialism from Ivan the Great to the Revolution* (New Brunswick, N.J., 1974), pp. 239–63.
7. On the first Russian penetration into Azerbaijan, see A. Abdurrakhmanov, *Azerbaidzhan vo vzaimootnosheniakh Rossii, Turtsii i Irana v pervoi polovine XVIII veka* (Baku, 1964), pp. 26–32.
8. D. M. Lang, *The Last Years of the Georgian Monarchy, 1685–1832* (New York, 1957), pp. 183–4; M. Atkin, *Russia and Iran, 1780–1828* (Minneapolis, 1980), pp. 22–45.
9. A. S. Sumbatzade and G. Mekhtiev, "Prisoedinenie Azerbaidzhana k Rossii i ego istoricheskoe znachenie," in A.N.Az.S.S.R., *Prisoedinenie Azerbaidzhana k Rossii i ego progressivnye posledstviia v oblasti ekonomiki i kul'tury* (Baku, 1955), p. 28.
10. N. Dubrovin, *Zakavkaz'e ot 1803 do 1906 g.* (St. Petersburg, 1866) p. 50.
11. On the siege of Ganja, see ibid., pp. 211–23; Baddeley, p. 67.
12. On Tsitsianov, see Atkin, pp. 71–85; Fadeev, p. 125.
13. On this Russo–Persian war, see Atkin, pp. 99–122.
14. *A.K.A.K.*, vol. 5, no. 377; Sumbatzade, Mekhtiev, *Prisoedinenie*, pp. 38–9.
15. For official documents on Azerbaijani attitudes in this war, see *A.K.A.K.*, vol. 6, part 2, no. 651; see also A.N.S.S.S.R., Institut Istorii, *Kolonial'naia politika rossiiskogo tsarizma v Azerbaidzhane v 20–60 gg. XIX veka* (Moscow and Leningrad, 1937).
16. A.N.S.S.S.R., Institut Istorii, *Kolonial'naia politika*, vol. 1, p. 16; A. Vambery, "The Turks in Persia and the Caucasus," *Asiatic Quarterly Review*, 4 (1886), 177.
17. M. A. Ismailov, "Ob uchastii azerbaidzhantsev v riadakh russkikh voisk v russko-iranskikh i russko-turetskikh voinakh pervoi treti XIX veka," *A.N.Az.S.S.R., Trudy* 4 (1954), 10; Kh. M. Ibragimbeili, *Rossiia i Azerbaidzhan v pervoi treti XIX veka* (Moscow, 1968), pp. 154–210; see also V. Potto, *Pervye dobrovol'tsy Karabaga* (Tiflis, 1902).
18. A. R. Ioannisian, *Prisoedinenie Zakavkaz'ia k Rossii i mezhdunarodnye otnosheniia v nachale XIX stoletiia* (Erivan, 1958), pp. 391–446.
19. Ibragimbeili, pp. 216–52; Ismailov, "Ob uchasti," pp. 14–19.
20. Vambery, "The Turks in Persia and the Caucasus," p. 174.
21. The incomplete statistical data published in 1836 estimated the "Tatar" male population of Transcaucasia at 319,000. See *Obozrenie rossiiskikh vladenii za Kavkazom v statisticheskom, topograficheskom i finansovom otnosheniiakh* (St. Petersburg, 1836), vol. 4, p. 361.
22. G. A. Bournoutian, *Eastern Armenia in the Last Decades of Persian Rule, 1807–1828: A Political and Socioeconomic Study of the Khanate of Erevan on the Eve of the Russian Conquest* (Malibu, Calif., 1982),

Notes to pp. 8–13 199

pp. 74–7; Z. T. Grigorian, *Prisoedinenie Vostochnoi Armenii k Rossii v nachale XIX veka* (Moscow, 1959), p. 160.
23. A.N.S.S.S.R., Institut Istorii, *Kolonial'naia politika*, vol. 2, p. 372.
24. L. Widerszal, *Sprawy Kaukaskie w polityce europejskiej* (Warsaw, 1934), p. 174, estimates the number of emigrants from the Caucasus and Transcaucasia in the years 1863–1864 at 220,000. For the population statistics in various years, see *Obozrenie rossiiskikh vladenii; Kavkazskii kalendar*; Kavkazskii Statisticheskii Komitet, *Sbornik svedenii o Kavkaze* (Tiflis, 1871).
25. For documentary material on the Shamil's movement, see A.N.S.S.S.R., Daghestanskii Filial, *Dvizhenie gortsov Severno-Vostochnogo Kavkaza v 20–50 godakh XIX veka* (Makhachkala, 1959). For monographic studies, see A. N. Smirnov, *Miuridizm na Kavkaze* (Moscow, 1963); M. Z. Hizaloğlu, *Şeih Şamil* (Ankara, 1958); S. K. Bushuev, *Bor'ba gortsev za nezavisimost' pod rukovodstvom Shamilia* (Moscow, 1939).
26. A.N.S.S.S.R., Institut Istorii, *Kolonial'naia politika*, vol. 2, p. 8.
27. Ibid.
28. A.N.S.S.S.R., Daghestanskii Filial, *Dvizhenie gortsev*, p. 115.
29. A. S. Sumbatzade, *Kubinskoe vosstanie 1837 goda* (Baku, 1961), pp. 11–12.
30. *A.K.A.K.*, vol. 2, no. 1491.
31. Ibid. 7, nos. 936, 937, 938.
32. Quoted in M. K. Rozhkova, *Ekonomicheskaia politika tsarskogo pravitel'stva na Srednem Vostoke vo vtoroi chetverti XIX veka i russkaia burzhuaziia* (Moscow, 1949), p. 94.
33. Mil'man, p. 146.
34. V. Potto, *Kavkazskaia voina v otdel'nykh ocherkakh, epizodakh, legendakh i biografiakh* (St. Petersburg, 1866), vol. 2, p. 712.
35. Atkin, p. 146.
36. Mil'man, pp. 67–75.
37. *A.K.A.K.*, vol. 8, no. 1.
38. A.N.S.S.S.R., *Kolonial'naia politika*, vol. 1, pp. 20–4; "Iz zapisok barona (v posledstvii grafa) M. A. Korfa," *Russkaia starina* 101 (1900), 33–9.
39. Mil'man, pp. 112–23.
40. I. Gasanov, "K istorii podgotovki reskripta 6 dekabria 1846 goda," *A.N.Az.S.S.R., Trudy* 4 (1954), 25–26; on the Russian settlers, see *A.K.A.K.*, vol. 10, nos. 6, 42, 82.
41. Quoted in Gasanov, "K istorii," p. 27.
42. Quoted in ibid., p. 27.
43. On Vorontsov, see L. H. Rhinelander, "Viceroy Vorontsov's administration of the Caucasus," in Suny, *Transcaucasia*, pp. 87–108; D. M. Lang, *A Modern History of Soviet Georgia* (New York, 1962), pp. 82–6.
44. For the text of the Rescript, see A.N.S.S.S.R., Institut Istorii, *Kolonial'naia politika*, vol. 2, pp. 105–7.
45. Ibid., vol. 2, p. 250.

46. Mil'man, p. 133.
47. Ibid., p. 141.
48. Ibid., p. 156.
49. B. Ischanian, *Nationaler Bestand berufmässige Gruppierung und Gliederung der kaukasischen Völker* (Berlin, 1914), pp. 52–4.
50. Mil'man, p. 217.
51. I. I. Vorontsov-Dashkov, *Vsepoddannieishii otchet za vosem' let upravleniia Kavkazom* (St. Petersburg, 193), p. 27.
52. S. Kurban, *Ali and Nino* (New York, 1972), p. 111.
53. Quoted in Rozhkova, p. 94.
54. Quoted in N. I. Enikopolova, *Griboedov i Vostok* (Erivan, 1954), p. 146.
55. Bartol'd, p. 10.
56. Sumbatzade, Mekhtiev, p. 51.
57. On the nineteenth-century industrialization of Azerbaijan, see A. S. Sumbatzade, *Promyshlennost' Azerbaidzhana v XIX veke* (Baku, 1964); idem, "K voprosu o kharakteristike razvitiia promyshlennogo kapitalizma v Azerbaidzhane vo vtoroi polovine XIX veka," in *A.N.Az.S.S.R., 10 let Akademii Nauk Az.S.S.R.* (Baku, 1957), pp. 623–34.
58. Ts. Agaian, *Krest'ianskaia reforma v Azerbaidzhane* (Baku, 158); A. S. Sumbatzade, *Sel'skoe khoziaistvo Azerbaidzhana v XIX veke* (Baku, 1958), pp. 151–4.
59. I. M. Gasanov, "O proizvodstvennykh otnosheniiakh v gosudarstvennoi derevne Azerbaidzhana v kontse XIX veka," *A.N.Az.S.S.R., Doklady*, no. 8 (1958), 604.
60. Sumbatzade, *Promyshlennost'*, p. 48.
61. For the statistical data on the growth of Azerbaijani towns, see ibid., p. 53.
62. K. A. Pazhitnov, *Ocherki po istorii bakinskoi neftedobyvaiushchei promyshlennosti* (Moscow, 1940); S. M. Lisichkin, *Ocherki po istorii razvitiia otechestvennoi neftianoi promyshlennosti* (Moscow, 1954); M. Ismailov, "Azärbayjan neft sänesindä ijaradarlïg sisteminin läghv edilmäsinä dair," *A.N.Az.S.S.R., Trudy* 2 (1952), 75–104. R. W. Tolf, *The Russian Rockefellers: The Saga of the Nobel Family and the Russian Oil Industry* (Stanford University Press, 1976), pp. 50–108.
63. B. Iu. Akhundov, *Monopolisticheskii kapital v dorevoliutsionnoi bakinskoi promyshlennosti* (Moscow, 1959); M. A. Musayev, *XIX äsrin sonlarïnda Bakï shähärinin tijaräti (1883–1900-ju illär)* (Baku, 1972), pp. 141–8.
64. *Baku po perepisi 22 oktiabria 1903 goda* (Baku, 1905), p. 30.
65. L. Villari, *The Fire and Sword in the Caucasus* (London, 1906), p. 181.
66. A. Alstadt-Mirhadi, "The Azerbaijani Turkish Community of Baku before World War I," Ph.D. dissertation, University of Chicago, 1983, pp. 49–92; I. V. Strigunov, "Bakï proletariatin täshäkkülü mäsäläsina dair," *A.N.Az.S.S.R., Trudy* 10 (1955), 42–77; Akhundov, *Monopolisticheskii kapital*, p. 223.

Notes to pp. 22–25 201

67. Alstadt-Mirhadi, pp. 60–5; R. G. Suny, *The Baku Commune, 1917–1918: Class and Nationality in the Russian Revolution* (Princeton, 1972), p. 7. See also W. Fabritius, "Die heutige Stadt Baku und die Naphtaindustrie in ihrer Umgegend," *Russische Revue* 10 (1877), 33–50.
68. G. Pichkian, "Kapitalisticheskoe razvitie neftianoi promyshlennosti v Azerbaidzhane," Zakavkazskii Kommunisticheskii Universitet, *Istoriia klassovoi bor'by v Zakavkazii* (Tiflis, 1930), pp. 108–10.
69. Musayev, pp. 156–67; D. B. Seidzade, *Iz istorii azerbaidzhanskoi burzhuazii v nachale XX veka* (Baku, 1978), pp. 23–38; Sumbatzade, *Promyshlennost'*, pp. 461–4.
70. On Taghiyev, see "Türk Rokfeleri," *Kurtuluş*, (1937), no. 32, 634. A. Novikov, "Zapiski gorodskogo golovy," *Obrazovanie*, no. 9, part 2 (1904), 126–7.
71. N. A. Tairzade, "Chislennost' i sostav uchashchikhsia russkikh uchebnykh zavedenii Azerbaidzhana v 40–50 gg XIX veka," *A.N.Az.S.S.R., Izvestiia, Ser.Ob.N.*, no. 1 (1964), 43–56.
72. A. G. Teregulov, "V Goriiskoi Uchitel'noi Seminarii," *A.N.Az.S.S.R., Izvestiia*, no. 8 (1945), 69–84.
73. For bibliographical guidance on Akhundzadä, see "M. F. Akhundov v vostokovedcheskoi literature," *A.N.Az.S.S.R., Izvestiia, Ser.Lit.Iaz.Issk.*, no. 2 (1967), 31–7; G. Tagiev, *Bibliografiia o M. F. Akhundove* (Baku, 1948). For monographic works, see Sh. Mamedov, *Mirovozzrenie M. F. Akhundova* (Moscow, 1962); D. Dzhafarov, *M. F. Akhundov* (Moscow, 1962); M. Rafili, *Akhundov* (Moscow, 1959); A. V. Yurtsever, *Mirza Fethali Ahundzadenin hayatı ve eserleri* (Ankara, 1950).
74. On Akhundzadä's plays, see: H. W. Brands, *Aserbaidschanische Volksleben und modernistische Tendenz in den Schauspielen Mirza Feth-Ali Akhundzades* (Wiesbaden, 1958); A. Sultanli, *Azärbayjan dramaturqiyasïnïn inkishafï tarikhindän* (Baku, 1964), pp. 87–134.
75. Quoted in M. F. Akhundov, *Asärläri* (Baku, 1961), vol. 2, p. 44. On the alphabet reform, see A. S. Levend, *Turk dilinde gelişme ve sadeleşme safhaları* (Ankara, 1949), p. 171; "Popytki zakavkazskikh muzul'man reformirovat' svoiu azbuku," *M.I.* 2 (1913), 831–44; R. Tansel, "Arap harflerinin ıslahı ve degiştirilmesi hakkında ilk teşebbüsleri ve neticeleri," *T.T.K. Belleten* 46 (1953), 224–49.
76. Akhundov, M. F., *Äsärläri*, vol. 2, p. 134.
77. Ibid., vol. 2, p. 18; see also F. Adamiyat, *Andishaha-i Mirza Fath 'Ali Akhundzadeh* (Tehran, 1349), pp. 147–8. On Akhundzadä's influence on Persian literature, see H. Algar, *Mirza Malkum Khan: A Study in the History of Iranian Modernism* (Berkeley, Calif., 1973), pp. 264–8; A. M. Aghakhi, "O vliianii M. F. Akhundova na razvitie obshchestvennoi mys'li v Irane," *A.N.Az.S.S.R., Izvestiia, Ser.Ob.N.*, no. 10 (1962), 75–85; H. Mämmadzadä, "M. F. Akhundov vä XIX äsr Iran maarifchilari," ibid., 25–7; A. M. Shoitov, "Rol' M. F. Akhundova v razvitii persidskoi progressivnoi litera-

tury," *A.N.S.S.S.R., Institut Vostokovedeniia, Kratkie soobshcheniia* 9 (1953), 58-65.
78. See Akhundov, vol. 2, pp. 262-83; Y. Akçuraoğlu, "Türkçülük," *Türk Yılı* (1928), 315-18.
79. Akhundov, vol. 2, p. 43.
80. S. Ä. Shirvani, *Äsärläri* (Baku, 1950), vol. 2, p. 8. On the views of Azerbaijani intellectual of the period, see Z. B. Qöyushov, *Azärbayjan maarifchilerinin etik qörüshläri (XIX äsrin ikinji yarïsï* (Baku, 1960).
81. D. Kuliev, "M. F. Akhundov i azerbaidzhanskii iazyk," *A.N.Az.S.S.R., Azerbaidzhanskii Filial, Izvestiia*, no. 6 (1938), 179-92.
82. A. Huseynzadä, *XIX äsrin ikinji yarïsïnda Azärbayjan tarikhshunaslïghï* (Baku, 1967), p. 32.
83. Akhundov, *Äsärläri*, vol. 3, p. 102.
84. H. b. Zardabi, *Sechilmish äsärläri* (Baku, 1976), pp. 219-21; D. Dzhafarov, *Teatr imenii Azizbekova* (Moscow, 1951), pp. 29-43; G. Mammädli, *Azärbayian teatrïnïn salnamäsi (1850-1920)*, Baku, 1975, pp. 45-60.
85. Akhundov, vol. 2, p. 233.
86. On the rise of the Azerbaijani tragedy, see Y. Garayev, "Dramaturqiyamizdä ilk fajiialar," *A.N.Az.S.S.R., Izvestiia, Ser.Ob.N.*, no. 6 (1962), 63-75; G. Yashar, *Azärbayjan ädäbiyyatïndä fajia zhanrï* (Baku, 1965). On Väzirov, see K. Mammädov, *Näjäf bäy Väzirov* (Baku, 1963); on Haqverdiyev, see K. Mammädov, *A. Hagverdiyev* (Baku, 1955). See also Sultanli, pp. 135-67.
87. Z. B. Geiushev, *Mirovozzrenie G. b. Zardabi* (Baku, 1962); see also H. Baykara, *Azerbaycanda yenileşme hareketi* (Ankara, 1966), pp. 132-7; G. Guseinov, *Iz istorii obshchestvennoi i filosofskoi mys'li v Azerbaidzhane* (Baku, 1958), pp. 296-304.
88. For monographic studies of the *Äkinchi*, see S. Huseynov, "Äkinchi gäzetinin izahlï bibliografisi," *A.N.Az.S.S.R., Izvestiia, Ser.Ob.N.*, no. 9 (1959), 81-92; B. S. Baydamirova, "Äkinchi gäzetinin meydana qälmäsi va onun Azärbayjan ijtimai-igtisadi fikir tarikhindä roluna dair," ibid., no. 5 (1963), 107-18; idem, "Äkinchi gazetindä känd tasarrufati mäsäläärinä dair," ibid., no. 1 (1965) 37-47. For general discussion of the newspaper, see D. Hajibeyli, "The Origins of the National Press in Azerbayjan," *A.R.* 25, no. 88 (1930), 758-67; A. Bennigsen and Ch. Lemercier-Quelqujay, *La presse et le mouvements nationaux chez les musulmans de Russie avant 1920* (Paris, 1960). See also T. Hasanzadä (ed.), *Äkinchi, 1875-1877: Tam mätin* (Baku, 1979).
89. A. H. Orujov, "Äkinchi gäzetinin dili haggïnda," *A.N.Az.S.S.R., Doklady* 2, no. 7 (1947), 410-18.
90. *Äkinchi* no. 1 (1877).
91. H. b. Zärdabi, "Rusyada ävvälinji türk gäzeti," *Häyat*, no. 129 (1905), nos. 2, 3 (1906); reprinted in H. b. Zärdabi, *Sechilmish äsärläri* (Baku, 1960), pp. 226-33.
92. Bennigsen and Quelqujay, *La presse*, pp. 27-30; Hajibeyli, "The Origins," pp. 758-67. For monographic studies of particular newspapers, see A. R. Zeynalov, "Ziya gäzetinin näshri tarikhïnä geid-

ler,"*A.N.Az.S.S.R., Doklady* 16, no. 5 (1960), 519–22; idem, "Käshkül zhurnalï va gäzetinin näshri tarikhindän," *A.N.Az.S.S.R., Izvestiia, Ser.Ob.N.*, no. 1 (1959), 75–89; Sh. Novruzov, "XX äsrin ilk Azärbayjan gäzeti Shärg-i Russ," in *A.N.Az.S.S.R., Materialy nauchno-teoreticheskoi konferentsii molodykh uchenykh* (Baku, 1967).
93. For data on *mäktäb*s, see *Kavkazskii Kalendar, 1870–1890*; see also N. A. Tahirzadä, "XIX äsrin 30–50–ji illärdä Azärbayjanda mäktäblar haggïnda," *A.N.Az.S.S.R., Izvestiia, Ser.Ob.N.*, no. 11 (1961), 43–59; A. Zakharov, "Narodnoe obuchenie u kavkazskikh Tatar," *S.M.O.M.P.K.*, part 2 (1890), 7–51.
94. A.N.Az.S.S.R., *Istoriia*, vol. 2, p. 334. Alstadt-Mirhadi, pp. 55–6, gives a higher literacy rate for the Baku Muslim population. On the criticism of the *mäktäb*s, see G. Vezirov, "O tatarskikh shkolakh," *S.M.O,M.P.K.*, part 2 (1890), 1–6.
95. Akhundov, vol. 2, p. 384.
96. D. Validov, *Ocherki istorii obrazovannosti i literatury Tatar*, (Moscow, 1923), pp. 46ff; G. v. Mende, *Der nationale Kampf der Russlandtürken* (Berlin, 1936), pp. 33–6.
97. S. Rybakov, "Novometodisty i starometodisty v russkom muzul'manstve," *M.I.*, 2 (1913), 852–73.
98. For monographic works on Gasprinski, see C. Seydahmet, *Gaspir-Ali Ismail bey* (Istanbul, 1934); E. Lezzerini, "Ismail bey Gasprinski and Muslim Modernism in Russian," Ph.D. dissertation, University of Washington, 1973. See also A. Fisher, *The Crimean Tatars* (Stanford, 1978), pp. 100–6; S. Zenkovsky, *Pan-Turkism and Islam in Russia* (Cambridge, Mass., 1960), pp. 24–36.
99. Guseinov, *Iz istorii*, p. 274.
100. *Käshkül*, no. 22 (1891).
101. For biographical information on Huseynzadä, see Akçuraoğlu, pp. 412–19; I. A. Gövsa, *Türk meşhurları ansiklopedisi* (Istanbul, 1946), p. 386.
102. A. B. Kuran, *Inkılâp tarihimiz ve Ittihad ve Terakki* (Istanbul, 1948), p. 61.
103. Gökalp, Ziya, *The Principles of Turkism* (Leiden, 1968), pp. 5–6; U. Heyd, *Foundations of Turkish Nationalism: The Life and Teachings of Ziya Gökalp* (London, 1950), pp. 107–8; E. B. Şapolyo, *Ziya Gökalp Ittihad ve Terakki ve meşrutiyet tarihi* (Istanbul, 1943), p. 99; N. Berkes, *Turkish Nationalism and Western Civilization: Selected Essays of Ziya Gökalp* (New York, 1959).
104. Anonymous, "Le panislamisme et panturkisme," *R.M.M.* 23 (1913), 179–220. T. Z. Tunaya, *Islamcilik cereyanı* (Istanbul, 1962); A. Arsharuni and Kh. Gabidullin, *Ocherki panislamizma i pantiurkizma v Rossii* (Moscow, 1931).
105. Arsharuni and Gabidullin, p. 3.
106. N. Keddie, *An Islamic Response to Imperialism: Political and Religious Writings of Sayyid Jamal ad-Din "al-Afghani"* (Berkeley, Calif., 1968); idem, *Sayyid Jamal ad-Din "al-Afghani": A Political Biography* (Berkeley, Calif., 1972).

107. Akçuraoğlu, pp. 419–34; F. Muslih, "The Life and Work of Agaoğlu Ahmet," *A.R.* 38 (1942), 177–8; S. Agaoğlu, *Babamdan hatıralar* (Ankara, 1940).
108. *Nouvelle revue* (Paris), (1893), 526.
109. Ibid. (1891), 389.
110. Seidzade, pp. 39–48.
111. For a biography of Topchibashev, see *Kavkaz*, nos. 10–11 (1934), 27–9.
112. Hajibeyli, "The Origins," p. 763; Novikov, "Zapiski," pp. 133–41.

Chapter 2. The 1905 Revolution and Azerbaijani political awakening

1. On the origins of the socialist movement in Baku, see S. T. Arkomed, *Rabochee dvizhenie i sotsial'demokratia na Kavkaze (s 80-kh gg. po 1903 g.)* (Moscow, 1923); A. M. Raevski, *Bol'sheviki i mensheviki v Baku v 1904–1905 gg.* (Baku, 1930).
2. E. L. Keenan, "Remarques sur l'histoire du mouvement révolutionnaire à Bakou (1904–1905)," *Cahiers du monde russe et sovietique* 3, no. 2 (1962), 243; Raevski, p. 98.
3. L. Nalbandian, *The Armenian Revolutionary Movement: The Development of Armenian Political Parties through the Nineteenth Century* (Berkeley, Calif., 1963), pp. 104–31; C. J. Walker, *Armenia: The Survival of a Nation* (New York, 1980), pp. 69–8.
4. P. N. Valuev, *Bol'sheviki Azerbaidzhana v gody pervoi russkoi revoliutsii* (Baku, 1963); Z. Ibragimov, *Revoliutsiia 1905–1907 gg. v. Azerbaidzhane* (Baku, 1955); see also a special issue of *A.Az.S.S.R., Trudy* 10 (1955); K.P.Az. Institut Istorii Partii, *Listovki bakinskikh bol'shevikov, 1905–1907* (Baku, 1955).
5. Quoted in Mil'man, p. 247.
6. U.S. Archives, RG 256, Special Memorandum, "The Nationality Problem in the Caucasus," Inquiry Doc. 770, p. 9.
7. Pichkian, p. 114.
8. A.N.Az.S.S.R., *Istoriia*, vol. 2, p. 255; Seidzade, p. 25.
9. Ischanian, p. 45.
10. Villari, p. 166.
11. *Tarjuman*, no. 46 (1896). A contemporary Western author confirms that in 1893–1894 Armenians were "without a rival" in the civil service in Transcaucasia. See H. F. Lynch, *Armenia: Travels and Studies* (London, 1901), vol. 1, p. 467.
12. Mil'man, p. 218.
13. Walker, pp. 69–72; S. Atamian, *The Armenian Community: The Historical Development of Social and Ideological Conflict* (New York, 1955), pp. 114–15.
14. I. I. Vorontsov-Dashkov, *Vsepoddanneishaia zapiska po upravleniiu Kavkazskim Kraem* (St. Petersburg, 1907), p. 14; see also

A.N.Az.S.S.R., Institut Istorii i Filosofii, *Rabochee dvizhenie v Baku v gody pervoi russkoi revoliutsii, Dokumenty i materialy* (Baku, 1956), pp. 99–110.
15. For the accounts of the fighting, see Villari, pp. 190ff. Walker, pp. 73–81; J. D. Henry, *Baku: An Eventful History* (London, 1905); E. Aknouni, *Political Persecutions: Armenian Prisoners of the Caucasus* (New York, 1911); for an Azerbaijani view, see A. Muhtar, "Hayes Turkes? Ermeniler tarafından yapılan Türk katliaminin 60-nci yıldönümü münasebetile," *T.K.* 3 (1965), pp. 529–35.
16. Aknouni, p. 30.
17. R. G. Hovannisian, *Armenia on the Road to Independence, 1918* (Berkeley, Calif., 1969), p. 264n.
18. Aknouni, p. 30.
19. Quoted in *Armenia*, 2, no. 2 (1906), 30–1.
20. S. Refik, "Azeri halk edebiyatında Deli Ali destanı," *A.Y.B.*, 2, no. 23 (1933), 415–19.
21. "Pis'ma I. I. Vorontsova-Dashkova Nikolaiu Romanovu, 1905–1915," *Krasnyi Arkhiv*, 26 (1928).
22. Ibid., p. 119.
23. D. M. Lang, *A Modern History of Georgia* (New York, 1962), p. 162.
24. "Bor'ba s revoliutsionnym dvizheniem na Kavkaze v epokhu stolypinshchiny, (Iz perepiski P. A. Stolypina s Gr. Vorontsovym-Dashkovym)," *Krasnyi Arkhiv* 34, no. 3 (1929), 187.
25. N. Keykurun, *Azerbaycan istiklâl mücadelesinin hatıraları* (Istanbul, 1964), pp. 10–15; Z. Ibragimov, p. 144.
26. Keykurun, p. 14.
27. Russia, *Gosudarstvennaia Duma. Vtoroi Sozyv* (St. Petersburg, 1907), p. 1229.
28. Seidzade, pp. 52, 71–2; V. Iu. Samedov, *Raspostranenie marksizma leninizma v Azerbaidzhane*, vol. 2, p. 58.
29. G. Aliev, "K voprosu o pomoshchi azerbaidzhanskoi demokratii mladoturetskomu dvizheniiu," *Tiurkologicheskii sbornik* (Moscow, 1975), pp. 187–91.
30. R. Pipes, *The Formation of the Soviet Union: Communism and Nationalism, 1917–1923* (Cambridge, Mass., 1970), p. 19; see also G. J. Libaridian, "Revolution and Liberation in 1892 and 1907 Programs of the Dashnaktsutiun," in Suny, *Transcaucasia*, pp. 185–96; A. Ter Minassian, "Nationalisme et socialisme dans le mouvement révolutionnaire arménien (1887–1912)," in Suny, *Transcaucasia*, pp. 141–84.
31. Seidzade, pp. 46–7.
32. For a detailed discussion of the petition, see ibid., pp. 59–62.
33. H. A. Orujov, "1905-ji ildä Azärbaijanda zemstvo kampaniyası," *A.N.Az.S.S.R., Izvestiia, Ser.Ist.Fil.Pr.*, no. 1 (1966), pp. 31–9.
34. *Tarjuman*, no. 41 (1905).
35. Arsharuni and Gabidullin, pp. 25–8; Zenkovsky, pp. 39–40.
36. S. M. Dimanshtein (Ed.), *Revoliutsiia i natsional'nyi vopros* (Moscow, 1930), vol. 3, pp. 283–92.

37. F. Georgon, *Aux origines du nationalisme turc.* Yusuf Akçura (Paris, 1980); B. Lewis, *The Emergence of Modern Turkey* (London, 1968), pp. 326-7.
38. Zenkovsky, p. 41.
39. Ibid., pp. 41-3.
40. Ibid., pp. 45-51; Arsharuni and Gabidullin, pp. 113-18.
41. Seidzade, pp. 119, 134.
42. K.P.Az, Institut Istorii Partii, *Listovki,* no. 115.
43. Russia, *Gosudarstvennaia Duma: Pérvyi Sozyv* (Moscow, 1906), pp. 116-17.
44. For the texts of the speeches, see Russia. *Gosudarstvennaia Duma: Pervyi Sozyv — Stenograficheskie otchety* (St. Petersburg, 1907).
45. S. M. Äfändiyev, "Himmätin yaranmasï," *Azärbayjan elmi savhasï,* nos. 1, 2 (1932), 83-9.
46. T. Shakhbazi, "Istoriia tiurskoi rabochei pechati," *Iz proshlogo: Stat'i i vospominaniia iz istorii bakinskoi organizatskii i rabochego dvizheniia v Baku* (Baku, 1932), p. 134. For a survey of the Himmät's history, see T. Świętochowski, "The Himmät Party: Socialism and the National Question in Russian Azerbaijan, 1904-1920," *Cahiers du monde russe et sovietique* 19, nos. 1, 2 (1978), 119-42.
47. Samedov, vol. 1, p. 659.
48. Ibid., p. 650; A. A. Sarkisov, "K istorii vozniknoveniia azerbaidzhanskoi bol'shevitskoi pechati," K.P.Az., Institut Istorii Partii, *Äsärlär-Trudy,* no. 23 (1959), 121-2.
49. On Narimanov, see M. Rafili, *Nariman Narimanov, vydaiushchiisia revoliutsioner i pisatel'* (Baku, 1956); V. Mammädov, *Näriman Närimanov* (Baku, 1957); T. Ahmädov, *Näriman Närimanov* (Baku, 1977). For a biography of Äzizbäkov, see M. Kaziev, *Zhizn' i revoliutsionnaia deiatel'nost' Mashadi Azizbekova* (Baku, 1956).
50. Quoted in Raevski, *Bol'sheviki i mensheviki,* p. 177.
51. K.P.Az., Institut Istorii Partii, *Listovki,* no. 112.
52. Äfändiyev, "Himmätin yaranmasï," p. 85.
53. K.P.Az., Institut Istorii Partii, *Listovki,* no. 79. This document was issued above the name of the Muslim Social Democratic Group of the Baku Social Democratic Organization.
54. Ibid., no. 85.
55. M. A. Resuloğlu, "Müsavat partisinin kuruluşu," *Milli Azerbaycan Müsavat Partısı, Bülteni,* no. 4 (1962), 9.
56. Bennigsen and Lemercier-Quelquejay, *La presse,* pp. 121-2.
57. A. G. Shakhgeldiev, "Legal'naia bol'shevitskaia gazeta Takammul," *Bakinskii rabochii,* December 29, 1957; N. M. Mikayilov, "Milli mäsälädä marksizm—leninizm ideyalari ughrunda Azärbayjan bol'shevik mätbuatinin mübarizäsi, 1905-1910 illär," *A.N.Az.S.S.R., Izvestiia, Ser.Ob.N.,* no. 1 (1963), 21-61.
58. S. M. Efendiev, "Razgrom musul'manskoi sotsial'-demokraticheskoi organizatsii Gummet," in *Iz proshlogo: Sbornik materialov po istorii*

Notes to pp. 55–63   207

 bakinskoi bol'shevitskoi organizatsii i oktiabrskoi revoliutsii v Azerbaidzane (Baku, 1924) pp. 21–3.
59. E. Bor-Rashenski, "Iranskaia revoliutsiia i bol'sheviki Zakavkaz'ia," *Krasnyi Arkhiv*, no. 2 (105) (1941), 51–3.
60. A.N.Az.S.S.R., Institut Istorii, *Rabochee dvizhenie Azerbaidzhana v gody nòvogo revoliutsionnogo pod'ema, 1910–1914 gg.* (Baku, 1967), vol. 2, p. 11.
61. N. M. Mikayilov, "Tarikh materializminin bazi mäsälärinin Azärbayjan bolshevik mätbuatïnda müdafia vä täblighi," *A.N.Az.S.S.R., Izvestiia, Ser.Ob.N.*, no. 2 (1963), 85–95.
62. Bennigsen and Lemercier-Quelquejay, *La presse*, p. 135. On the educational and cultural activities in the period, see A. Alstadt-Mirhadi, "The Azerbaijani Bourgeoisie and the Cultural Enlightenment Movement in Baku: First Steps toward Nationalism," in Suny, *Transcaucasia*, pp. 197–207.
63. For a survey of the Azerbaijani press of the period, see ibid., pp. 104–33; on the *Molla Näsr al-din*, see N. Akhundov, *Molla Näsraddin zhurnalinin näshri tarikhi* (Baku, 1959); on the *Häyat*, see O. Bayramova, "Häyat gäzetinin ideya istigamäti haggïnda," *A.N.Az.S.S.R., Izvestiia, Ser.Lit.Iaz.Issk.*, no. 2 (1982), 35–44.
64. Hajibeyli, p. 351.
65. *Irshad*, no. 283 (1906).
66. Ibid., no. 211 (1906).
67. *Täräqqi*, no. 16 (1909).
68. Ibid., no. 22 (1909).
69. Akçuraoğlu, p. 417; Heyd, *Foundations*, p. 149; M. Hartmann, "Aus der neuren osmanischen Dichtung," *M.S.O.S.* 20 (1917), 134.
70. *Füyuzat*, no. 23 (1907).
71. See Mämmad Jäfär, *Azärbayjan ädäbiyyatïnda romantizm* (Baku, 1963), pp. 178–86.
72. *Häyat*, no. 77 (1906).
73. *Füyuzat*, no. 20 (1907).
74. Ibid., no. 21. On Ahmad Kemal's activity in Azerbaijan, see D. Akünal, "Azerbaycan için calışanlardan Ahmet Akünal," *Türk Amacı* 2, no. 8 (1943), 349–55.
75. A. Vambery, *Western Culture in Eastern Lands* (New York, 1906), p. 279.
76. *Molla Näsr al-din*, no. 11 (1906).
77. *Täräqqi*, no. 49 (1909).
78. *Shälälä*, no. 21 (1913). On the *Yeni Lisan* movement in Turkey, see Levend, pp. 331–43; Heyd, pp. 115–21. See also idem, *Language Reform in Turkey* (Jerusalem, 1954).
79. *Molla Näsr al-din*, no. 32 (1909).
80. *Iqbal*, no. 44 (1912).
81. *Molla Näsr al-din*, no. 22 (1913).
82. Ibid., no. 23 (1913).

Chapter 3. The era of war and revolutions: ideologies, programs, and political orientations

1. H. Taqizadeh, "The Background of the Constitutional Movement in Azerbaijan," *M.E.J.*, 14 (1960), 462.
2. Strigunov, p. 53. In addition, some sixty to one hundred thousand illegal immigrants crossed the frontier annually; see S. Ravasani, *Sowjetrepublik Gilan: Die sozialistische Bewegung in Iran seit Ende des 19Jh. bis 1922* (Berlin, n.d.). On the trade between Baku and Persia, see M. A. Musayev, *XIX äsrin sonlarïnda Baki shähärinin tijaräti* (Baku, 1972) pp. 98–111.
3. G. M. Gasanov, "Iz istorii internatsional'nykh sviazei bol'shevikov Azerbaidzhana s iranskim revoliutsionerami (1905–1911 gg)," *K.P.Az., Institut Istorii Partii, Äsärlär-Trudy*, no. 26 (1967), 26.
4. For a monographic work on the Russo–British rivalry in Persia, see F. Kazemzadeh, *Russia and Britain in Persia, 1864–1914: A Study in Imperialism* (New Haven, 1968).
5. For a survey of the Persian Revolution, see E. G. Browne, *The Persian Revolution of 1905–1909* (Cambridge, 1910); M. S. Ivanov, *Iranskaia revoliutsiia 1905–1911 gg.* (Moscow, 1957). See also E. Abrahamian, *Iran between two Revolutions* (Princeton, 1982), pp. 50–92.
6. Browne, *Revolution*, p. 146.
7. T. A. Ibrahimov, *Iran Kommünist Partiyasïnïn yaranmasï* (Baku, 1963), p. 78; Ravasani, pp. 134–6; see also Z. Z. Abdullaev and S. Sh. Aslani, "K voprosu o nachale sotsial'-demokraticheskogo dvizheniia v Irane," *A.N.Az.S.S.R., Izvestiia, Ser.Istorii, Fil.Prava* (1970), 118–128; A. U. Martirosov, "Novye materialy o sotsial-demokraticheskom dvizhenii v Irane v 1905- 1911 godakh," *Narody Azii i Afriki*, no. 2 (1973), 116–22.
8. Gasanov, pp. 75–6.
9. M. Jäfär, p. 141. See also M. Kiazimov, "Tema Azerbaidzhana v tvorchestve Abul'Kasema Lakhuti," *A.N.Az.S.S.R., Izvestiia, Ser. Lit., Iaz., Isk.*, no. 2 (1982), pp. 47–51.
10. Taqizadeh, p. 460.
11. E. G. Browne, *The Press and Poetry of Modern Persia* (Cambridge, 1914), p. 102. See also A. Agaoğlu, *Iran ve inkılâbı* (Ankara, 1941), pp. 96–100.
12. On the influence of *Molla Näsr al-din* on the Persian public and press, see ibid., p. 16; for monographic studies, see V. Kliashtorna, "Zhurnal Molla Näsraddin i persidskaia politicheskaia satira perioda revoliutsii 1905–1911 godov," *A.N.S.S.R., Institut Vostovedeniia, Kratkie soobshcheniia* 27, no. 10 (1958), 31–41; M. Alizade, "Pervaia russkaia revoliutsiia i persidskaia demokraticheskaia literatura," *Az.G.U., Uchenye zapiski*, no. 10 (1955), pp. 119–71.
13. On reflections of the Persian revolution in Sabir's poetry, see M. Aghamirov, *M. A. Sabirin dünyaqörüshü* (Baku, 1962), pp. 41–70.

14. A. S. Sumbatzada (ed.), *Qorkämli ingilabchï Sattar Khan* (Baku, 1972), p. 3. See also I. Amir-Khizi, *Qiyam-i Azerbaijan va Sattar Khan* (Tabriz, 1960).
15. M. Jafar, p. 140.
16. Browne, *Revolution*, p. 250n; see also Abrahamian, p. 91.
17. Browne, *Revolution*, p. 250.
18. Kazemzadeh, *Russia and Britain*, p. 532.
19. E. Bor-Rashenski, "K voprosu o roli bol'shevikov Zakavkaz'ia v iranskoi revoliutsii 1905–1911 godov," *Istorik-marksist*, no 11 (1940), pp. 84–99; C. von Hahn, "Der Kaukasus und die Revolution in Persien," *Asien*, no. 8 (1909), pp. 117–18; see also I. Spector, *The First Russian Revolution and Its Impact on Asia* (New York, 1962).
20. *Novoe Vremiia*, October 18, quoted in Bor-Rashenski, p. 91.
21. V. Tria, *Kavkazskie sotsial-demokraty v persidskoi revoliutsii* (Paris, 1910), pp. 9–10; M. S. Ivanov, "Novye materialy o sotsial'-demokraticheskoi gruppe v Tabrize v 1908 godu," *Problemy vostokovedeniia*, no. 5 (1950), pp. 179–83.
22. For biographical information on Räsulzadä, see C. Hostler, *Turkism and the Soviets* (London, 1957), pp. 215–17; *Milli Azerbaycan Musavat Partisi, Bülteni*, no. 4 (1962), 5–6.
23. Browne, *The Press and Poetry*, p. 52; for further discussion on Rasulzadä and *Iran-i nou*, see M. Pavlovich and S. Iranski, *Persiia v bor'be za nezavisimost'* (Moscow, 1925), pp. 47-8; Abrahamian, pp. 103–4; Ravasani, pp. 156–8.
24. On the Turkish revolution of 1908, see A. Feroz, *The Young Turks: The Committee of Union and Progress in Turkish Politics, 1908–1914* (Oxford, 1969); B. Lewis, *The Emergence of Modern Turkey* (London, 1968), pp. 210–38. See ibid. for bibliographic guidance.
25. On the growth of Turkism in the Ottoman Empire after 1908, see Akchuraoghlu, pp. 434–50; J. Landau, *Pan-Turkism in Turkey: A Study of Irredentism* (London, 1981), pp. 30–55; K. Karpat, *Turkey's Politics: The Transition to a Multi-Party System* (Princeton, 1959).
26. Quoted in U. Heyd, *Foundations of Turkish Nationalism: The Life and Teachings of Ziya Gökalp* (London, 1950), p. 126.
27. Z. Gökalp, *The Principles of Turkism* (Leiden, 1968), p. 17.
28. See P. Dumont, "La revue Türk Yurdu et les Musulmans de l'Empire Russe, 1911–1914," *Cahiers du monde russe et sovietique*, 15, nos. 3, 4 (1974), pp. 315–31.
29. *Türk Yurdu*, no. 10 (1912), 293.
30. Ibid., no. 14 (1912), 419.
31. Ibid., no. 17 (1912), 547.
32. Ibid., 545.
33. Vorontsov-Dashkov, p. 9.
34. M. A. Resuloğlu, "Musavat partisinin kuruluşu," *Musavat Bülteni*, no. 4 (1962), pp. 9–14.
35. M. A. Räsulzadä, *Azerbayjan Jumhuriyeti* (Istanbul, 1341), p. 22.
36. M. Mirza-Bala, *Milli Azerbaycan hareketi: Milli Azerbaycan Musavat*

Fırkasının tarihi (Berlin, 1938), p. 64; M. D. Guseinov, *Tiurskaia Demokraticheskaia Partiia federalistov Musavat v proshlom i nastoiashchem* (Tiflis, 1927), p. 9.
37. Guseinov, *Musavat*, p. 77.
38. "Sotsial'naia sushchnost' musavatizma," in *Pervaia vsesoiuznaia konferentsiia istorikov-marksistov: Trudy* (Moscow, 1930), pp. 501–20.
39. Mirza-Bala, *Musavat*, p. 67; Resuloğlu, p. 10.
40. *Shälälä*, nos. 21, 37 (1913),
41. *Dirilik*, no. 3 (1914),
42. Zenkovsky, p. 124; Suny, p. 19.
43. A.N.Az.S.S.R., *Istoriia*, vol. 2, pp. 746–8.
44. A. N. Kurat, *Türkiye ve Rusya: XVIII yüzyıl, sonundan kurtuluş savaşına kaolar türk–rüs ilišikleri* (Ankara, 1970), p. 256.
45. Quoted in G. Jaschke, "Der Turanismus der Jungturken," *W.I.* 23, nos. 1, 2 (1941), 12.
46. W. Bihl, *Die Kaukasuspolitik der Mittelmächte* (Vienna, 1975), pp. 74–82.
47. Hovannisian, *Armenia*, p. 41.
48. Halil Paşa [Kut], *Bitmiyen savaş* (Istanbul, 1972), p. 136; W.E.D. Allen and P. Muratoff, *Caucasian Battlefields: A History of the Wars on the Turco–Caucasian Border, 1928–1921* (Cambridge, 1953), p. 289.
49. Allen and Muratoff, p. 248; E. K. Sarkissian, *Ekspansionistskaia politika Osmanskoi Imperii v Zakavkaz'e nakanune i v gody pervoi mirovoi voiny* (Erivan, 1962), p. 183.
50. Bihl, p. 223; see also pp. 349–50 for a bibliography of the war in the Caucasus.
51. For a recent work discussing Ottoman policy toward the Armenians in 1915 and for bibliographical information see Walker, pp. 197–240.
52. Lang, *Soviet Georgia*, p. 185.
53. Allen and Muratoff, p. 296.
54. R. K. Ramazani, *The Foreign Policy of Iran: A Developing Nation in World Affairs, 1500–1941* (Charlottenville, Va., 1966), p. 136.
55. Jäschke, *Der Turanismus*, p. 15n.
56. On strategical significance of Persian Azerbaijan for Pan-Turanian designs, see U.S. Archives, RG 256,891.00/4.
57. Bihl, p. 241.
58. Resuloğlu, pp. 11–12; Sarkissian, pp. 200–14.
59. Hovannisian, *Armenia*, p. 47.
60. Jäschke, *Der Turanismus*, p. 16.
61. Bihl, p. 70.
62. Ibid., p. 71.
63. English translation quoted in *The National Question in Russian Duma* (London, 1915), pp. 9–10.
64. *Achïq Söz*, no. 1 (1915).
65. Kurban Said, *Ali and Nino*, p. 111.
66. *Kaspiy*, no. 7 (1917).

Notes to pp. 84–91

67. Kurat, pp. 501–5; Bihl, p. 242; see also G. Jäschke, "Zwei Denkschriften der Kaukasustürken von 1915," *W.I.* 24 (1942), 132–6.

Chapter 4. Transition to nationhood: in quest of autonomy

1. Dimanshtein, vol. 2, p. 53.
2. The list of the Ozakom members is based on Hovannisian, *Armenia*, p. 76, and differs slightly from that in F. Kazemzadeh, *The Struggle for Transcaucasia* (New York and Oxford, 1951), p. 34.
3. Suny, *The Baku Commune*, p. 74.
4. S. Belen'ki and A. Manvelov, *Revoliutsiia 1917 goda v Azerbaidzhane: Kronika sobytii* (Baku, 1927), p. 27.
5. Ibid., p. 26.
6. A. B. Kurban, *Inkilâp tarihimiz ve Jön Türkler* (Istanbul, 1945), pp. 192–3.
7. Mirza-Bala, *Musavat*, p. 78; N. Keykurun, "Türk Ademi Merkeziyet Firkasinin faaliyeti ve Musavat Partisiyle birleşmesi," *Musavat Bülteni* 4 (1962), 19–21.
8. K.P.Az., Institut Istorii Partii, *Bol'sheviki v bor'be za pobedu sotsialisticheskoi revoliutsii v Azerbaidzhane: Dokumenty i materialy, 1917–1918 gg.* (Baku, 1957), no. 1.
9. Ravasani, pp. 248–51; Ibrahimov, pp. 121–33.
10. K.P.Az., Institut Istorii Partii, *Bol'sheviki v bor'be*, no. 55.
11. Dimanshtein, vol. 3, p. 340.
12. M S. Iskenderov, *Iz istorii bor'by Kommunisticheskoi Partii Azerbaidzhana za pobedu sovetskoi vlasti* (Baku, 1958), pp. 174–5. On Aghamalïoghlï, see Kh. Näjäfov, *S. Aghamalïoghlunun ijtimaisi-yasi va ateist qörüshläri* (Baku, 1968); G. Imart, "Un intellectuel azerbaidjanais face à la revolution de 1917: Samad aga Agamaly-oglu," *Cahiers du monde russe et sovietique* (1967), 528–59.
13. A.N.Az.S.S.R., *Istoriia*, vol. 3, p. 59.
14. *Kaspiy*, no. 259 (1917),
15. See Mirza-Bala, *Musavat*, p. 155; for further discussion of the Ittihad, see K. Karabekir, *Istiklâl harbimiz* (Istanbul, 1960), p. 492; see also D. B. Guliev, *Bor'ba kommunisticheskoi partii za osushchestvlenie leninskoi natsional'noi politiki v Azerbaidzhane*, (Baku, 1970), pp. 143–4.
16. Belen'ki, Manvelov, p. 36.
17. Ibid., pp. 35-6.
18. For a discussion of Russian Muslim movement in 1917, see Dimanshtein, pp. 287 ff.; A. Bennigsen and C. Lemercier-Quelqujay, *Islam in the Soviet Union* (New York, 1967), pp. 65-80.
19. For a detailed discussion of the congress, see Zenkovsky, pp. 142-50.
20. For the text of Tsalikov's speech, see *Der Neue Orient*, no. 10 (1917), 527.

212 *Notes to pp. 92–105*

21. For the text of Räsulzadä's speech, see ibid., p. 526-7.
22. See ibid., 526.
23. Dimanshtein, p. 294.
24. Ibid., pp. 299, 304.
25. For the text of the provisional program, see ibid., pp. 341-5.
26. Belen'ki and Manvelov, p. 66.
27. Quoted in *Pervaia vsesoiuznaia konferentsiia istorikov marksistov*, p. 512.
28. G. Katkov, *The Kornilov Affair: Kerensky and the Break-up of the Russian Army* (London, 1980), pp. 93-120.
29. Belen'ki and Manvelov, p. 66.
30. A. L. Popov, "Iz istorii revoliutsii v Vostochnom Zakavkaz'e," *Proletarskaia Revoliutsiia*, 7, no. 30 (1924), 117.
31. Suny, *The Baku Commune*, p. 140.
32. Ibid., p. 139.
33. Belen'ki and Manvelov, p. 174.
34. Popov, "Iz istorii revoliutsii v Vostochnom Zakavkaz'e," p. 131.
35. For a discussion of the Provisional Government's nationality policy, see Dimanshtein, pp. 56 ff.; see also Pipes, pp. 50-1.
36. For further discussion of Lenin's views on the nationality question, see Pipes, pp. 41-9.
37. Dimanshtein, p. 26; see also A. Bennigsen and C. Lemercier-Quelquejay, *Islam*, pp. 67-8.
38. K.P.Az., *Bolsheviki v Bor'be*, no. 172.
39. Mirza-Bala, *Musavat*, pp. 85-6.
40. Ibid., p. 86. On the Musavat congress, see also M. D. Guseinov, *Musavat*, p. 30.
41. M. Florinsky, *Russia: A Short History* (New York, 1964), p. 452.
42. Quoted in Bennigsen and Lemercier-Quelquejay, *Islam*, p. 82.
43. On the crisis within the Baku Soviet following the Bolshevik coup, see Suny, *The Baku Commune*, pp. 147 ff.
44. Ibid., p. 163.
45. Belen'ki and Manvelov, p. 196.
46. Ibid., p. 181.
47. Popov, "Iz istorii revoliutsii v Vostochnom Zakavkaz'e," p. 136.
48. Suny, *The Baku Commune*, p. 188.
49. These figures are based on A.N.Az.S.S.R., *Istoriia*, vol. 3, p. 83. They differ slightly from those in Belen'ki and Manvelov, p. 233.
50. Ia. Ratgauzer, *Revoliutsiia i grazhdanskaia voina v Baku* (Baku, 1927), p. 107.
51. Stepan Shaumian, *Izbrannye proizvedeniia* (Moscow, 1957-58), vol. 2, pp. 182-3.

Chapter 5. Transition to nationhood: Transcaucasian federalism

1. Gruziia, *Dokumenty i materialy po vneshnei politike Zakavkaz'ia i Gruzii* (Tiflis, 1919) (hereafter cited as *Dokumenty*), no. 3. p. 2.

2. Ibid., no. 6. p. 7.
3. Ibid., no. 6. p. 7.
4. Ibid., no. 7. p. 8.
5. Ibid., no. 7. p. 9.
6. Hovannisian, *Armenia*, p. 108.
7. Belen'ki and Manvelov, p. 219.
8. Suny, *The Baku Commune*, p. 178.
9. Ibid., p. 194.
10. Pipes, p. 111.
11. Hovannisian, *Armenia*, p. 126.
12. See Narimanov's article "What should we do?" *Himmät*, 1 (1918).
13. Mirza-Bala, *Musavat*, p. 106. For the list of the Azerbaijani members of the Seim, see D. Demir, "On yıl evvel," *Azeri Türk*, no. 4 (1928), 28-30. On the organization and work of the Seim, see S. Kheifets, "Zakavkaz'e v pervuiu polovinu 1918 goda i zakavkazskii Seim," *Byloe*, no. 21 (1923), 298-310.
14. Mirza-Bala, p. 108.
15. Hovannisian, *Armenia*, p. 128.
16. Ibid., p. 127.
17. Mirza-Bala, *Musavat*, p. 109.
18. Ibid., pp. 109-10.
19. On the involvement of the Western powers' representatives in creating a Transcaucasian army for the the purpose of continuing the war against Turkey, see Hovannisian, *Armenia*, pp. 117-9; Kazemzadeh, *Struggle*, pp. 53, 78-80. For a Soviet view G. Gambashidze, *Iz istorii politiki S.Sh.A. v otnoshenii Gruzii, 1719-1920* (Tiflis, 1960); G. Galoian, *Bor'ba za sovetskuiu vlast' v Armenii* (Moskva, 1957).
20. Republic of Azerbaijan, *Economic and Financial Situation of Caucasian Azerbaijan* (Paris, 1919), p. 16; S. E. Sef, "Bakinskii oktiabr'," *Proletarskaia Revoliutsiia*, no. 11 (1930), pp. 73-4.
21. For a statement of the Bolshevik view, see Shaumian, vol. 2, pp. 181-4.
22. Ibid., vol. 2, pp. 185-6; Sef, "Bor'ba za oktiabr'," pp. 86-90; Ia. Shafir, *Ocherki gruzinskoi Zhirondy* (Moscow, 1925), pp. 53-4; A. Ziatkhan, *Aperçu sur l'histoire, la litterature, et la politique de l'Azerbaidjan* (Baku, 1919), pp. 57-62.
23. The leadership of the National Council in Ganja was in the hands of Ziyatkhanov, Rustambäkov, Safikiurdski, A. Khasmammädov, and Ussubäkov; see Shaumian, vol. 2, p. 167.
24. Gruziia, *Dokumenty*, nos. 59, 61, 62; J. Elder, "Memories of the Armenian Republic," *Armenian Review* 6, no. 1 (1953), 3-19.
25. Shaumian, vol. 2, p. 192.
26. A. Baikov, "Vospominaniia o revoliutsii v Zakavkazii," *Arkhiv Russkoi Revoliutsii* 9 (1923), 191.
27. Hovannisian, *Armenia*, pp. 112-13.
28. Popov, *Iz istorii*, p. 154. According to 1916 statistics, Muslim in-

habitants of Baku numbered 95,000; Russians numbered 90,000, Armenians 63,000. See Suny, p. 20.
29. Shaumian, vol. 2, p. 188.
30. K.P.Az., Institut Istorii Partii, *Bol'sheviki v bor'be*, no. 298.
31. See Kazemzadeh, *Struggle*, p. 70.
32. An oblique attack on Narimanov's role in this crisis appeared in A. S. Surguladze, *Zakavkaz'e v bor'be za pobedu sotsialisticheskoi revoliutsii* (Tiflis, 1971), p. 381, with the remark that "some nationalistically minded Himmätists sabotaged the struggle against the mutineers."
33. N. Narimanov, *Stat'i pis'ma* (Moscow, 1925), p. 6.
34. Shaumian, vol. 2, p. 209.
35. Great Britain, F.O. 371/3300, April 23, report of Vice-Consul McDonell; Suny, *The Baku Commune*, pp. 214-33; Popov, *Iz istorii*, pp. 157-9; idem, "Nationalism and Social Class in the Russian Revolution," in Suny, *Transcaucasia*, pp. 239-58; Suren Shaumian, *Bakinskaia Kommuna* (Baku, 1927), pp. 14-16; Korganoff, *La participation des Arméniens à la guerre mondiale sur le front du Caucase, 1914-1918* (Paris, 1927), pp. 174-6.
36. K.P.Az., Institut Istorii Partii, *Bol'sheviki v bor'be*, no. 341.
37. Narimanov, p. 6. A similar tone is found in Afändiyev, *Zhizn' Natsional'nostei* (1919) no. 25 (33).
38. Stepan Shaumian, vol. 2, p. 209. This figure differs sharply from the Azerbaijani claim that twelve thousand lives were lost in the "March Days." See *La République de l'Azerbaidjan du Caucase* (Paris, 1919), p. 19.
39. S. E. Sef, "Bakinskii Oktiabr," *Proletarskaia Revoliutsiia*, no. 11 (1930), p. 76.
40. Ibid., p. 77.
41. Stepan Shaumian, vol. 2, p. 211.
42. Suny, *The Baku Commune*, p. 226.
43. Ibid., p. 228.
44. Ibid., pp. 231-2.
45. K.P.Az. Institut Istorii Partii, *Bol'sheviki v bor'be*, no. 343.
46. Gruziia, *Dokumenty*, no. 14, pp. 18-23.
47. Jäschke, *Der Turanismus*, p. 22; see also Kurat, pp. 506-7.
48. Jäschke, *Der Turanismus*, p. 25.
49. Hovannisian, *Armenia*, p. 120.
50. Ibid., p. 120.
51. Allen, Muratoff, pp. 460-1; E. F. Ludshuveit, *Turtsiia v gody pervoi mirovoi voiny* (Moscow, 1966), p. 170.
52. Quoted in Iu. Semenov, "Zakavkazskaia Respublika," *Vozrozhdenie* 1 (1949), 146.
53. Gruziia, *Dokumenty*, no. 46, 83; see also S. T. Arkomed, *Materialy po istorii otpadeniia Zakavkaz'ia ot Rossii* (Tiflis, 1931), p. 20; O. Minasian, "Vneshnaia politika zakavkazskoi kontrrevoliutsii v pervoi polovine 1918 goda," *Istorik-marksist*, no. 6 (1938), 53-86.
54. Gruziia, *Dokumenty*, no. 46, p. 84.

55. Hovannisian, *Armenia*, p. 134.
56. Gruziia, *Dokumenty*, no. 47, p. 85.
57. Ibid., no. 53, pp. 89-90.
58. Ibid., no. 69, p. 145.
59. Arkomed, *Materialy*, pp. 42-4.
60. Ibid., p. 42; Minasian, "Vneshnaia politika," p. 68.
61. Ibid., p. 55.
62. Gruziia, *Dokumenty*, no. 82, p. 165.
63. Ibid., no. 83, p. 174.
64. Ibid., no. 83, p. 177.
65. Ibid., no. 86, p. 187.
66. Arkomed, *Materialy*, pp. 62-3.
67. Quoted in ibid., p. 68.
68. Gruziia, *Dokumenty*, no. 99, pp. 200-222; Kazemzadeh, *Struggle*, p. 106.
69. Gruziia, *Dokumenty*, no. 99, p. 214.
70. Ibid., no. 100, p. 222.
71. Ibid., no. 108, p. 229.
72. Ibid., no. 108, pp. 230-33.
73. Ibid., no. 108, pp. 233-4.
74. W. Zürrer, "Deutschland und die Entwicklung Nordkaukasiens im Jahre 1918," *Jahrbücher für Geschichte Osteuropas*, no. 1 (1978), pp. 31-50; H. Bammate, *Le Caucase et la révolution russe* (Paris, 1929), pp. 38-9.
75. Gruziia, *Dokumenty*, no. 159, pp. 314-16.
76. Z. Avalov, *Nezavisimost' Gruzii v mezhdunarodnoi politike, 1918-1921 gg.* (Paris, 1924), pp. 41-2; G. Jäschke, "Entwurf zu einem Freundschaftsvertrag zwischen dem Osmanischen Reich und der Föderativen Transkaukasischen Republik," *W.I.* 23, no. 314 (1941), 170-4.
77. Hovannisian, *Armenia*, pp. 174-6.
78. Quoted in Zürrer, "Deutschland," p. 39n.
79. Kazemzadeh, *Struggle*, p. 114.
80. On the conflicting interests of Germany and Turkey in Transcaucasia, see Trumpener, pp. 167-99; C. Mühlman, *Das deutsch–türkische Waffenbündniss im Weltkriege* (Leipzig, 1940), pp. 196-9; J. Pomiankowski, *Der Zusammenbruch des Ottomanischen Reiches: Errinerungen an die Türkei der Zeit des Welkrieges* (Leipzig, 1928), pp. 359-75; K. Ziemke, *Die neue Türkei: Politische Entwicklung* (Stuttgart, 1930), pp. 51-3.
81. Gruziia, *Dokumenty*, no. 147, p. 293.
82. Ibid., no. 148, pp. 296-301.
83. Kazemzadeh, *Struggle*, p. 116.
84. Avalov, p. 57.
85. Trumpener, p. 180.
86. I. Tsereteli, *Séparation de la Transcaucasie de la Russie et independence de la Georgie: Discours prononcé à la Diète Transcaucasienne* (Paris, 1919), p. 46.
87. Ibid., p. 47.

Chapter 6. The Azerbaijani nation-state

1. "Milli Azerbaycanin onbeş yıllığı," *A.Y.B.* 2, no. 17 (1933), pp. 113–14.
2. I. A. Guseinov, "Istoricheskie znachenie lozunga 'Nezavisimyi Sovetskii Azerbaidzhan,'" *Azerbaidzhanskii Gosudarstvennyi Universitet, Uchenye zapiski*, no. 10 (1957), p. 67.
3. See *A.Y.B.*, 2, no. 17 (1933), 194.
4. G. Jäschke, "Der türkisch–aserbaidschanisch Freundschaftsvertrag vom 4 Juni 1918," *Vorderasien: Studien zur Auslandkunde*, no. 1 (1944), 64. See also Räsulzadä, *Azerbaycan Cumhuriyeti*, p. 61; Kurat, pp. 662 ff.
5. On the Army of Islam, see K. Rüştü, "Büyük harpte Kafkas yollarında 5-nci piyade fırkası," *Askeri mecmua*, no. 93, (Tarih kismi, no. 34) (1934), 5–6; see also Ludshuveit, pp. 209–11.
6. Rüştü, p. 5.
7. Mirza-Bala, *Musavat*, p. 139. See also A. Raevski, *Musavatskoe pravitel'stvo na versal'skoi konferentsii. Doneseniia predseatelia musavatskoi delegatsii* (Baku, 1930), pp. 3–4.
8. On the Azerbaijani reactions to Ottoman interference, see Mirza-Bala, *Musavat*, p. 148; Guliev, *Bor'ba*, pp. 74–5.
9. Guliev, *Bor'ba*, pp. 73–4. For the list of the cabinet members, see *Le 28 Mai 1919* (Baku, 1919), p. 9.
10. Pipes, p. 205.
11. Sh. A. Tagieva, *Natsional 'no-osvoboditel'noe dvizhenie v iranskom Azerbaidzhane v 1917–1920 gg* (Baku, 1956), p. 37. For a contemporary account of the Ottoman policy in Persian Azerbaijan, see *Der neue Orient* (1918), vol. 3, p. 378.
12. Such reinterpretation of Pan-Turkism with reference to the experience of the Ottoman occupation of Azerbaijan will be found in M. E. Resulzade [Räsulzadä], *O panturanizme v sviaz'i s kavkazskoi problemoi* (Paris, 1930).
13. Suny, *The Baku Commune*, p. 269.
14. Allen, Muratoff, pp. 486–8; Korganoff, pp. 186–8.
15. A.N.S.S.S.R., Institut Istorii, *Dokumenty po istorii grazhdanskoi voiny v S.S.S.R.* (Moscow, 1940), vol. 1, p. 381.
16. Quoted in U.S.S.R., Ministerstvo Inostrannykh Del, *Dokumenty vneshnei politiki S.S.S.R.* (Moscow, 1940), vol. 1, p. 381.
17. Quoted in Mühlman, p. 207.
18. J. W. Wheeler-Bennet, *Brest-Litovsk: The Forgotten Peace* (London, 1938) p. 433.
19. Quoted in Mirza-Bala, *Musavat*, p. 147.
20. For a monograph of the Commune, see Suren Shaumian, *Bakinskaia Kommuna*; see also Suny, pp. 331 ff. On the reforms undertaken by the Baku Sovnarkom, see P. A. Azizbekova and M. A. Gaziev, "Bakï Khalg Komissarläri Sovetinin 1918-nji ildä sosialist

tädbirläri," in A.N.Az.S.S.R., *Böyük Oktiabr va soviet hakimiyyäti ughrunda mubarizä* (Baku, 1958), pp. 204–16.
21. Suny, *The Baku Commune*, p. 238.
22. Ratgauzer, *Revoliutsiia i grazhdanskaia voina*, p. 177.
23. On the peasants' violence in the Azerbaijani countryside, see Stepan Shaumian, vol. 2, pp. 157–9. At that time (February 1918) Shaumian appealed to the peasants to refrain from killing and burning. See also Suny *The Baku Commune*, pp. 293–4.
24. Iskenderov, p. 214.
25. Quoted in K.P.Az., Institut Istorii Partii, *Bol'sheviki v bor'be*, no. 456.
26. Quoted in ibid., no. 452.
27. Ibid., no. 506.
28. Suny, *The Baku Commune*, p. 296.
29. Suren Shaumian, pp. 29–30; Ludshuveit, p. 219.
30. On Dunsterville's expedition to Baku, see L. C. Dunsterville, *The Adventures of Dunsterforce* (London, 1932). See also Kazemzadeh, *Struggle*, pp. 139–43; R. G. Ullman, *Anglo-Soviet Relations, 1917–1921*, vol. 1, *Intervention and the War* (Princeton, 1961), pp. 305–7; G. A. Brinkley, *The Volunteer Army and the Allied Intervention in South Russia, 1917–1921* (Notre Dame, Ind., 1966), pp. 60–3. For monographic works, see A. H. Arslanian, "The British Decision to Intervene in Transcaucasia during World War I," *Armenian Review* 27 (Summer 1974), 146–59; see also idem, "Dunsterville's Adventure: A Reappraisal," *I.J.M.E.S.* 12 (1982), 199–216; idem, "Britain and the Transcaucasian nationalities during the Russian Civil War," in Suny, *Transcaucasia*, pp. 293–304.
31. See Great Britain, F.O.371/42519, Caucasus File, 512. The report of R. McDonell, British vice-consul in Baku, seems to indicate that the Bolsheviks were not always vehemently against the idea of inviting the British.
32. On Bicherakhov's role in the defence of Baku, see Suren Shaumian, pp. 33–4; Ratgauzer, pp. 195–200.
33. Suny, *The Baku Commune*, p. 318.
34. Kazemzadeh, *Struggle*, pp. 138–9.
35. There is some discrepancy between Allen and Muratoff, p. 492, Ludshuveit, p. 248, and Dunsterville, p. 284, as to the numerical strength of the British forces that arrived in Baku; all three sources agree, however, that the British were too weak for the task of defending the city.
36. Dunsterville, p. 309.
37. Mühlman, p. 270; Pomiankowski, 374.
38. Kazemzadeh, *Struggle*, pp. 143–4, gives the total of 8,988 persons killed, the figure arrived by analyzing Armenian sources. Other authors give much higher figures: Korganoff, p. 204, estimates the number of killed to be 15,000–30,000, Walker, p. 261, to be 20,000. On the September 15 massacre in Baku, see also U.S.

Archives, RG 256, "The Caucasus," Confidential Volume, chap. 3, "Massacres in Baku," no. 861. K.00/5.
39. A. S. Bukshpan (ed.), *Poslednie dni komissarov bakinskoi kommuny* (Baku, 1928); "Pamiatii 26 bakinskikh komissarov," *Krasnyi arkhiv*, nos. 4–5 (89–90) (1938), 3–29.
40. Ludshuveit, p. 262; Allen and Muratoff, p. 495.
41. A. L. Popov, "Iz epokhi angliiskoi interventsii v Zakavkaz'e," *Proletarskaia Revoliutsiia* (1923), 225.
42. Ziemke, p. 475; Jäschke, *Der Turanismus*, pp. 45–7.
43. Trumpener, p. 197.
44. Hovannisian, *Armenia*, p. 239.
45. E. Kurtulan, "Türk ordusunun Azerbaycanda kalması meselesi," *Azerbaycan*, nos. 4–6 (1964), 15; Mirza-Bala, *Musavat*, pp. 149–50.
46. Raevski, *Angliiskaia interventsiia*, p. 33.
47. U.S. Archives, RG 256.184.02102/6, Harbord Report, app. A, exh. B.
48. Mirza-Bala, *Musavat*, p. 151; see also Baikov, p. 150.
49. Great Britain, F.O. 371/24819, R.I.G. Gorton, Brig. General, "Notes on the Situation in Azerbaijan," December 8, 1918.
50. For a monographic work on the Karabagh dispute, see R. Hovannisian, "The Armeno–Azerbaijani Conflict over Mountainous Karabagh," *Armenian Review* 24 (Summer 1971), 3–24; idem, *The Republic of Armenia: The First Year, 1918–1919* (Berkeley, Calif. 1974) (hereafter cited as *Republic*), pp. 156–97.
51. Hovannisian, *Republic*, 169–70.
52. Great Britain, F.O. 371/3658, March 18, 1919.
53. See Ullman, pp. 223–4; Hovannisian, *Republic*, p. 157; Great Britain, F.O. 371/E8378/308, "Outline of Events in Transcaucasia," May 31, 1922.
54. See ibid.
55. See Ullman, pp. 78–9. For the Soviet view, see A.N.Az.S.S.R., *Istoriia*, vol. 3, pp. 167–8; Raevski, *Angliiskaia interventsiia*, pp. 20–2; D. Enukidze, *Krakh imperialisticheskoi interventsii v Zakavkaz'e* (Tiflis, 1954). For the British view, see F.O. 371/3690; see also U.S. Archives, RG 265, 861 K.00/5; RG 256, 184.021/371.
56. U.S. Archives, RG 256, 861,K.00/5, "The Caucasus," Confidential Volume, "Reorganization of Baku Branch of Russian State Bank."
57. Great Britain, F.O., 371/E 8378/308, "Outline of Events."
58. U.S. Archives, RG 256, 184.02102/6, Harbord Report, app. A, contains this comment on the policy of Great Britain in Transcaucasia: "British policy during the period of occupation was difficult to understand. In fact, there seems to have been no set policy."
59. *Le 28 mai 1919*, p. 15.
60. D.Z.T., "La premiere république musulmane: l'Azerbaidjan," *R.M.M.* 36 (1918–19), 231; see also A.A.A., "Eshche in pechal'nogo proshlogo: Proiskhozhdenie azerbaidzhanskogo parlamenta," *Kavkaz* 12/24 (1935), 28–9.

Notes to pp. 145–150

61. Mirza-Bala, *Musavat*, p. 155; slightly different figures are given by A.N.Az.S.S.R., *Istoriia*, vol. 3, p. 169.
62. Guliev, *Bor'ba*, pp. 143–52.
63. U.S. Archives, RG 256, 184.02102/8, Harbord Report, app. C, October 16, 1919.
64. For the names of the members of the second and third Khoiski cabinets, see *Le 28 mai 1919*, pp. 9, 18–9. For those of the first Ussubäkov cabinet, see U.S. Archives, RG 256, 184.01602/23; for those of his second cabinet, see Karabekir, p. 493.
65. A.N.Az.S.S.R., Sektor Filosofii, *Istoriia gosudarstva i prava Azerbaidzhanskoi S.S.R.* (Baku, 1964), p. 278.
66. Mirza-Bala, *Musavat*, pp. 159–64.
67. Ibid., p. 163.
68. A. G. Karaev, *Iz nedavnogo proshlogo* (Baku, 1926), p. 81.
69. For monographic studies of the agrarian question of the period, see N. Pchelin, *Krest'ianski vopros pri Musavate* (Baku, 1931); I. A. Guseinov, "Krestianskoe dvizhenie v Azerbaidzhane 1917–1920 gg," in A.N.Az.S.S.R., *Böyük Oktiabr*, pp. 217–65.
70. D.Z.T., "La premier république," p. 264.
71. U.S. Archives, RG 256, 184.02101/8, Harbord Report, app. C, October 16, 1919.
72. Baikov, p. 156.
73. A. Azeri, "Die Errungschaften der nationalen Republik Aserbaidschan," *Die Befreiung* 2 (1939), 58–9; M. A. Räsulzadä, "Kafkasya Türkleri," *Türk Yılı* (1928), 527–9.
74. Azerbaidzhanski Gosudarstvennyi Universitet, *Pervoe desiatiletie* (Baku, 1930), pp. 1–10.
75. Azeri Türk 18 (1928), 4.
76. On Sulkiewicz, see Fisher, pp. 123–6.
77. K.P.Az., Institut Istorii Partii, *Bor'ba za pobedu sovetskoi vlasti v Azerbaidzhane, 1918–1920: Dokumenty i materialy* (Baku, 1967), no. 347, p. 292.
78. Mirza-Bala, *Musavat*, p. 163. Other sources give different figures: A.N.Az.S.S.R., *Istoriia*, 20,000, and Baikov, 50,000; see also E. Kurtulan, 'Azerbaycan ordu teşkilatı," *Azerbaycan*, nos. 7–9 (1964), 13–15.
79. Republic of Azerbaijan, Delegation to the Paris Peace Conference, *Economic and Financial Situation of Caucasian Azerbaijan* (Paris, 1919), p. 7.
80. A. Dubner, *Bakinskii proletariat v gody revoliutsii* (Baku, 1931), pp. 112–3. See ibid. for data on the population's standard of living.
81. Republic of Azerbaijan, Delegation to the Paris Peace Conference, *Economic and Financial Situation*, p. 7.
82. U.S. Archives, RG 256, 184.01602/23, "Supplementary Report on the Situation in Azerbaijan," May 1, 1914.
83. Republic of Azerbaijan, Delegation to the Paris Peace Conference, *Economic and Financial Situation*, p. 9.
84. For Western views of Azerbaijan's economic potential, see Great

Britain, F.O. 371/3662/72735; U.S. Archives, RG 256. 184.01602/2.
85. Quoted in Raevski, *Angliiskaia interventsiia*, p. 160.
86. Great Britain, F.O. 371/3662, "Notes on Present Conditions in the Caucasus," July 26, 1919. See also K. Agaev, *Osobaia morskaia ekspeditsiia* (Baku, 1967), pp. 36-44.
87. G. A. Brinkley, p. 155.
88. Great Britain, F.O. 371/808, "Outline of Events," p. 14.
89. Raevski, *Angliiskaia interventsiia*, pp. 94-5; Kazemzadeh, *Struggle*, p. 242.
90. Quoted in A. I. Denikin, *Ocherki russkoi smuty* (Berlin, 1925), vol. 4, p. 125.
91. Great Britain, F.O. 371/3662/113022; D.Z.T., *La premiere république*, p. 266. For a discussion of the Armenian position, see Hovannisian, *Republic*, pp. 379-84.
92. Great Britain, F.O. 371/E 8378/808, "Outline of Events," p. 14; Brinkley, p. 161-3.
93. Denikin, vol. 4, pp. 137-8.
94. Great Britain, F.O. 371/3667, 23445.
95. Kazemzadeh, *Struggle*, p. 266; Hovannisian, *Republic*, pp. 289-91.
96. Quoted in I. A. Guseinov, *Istoricheskie znachenie*, p. 71.
97. Great Britain, F.O. 371/E 8378/808, "Outline of Events," p. 12.
98. Republic of Armenia, Delegation to the Peace Conference, *La République Arménienne et ses voisins: Questions territoriales* (Paris, 1919), pp. 9-11.
99. *Claims of Persia before the Conference of the Preliminaries of Peace at Paris* (Paris, 1919), pp. 9-10.
100. Quoted in I. A. Guseinov, *Istoricheskie znachenie*, p. 68.
101. *Claims of the Peace Delegation of the Republic of Caucasian Azerbaijan presented to the Peace Conference* (Paris, 1919), p. 9.
102. Ibid., p. 49.
103. Great Britain, F.O. 371/E 8378/808, "Outline of Events," p. 13.
104. Great Britain, CAB, 45/107, Thomson, "Notes on Transcaucasia," May 26, 1919.
105. Great Britain, F.O. 371/3662, July 26, 1919.
106. Great Britain, F.O. 371/E 8378/808, "Outline of Events," p. 13; U.S. Archives, RG 246, 184.01602/97; B. B. Moore to R. Tyler, July 24, 1919.
107. K.P.Az., Institut Istorii Partii, *Bor'ba za pobedu*, no. 383. pp. 321-2.
108. Kazemzadeh, *Struggle*, p. 229.
109. Raevski, *Angliiskaia interventsiia*, pp. 62-3.
110. For a Western proposal of uniting Russian Azerbaijan with Persia, see U.S. Archives, RG 256, 869.00/2, Memorandum of Samuel Edelman, December 12, 1918.
111. Mirza-Bala, p. 178.
112. On the rise of Khiabani's movement, see Tagieva, pp. 82-116; Cottam, pp. 122-4.

Notes to pp. 159–166   221

113. Kazemzadeh, *Struggle*, pp. 174–82.
114. For a detailed discussion of the Nakhichevan problem, see Hovannisian, *Republic*, pp. 235–49.
115. Avalov, p. 244.
116. Ibid., p. 244
117. Brinkley, p. 214, Ullman, 294–304.
118. Avalov, p. 241.
119. On the Armenian policy in the face of the Azerbaijani and Turkish threats, see ibid., pp. 262,281. See also R. Hovannisian, "Caucasian Armenia between Imperial and Soviet Rule: The Interlude of National Independence," in Suny, *Transcaucasia*, pp. 227–92. On the Karabagh uprising, see Mirza-Bala, *Musavat*, p. 171.
120. R. G. Hovannisian, "Armenia and the Caucasus in the Genesis of the Soviet–Turkish Entente," *I.J.M.E.S.* 4 (1973), 2,129–47; G. Jäschke, "La rôle du communisme dans les relations russo–turque," *Orient* 7 (1963), 26, 31–46.
121. A. A. Cruinkshank, "The Young Turk Challenge in Postwar Turkey," M.E.J., 22 (Winter 1968), 17–18.
122. S. S. Aydemir, *Makedonyadan Ortaasya'ya Enver Paşa* (Istanbul, 1978), vol. 3, p. 446.
123. Hovannisian, *Armenia and the Caucasus*, p. 138.
124. Ibid., p. 140; Karaev, p. 60.
125. Great Britain, F.O. 371/E 8378/808, "Outline of Events," p. 19.
126. Quoted in Karabekir, p. 359.
127. Jäschke, *La role du communisme*, pp. 33–4.
128. U.S. Archives, RG 256, 184.0602/95, July 23, 1919; Karabekir, pp. 328–30. Halil Pasha's participation in the Nakhichevan fighting should not be confused with the role of Major Halil bey, the commander of Turkish–Azerbaijani volunteers in the area.
129. *Der Neue Orient* 4 (1919), 22.
130. G. Jäschke, "Beiträge zum türkischen Freiheitskampf," *W.I.*, nos. 4, 5 (1956), 46; U.S. Archives, RG 256.18401602/19, 1/2, Bristol to Churchill from Constantinople, April 11, 1919.
131. Karabekir, pp. 466–7.
132. Mirza-Bala, *Musavat*, p. 180.
133. Karabekir, p. 611.

Chapter 7. The coming of Soviet power

1. *Azärbaijan*, 60 (1918), December 14.
2. Iskenderov, p. 344.
3. A.N.Az.S.S.R., *Istoriia*, vol. 3, part 1, p. 176.
4. Ibid., pp. 185–7.
5. K.P.Az., Institut Istorii Partii, *Bor'ba za pobedu*, no. 173.
6. Ibid., no. 173. p. 138.
7. Quoted in Guliev, *Bor'ba*, p. 408.

Notes to pp. 166–172

8. A. Mikoyan, "Bakinskoe podpol'e pri angliiskoi okkupatsii," *Iunost'* 10 (1968), 93.
9. K.P.Az., Institut Istorii Partii, *Bor'ba za pobedu*, no. 328, p. 275.
10. Guliev, *Bor'ba*, pp. 407–8.
11. Ibid., 412.
12. Ravasani, p. 253.
13. Karaev, pp. 54–5.
14. E———v [Efendiev], "Gazeta Gummet Tsentral'nogo Biuro Muzul'man Kommunistov Kavkaza," *Zhizn' natsional'nostei* 22 (1919).
15. A. Talibov, "Milli müstemläka mäsäläsi haggïnda marksizm–leninizm näzäriyäsinin S. M. Äfändiyev tarafïndan müdafia edilmäsi va täblighi," *A.N.Az.S.S.R., Izvestiia, Ser.Ob.N.* 10 (1961), 3–14.
16. Narimanov, p. 20.
17. K.P.Az., Institut Istorii Partii, *Bor'ba za pobedu*, no. 347. p. 291.
18. Ibid., no. 173. p. 138.
19. Guliev, *Bor'ba*, p. 284; see also S. Blank, "Bolshevik Organizational Development in Early Soviet Transcaucasia," in Suny, *Transcaucasia*, pp. 317–20.
20. Guliev, *Bor'ba*, p. 284.
21. Karaev, p. 54.
22. At the First All-Russian Congress of Muslim Communists in November 1918 Sultan Galiev argued for the need to create a separate Muslim Communist Party with its own Central Committee. Although rejected by the congress, these ideas enjoyed popularity among some Muslim Communists, including those in Azerbaijan, where Sultan Galiev had once lived. For a monographic work on Sultan Galiev, see A. Bennigsen and C. Lemercier-Quelquejay, *Le sultan galievisme au Tatarstan* (Paris, 1960).
23. K.P.Az., Institut Istorii Partii, *Ocherki istorii Kommunisticheskoi Partii Azerbaidzhana* (Baku, 1963), p. 321. For Mikoyan's recollection of the improper attitude of the Himmätists, see *Bakinskii rabochii* 75, April 25, 1925.
24. Ia. Ratgauzer, *Bor'ba za sovetskii Azerbaidzhan* (Baku, 1928), p. 61.
25. Guliev, *Bor'ba*, p. 430.
26. Iskenderov, p. 419; Pipes, pp. 218–19.
27. S. M. Kirov, *Stat'i i rechi* (Moscow, 1937), vol. 1, p. 201.
28. Ravasani, p. 254.
29. K.P.Az., Institut Istorii Partii, *Azärbayjan Kommunist Partiyasïnïn tarikhi* (Baku, 1958). vol. 1, p. 374. *Bakinskii rabochii*, 100, April 27, 1928, cites some evidence that the call to convene the first congress of the AzCP(B), on the initiative of the Himmät, was unexpected by the Baku Committee. This might explain why the Muslims made such a strong showing at the Congress, while the Russians, who had been given short notice, were underrepresented. See also Guliev, *Bor'ba*, p. 473.
30. K.P.Az., Institut Istorii Partii, *Ocherki istorii K.P.Az.*, p. 324.
31. Bennigsen, Quelquejay, *La presse*, p. 329.
32. *Fuqara Sädasi* August 27, 1919.

33. Ibid. August 24, 1919.
34. K.P.Az., Institut Istorii Partii, *Ocherki istorii K.P.Az.*, p. 326.
35. K.P.Az., Institut Istorii Partii, *Bor'ba za pobedu*, no. 494. p. 421.
36. Ibid., no. 523, p. 446.
37. Karabekir, p. 493.
38. Karaev, p. 100.
39. *Ittihad* 1 (1919), as quoted in Guliev, *Bor'ba*, p. 143.
40. Ibid. 6 (1919), as quoted in p. 143.
41. Quoted in Kazemzadeh, *Struggle*, p. 279.
42. Raevski, *Angliiskaia intereventsiia*, pp. 181–2.
43. Kazemzadeh, *Struggle*, p. 280.
44. Guliev, *Bor'ba*, pp. 331–2.
45. Popov, *Iz epokhi*, pp. 211–12.
46. Quoted in Guliev, *Bor'ba*, p. 335.
47. Ibid., p. 332.
48. There are two accounts of the Hajinski's episode written by the same author, but differing in some details: S. Rustambeyli [Rustambäkov], "27 Nisan hatırası," *A.Y.B.* 2 (1933), 176–80; Sh. Rustambekov, "Iz pechal'nogo proshlogo," *Kavkaz*, 7–9 (19–20) (1935), pp. 7–11.
49. Rustambeyli, p. 183.
50. Baikov, p. 174.
51. H. b. Agaev, "Pis'mo Enver Pashe," *Kavkaz* 9 (45) (1937), 27.
52. V. I. Lenin, *Polnoe sobranie sochinenii*, vol. 51, pp. 163–4.
53. Pipes, p. 224.
54. Rustambeyli, p. 184.
55. Karabekir, p. 663.
56. Kazemzadeh, *Struggle*, pp. 280–1.
57. On the rise of the Turkish Communist organization in Baku, see G. S. Harris, *The Origins of Communism in Turkey* (Stanford, Calif., 1967), p. 58; Karabekir, pp. 609–12; F. Tevetoğlu, *Türkiyede sosyalist ve komünist faaliyetler, 1910–1960* (Ankara, 1967), p. 229.
58. Karabekir, p. 610.
59. Ibid., pp. 633–4.
60. G. Jäschke, "Neues zur russisch–turkischen Freundschaft von 1919–1939," *W.I.* (New series) 6 (1961), 205–6.
61. Karaev, pp. 123–4.
62. Agaev, "Pis'mo Enver Pashe," p. 25.
63. G. Jäschke, "Transkaukasien: Ein Musterbeispiel sowjetrussischer Eroberungspolitik," *Osteuropa* 11 (1936), 26.
64. Karaev, pp. 115–16; Mirza-Bala, pp. 180–1; Nuh-Oğlu, "27 Nisan," *Kurtuluş* (1936), 514–17; Kazemzadeh, *Struggle*, p. 282.
65. Rustambeyli, p. 185.
66. K.P.Az., Institut Istorii Partii, *Bor'ba za pobedu*, no. 539, p. 460.
67. Years later, the commander of the armored train, M. G. Efremov, explained that his haste in moving on to Baku had been due to the need to prevent the destruction of the oilfields. See *Bakinskii rabochii* 93, April 23, 1925.

224   *Notes to pp. 181–188*

68. Iskenderov, p. 440.
69. Agaev, "Pis'mo Enver Pashe," p. 27; Iu. A. Bagirov, *Iz istorii sovetsko-turetskikh otnoshenii* (Baku, 1965), pp. 29–32.
70. Rustambeyli, p. 186.
71. Quoted in Mirza-Bala, *Musavat*, p. 200.
72. Rustambeyli, p. 186.
73. Quoted from an archival source by Iskenderov, p. 442.
74. K.P.Az., Institut Istorii Partii, *Bor'ba za pobedu*, no. 541, pp. 461–2.
75. Ibid., no. 555, p. 471.
76. Ibid., no. 543, pp. 462–3.
77. Ibid., no. 544, p. 463.
78. Lenin, vol. 40, p. 332.
79. A.N.Az.S.S.R., *Istoriia*, vol. 3, part 2, p. 243.
80. Ibid., p. 240.
81. Mirza-Bala, *Musavat*, p. 203.
82. Ibid., p. 204; Guliev, *Bor'ba*, pp. 547–8.
83. For a biography of Räsulzadä, see Hostler, pp. 215–17.
84. Mirza-Bala, *Musavat*, p. 213.
85. Kazemzadeh, *Struggle*, p. 209.
86. Ibid., p. 219.
87. Pipes, p. 228.
88. Benab, p. 14.
89. Ibid., p. 13.
90. For monographic works on Khiabani's movement, see A. Azari, *Qiyam-i Khiabani dar Tabriz* (Tahran, 1329); A. Vishnegradova, "Revoliutsionnoe dvizhenie v Persidskom Azerbaidzhane," *Novyi Vostok*, 2 (1922), 249–55. See also Tagieva, pp. 82–116; G. Lenczowski, *Russia and the West in Iran: A Study in Great Powers Rivalry, 1918–1948* (Ithaca, N.Y., 1949), pp. 61–4; P. Homayounpour, *L'affaire d'Azerbaidjan* (Lausanne, n.d.), pp. 29–46; A. Kasravi, *Tarikh-i hijdah sala-yi Azerbajan* (Tehran, 1340/1961), pp. 870 ff.; G. Nollau and H. J. Wiehe, *Russia's South Flank* (London, 1963), pp. 156–8.
91. See Mämmäd Jafar, pp. 139–92.
92. See Ravasani, pp. 279–332; S. Zabih, *The Communist Movement in Iran* (Berkeley, Calif., 1966) pp. 13–19; S. Blank, "Soviet Politics and the Iranian Revolution of 1919–1921," *Cahiers du Monde Russe et Sovietique* 21, no. 2 (1980), 173–94.
93. S. F. Fatemi, *Diplomatic History of Persia, 1917–1923* (New York) p. 250. See ibid. for a discussion of Khiabani's statements.
94. Mirza-Bala, *Musavat*, pp. 213–15; Guliev, *Bor'ba*, p. 552.
95. For the Soviet view of the political background of the Ganja uprising, see F. Makharadze, "Oktiabrskaia Revoliutsiia i sotsialpredateli," *Proletarskaia revoliutsiia* no. 10 (1922).

96. A. B. Kadishev, *Interventsiia i grazhdanskaia voina v Zakavkaz'e* (Moscow, 1960), p. 294.
97. Ibid., p. 298; see also P, Gentizon, *La résurrection georgienne* (Paris, 1921), p. 215.
98. Mirza-Bala, *Musavat*, p. 213.
99. Kadishev, p. 292.
100. Ibid., p. 293.
101. Ibid., p. 304.
102. Ibid., p. 300; Guliev, *Bor'ba*, p. 552.
103. Kadishev, p. 301.
104. Allen and Muratoff, p. 511.
105. Kadishev, pp. 350 ff.

Conclusion

1. Narimanov, *Stat'i i pis'ma*, p. 20.

Bibliography

ARCHIVAL SOURCES

great britain: public records office
Cabinet Office Archives
Foreign Office Archives
War Office Archives

united states: national archives
General Records of the Department of State
Records of the American Commission to Negotiate Peace

OFFICIAL PUBLICATIONS AND COLLECTIONS OF DOCUMENTS

Akademiia Nauk Azerbaidzhanskoi, S.S.R., Institut Istorii i Filosofii. *Rabochee dvizhenie v Baku v gody pervoi russkoi revoluitsii: Dokumenty i materialy.* Baku, 1956.
Akademiia Nauk S.S.S.R., Daghestankii Filial, Institut Istorii, Iazyka i Literatury. *Dvizhenie gortsov Severo-Vostochnogo Kavkaza v 20–50 gg. XIX veka.* Makhachkala, 1959.
Glavnoe Arkhivnoe Upravlenie. *Revoliutsiia 1905–1907 gg v Rossi. Dokumenty i materialy.* Pankratova, A.M. (ed.). Moscow, 1955.
Gruzinskii Filial, Institut Iazyka, Istorii i Material'noi Kul'tury imenii N.I. Marra. *Ukazy kubinskikh khanov.* Tbilisi, 1937.
Institut Istorii. *Kolonial'naia politika rossiiskogo tsarizma v Azerbaidzhane v 20–60 gg. XIX veka.* Moscow and Leningrad, 1937.
Baku po perepisi 22 oktiabria 1903 goda. Baku, 1905.
"Bor'ba s revoluitsionnym dvizheniem na Kavkaze v epokhu stolypinshchiny (Iz perepiski P.A. Stolypina s Gr.I.I. Vorontsovym-Dashkovym." *Krasnyi arkhiv* 34, no. 3 (1929), 184–221; 35, no. 4 (1929), 128–50.

Dimanshtein, S.M. (ed.). *Revoliutsiia i natsional'nyi vopros*, vol. III. Moscow: Kommunisticheskaia Akademiia, 1930.
Kavkazskaia Arkheograficheskaia Kommissiia. *Akty sobrannye Kavkazskuiu Arkheograficheskuiu Kommissieiu*. Tiflis, 1866-1885.
Kavkazskii Statisticheskii Komitet. *Sbornik svedenii o Kavkaze*. Tiflis, 1871.
Kommunisticheskaia Partiia Azerbaidzhana, Institut Istorii Partii. *Listovki bakinskikh bol'shevikov, 1905-1907*. Baku: Azgosizdat, 1955.
Bol'sheviki v bor'be za pobedu sotsialisticheskoi revoliutsii v Azerbaidzhane: Dokumenty i materialy. Baku: Izd-vo A.N.Az.S.S.R., 1957.
Bor'ba za pobedu sotsialisticheskoi revoliutsii v Azerbaidzhane. Dokumenty i materialy. Baku, 1967.
Obozrenie rossiiskikh vladenii za Kavkazom v statisticheskom, etnograficheskom i finansovom otnosheniiakh. St. Petersburg, 1936.
Persia, Delegation to the Paris Peace Conference, *Claims of Persia before the Conference of the Preliminaries of Peace at Paris*. Paris, 1919.
Pervaia Vseobshchaia Perepis' Rossiiskoi Imperii, 1897. *Raspredelenie rabochikh i prislug po gruppam zaniatii i po mestu rozhdeniia*. St. Petersburg, 1905.
"Pis'ma I.I. Vorontsova-Dashkova Nikolaiu Romanovu, 1905-1915." *Krasnyi Arkhiv* 26 (1928) 97-126.
Republic of Armenia, Delegation to the Peace Conference. *Donnés statistique des populations de la Transcaucasie*. Paris, 1919.
La République Arménienne et ses voisins: Questions territoriales. Paris, 1919.
Republic of Azerbaijan. *Le 28 mai 1919*. Baku, 1919.
Claims of the Peace Delegation of Caucasian Azerbaijan Presented to the Peace Conference in Paris. Paris, 1919.
Composition antropologique et ethnique de la population de l'Azerbaidjan du Caucase. Paris, 1919.
Economic and Financial Situation of Caucasian Azerbaijan. Paris, 1919.
La République de l'Azerbaidjan du Caucase. Paris, 1919.
Republic of Georgia. *Dokumenty i materialy po vneshnei politike Zakavkaz'ia i Gruzii*. Tiflis, 1919.
Russia. *Polnoe sobranie zakonov Rossiiskoi Imperii*. 2nd series. St. Petersburg, 1830-85.
Gosudarstvennaia Duma Pervogo Prizyva. Moscow, 1906.
Gosudarstvennaia Duma: Stenograficheskie otchety. Sozyv I, II. N.d.
USSR, Ministerstvo Inostrannykh Del. *Dokumenty vneshnei politiki S.S.S.R.* Moscow, 1957.
Vorontsov-Dashkov, I.I. *Vsepoddanneishaia zapiska po upravleniiu Kavkazskim Kraem generala ad'iutanta grafa Vorontsova-Dashkova*. St. Petersburg, 1907.
Vsepoddanneishii otchet za vosem' let upravleniia Kavkazom. St. Petersburg, 1913.

SECONDARY SOURCES

A.A.A., "Eshche iz pechal'nogo proshlogo. Proiskhozhdenie azerbaidzhanskogo parlamenta," *Kavkaz*, no.12/24, (1935), 28-9

Bibliography

Abdullaev, G.B. *Iz istorii Severo-Vostochnogo Azerbaidzhana v 60–80 gg. XVIII veka.* Baku: Izd-vo A.N.Az.S.S.R., 1958.
Azerbaidzhan v XVIII veke i vzaimootnosheniia s Rossiei. Baku: Izd-vo A.N.Az.S.S.R., 1976.
Abdullaev, Z.Z. "1905–1907-ji illär rus ingilabinin iakhïn va orta shärq ölkärinä tä'siri." *A.N.Az.S.S.R., Trudy* 10 (1955), 235-63.
Abdurrahmanov, A. *Azerbaidzhan vo vzaimootsheniiakh Rossii, Turtsii i Irana v pervoi polovine XVIII veka.* Baku: Izd-vo A.N.Az.S.S.R., 1964.
Abrahamian, E. *Iran between Two Revolutions.* Princeton: Princeton University Press, 1964.
Abramishvili, A.Z. "Iz istorii azerbaidzhanskoi periodicheskoi pechati." *Az.G.U., Uchenye zapiski,* no.10, (1957), 69-80.
Adamiyat, F. *Andishahha-i Mirza Fath 'Ali Akhundzadeh.* Tehran, 1349/ 1970.
Adilov, M.I. "M.F. Akhundovun dili va dram sänätkarlïghï haggïnda bä'zi geydlär" *A.N.Az.S.S.R., Izvestiia, Ser.Ob.N.,* no.10 (1962), 57-65.
Äfändiyev, S.M. (Efendiev). "Himmätin yaranmasï." *Azärbayjan elmi savhasï,* nos.1, 2 (1932), pp. 83–9.
Sechilmish äsärläri. Baku: Azärbayjan Dövlat Näshriyyätï, 1977.
Afşeranli, "Milli Azerbaycan ordusunun harb kabiliyeti." *Kurtuluş,* no. 16 (1936), 454-6.
Agaev, G.b. "Pis'mo Enver Pashe" *Kavkaz,* no. 9 (1937), 25-9.
Agaev, K. *Osobaia morskaia ekspeditsiia.* Baku: Azgosizdat, 1967.
Agaian, Ts.P. *Krest'ianskaia reforma v Azerbaidzhane.* Baku: Iz-vo A.N.Az.S.S.R., 1956.
Aghakhi, A.M. "O vliiani M.F. Akhundova na razvitie progessivnoi obshchestvennoi mys'li v Irane." *A.N.Az.S.S.R., Izvestiia, Ser.Ob.N.,* no.10 (1962), 75-85.
Aghamirov, M. *M.A. Sabirin dünyaqörüshü.* Baku: Elm Nashriyyati, 1962.
Birinji rus ingilabi illärinda Azärbayjan ijtimai fikrindä milli mäsäläyä dair. Baku: Iz-vo A.N.Az.S.S.R., 1963.
Agaoğlu, S. *Babamdan hatıralar.* Ankara: Zerbamat Basımevi, 1940.
Akademiia Nauk Azerbaidzhanskoi S.S.R., Institut Istorii. *Istorii Azerbaidzhana.* 3 vols. Baku: Izd-vo A.N.Az.S.S.R., 1958-63.
Prisoedinenie Azerbaidzhana k Rossii i ego progressivnye posledstviia v oblasti ekonomiki i kul'tury. Baku: Izd-vo A.N.Az.S.S.R., 1955.
Bol'sheviki Azerbaidzhana v pervoi russkoi revoliutsii. Baku: Izd-vo A.N.Az.S.S.R., 1963.
Böyük Oktiabr va Azärbayjanda soviet hakimiyyäti ughrunda mübarizä. Baku: Izd-vo A.N.Az.S.S.R., 1958.
Akademiia Nauk Azerbaidzhanskoi, Sektor Filosofii, *Istoriia gosudarstva i prava Azerbaidzhanskoi S.S.R.* Baku: Izd-vo A.N.Az.S.S.R., 1964.
Akademiia Nauk Azerbaidzhanskoi, Institut Iazyka i Literatury. *Azärbayjan ädäbiyyäti tarikhi.* 3 vols. Baku: Izd-vo A.N.Az.S.S.R., 1960-63.
Akchuraoghlu, Y. (Akçuraoğlu). "Türkçülük" *Türk yılı* (1928), 289-455.

Akhundov, B.Iu. *Monopolisticheskii kapital v dorevoliutsionnoi bakinskoi promyshlennosti.* Moscow, 1959.
Akhundov, M.F. *Äsärläri.* 3 vols. Baku: Izd-vo A.N.Az.S.S.R., 1958-62.
Akhundov, N.*Molla Näsraddin'zhurnalinin näshri tarikhi.* Baku: Azärbayjan Dövlat Näshriyyäti, 1959.
Azärbayjanda dövri mätbuat, 1832-1920: Bibliografiya. Baku: Izd-vo A.N.Az.S.S.R., 1965.
Azärbayjan satira zhurnallarï, 1906-1920. Baku: Izd-vo A.N.Az.S.S.R., 1968.
Aknouni, E. *Political Persecutions: Armenian Prisoners of the Caucasus.* New York, 1911.
Akünal, D., "Azerbaycan için calışanlardan Ahmet Kemal Akünal." *T.A.* 2, no.8 (1943), 349-55.
Alektorov, A. "Novye techeniia v zhizni magometanskikh shkol." *M.N.P.*, *Zhurnal* (1909), 187-203.
Algar, H. *Mirza Malkum Khan: A Study in the History of Iranian Modernism*, Berkeley: University of California Press, 1973.
"Malkum Khan: Akhunzadä and the proposed reform of the Arabic alphabet." *Middle Eastern Studies* 5, no.2 (1969), 116-30.
Aliev, G., "K voprosu o pomoshchi azerbaidzhanskoi demokratii mladoturetskomu dvizheniiu." *Tiurkologicheskii sbornik.* Moscow: Izd-vo Nauka, 1966.
Alieva, A.A. "1905-nji ildä Bakïnïn teatr hayatï." *A.I.S.*, 11 (1965), 104-29.
Ali-zade A.K. *Sotsial'no-ekonomicheskaia i politicheskaia istoriia Azerbaidzhana XII-XIV.* Baku: Izd-vo A.N.Az.S.S.R., 1956.
Alizade, M. "Pervaia russkaia revoliutsiia i persidskaia demokraticheskaia literatura." *Az.G.U., Uchenye Zapiski*, no.10 (1955), 119-29.
Allen, W.E.D., and Muratoff, P. *Caucasian Battlefields.* Cambridge: Cambridge University Press, 1953.
Allworth, E. *Central Asian Publishing and the Rise of Nationalism: An Essay and a List of Publications in the New York Public Library.* New York: New York Public Library, 1965.
Nationalities of the Soviet East – Publications and Writing Systems: A Bibliographical Directory and Transliteration Tables for Iranian and Turkic-language publications, 1918-1945, Located in US libraries. New York and London: Columbia University Press, 1971.
Alstadt-Mihradi, A. "The Azerbaijani–Turkish Community of Baku before World War I." Ph.D. Dissertation, University of Chicago, 1983.
"The Azerbaijani Bourgeoisie and the Cultural-Enlightenment Movement in Baku: First Steps toward Nationalism," in Suny, R.G. (ed.), *Transcausasia: Nationalism and Social Change.* Ann Arbor: University of Michigan, 1983, pp. 197-208.
Arkomed, S.T. *Rabochee dvizhenie i Sotsial–Demokratiia s 80–kh gg. po 1903 v Kavkaze.* Moscow: Gosudarsvennoe Izd-vo, 1923.
Materialy po istorii otpadeniia Zakavkaz'ia ot Rossii. Tiflis: Gosudarsvennoe Izd-vo, Gruziia, 1931.

Arsharuni, A., and Gabidullin, Kh. *Ocherki panislamizma i pantiurkizma v Rossii.* Moscow: Bezbozhnik, 1931.
Arslanian, A.H. "The British Decision to Intervene in Transcaucasia during World War I." *Armenian Review,* no.27 (Summer 1974), 146-59.
——— "Dunsterville's Adventure: A Reappraisal." *I.J.M.E.S.,* no.12 (1980), 199-216.
——— "Britain and the Transcaucasian Nationalities during the Russian Civil War." In Suny, R.G. (ed.), *Transcausasia: Nationalism and Social Change.* Ann Arbor: University of Michigan, 1983, pp. 293-304.
Arslanian, A.H., and Nichols, R.L. "Nationalism and the Russian Civil War. The Case of Volunteer Army–Armenian relations, 1918-20." *Soviet Studies* 31, no.4 (1979), 559-73.
Atamian, S. *The Armenian Community.* New York: Philosophical Library, 1955.
Atkin, M. *Russia and Iran, 1780-1828.* Minneapolis: University of Minnesota Press, 1980.
Avalov, Z. *Nezavisimost' Gruzii v mezhdunarodnoi politike, 1918-1921 gg.* Paris, 1924.
Aydemir, S.S. *Makedonyadan Ortaasya'ya Enver Paşa,* vol. 3. Istanbul: Remzi Kitabevi, 1978.
Azerbaidzhanskii Gosudarstvennyi Universitet imenii Lenina. *Pervoe desiatiletie.* Baku: Izd-vo Gosudarstvennogo Universiteta, 1930.
Azeri, A. "Die Errungenschaften der nationalen Republik Aserbaidschan." *Die Befreiung,* no.2 (1939), 57-61.
Azeri, A. *Qiyam–i Khiabani.* Tehran: Safi 'Ali Shah, 1950.
Azimov, H. "Azärbayjan gäzalarïnda sovetlärin faaliyyatina dair, (iyul-oktiabr 1917)." *A.N.Az.S.S.R., Izvestiia, Ser.Ob.N.,* no.6 (1965), 24-35.
——— *Azärbayjan gäzalarïnda sovetlär (1917-1918-ji illär).* Baku: Elm, 1971.
Azizbekova, P.A. "Bakï Khalq Komissarläri Sovetinin 1918-ji ildä sosyalist tadbirläri." In A.N.Az.S.S.R., *Böyuk oktiabr va sovet hakimiyyäti ughrunda mubarizä.* Baku: Izd-vo A.N.Az.S.S.R., pp. 204-16.
Badalbeyli, A., and Kasumov, K. *Azerbaidzhanskii Gosudarsvennyi ordena Lenina Teatr Opery i Baleta im.M.F.Akhundova: Kratkii ocherk.* Moscow, 1959.
Baddeley, J.F. *The Russian Conquest of the Caucasus.* London: Longmans, 1908.
Bagirov, Iu. *Iz istorii sovetsko–turetskikh otnoshenii v 1920-1922 gg.* Baku: Izd-vo A.N.Az.S.S.R., 1965.
Bagirov, M. *Iz istorii bol'shevitskikh organizatsii Baku i Azerbaidzhana.* Moscow: Gosudarstvennoe Izd-vo Pollit. Literatury, 1946.
Baikov, A. "Vospominaniia o revoliutsii v Zakavkazii." *Arkhiv russkoi revoliutsii* 9 (1923), 91-194.
Bammate, H. *Le Caucase et la revolution russe,* Paris, 1929.
Baydamirova, B.S. "Äkinchi gäzetenin meydana qälmäsi vä onun Azärbayjan ijtimai-igtisadi fikir tarikhindä roluna dair." *A.N.Az.S.S.R. R., Izvestiia, Ser.Ob.N.,* no.5 (1963), 107-18.

"Äkinchi gäzeti känd täsärrufatï mäsälälärinä dair." *A.N.Az.S.S.R., Izvestiia, Ser.Ob.N.*, no.1 (1965), 37-47.
Bartol'd, V. *Mesto prikaspiiskikh oblastei v istorii muzul'manskogo mira.* Baku: Istoriko-etnograficheskaia sektsiia obsledovaniia i izucheniia Azerbaidzhana, 1925.
Baykara, H. *Azerbaycanda yenileşme hareketleri.* Ankara: Türk Kültürünü Araştırma Enstitusü, 1966.
Azerbaycan istiklâl tarihi. Istanbul: Azerbaycan Halk Yayınları, 1975.
Bayramova, O. "Häyat gäzetinin ideya istigamäti haggïnda." *A.N.Az.S.S.R., Izvestiia, Ser.Lit. Iaz. Issk.*, no.2 (1982), 35-43.
Belen'ki, S., and Manvelov, A. *Revoliutsiia 1917 goda v Azerbaidzhane (Kronika sobytii).* Baku: Azgiz, 1927.
Benab, Y.P. "Tabriz in Perspective: A Historical Analysis of the Current Struggle of Iranian Peoples." *Review of Iranian Political Economy and History*, 2, no.2 (1978), 1-42.
Bennigsen, A., and Lemercier-Quelqujay, Ch.
Les mouvements nationaux chez les musulmans de Russie: Le'Sultangalievisme' au Tatarstan. Paris and The Hague: Mouton, 1960.
La presse et les mouvements nationaux chez les musulmans de Russie avant 1920. Paris and The Hague: Mouton, 1964.
Islam in the Soviet Union. New York: Praeger, 1967.
Bennigsen, A., and Wimbush, S.E. *Muslim National Communism in the Soviet Union: A Revolutionary Strategy for the Colonial World.* Chicago: University of Chicago Press, 1979.
Berkes, N. *Turkish Nationalism and Western Civilization: Selected Essays of Ziya Gökalp.* New York: Columbia University Press, 1959.
Bihl, W. *Die Kaukasuspolitik der Mittelemächte.* Vienna: Komission für neuere Geschichte Osterreichs, 1975.
Birgen, M. "Türk ordusunun Azerbaycana yardımı." *Yakın tarihimiz*, 2, no.5 (1962), 44-5.
"Bizimkiler ve Azerbaycan." *Yakın Tarihimiz*, 2, no.18 (1962), 157-8.
Bıyıklıoğlu, T. *Atatürk Anadoluda 1919-1921).* Ankara, 1959.
Blank, S. "Soviet Politics and the Iranian Revolution of 1919-1921." *Cahiers du Monde Russe et Sovietique* 21, no.2 (1980), 173-94.
"Bolshevik Organizational Development in Early Soviet Transcaucasia." In Suny, R.G. (ed.), *Transcausasia: Nationalism and Social Change.* Ann Arbor: University of Michigan, 1983, pp. 305-38.
Bor-Rashenski, E., "K voprosu o roli bol'shevikov Zakavkaz'ia v iranskoi revoliutsii 1905-1911 godov." *Istorik-marksist*, no. 11 (1940), 84-99.
"Iranskaia revoliutsiia 1905-1911 gg. i bol'sheviki Zakavkaz'ia," *Krasnyi arkhiv*, no. 5 (1941), 33-70.
Bournoutian, G.A. *Eastern Armenia in the Last Decades of Persian Rule, 1807-1828: A Political and Socioeconomic Study of the Khanate of Erevan on the Eve of the Russian Conquest.* (Malibu, Calif., 1982.)
"The Ethnic Composition and the Socio-Economic Condition of Eastern Armenia in the First Half of the Nineteenth Century." In Suny, R.G. (ed.), *Transcausasia: Nationalism and Social Change.* Ann Arbor: University of Michigan, 1983, pp. 69-88.

Bibliography

Brands, H.W. *Azerbaidschanische Volksleben und modernistische Tendez in den Schauspielen Mirsa Feth-Ali Ahundzades*. The Hague: Mouton, 1958.
Brinkley, G.A. *The Volunteer Army and Allied Intervention in South Russia*. Notre Dame, Ind.: Notre Dame University Press, 1966.
Browne, E.G., *The Persian Revolution, 1905-1909*. London: Cambridge University Press, 1912.
The Persian Crisis of December, 1911. London: Cambridge University Press, 1914.
Poetry and Press in Modern Persia. London: Cambridge University Press, 1914.
Bukshpan, A.S. (ed.). *Poslednie dni komissarov bakinskoi kommuny*. Baku, 1928.
Butkov, P. *Materialy po novoi istorii Kavakaza*. St. Petersburg, 1869.
Caferoğlu, A. "Azeri edebiyatında istiklâl mücadelesi izleri." *A.Y.B.* 1 (1932), 291-305, 339-48, 361-71, 426-34.
"Ismail bey Gasprinski." *A.Y.B.* 2 (1933), 165-9.
Azerbaycan. Istanbul: Cumhuriyet Matbaası 1940.
"Çarlık Rusyanın Azerbaycanda yaptığı istila savaşları." *T.K.* 2 no.19 (1964), 10-17.
"Ziya Gökalp'in Azerbaycan Türklüğü üzerindeki tesiri." *T.K.* 2 no. 24 (1964), 10-16.
Cebesoy, A.F. *Moskova hatırları*. Istanbul: Vatan Neşriyati, 1955.
Cottam, R.W. *Nationalism in Iran (Updated through 1978)*. Pittsburgh: University of Pittsburgh Press, 1979.
Cruickshank, A.A. "The Young Turk Challenge in Postwar Turkey." *M.E.J.* 22 (Winter 1968), 17-28.
Denikin A.I. *Ocherki russkoi smuty*. 5 vols. Paris and Berlin, 1921-26.
Dubner, A. *Bakinskii proletariat v gody revoliutsii*. Baku: Azgnin, 1931.
Dubrovin, N. *Zakavkaz'e ot 1803 do 1806 goda*. St. Petersburg, 1866.
Istoriia voiny i vladychestva russkikh na Kavkaz'e. 4 vols. St. Petersburg: N.N. Skorokhodov, 1871-88.
Dunsterville, L.C. *The Adventures of Dunsterforce*. London, 1932.
Dzhafarov, D. *Teatr imenii Azizbekova*. Moscow: Isskustvo, 1951.
D.Z.T. "La prémiere republique musulmane." *R.M.M.* 36 (1918-19), 229-36.
Efendiev, S. M. (Afändiyet). "Ob organizatsii Gummet." *Zhizn' natsinal'nostei*, no. 28 (36) 1919.
"Iz istorii revoliutsionnogo dvizheniia tiurskogo proletariata," *Iz proshlogo*. Baku, 1923, pp. 39-57.
"Razgrom musul'manskoi sotsial–demokraticheskoi organizatsii Gummet." In *Iz proshlogo: Sbornik materialov po istorii bakinskoi bol'shevitskoi organizatsii i oktiabrskoi Revoliutsii v Azerbaidzhane*. Baku, 1924, pp. 21–3.
Enikopolova, I. K. *Griboedov i vostok*, Erivan: Aiastan, 1974.
Ertürk, H. *Iki devrin perde arkası*. Istanbul: Hilmi Kitabevi, 1957.
Fabritius, W. "Die heutige Stadt Baku und die Naphtaindustrie in ihrer Umgegend," *Russische Revue* 10 (1877), 33–50.

Bibliography 233

Fadeev, A. V. *Rossiia i Kavkaz v pervoi tretii XIX veka.* Moscow: Izd-vo A.N.Az.S.S.R., 1960.
Fatemi, N. S. *Diplomatic History of Persia, 1917–1923: Anglo–Russian Power Politics in Iran.* New York: R. F. Moore, 1952.
Feroz, A. *The Young Turks: The Committee of Union and Progress in Turkish Politics, 1908–1914.* Oxford: Clarendon Press, 1969.
Fisher, A. *The Crimean Tatars.* Stanford, Calif.: Hoover Institution Press, 1978.
Gadzhinski, I. b. "Zhizn' Fet-Ali-Khana Kubinskogo." *Sbornik gazety Kavkaz* (Tiflis), (1847), 213–33.
Galoian, G. *Bor'ba za sovetskuiu vlast' v Armenii.* Moscow: Gos. Izd-vo Politicheskoi Literatury, 1957.
Garayev, Y. "Dramaturqiyamizdä ilk fajiälär." *A.N.Az.S.S.R., Izvestiia Ser.Ob.N.*, no. 6 (1962), 63–75.
Gasanov, G. M. Iz istorii internatsional'nykh sviazei bol'shevikov Azerbaidzhana s iranskimi revoliutsionerami (1905–1911 gg)," Institut Istorii Partii, Baku, *Trudy-Äsärlär*, no. 26 (1967), 74–85.
Gasanov, G. and Sarkisov, N. "Sovetskaia vlast' v Baku v 1918 godu (Bakinskaia Kommuna)." *Istorik-marksist*, no. 5 (1938), 32–70.
Gasanov, I. M., "Iz istorii feodal'nykh otnoshenii v Azerbaidzhane: Randzhbary v XIX veke." *A.N.Az.S.S.R., Trudy*, 9 (1956), 26–92.
"Iz istorii podgotovki reskripta 6 dekabria 1846 g." *A.N.Az.S.S.R., Trudy* 4 (1956), 21–39.
"O proizvodstvennykh otnosheniiakh v gosudarstvennoi derevne Azerbaidzhana v kontse XIX veka." *A.N.Az.S.S.R., Doklady*, no. 8 (1956), 604–17.
Chastnovladel'cheskie krest'iane v Azerbaidzhane pervoi poloviny XIX veka. Baku: Izd-vo A.N.Az.S.S.R., 1957.
"Iz istorii krest'ianskogo dvizheniia v Azerbaidzhane v gody pervoi russkoi revoliutsii." In A.N.Az.S.S.R., Institut Istorii, *Azerbaidzhan v gody pervoi russkoi revoliutsii.* Baku: Izd-vo A.N.AZ.S.S.R., 1955, pp. 160–200.
Gasimov, G., "Azärbayjanda ilk teatr tamashalari haggïnda." *A.N.Az.S.S.R., Doklady*, no. 7 (1957), 815–18.
Gasimov, M. R. "Rus ingilabi va onun Molla Näsräddin zhurnalinda in'ikasi." *A.N.Az.S.S.R., Trudy* 10 (1955), 266–300.
Gasimzadä F., *XIX-nju äsir Azärbayjan ädäbiyyäti tarikhi.* Baku: Maarif, 1974.
Geiushev, Z. B. "Kritika feodal'no – religioznoi morali azerbaidzhanskimi prosvetiteliami vtoroi poloviny XIX veka." *A.N.Az.S.S.R., Trudy* 13 (1958), 260–305.
Mirovozzrenie G. b. Zardabi. Baku: Izd-vo A.N.Az.S.S.R., 1920.
Germany, Reichsicherheitshaupamt. *Kaukasus.* Wannsee-Institut. 1920.
Gökalp, Z., *The Principles of Turkism.* Leyden: Brill, 1968.
Gökçe, C. *Kafkasya ve Osmanli İmparatoluğunun Kafkasya siyaseti.* Istanbul, n.d.
Golden, P. B., "The Turkic Peoples of Transcaucasia." In Suny, R. G.

(ed.), *Transcausasia: Nationalism and Social Change*. Ann Arbor: University of Michigan, 1983, pp. 45-68.
Gönlübol, M. *Atatürk ve Türkiyenin diş politikası (1919-1938)*. Istanbul, 1963.
Gövsa, I. A. *Türk meşhurlari ansiklopedisi*. N.d.
Grigorian, A. T. *Prisoedinenie vostochnoi Armenii k Rossii*, Moscow: Izdvo Sotsial'no-Ekonomicheskoi Literatury, 1959.
Guliev, D. B. *Bor'ba kommunisticheskoi partii za osuschchestvlenie leninskoi natsional'noi politiki v Azerbaidzhane*. Baku: Azernäshr, 1970.
Gurko-Kriazhin, V. A. "Angliiskaia interventsiia v 1918-19 gg. v Zakaspii i Zakavkaz'e." *Istorik-marksist* 2 (1926), 115-39.
Guseinov, G. *Iz istorii obshchestvennoi i filosofskoi mys'li v Azerbaidzhane*. Baku: Azerbaidzhanskoe Gosudartvennoe Izd-vo, 1958.
Guseinov, I. A. "Istoricheskoe znachenie lozunga "nezavisimyi sovetskii Azerbaidzhan." *Az.G.U., Uchenye Zapiski*, no. 10 (1957), 66.
"Krest'ianskoe dvizhenie v Azerbaidzhane, 1917-1920 gg." In A.N.Az.S.S.R., *Böyük oktiabr va Azärbayjanda sovet hakimiyyäti ughrunda mübarizä*. Baku: Izd-vo A.N.Az.S.S.R., 1956, pp. 217-75.
Guseinov, M. D. *Tiurskaia Demokraticheskaia Partiia Federalistov Musavat v proshlom i nastoiashchem*. Baku, 1927.
Guseinov, T. *Oktiabr' v Azerbaidzhane*. Baku: Azgiz, 1927.
Hahn, C. v. "Der Kaukasus und die Revolution in Persien." *Asien*, no. 8 (1909), 117-18.
Hajibeyli, D. "The Origins of National Press in Azerbaijan." *A.R.* 25 (1930), 758-67.
Halil Paşa (Kut). *Bitmiyen savaş*. Istanbul, 1972.
Harris, G. S. *The Origins of Communism in Turkey*, Stanford, Calif.: Hoover Institution Press, 1967.
Hartmann, M. "Aus der neuren osmanischen Dichtung," *M.S.O.S.* 19 (1916), 124-79; 20 (1917), 88-149.
Häsänov, H. I. "Birinji dünya muharibäsi illärindä Azärbayjan ijtimai fikrindä panislamizmä va panturkizmä garshï mubarizä." *A.N.Az.S.S.R., Izvestiia, Ser.Ob.N.*, no. 2 (1962), 89-99.
Häsänzadä, T. (ed.), *Äkinchi, 1875-1877: Tam mätin*. Baku: Azärbayjan Dövlet Näshriyyati, 1979.
Hasmahmetli, H. "Ismail-bey Gasprinski'ye ait bir hatira." *A.Y.B.* 2 (1933), 149-53.
Heyd, U. *Language Reform in Modern Turkey*. Jerusalem: Israel Oriental Society, 1954.
Foundations of Turkish Nationalism: The Life and Teachings of Ziya Gökalp. London: Luzac, 1950.
Homayounpour, P. *L'affaire d'Azerbaidjan*. Lausanne: Payot, 1967.
Hostler, Ch. W. *Turkism and the Soviets: The Turks of the World and Their Political Objectives*. London: Allen & Unwin, 1954.
Hourani, A. *The Arabic Thought in the Liberal Age, 1798-1939*. London: Oxford University Press, 1970.
Hovannisian, R.G. "The Allies and Armenia." *Armenian Review* 17 (Winter 1964), 20-39.

Armenia on the Road to Independence, 1918. Berkeley, University of California Press, 1969.
"The Armeno-Azerbaijani Conflict over Mountainous Karabagh, 1918–1919." *Armenian Review* 24 (Summer 1971), 3–24.
"Caucasian Armenia between Imperial and Soviet Rule: The Interlude of National Independence." In Suny, R. G. (ed.), *Transcausasia: Nationalism and Social Change*. Ann Arbor: University of Michigan, 1983, pp. 45–68.
The Republic of Armenia: The First Year, 1918–1919. Berkeley: University of California Press, 1971.
"Armenia and the Caucasus in the Genesis of the Soviet-Turkish Entente." *I.J.M.E.S.*, 4, no. 2 (1973), 129–47.
Huseynov, S. "Äkinchi gäzetinin izahlï bibliografisi. *A. N. Az. S. S. R, Izvestiia, Ser.Ob.N.* no. 9 (1959), 81–92.
XIX äsrin ikinji yaïsïndaAzärbayjan tarikhshunaslïghï. Baku, 1967.
Huseynzadä, A. "M. F. Akhundovun tarikhä dair mulahizalari." *A. Az. S. S. R., Izvestiia, Ser.Ob.N.*, no. 1 (1958), 41–53.
Iakhia-zade, S. M. "K voprosu o strukture i tematike gazety Ekinchi." *A.N.Az.S.S.R., Doklady*. no. 7 (1956), 325–29.
Ibragimbeilil,Kh. M. *Rossia i Azerbaidzhan v pervoi treti XIX veka*. Moscow: Nauka, 1969.
Ibragimov, D. *Feodal'nye gosudarstva na territorii Azerbaidzhana XV veka*. Baku: Azerbaidzhanskii Gosudarstvennyi Pedag. Institut, 1962.
Ibragimov, Z. *Revoliutsiia 1905–1907 gg. v Azerbaidzhane*. Baku: Azgosizdat, 1955.
Ibrahimov, M. *Böyük demokrat*. Baku: Elm Näshriyyati, 1957.
Ibrahimov, T. A. *Iran Kommunist Partiyasïnïn yaranmasï*. Baku, 1963.
Imart, G. "Un intellectuel azerbaidjanais face à la revolution de 1917: Samad Aga Agamaly-oglu." *Cahiers du monde russe et sovietique* (1967), 528–59.
Ioannisian, A. R. *Prisoedinenie Zakavkaz'ia k Rossii i mezhdunarodnye otnosheniia v nachale XIX stoletiia*. Erivan: Izd-vo Akademiia Nauk Armianskoi S.S.R., 1958.
Ischanian, B. *Nationaler Bestand berufmässige Gruppierung und Gliederung der kaukasischen Völker*. Berlin: G. J. Goschen, 1914.
Iskenderov, M. S. *Iz istorii bor'by Kommunisticheskoi Partii Azerbaidzhana za pobedu sovetskoi vlasti*. Baku: Azgosizdat, 1958.
Ismailov, M. "Ob uchasti azerbaidzhantsev v riadakh russkikh voisk v russko-iranskikh i russko-turetskikh voinakh pervoi treti XIX veka." *A.N.Az.S.S.R., Trudy* 11 (1957), 5–20.
Ismailov, M. A. "Gosudarstvennye krest'iane Azerbaidzhana v kontse XIX veka." *A.N.Az.S.S.R., Trudy* 11 (1957), 111–56.
Ismayilov, M. "Äzärbayjanin neft sanäesinda ijaradarligh sisteminin läghv edilmäsinä dair." *A.N.Az.S.S.R., Trudy* 2 (1952), 75–104.
Ismayilov, M. A. *XX äsrin ävvälärindä Azärbayjanïn känd täsarrufati*. Baku: Elm, 1960.
Israfil-bey. "Azerbaycan ordusu hakkında." *Azeri Türk*, no. 9 (1928), 20–3.

Ivanov, M. S. *Iranskaia revoliutsiia 1905–1911 gg.* Baku: IMO, 1957.
"Novye materialy o sotsial-demokraticheskoi gruppe v Tabrize v 1908 godu." *Problemy vostokovedeniia*, no. 5 (1959), 179–83.
"Iz zapisok barona (v posledstvii grafa) M. A. Korfa." *Russkaia starina* 101 (1899), 25–58.
Jahanqirov, M. *Azärbayjan milli ädäbi dilinin täshäkkulu.* Baku: Elm Näshriyyäti, 1978.
Jäschke, G. "28 Mayistan 27 Nisana kadar." *Kurtuluş*, no. 19 (1936), 543–7; no. 20 (1936), 21–5.
"Entwurf zu einem Frieden und Freundschaftsvertrag zwischen dem Osmanischen Reich und der Föderativen Transkaukasischen Republik." *W.I.* 22, nos. 3–4 (1941), 170–4.
"Die republik Aserbeidschan: Geschichtskalender." *W.I.* 23, no. 1–2 (1941), 55–69.
"Der Turanismus der Jungtürken." *W.I.* 23, nos. 1–2 (1941), 1–54.
"Der türkisch-aserbaidschanisch Freundschaftsvertrag vom 4 Juni 1918." *Vorderasien. Studien zur Auslankunde*, no. 1 (1944).
"Beiträge zum türkischen Freiheitskampf." *W.I.*, 5 (1958), 1–64.
"La role du communisme dans les relations russo-turque." *Orient* 7, no. 26 (1963), 31–44.
Kadishev, A. B. *Interventsiia i grazhdanskaia voina v Zakavkaz'e.* Moscow: Voennoe Izd-vo, 1960.
Karabekir, K. *Istklâl harbimiz.* Istanbul: Türkiye Yayınevi, 1960.
Karaev, A. G. *Iz nedavnogo proshlogo.* Baku: Bakinskii rabochii, 1926.
Kasimov, K. "K istorii azerbaidzhanskogo teatra." *A.N.Az.S.S.R., Doklady* 6, no. 6 (1955), 422–44.
Kasravi, A. *Tarikhi-hijdah sala-yi Azarbayjan ya dastan-i mashrut dar Iran.* 6 vols. Tehran, 1313–20/1934–41.
Kasumov, M. M. "G. Zardabi – vydaiushchiisia azerbaidzhanskoi prosvetitel." *A.N.Az.S.S.R., Trudy* 8 (1955), 136–78.
"Gasan bek Zardabi – pitomets Moskovskogo Universiteta Az.G.U." *Uchenye zapiski*, no. 8 (1955), 30–43.
Katkov, G. *The Kornilov Affair: Kerensky and the Break-up of the Russian Army.* London: Longmans, 1980.
Keddie, N. *An Islamic Response to Imperialism: Political and Religious Writings of Sayyid Jamal ad-Din "al-Afghani,"* Berkeley: University of California Press, 1968.
Sayyid Jamal ad-Din "al-Afghani": A Political Biography. Berkeley: University of California Press, 1972.
Keykurun, N. "Türk Ademi Merkeziyet Fırkasının faaliyeti ve Musavat Partisiyle birleşmesi." *Musavat Bülteni* 4 (1962), 19–21.
Azerbaycan istiklâl mücadelesinin hatıraları. Istanbul: Azerbaycan Gençlik Derneği, 1964.
Kaukasielli. *Der Kaukasus im Weltkrieg.* Weimar: Verlag Gustav Kiepenheuer, 1916.
Kazemzadeh, F. *The Struggle for Transcaucasia (1917–1921).* New York: Philosophical Library, 1951.

Bibliography 237

Russia and Britain in Persia, 1864–1914. New Haven: Yale University Press, 1968.
"Russian Penetration of the Caucasus." In Hunczak, T. (ed.), *Russian Imperialism from Ivan the Great to the Revolution.* New Brunswick, N.J.: Rutgers University Press, 1974, pp. 239–63.
Kaziev, M. *"Zhizn' i revoliutsionnaia deiatel'nost' Meshadi Azizbekova.* Baku: Izd-vo Iunost', 1956.
Khachapuridze, G. *Bol'sheviki Gruzii v boiakh za pobedu sovetskoi vlasti.* Moscow, 1951.
Keenan, E. L. "Remarques sur l'histoire du movement revolutionnaire à Bakou (1904–1905)." *Cahiers du monde russe et sovietique* 3 (1962), 224–60.
Kheifets, S. Ia. "Zakavkaz'e v pervuiu polovinu 1918 goda i Zakavkazskii Seim." *Byloe,* no. 21 (1923), 298–310.
Khudadov, V. "Sovremennyi Azerbaidzhan." *Novyi vostok* 3 (1923), 156–61.
Kiazimov, M. "Tema Azerbaidzhana v tvorchestvie Abulkasema Lakhuti." *A.N.Az.S.S.R., Izvestiia, Ser.Lit.Iaz.Issk.,* no. 2 (1982), 47–51.
Kirimli, C.S.A. "Ismaiil-bey Gasprinski." *A.Y.B.,* 2 (1933), 156–61.
Kirov, S. M. *Rechi i stat'i.* 2 vols. Moscow: Gosudarstvennoe Sots-Ekonomicheskoe Izd-vo, 1937.
"K istorii musul'manskogo obrazovatel'nogo dvizheniia v Rossii v XIX i XX stoletiakh." *M.I.* 2, no. 5 (1913), 302–31.
Kliashtorna, V. "Zhurnal Molla Näsraddin i persidskaia politicheskaia satira perioda revoliutsii 1905–1911 godov." *A.N.S.S.R., Institut Vostovedeniia, Kratkie soobshcheniia* 27, no. 10 (1958), 31–41.
Klimovich, L. *Islam v tsarskoi Rossii.* Moscow: Izd-vo Bezbozhnik, 1936.
Köchärli, F. b. *Sechilmish äsärläri.* Baku: Elm Näshriyyati, 1963.
Köchärli, F. K. *Nariman Narimanov.* Baku: Iz-vo A.N.Az.S.S.R., 1965.
Kommunisticheskaia Partiia Azerbaidzhana, Institut Istorii Partii. *Aktivnye bortsy za sovetskuiu vlast'v Azerbaidzhane.* Baku, 1957.
Istoriia Kommunisticheskoi Partii Azerbaidzhana. Baku, 1958.
Korganoff, G. *La participation des Armeniens à la guerre mondiale sur le front du Caucase, 1914–1918.* Paris: Massis. 1927.
Kovalevski, P. I. *Zavoevanie Kavkaza Rossiei.* St. Petersburg, n.d.
Kozlov, V. I. *Natsional'nosti S.S.S.R. Etnodemograficheskii obzor.* Moscow: "Finansy i statistika," 1982.
Kuliev, D. "M. F. Akhundov i azerbaidzhanskii iazyk." *A.N.Az.S.S.R., Azerbaidzhanskii Filial, Izvestiia,* no. 6 (1938), 179–92.
Kuliev, M. *Vragi oktiabria v Azerbaidzhane.* Baku: Azgiz, 1927.
Kuran, A. B. *Inkılâp tarihimiz ve Ittihad ve Terakki.* Istanbul, 1948.
Kurat, A. N. *Türkiye ve Rusya: XVIII yüzyıl sonundan kurtuluş savaşına kadar türk–rus ilişikleri.* Ankara Üniversitesi Yayınları, 1970.
Kurtulan, E. "Türk ordusunun Azerbaycanda kalması meselesi," *Azerbaycn,* nos. 4–6 (1963), 13–17.
"Azerbaycan ordu teşkilâtı." *Azerbaycan,* nos. 7–9, (1964), 13–16.
Kushner, D. *The Rise of Turkish Nationalism, 1876–1908.* London: Cass, 1977.

"K voprosu o panislamizme." *M.I.* 2, no. 1 (1913), 1-12.
La Chesnais, P.G. *Les peuples de la Transcaucasie pendant la guerre et devant la paix.* Paris, 1921.
Landau, J. M. *Pan-Turkism in Turkey: A Study of Irredentism.* London: Hurst, 1981.
Lang, D. M. *The Last Years of the Georgian Monarchy, 1685-1832.* New York: Columbia University Press, 1957.
A Modern History of Soviet Georgia. New York: Grove Press, 1962.
Lenczowski, G. *Russia and the West in Iran: A Study in Great Powers Rivalry, 1918-1948.* Ithaca, N.Y.: Cornell University Press, 1968.
Levend, A.S. *Türk dilinde gelişme ve sadeleşme safhaları.* Ankara: Turk Tarih Kurumu Yayınları, 1949.
Lazzerini, E. "Ismail bey Gasprinski and Muslim Modernism in Russia." Ph.D. dissertation, University of Washington, 1973.
Leviator, V. N. *Ocherki po istorii Azerbaidzhana v XVIII veke.* Baku: 1948.
Lewis, B. *The Emergence of Modern Turkey.* London: Oxford University Press, 1968.
Libaridian, G. J. "Revolution and Liberation in the 1892 and 1907 Programs of the Dashnaktsutiun." In Suny, R. G. (ed.), *Transcausasia: Nationalism and Social Change.* Ann Arbor: University of Michigan, 1983, pp. 185-96.
Lisichkin, S. M. *Ocherki po istorii razvitiia otechestvennoi neftianoi promyshlennosti.* Moscow: Gostoptekhizdat, 1954.
Ludshuveit, E. F. *Turtsiia v gody pervoi mirovoi voiny.* Moscow: Izd-vo Moskovskogo Universiteta, 1966.
L'vov, A. "1905 god v Baku (Kratkii obzor)." *Novyi vostok,* nos. 13-14, (1925), 132-57.
Mädätov, I. *1905-ji ildä Bakï proletariatïnïn ingilabi tä'til häräkätï tarikhindän.* Baku: Azärbayjan Dövlat Näshriyyäti, 1965.
Makharadze, F. *Ocherki revoliutsionnogo dvizheniia v Zakavkaz'e.* Tiflis, 1927.
Mamedov, Sh. *Mirovozzrenie M. F. Akhundova.* Moscow: Izd-vo Moskovskogo Universiteta, 1962.
Mammäd Jäfär. *Azärbayjanda romantizm.* Baku: Izd-vo A.N.Az.S.S.R., 1966.
Mammädov, K. *A. Hagverdiyev.* Baku, 1955.
"Burzhua akhlaghïnï ifsha edän pyes." *A.N.Az.S.S.R., Izvestiia, Ser.Ob.N.,* (1962), no. 3, 71-81.
Näjäf bäy Väzirov. Baku: Izd-vo A. N. Az. S. S. R., 1963.
Mammädov, M. "A. Hagverdiyevin yaradïjïlïghïnda din va mövhumat aleyhinä mübarizä mäsäläri." *A.N.Az.S.S.R., Izvestiia, Ser.Ob.N.,* no. 3 (1962), 89-99.
J. Mammadguluzadä din va mövhumat aleyhinä. Baku: Elm, 1962.
Mammädov, V. *Nariman Narimanov.* Baku, 1957.
Mammädzadä, H. R. "M. F. Akhundov vä XIX-nju äsr Iran maarifchiläri."*A.N.Az.S.S.R., Izvestiia, Ser.Ob.N.,* no. 10 (1962), 25-37.
Martirovsov, A. U. "Novye materialy o sotsial-demokraticheskom dvi-

zhenii v Irane v 1905–1911 godakh." *Narody Azii i Afriki*, no. 2 (1973), 116–22.

Mende, G. v. *Der nationale Kampf der Russlandstürken: Ein Beitrag zur nationalen Frage in der Sovjetunion.* Berlin: Weidman, 1936.

Mikayïlov, N. M. "Milli mäsälädä marksizm-lenininizm ideyalarï ughrunda Azärbayjan bolshevik mätbuatïnïn mübarazäsi (1905–1910 illär)." *A.N.Az.S.S.R., Izvestiia, Ser.Ob.N.*, no. 1 (1963), 21–31.

"Milli Azerbaycan Cumhuriyetinin onbeş yıllığı." *A.Y.B.* 2 (1933), 193–5.

Mil'man, A. S. *Politicheskii stroi Azerbaidzhana v XIX–nachale XX vekov.* Baku: Azerneshr, 1966.

Minasian, O. "Vneshnaia politika zakavkazskoi kontrevoliutsii v pervoi polovine 1918 goda." *Istorik-marksist*, no. 6 (1938), 53–86.

Mirahmädov, A. "XIX äsrdä Azärbayjan mädäniyyäti." *A.N.Az.S.S.R., Trudy* 6 (1955), 56–106.

"Molla Näsraddin zhurnalïnïn yayïlmasï vä tä'siri haggïnda." *A.N.Az.S.S.R., Izvestiia, Ser.Ob.N.*, (1958), no. 1, 65–76.

Mirza-Bala, M. *Azerbaycan Misak-i Milli: 28 Mayis istiklal beyannamesinin tahlili.* Istanbul: Istikbal Matbaasi, 1927.

"Milli hars hakkında." *Azeri Türk*, no. 3–4 (1928).

"Takvim nasıl yazılıyor? (27 Nisan istilasi munasebetile)." *Kurtuluş*, no. 18 (1936), 514–17.

Milli Azerbaycan hareketi: Milli Azerbaycan Musavat Halk Firkasının tarihi. Berlin: Fïrka Divani, 1938.

Mochalov, V. D. *Krest'ianskoe khoziaistvo v Zakavkaz'e v kontse XIX veka.* Moscow: Izd-vo A.N.S.S.S.R., 1958.

Mühlman, C. *Das deutsch-türkische Waffenbündniss im Weltkrieg.* Leipzig: Koehler & Amelan, 1940.

Muhtar, A. "Hayes Turkes? Ermeniler tarafından yapılan Türk katliamin 60-nci yıldönümü münasebetile." *T.K.* 3, no. 32 (1965), 529–35.

Musayev, M. A. "XIX äsrin birinji otuz illärda Bakï shähärinin tijarät alagalari tarikhindän." *A.N.Az.S.S.R., Izvestiia, Ser.Ob.N.*, no. 5 (1961), 15–27.

XIX äsrin sonlarïnda Bakï shähärinin tijaräti (1883–1900-ju illär). Baku: Elm, 1972.

XX äsrin ävvällärindä Bakï shähärinin tijaräti (1900–1917-ji illär). Baku: Elm, 1975.

Muslih, F. "The Life and Work of Agaoğlu Ahmet." *A.R.* 38 (1942), 177–8.

Nalbandian, L. *The Armenian Revolutionary Movement: The Development of Armenian Political Parties through the Nineteenth Century.* Berkeley: University of California Press, 1963.

Narimanov, N. *Stat'i i pis'ma.* Moscow, 1925.

Sechilmish äsärläri. Baku: Elm, 1973.

Näjäfov. Kh. S. *Aghamalïoghlunun ijtimai-siyasi va ateist qörüshläri.* Baku, 1968.

Nikuradse, S. *Kaukasien.* Munich: Hoheneichen-Verlag, 1942.

Nollau, G., and Wiehe, H. J. *Russia's South Flank*. New York, 1963.
Novikov, A. "Zapiski gorodskogo golovy." *Obrazovanie*, nos. 9, 10–12 (1904).
Novosel'tsev, A. P. "Goroda Azerbaidzhana i Vostochnoi Armenii v XVII–XVIII vv." *Istoriia S.S.S.R.*, 3, no. 1 (1959), 87–100.
Novruzov, Sh. "XX äsrin ilk Azärbayjan gäzeti Shärg-i rus." In A.N.Az.S.S.R., *Materialy nauchno-teoreticheskoi konferentsii molodykh uchenykh*. Baku, 1967, pp. 66–8.
Nuh-Oğlu, V. "27 Nisan." *Kurtuluş*, no. 18 (1936), 505–6.
Ordubadi, M. S. *Dumanlï Tabriz*. Baku, 1964.
Orujov, G. A. "1905-ji ildä Azärbayjanda zemstvo kampanyasï." *A.N.Az.S.S.R., Izvestiia, Ser.Ist.Fil.Pr.*, no. 1 (1966), 31–9.
"Pamiati 26 bakinskikh komissarov." *Krasnyi arkhiv*, nos. 4–5 (89–90) (1938), 3–29.
"Pantiurkizm v Rossii." *M.I.* 2, no. 1 (1913), 13–30.
Pavlovich, M., and Iranski, S. *Persiia v bor'be za nezavisimost'*. Moscow, 1925.
Pazhitnov, K. A. *Ocherki po istorii bakinskoi neftedobyvaiushchei promyshlennosti*. Moscow and Leningrad: Gospottekhizdat, 1940.
Pchelin, N. *Krest'ianskii vopros pri Musavate*. Baku: Azgnin, 1931.
"Pervaia musul'manskaia gazeta na Kavkaze." *M.I.* 2, no. 12 (1913), 882–7.
Petrushevski, I. P. "Persidskie ofitsial'nye dokumenty kak istochnik dlia istorii feodal'nykh otnoshenii v Azerbaidzhane i Armenii." *Problemy istochnikovedeniia* 3 (1940), 5–44.
Ocherki po istorii feodal'nykh otnoshenii v Azerbaidzhane i Armenii v XVI–nachalo XIX vv. Leningrad, 1949.
Pichkian, G. "Kapitalisticheskoe razvitie neftianoi promyshlennosti v Azerbaidzhane." In Zakavkazskii Kommunisticheski Universitet, *Istoriia klasovoi bor'by v Zakavkazii*. Tiflis, 1930, pp. 71–122.
Pipes, R., *The Formation of the Soviet Union: Communism and Nationalism, 1917–1923*. Rev. ed. Cambridge: Harvard University Press, 1964.
Pomiankowski, J. *Der Zusammenbruch des ottomanischen Reiches*, Zurich: Almathea Verlag, 1928.
Popov, A. "Iz epokhi angliiskoi interventsii v Zakavkaz'e." *Proletarskaia revoliutsiia*, nos. 6–7 (18–19), (1923), 223–74.
"Revoliutsiia v Baku, (ocherk pervyi)." *Byloe*, no. 22 (1923), 278–312.
"Iz istorii revoliutsii v Vostochnom Zakavkaz'e." *Proletarskaia revoliutsiia*, no. 5 *(28)*, (1924), 13–35.
"Popytki zakavkazskikh musul'man reformirovat' svoiu azbuku." *M.I.* 2, no. 12 (1913), 831–44.
Potto, V. *Pervye dobrovol'tsy Karabaga*. Tiflis, 1902.
"Pravila o merakh k obrazovanniu naseliaiushchikh Rossiu inorodtsev." *M.I.* 2, no. 4 (1913), 264–70.
Qöyushov, Z. B. *Azärbayjan maarifchilerinin etik qörüshläri XIX äsrin ikinji yarïsï*. Baku, 1960.
Raevski, A. *Angliiskie "druz'ia" i musavatskie "patrioty."* Baku, 1927.

Bibliography

Angliiskaia interventsiia i musavatskoe pravitel'stvo. Iz istorii interventsii i kontrrevoliutsii v Zakavkaz'e. Baku: Krasnyi Vostok, 1927.
Partiia Musavat i ee kontrrevoliutsionna rabota. Baku: 1929.
Bol'sheviki i mensheviki v Baku v 1904–1905 godakh. Baku: Azgnin, 1930.
Musavatskoe pravitel'stvo na versal'skoi konferentsii: Doneseniia predsedatelia azerbaidzhanskoi musavatskoi delegtsii. Baku, 1930.
Rafili, M. "Bor'ba M. F. Akhundova za opublikovanie svoikh filosofsko-politicheskikh 'Pisem.' " *A.N.Az.S.S.R., Azerbaidzhanskii Filial, Izvestiia*, no. 6 (1938), 163–76.
Nariman Narimanov – vydaiushchiisia revoliutsioner i pisatel' Baku, 1956. *Akhundov*. Moscow: Molodaia Gvardiia, 1959.
Ramazani, R. K. *The Foreign Policy of Iran: A Developing Nation in World Affairs, 1500–1941*. Charlottesville: University of Virginia Press, 1966.
Ramsaur, E. E. *The Young Turks: Prelude to the Revolution of 1908*. Princeton: Princeton University Press, 1957.
Räsulzadä, M. A. *See* Resulzade, M. E.
Ratgauzer, Ia. A. *Revoliutsiia i grazhdanskaia voina v Baku, 1917–1918*. Baku: Krasnyi Vostok, 1927.
Bor'ba za sovetskii Azerbaidzhan: K istorii aprel'skogo perevorota. Baku, 1928.
Ravasani, S. *Sowjetrepublik Gilan: Die sozialistische Bewegung in Iran sei Ende des 19 Jhdt. bis 1922*. Berlin: Basis-Verlag, 1973.
Refik, S. "Azeri halk edebiyatında Deli Ali destanı." *A.Y.B.*, 2 (1933), 163–6.
Resuloğlu, M. A. "Musavat Partisinin kuruluşu." *Milli Azerbaycan Musavat Partisi Bülteni*, no. 4 (1962), 9–14.
Resulzade, M. E. *Azerbaycan Cumhuriyeti*. Istanbul: 1339/1923.
"Kafkasya Türkleri." *Türk yılı* (1928), 474–522.
O pantiurkizme v sviazi z kavkazskoi problemoi. Paris, 1930.
"Azeri edebiyatında Sabir." *A.Y.B.* 3 (1934), 334–40.
"Milli Azerbaycan hareketinin karakteri." *A.Y.B.* 3 (1934), 163–6.
"Literatura Azerbajdżanu." *Wschòd-Orient* 2 (1936), 63–70.
Das Problem Aserbaidschans. Berlin: Kurtulusch-Verlag, 1938.
Azerbaycan kültür gelenekleri. Ankara, 1949.
Reychman, J. "Pol'sko-azerbaidzhanskie literaturnye otnosheniia v XIX veke." *A.N.Az.S.S.R., Izvestiia, Ser.Ob.N.*, no. 2 (1963), 109–12.
Rhinelander, L. H. "Russia's Imperial Policy: The Administration of the Caucasus in the First Half of the Nineteenth Century." *Canadian Slavonic Papers* 17 (1975), 218–35.
"Viceroy Vorontsov's Administration of the Caucasus." In Suny, R. G. (ed.), *Transcausasia: Nationalism and Social Change*. Ann Arbor: University of Michigan, 1983, pp. 87–108.
Rozhkova, M. K. *Ekonomicheskaia politika tsarskogo pravitel'stva na Srednem Vostoke vo vtoroi chetvert'i XIX veka i russkaia burzhuaziia*. Moscow: Izd-vo AN.S.S.R., 1949.
Rustambekov, Sh. "Iz pechal'nogo proshlogo." *Kavkaz*, no. 7–9 (19–20) (1935), 7–11.

Rustambeyli, S. "27 Nisan hatırası." *A.Y.B.*, 2 (1933), 176–80.
Rüştü, K. "Büyük harpte Baku yollarında 5-nci piyade fırkası." *Askeri mecmua* (1934), 1–49.
Rybakov, S. "Novometodisty i starometodisty v russkom musul'manstve." *M.I.* 2 (1913), 852–73.
Sadykhzade, R. M. "Iz istorii proniknoveniia angliiskogo kapitala v neftianuiu promyshlennost' Azerbaidzhana." *A.N.Az.S.S.R., Izvestiia, Ser.Ob.N.*, no. 4 (1956), 25–35.
Samedov, V. Iu. *Raspostranenie marksizma-leninizma v Azerbaidzhane.* 2 vols. Elm, 1962–66.
Şapolyo, E. B. *Ziya Gökalp, Ittihad ve Terakki ve meşrutiyet tarihi.* Istanbul, 1954.
Sarkisian, E. K. *Ekspansionistskaia politika Osmanskoi Imperii v Zakavkaz'e nakanune i v gody pervoi mirovoi voiny.* Erivan: Izd-vo A.N. Armianskoi S.S.R., 1962.
Sef, S. E. *Kak bol'sheviki prishli k vlasti v 1917–1918 gg. v bakinskom raione.* Baku, 1927.
——— *Bor'ba za oktiabr' v Zakavkaz'i.* Tiflis, 1932.
Seidov, A. *Azärbayjanda pedagozhi fikrinin inkishafi tarikhindän.* Baku: Maarif, 1968.
Seidzade, D. B. *Iz istorii azerbaidzhanskoi burzhuazii v nachale XX veka.* Baku: Elm, 1978.
Seid-Zade, A. A. "K pedagogicheskoi deiatel'nosti Seid Azima Shirvani." *A.Az.S.S.R., Trudy* 9 (1956), 307–19.
Selek, S. *Milli mücadele. Anadolu ihtilâli.* Istanbul, 1963.
Semenov, Iu. F. "Zakavkazskaia Respublika." *Vozrozhdenie* (Paris), (1949), 121–39.
Seydahmet, C. *Gaspirali Ismail bey.* Istanbul, 1934.
Sharif, A. A. "50 let so dnia osnovania zhurnala Molla Nasraddin." *A.N.Az.S.S.R., Institut Vostokovedeniia, Kratkie soobshcheniia* 27 (1958), 25–37.
Shafir, Ia. *Ocherki gruzinskoi zhirondy.* Moscow, 1925.
Shakhbazi, T. "Istoriia tiurskoi rabochei pechati." *Iz proshlogo* (Baku), (1923), 134–42.
Shaumian, Stepan. *Izbrannye proizvedeniia.* Moscow, 1957.
Shaumian, Suren. *Bakinskaia Kommuna.* Baku, 1927.
Shirvani, S. Ä. *Äsärlär.* 3 vols. Baku: Elm, 1967–74.
Shoitov, A. M. "Rol' M. F. Akhundova v razvitii persidskoi progressivnoi literatury." *A.N.S.S.S.R., Institut Vostokovedeniia, Kratkie soobshcheniia* 9 (1953), 58–65.
Simonovich, V. *Neft i neftianaia promyshlennost'.* St. Petersburg, 1884.
Smirnov, N. A. *Politika Rossii na Kavkaze v XVI-XIX vekakh.* Moscow: Izd-vo Sotsial'no-Ekonomicheskoi Literatury, 1958.
——— *Miuridizm na Kavkaze.* Moscow: Izd-vo A.N.Az.S.S.R., 1963.
"Sotsial'naia sushchnost' musavatizma." In *Pervaia vsesoiuznaia konferentsiia istorikov-marksistov, Trudy.* Moscow: Kommunisticheskaia Akademiia, 1930, pp. 501–20.

Startsev, G. E. *Bakinskaia neftianaia promyshlennost': Istoriko-statisticheskii ocherk*. Baku, 1901.
Strigunov, I. V. "Bakï proletariatinin täshäkkülü mäsäläsinä dair." *A.N.Az.S.S.R., Trudy* 10 (1955), 42–77.
Sultanlï, A. *Azärbayjan dramaturqiyasïnin inkishafi tarikhindän*. Baku: Azärbayjan Dövlät Näshriyyäti, 1964.
Sumbatzade, A. S. "Razvitie kapitalizma v Rossii i ego vliiane na ekonomiku Azerbaidzhana vo vtoroi polovine XIX veka." In *A.N.Az.S.S.R., Institut Istorii i Filosofii, Prisoedinenie Azerbaidzhana k Rossii i ego progressivnye posledstviia v oblasti ekonomiki i kul'tury*. Baku: Izd-vo A.N.Az.S.S.R., 1955.
"K vosprosu o kharaktere razvitiia promyshlennego kapitalizma v Azerbaidzhane vo vtoroi polovine XIX veka." In *10 let Akademii Nauk AzS.S.R.*, Baku: Izd-vo A.N.Az.S.S.R, 1957, pp. 623–34.
Sel'skoe khoziaistvo Azerbaidzhana v XIX veke. Baku, 1958.
Kubinskoe vosstanie 1837 g. Baku: Izd-vo A.N.S.S.R., 1961.
Promyshlennost' Azerbaidzhana v XIX veke. Baku, 1964.
(ed) *Qörkämli ingilabchï Sattarkhan*. Baku: Azernashr, 1972.
Sümer, F. "Azerbaycanın türkleşmesi tarihine umumi bir bakış." *T.T.K., Belleten* 21, no. 83 (1957), 429–47.
Suny, R. G. *The Baku Commune, 1917–1918: Class and Nationality in the Russian Revolution*. Princeton: Princeton University Press, 1972.
(ed.) *Transcaucasia: Nationalism and Social Change*. Ann Arbor: University of Michigan, 1983.
"Nationalism and Social Class in the Russian Revolution: The Cases of Baku and Tiflis." In Suny, R. G. (ed.), *Transcausasia: Nationalism and Social Change*. Ann Arbor: University of Michigan, 1983, pp. 239–58.
Swietochowski, T. "The Himmät Party: Socialism and the Nationality Question in Russian Azerbaijan, 1904–1920." *Cahiers du monde russe et sovietique* 19 (1978), 119–42.
"National Consciousness and Political Orientations in Russian Azerbayjan, 1905–1920." In Suny, R. G. (ed.), *Transcausasia: Nationalism and Social Change*. Ann Arbor: University of Michigan, 1983, pp. 209–38.
Tagieva, Sh. A. "Tebrizskoe vosstanie 1920 g." *A.N.Az.S.S.R., Trudy* 7 (1955), 89–134.
Natsional'no osvoboditel'noe dvizhenie v iranskom Azerbaidzhane v 1917–1920 gg. Baku: Izd-vo A.N.Az.S.S.R., 1956.
Tahir-Zadeh, B. K. *Qiyam-i Azarbaijan dar inqilab-i mashrutiyat*. Tehran: Eqbal, 1334.
Tahirzadä, N. A. "XIX-nju äsrin 30–50-ji illärda Azärbayjanda mäktäblär haggïnda." *A.N.Az.S.S.R., Izvestiia, Ser.Ob.N.*, no. 11 (1961), 43–59.
Tairzade, N. A. "K istorii sozdaniia uchebnykh posobii po azerbaidzhanskomu iazyku dlia russkikh uchebnykh zavedenii Zakavkazia v 30–50 godakh XIX veka." *A.N.Az.S.S.R., Iavestiia, Ser.Ob.N.*, no. 2 (1963), 39–54.

"Chislennost' i sostav uchashchikhsia russkikh uchebnykh zavedenii Azerbaidzhana v 40-50 gg. XIX veka." *A.N.Az.S.S.R., Izvestiia, Ser.Ob.N.*, no. 1 (1964), 43-56.

"K uchastiiu studentov moskovskogo universiteta v revoliutsionnom dvizhenii Rossi v kontse 60-kh godov XIX veka." *A.N.Az.S.S.R., Izvestiia, Ser.Ob.n.*, no. 4 (1964), 27-43.

Talibov, A. "Milli müstemläka mäsäläsi haggïnda marksizm-leninizm näzäriyesinin S. M. Äfändiyev täräfindän mudafiä edilmäsi va tablighi." *A.N.Az.S.S.R., Izvestiia, Ser.Ob.N.*, no. 10 (1961), 3-14.

Tansel, F. "Arab harflerinin ıslahı ve degiştirilmesi hakkında ilk teşebbüsler ve neticeleri." *T.T.K. Belleten*, no. 66 (1953), 224-49.

Taqizadeh, S. H. "The Background of the Constitutional Movement in Azerbaijan: Document." *M.E.J.* 14, no. 4 (1960), 456-65.

Ter Minassian, A. "Nationalisme et socialisme dans le mouvement revolutionnaire arménien (1887-1912)." In Suny, R. G. (ed.), *Transcausasia: Nationalism and Social Change*. Ann Arbor: University of Michigan, 1983, pp. 141-84.

Tevetoğlu, F. *Türkiyede sosyalist ve kommunist faaliyetler, 1910-1960*. Ankara, 1967.

Ömer Naci, Istanbul: Milli Eğitim Basimevi, 1971.

Tokarzhevski, E. *Iz istorii inostrannoi interventsii i grazhdanskoi voiny v Azerbaidzhane*. Baku, 1957.

Tria, V. *Kavkazskie sotsial-demokraty v persidskoi revoliutsii*. Paris: Izd-vo Sotsialdemokrat, 1910.

Trumpener, U. *Germany and the Ottoman Empire, 1914-1918*. Princeton: Princeton University Press, 1968.

Tsereteli, I. *Separation de la Transcaucasie de la Russie et independence de la Georgie: Discours prononcé à la Diete Transcaucasienne*. Paris: Chaix, 1919.

Tunaya, T. Z. *Türkiyede siyasi partiler, 1859-1952*. Istanbul, 1952.

Islamcilik cereyanı: Ikinci meşrutiyetin siyasi hayatı boyunca gelişmesi ve bugüne bıraktığı meseleler. Istanbul: Baha Matbbasi, 1962.

Ullman, R. H. *Anglo-Soviet Relations, 1917-1922: Britain and the Russian Civil War, November 1918-February 1920*, Princeton: Princeton University Press, 1968.

Validi, A. Z. "Türklerde hars buhrani." *Türk Yurdu* (1924), 501-42.

Validov, D. *Ocherki istorii obrazovannosti i literatury Tatar*. Moscow: Gosudarstvennoe Izdatel'stvo, 1923.

Vambery, A. "The Turks in Persia and the Caucasus." *Asiatic Quarterly Review* (1866), 165-79.

La Turquie d'aujourd'hui et avant quarante ans. Paris, 1898.

Western Culture in Eastern Lands, New York, 1906.

Vezirov, M.G.b. "O tatarskikh shkolakh." *S.M.O.M.P.K.*, part 2 (1890), 1-6.

Villari, L. *The Fire and Sword in the Caucassus*. London: Allen & Unwin, 1906.

Vishnegradova, A. "Revoliutsionnoe dvizhenie v persidskom Azerbaidzhane." *Novyi Vostok* 2 (1922), 249-55.

Bibliography

Walker, C. J. *Armenia: The Survival of a Nation*, New York: St. Martin's Press, 1980.
Wheeler-Bennet, J. W. *Brest-Litovsk: The Forgotten Peace*. London: Macmillan, 1939.
Widerszal, L. *Sprawy kaukaskie w polityce europejskiej*. Warsaw, 1934.
Wimbusch, S. E. "Divided Azerbaijan: Nation Building, Assimilation, and Mobilization between Three States." In McCagg, W. O., Jr., and Silver, B. D. (eds.), *Soviet Asian Ethnic Frontiers*. New York: Praeger, 1980, pp. 61–81.
Yacoub-Mir, *Le problème du Caucase*. Paris: Librairie Orientale et Americaine, 1933.
Yashar, G. *Azärbayjan ädäbiyyätïndä fajia zhanri*. Baku: Izd-vo A.Az.S.S.R., 1965.
Yurtsever, A. V. *Mirza Fethali Ahundzadenin hayatı ve eserleri*. Ankara: Azerbaycan Kultur Derneği yayınları, 1950.
Azerbaycan dram edebiyati. Ankara: Azerbaycan Kültür Derneği yayınları, 1951.
Zabih, S. *The Communist Movement in Iran*. Berkeley: University of California Press, 1966.
Zakharov, A. "Narodnoe obuchenie u zakavkazskikh Tatar." *S.M.O.M.P.K.*, part 2 (1890), 7–51.
Zärdabi, H. b., *Sechilmish äsärläri*. Baku: Azärbayjan Dövlat Näshriyyäti, 1964.
Zarevand, *Turtsiia i panturanism*. Paris, 1930.
United and Independent Turania. Leiden: E. J. Brill, 1971.
Zenkovsky, S. *Pan-Turkism and Islam in Russia*. Cambridge: Harvard University Press, 1960.
Zeynalov, A. R. "Käshkül zhurnalï vä gäzetini näshri tarikhindän." *A.N.Az.S.S.R., Izvestiia, Ser.Ob.N.*, no. 11 (1959), 75–89.
"Ziya gäzetinin näshri tarikhina geidlär." *A.N.Az.S.S.R., Doklady* 16, no. 5 (1960), 519–22.
Käshküldä badii ädäbiyyät. Baku: Elm, 1978.
Zeynalov, N. *Azärbayjan mätbuati tarikhi*. Baku, 1974.
Ziatkhan, A. *Aperçue sur l'histoire, la litterature, et la politique de l'Azerbaidjan*. Baku, 1919.
Zürrer, W. "Deutschland und die Entwicklung Nordkaukasiens im Jahre 1918." *Jahrbücher für Geschichte Ost Europas* 26 (1978), 31–59.

NEWSPAPERS

Äkinchi (Baku), 1875–1877.
Füyuzat (Baku), 1906–1907.
Irshad (Baku), 1906–1907.
Kaspiy (Baku), 1892–1917.
Käshkül (Tiflis), 1884–1891.
Molla Näsr al-din (Tiflis), 1906–1913.

Shälälä (Baku), 1912.
Sharq-i rus (Tiflis), 1903-1904.
Täräqqi (Baku), 1909.
Tarjuman (Bakhchisarai), 1893-1907.
Ziya (Tiflis), 1879-1881.

Index

Abashidze, Kita, Prince, 85
Abbas Mirza, 5
Abdulhamid II, Sultan (1876–1909), 33, 34, 70
Abilov, Ibrahim, M. (1881–1923), 55, 88, 165, 185
Ädalät: and constituent congress of AzCP(B), 171; formation of, 87; and Himmät, 166, 167, 170, 171; and Khiabani, 158; in Muslim Socialist Bureau, 119
Adäm-i Märkaziyyät, Türk Firqasï: and agrarian question, 100; formation of, 86; and Musavat, 90; and Muslim Congress of the Caucasus, 89; unification with Musavat, 93
Äfändiyev, Hafiz, 189, 190
Äfändiyev, Sultan Majid, 52, 55, 136, 168, 173
Aghamalïoghlï, Samäd, Agha (1867–1930), 88, 165, 182, 185
Aghayev, Ahmäd bäy, (Agaoğlu), 35, 57, 58, 70, 76, 141, 154; as adviser to Nuri Pasha, 131; in Committee for Defense of Rights of Muslim Turco-Tatars in Russia, 83; on intercommunal violence, 44; on nationalism and socialism, 58
Aghazadä, Hasan, Dr., 44, 86, 93, 111, 185
Agrarian reform, 19, 146; Adäm-i Märkaziyyät and, 93; First Congress of Musavat and, 100; Right and Left Musavat on, 146–7; Second Congress and, 173
Ahrar party, 145, 181
Ajars, 77, 78, 79, 81, 82,

Akchuraoghlu (Akchurin, Akçuraoğlu), Yusuf, 48, 71, 206 n37
Akhalkalak, 126
Akhaltsik, 7, 126
Akhundov, Ruhullah, A. (1897–1938), 167, 171
Akhundzadä (Akhundov), Mirza Fath ʿAli, 24–7; and alphabet reform, 24, 201 n75; and Azerbaijani literary revival, 25–7; on learning Russian, 30; and theatre, 27, 201 n74
Äkinchi, Baku newspaper, 28–9; and Azerbaijani language, 28; and Russo–Ottoman war, 29; *see also* Zärdabi, Hasan bäy
Äkinchi, Muslim Left SR organization, 118–19, 166–7
al-Afghani, Sayyid Jamal al-din, 34, 68, 75; *see also* Pan-Islamism
Alekseev-Mekhtiev, 106
Alexander I, tsar of Russia, 4
Alexander III, tsar of Russia, 15
Alexandropol, 126
Aliyev, Ashum, 165
Allied Supreme Council, 156, 159; recognition of Azerbaijani Republic, 174
All-Russian Muslim Congresses, *see* Congress, All-Russian Muslim
Anatolia, 160, 161, 162, 181
Andranik, Ozanian, General, 112, 143
Ankara, 178, 179
Apsheron Peninsula, 21, 133
Araxes River, 4, 32, 64, 66, 132, 187
Ardahan, 78, 113, 122

248 Index

Armenia, Republic of: and dispute over Borchalu, 159; and fighting in Nakhichevan, 159; and regional cooperation, 158–9; and resistance to Communist takeover, 186; and territorial claims at Versailles, 155; and treaty with Turkey, 130
Armenia, Turkish (Eastern Anatolia), 43, 79, 121
Armenian–Muslim antagonism, 39–46, 114–17, 139
Armenian National Corps, 112
Armenian *oblast'*, 7
Armenians: in Baku, 21; immigration from Persia and Turkey, 7, 198 n2; in Mountainous Karabagh, 14, 143; 1915 deportations of, 79; in oil industry, 22; Russian orientation of, 43, 114, 153
Army of Islam, 130, 133, 134
Ashurbäkov, Isa, 57, 89
Assadullayev, 22
Astrakhan, 139, 151, 168
Autonomy, 46, 50, 86; cultural, 46, 91; territorial, 91–2, 98–9, 102, 104, 111, 119, 168, 192–3
Avetisian, Z., Colonel, 137
Azadistan, 186–7; *see also* Azerbaijan, Persian
Azärijilär, 61–2, 75
Azerbaijan: early history of, 1–2, 93, 153, 197 n1, 2, 3; and Ottoman war plans 77–8; 99, 114, 121; partition of, 7; with Russian market, 19, 200 n57; strategic role of, 10; and territorial consolidation, 17
Azerbaijan, Persian, 64–5, 74, 79; Khiabani's uprising in, 186–7; in Ottoman war plans, 80–1, 139; *see also* Tabriz, Tabriz province
Azerbaijan, Republic of: and proclamation of independence, 129; recognition of by the Allies, 159; and relations with Persia, 155–8; and relations with Turkey, 160–4; territorial claims of, 155; and treaty with Georgia, 153; and treaty with Turkey, 130
Azerbaijani cabinets, 145, 219 n64
Azerbaijani Communist Party (Bolsheviks) (AzCP[B]), formation of, 171–2, 173, 175, 181

Azerbaijani ("Azeri") language, 1, 26, 28, 29, 60–3, 148, 202 n89
Azerbaijani National Council, 129, 131–2, 144–5
Azerbaijani Sovnarkom, formation of, 183
Azerbaijanis: and Baku Sovnarkom, 119; and elections to Constituent Assembly, 108; and independence of Transcaucasia, 122; and Oghusianism, 72, 78; in Russia's Muslim movement, 48–9; in World War, 83
Azrevkom (Azerbaijani Revolutionary Committee), 181, 182, 183–4, 185
Äzizbäkov, Mäshadi, A., 52, 55, 58, 136, 139

Baikov, A., 114
Baku: city, growth of, 18, 21–3, 200 n64, 66; *guberniia*, 14, 16, 39, 80; khanate, 2, 4, 5; labor unrest in, 37–8; "oil revolution" in, 20–3; population of, 21; *uezd*, 108, 134
Baku, Armenian National council, 118, 138
Baku-Batum rail line, 124, 143
Baku Committee of RSDWP, 53; *see also* RSDWP
Baku Committee of RCP(B), 166–7, 170–1
Baku Commune, 135, 137
Baku *duma*, 15, 23, 46, 103, 118
Baku: "March Days," 1918, 114–17; September 1918 massacre, 139
Baku Soviet, 85, 95, 101–2, 104, 108, 113, 135, 137
Baku Sovnarkom, 118, 119, 133, 135–7
Baku, twenty-six Commissars, 139
Baku University, 148
Balkan wars, 72, 74
Bashkiria, 91, 99
Batum, 120, 122–4, 130; peace conference of, 125–7
Bicherakhov, Lazar, Colonel, 137, 141, 152–3
Birlik, Organization of Volga Tatars, 87
Bolsheviks, *see also* RSDWP, RCP(B): and Baku bureau, 166; in the Baku *duma*, 103; in the Baku So-

viet, 95, 101–2; in the Baku Sovnarkom, 118; and the Caucasus nationality problem, 98; elections of to the Constituent Assembly, 107–8; and national strife in Baku, 101, 114–19; opposed to inviting Dunsterville, 137; rapprochement of with the Dashnakists, 114
Brest-Litovsk Peace Conference, 111; Treaty, 122, 123, 127
British occupation of Azerbaijan, see Great Britain
Browne, E.G., 68
Buniatzadä, Dadash, H., 55, 87, 167, 181

Catherine II, Empress of Russia, 3
Caucasus front, 78, 81, 83, 107, 112–13, 139
Chernishevski, A.I., 12–13
Chicherin, G., notes to Azerbaijani government, 174–5
Chkheidze, Nikolai, 105
Chkhenkeli Akakii, L., 85, 106, 121, 123–7
Congress, All-Russian Muslim, First, 1905, 48–9; All-Russian Muslim First, 1917, 91–2; Second, 1906, 49; Third, 1906, 49
Communists, Azerbaijani, 167, 170, 172, 179–81
Committee of Union and Progress (CUP), 70, 71, 76–7, 79, 119, 140; see also Young Turks
Constituent Assembly, of Russia, 84, 96, 105–6, 107; dispersed, 108; elections to, 107
Crimea, 91
Crimean Tatars, 99

Daghestan, 8, 9, 77, 80, 89, 121, 125, 146; anti-Soviet uprisings in, 190; and occupation by Denikin, 153; and occupation by Ottomans, 139; occupation by Red Army, 177; see also Ghazavat; Murids
Däli 'Ali, 42
Dashnaktsutiun, 37; in the Azerbaijani Parliament, 145; and the Baku Sovnarkom, 136; and Bolsheviks, 114–15; and conflict with the Tsardom, 40–1; 1914 congress of, 77;

and elections to the Baku Soviet, 102, 104; formation and goals of, 40; intercommunal violence in, 42; and "March Days, 116–17; in the Seim, 110; and Tabriz uprising, 68
December Rescript of 1846, 13, 199 n44; see also, Vorontsov
Democratic Party of Azerbaijan (Persian), 132, 186
Democratic Party of Iran, 69
Denikin, Anton, I., General, 152–3, 159, 169, 174
Derbent, khanate, 2; military province, 11; guberniia, 14
Difai: and Adem-i-Märkaziyyät; and Dashnaktsutiun, 45; formation of, 43–4; intercommunal violence in, 44; and the Ottoman League of Decentralization, 45
Dondukov, A.M., Prince, Governor General of the Caucasus, 15
Dunsterville, Lionel, C., General, 137–8, 141
Dzhaparidze, Prokofii, A., 54, 103–4, 116, 118, 135, 139

Eastern Transcaucasia, 14, 17, 19, 22, 50, 85, 142–3; see also Azerbaijan
Education, Muslim, 29–32, 203 n93, 94; see also Mäktäbs
Eleventh (Red) Army, 177–9, 180, 186, 188
Elizavetpol, 4; guberniia, 14, 19, 42, 80, 142, 155
Enver Pasha, Vice-Generalissimo, 77–8, 80, 119, 161; and Transcaucasia, 130–36; see also Caucasus front
Enzeli, 141–2, 187
Erivan, khanate, 2, 6, 7; guberniia, 15, 19, 41, 113, 149
Ermolov, A.P., General, 6, 10
Erzerum, 7, 79, 83
Erzincan, 79, 120; armistice of, 119, 120
Etchmiadzin, 5, 42; uezd, 126

Fath ʿAli Khan of Kuba, 3, 197 n5
Fath ʿAli, Shah of Persia, 5
Füyuzat: literary review, 56, 59, 60;

Index

literature, 59; Ottomanization of language; *see also* Turkism

Gabba, M. Colonel, 157
Galiev, Sultan, 170
Gallipoli operation, 78
Ganja, 16, 18, 41, 147; and *Difai*, 44–5; khanates in, 2, 4, 10; siege of, 1804, 4, 198 n11; as temporary capital of Azerbaijan, 130; uprising in, 188
Ganja Muslim National Council, 113
Garayev (Karaev), Ali, Haidar, 88, 165, 166, 172, 181, 183
Gasprinski (Gaspir Ali), Ismail bey, 31–2, 48–9, 71, 203 n98; *see also* Turkism; Jadidism
Gayret (clandestine association), 45
Gegechkori, Evgenii, Chairman of Zakavkom, 106
Geokchai, 133
Georgia, Republic of: and defense pact with Azerbaijan, 153; and dispute with Armenia, 159; and resistance to the Eleventh Army, 186; and Transcaucasian conferences, 158–9; and treaty with Soviet Russia, 186; and treaty with Turkey, 130
Georgian *guberniia*, 4
Georgian Legion, 77
Georgian Mensheviks, 68, 88, 105, 120; and break-up of Transcaucasian Federation, 127–8; and convocation of Seim, 109–11; elections to the Constituent Assembly of, 107–8; manifesto to to the Russian proletariat of, 124
Georgian separatists, 77
Georgian Social Federalists, 45, 107, 110
Germany: and disagreements with Turkey, 124–8; and German-Ottoman Protocol, 140; and German–Soviet talks on Baku, 134; interest in Baku oil of, 133; and supplement to the Brest-Litovsk Treaty, 134; and support for the Ottoman seizure of Baku, 138
Ghazavat, 8; *see also* Shamil
Gilan, province of, 69, 186–7
Gilani, Sayyid Ashraf, 66

Golitsyn, Grigorii, Prince, 40
Gotsinski, Imam, Najm ul-din, 113, 117, 190
Great Britain: and Anglo-Persian Treaty of 1919, 157–8; and the Baku oil, 143–4, 157; and decision to evacuate Transcaucasia, 156–7; and embargo on oil shipments to Russia, 151; and the issue of Mountainous Karabagh, 142–3; and martial law in Baku, 143; and mediation between Transcaucasian Republics and Denikin, 152–3; occupation of Azerbaijan by, 141–4; support for the Azerbaijani government by, 143; and views on the Muslims of Transcaucasia, 143; *see also* Thomson, Karabagh, Transcaucasia
Griboedov, A.S., 17
Gulistan Treaty of, 5, 198 n14

Hahn, P.V., Baron, administrative reforms of, 12–13, 199 n39
Haidarov, Ibrahim, 108, 125, 131
Hajibäyli, Jäyhun, 154
Hajibäyli, Uzeir, 56
Hajinski, Mammäd, Hasan, 52, 55, 85, 122, 124; attempts to form a cabinet by, 178, 180, 198 n48; in the Batum Conference, 125; in Himmät, 51; and the "placate Russia" policy, 175–6
Halil bey, Ottoman delegate at Batum Conference, 126
Halil bey (then Halil Pasha, Kut), Ottoman general, 78, 138, 162; in last days of Republic, 179–80; support for Hajinski by, 178
Haqvärdiyev, ʿAbd ul-Rahman, 27–8, 50
Häyat, Baku newspaper, 56, 59
Himmät, clandestine publication, 52
Himmät, 35, 51–6, 86–8; Bolshevik and Menshevik factions, 165, 167; relationship to RSDWP, 53
Himmät-Bolsheviks, 88, 114, 158
Himmät-Left, Azerbaijani Communist Party, 165, 167; cells of absorbed by the RCP(B); and formation of AzCP(B), 171; and is-

Index 251

sue of party name, 168; and the Kraikom, 170
Himmät-Mensheviks (Social Democratic Workers Party, Himmät), 88, 109, 166–9, 178, 185; and elections to Constituent Assembly, 107; in the Parliament, 145; and withdrawal from the National Council, 131
Himmätists: as commissars in the Baku Commune, 136; in Tabriz uprising of 1908, 68
Hinchak Party, 37, 54
Huseynov, Mirza Davud, 165–6, 170, 172, 181, 183
Huseynzadä, 'Ali bäy, 33, 59, 70; debate on literary language, 62; on the future of Transcaucasia, 120; on national identity, 59–60

Ibrahimov, Rashid, 48
Ijtima-i Amiyyun, Persian Social-Democratic organization, 66, 87
Ilminski, N.I., Russian educator, 63
Irakli II, king of Kakheti-Kartli, 3, 198 n8
Irshad, Baku newspaper, 56; and Persian revolution, 66
Ismail, Khan of Sheki, 11
Israfilbäkov, Movsum, N., 87, 136, 168
Italy, mandate over Transcaucasia, 156
Ittifaq (Union of Russian Muslims), 48, 51; in the State Duma, 50; transformed into a party, 49; *see also* Kadets
Ittihad (Rusyada Musulmanlïq-Ittihad), 88, 123, 174, 178, 181, 185; and elections to Constituent Assembly, 107–8; formation and ideology of, 88–9; and rapprochement with the Bolsheviks, 174
Ittihad-i Osmaniyye, clandestine Ottoman organization, 33
Iudenich, N.N., General, 78

Jadidism, 30–1; *see also* Education; Gasprinski; Turkism
Jafarov, Muhammad; in the Azerbaijani cabinet, 132; in the Ozakom, 85; in the State Duma, 81; in the Zakavkom, 106

Jar–Belokan, 4, 9, 10
Jävad Khan of Ganja, 4
Jihad, 76
Julfa, 126

Kachaznuni, Hovannes, 111, 125
Kadets (Constitutional–Democratic Party), 49–50, 110, 142
Kankrin, T.E., Russian finance minister, 10, 17, 200 n53
Karabagh: khanate, 2, 4, 5; province, 147
Karabagh, Mountainous, 130, 142–3, 159, 173; Armenian uprising in, 160, 177; anti-Soviet uprising in, 189
Karabäkov, Karabäy, 70, 89
Karabekir, Kâzim Pasha, Ottoman General, 161–2, 179
Kars, 78, 120, 122, 124
Käshkül, literary magazine, 29, 32
Kaspiy, Baku newspaper, 35, 46, 83
Katkov, M.N., 31
Kavbiuro (Caucasian Bureau of RCP[B]), 177, 184
Kazakh, 6
Kazimzadä, Abbas, 52, 73
Kedabek, copper mines, 18
Kemal Pasha, Mustafa, 160–4; on "Caucasus barrier," 163; on the future of Transcaucasian republics, 162; and letter to Lenin, 179; and rivalry with the Young Turks, 160; and Soviet Russia, 161
Kemalist Turks, in Baku, 177–9
Kerenski, regime of, 99, 109, 112; *see also* Provisional Government
Khasmammädov, Alakpär, 50–1
Khasmammädov, brothers, 44, 86
Khiabani, Shaikh Muhammad, 132, 158; seizure of power in Tabriz by, 186–7; *see also* Azerbaijan, Persian; Tabriz
Khoiski, Aslan Khan, 80–1; *see also* Enver Pasha; Caucasus front
Khoiski, Fath 'Ali Khan, 50–1, 83, 86, 122, 140, 151–2, 185; as Azerbaijani prime minister, 130, 144–5; as chairman of the Baku *duma*, 103; Chicherin's diplomatic offensive and, 175, 178; as foreign min-

ister, 173; opposition to Hajinski by, 178
Kirghzia, 91, 99
Kirov, S.M., 170, 177
Köchärli, Färidun bäy, 62
Köprüköy, battle of, 78
Kornilov, L.G., General 94–5
Kraikom (Regional Committee of the RCP(B)), 167, 170–1, 173, 177
Kress von Kressenstein, Colonel, 127
Kuba, khanate, 2, 5; town, 18
Kuchuk Khan, Mirza, 137, 187
Kutaisov, P.I., Senator, 11
Kvantaliani, E., A., 179

Lazes, 78–9
League of Nations, 146, 154, 156
Lenin, Vladimir I.: advice to Shaumian on Baku situation, 115; and Declaration of the Rights of Peoples of Russia, 100; dispersing of the Constituent Assembly by, 108; ending of hostilities against Georgia by, 186; endorsement of German mediation on Baku by, 133; on federalism, 108–9; on importance of seizing Baku, 184; and Manifesto to the Toiling Muslims of Russia and the Orient, 101; on national self-determination, 97–8
Lenkoran, 3, 11, 115, 190
Levandovski, Commander of the Eleventh Army, 180, 183
Lezghians, 7, 39, 53, 113
Liakhov, General, 79
Liberalism, Azerbaijani, 35, 46–51; in All-Russian Muslim movement, 47–9; in 1905 Petition, 47; *see also* All-Russian Muslim Congresses; Kadets; Muslim Constitutional Party
Lordkipanidze, Ivane, 124
Lossov, von, Otto, General, 126–7

Mahal, 2, 11, 12
Mahdi Qulu, khan of Karabagh, 11
Makhmändiarov, Samäd bäy, General, 76, 148–9, 173, 176, 181
Mäkhtiyev, Yaqub Mir, 111, 122
Mäktäbs, 29–30, 35; *see also* Education; Jadidism
Malik-Aslanov, Khudad, 106, 125

Mammäd Jäfär, 66
Manifesto to the Toiling Muslims of Russia and the Orient, 101; *see also* Lenin
Mdivani, Budu, 117
Mechnikov, P.I., Senator, 11
Mehmed VI, Ottoman Sultan (1918–1922), 160
Mesopotamia, front, 79, 112, 127
Mikoyan, Anastas, I., 166, 171
Military government, 11, 12, 199 n33
Millät, 32, 60, 62, 75, 191
Mir Hasan, khan of Talysh, 9
Molla Näsr al-din, satirical-literary journal, 57; language debate, 61–2; and Persian revolution, 66
Mudros Armistice, 140
Mugan Steppe: intercommunal clashes in, 113, 115, 149; Russian settlers in, 16
Muhammad ʿAli, shah of Persia, 67, 69
Municipal reform, 16, 200 n50
Murids, 8, 9
Musabäkov, H.M., 168, 181
Musavat, 74, 85–6, 89, 96, 98, 102, 108, 113; and Adäm-i Märkaziyyät, 90, 93; and agrarian reform, 93, 100, 173, 146–7; and elections to the Baku Soviet, 95, 104; and elections to Constituent Assembly, 107; First Congress and 1917 program of, 99–100; formation of and program, 73; in "Kornilov Days," 94–5; and Left or Baku Musavatists, 93–4; 100, 106, 147, 173, 185; 1918 party program of, 146; in Parliament, 145; and party representation in Seim, 109–10; and rapprochement with Bolsheviks, 96–103, 106, 108; and Räsulzadä, 74; and Right or Ganja Musavatists, 93–4, 100, 104, 147, 173, 180; Second Congress of, 173; and strain in relations with Bolsheviks, 104, 113–15
Müsävi, Mir Fattah (1891–1919), 165, 167
Muslim–Armenian clashes, 41, 113, 116–17, 139, 205 n15; Aghayev on, 44; Ziyatkhanov's declaration on, 44; *see also* Armenian–Muslim antagonism

Index

Muslim Constitutional Party, 50; see also Kadets
Muslim National Corps, 112, 130, 148
Muslim Socialist Bloc, 107–8, 131, 145
Mustafa, khan of Shirvan, 11
Muzaffar al-din, shah of Persia, 65, 67

Nadir, shah of Persia, 2, 3, 198 n7
Naji, Ömer, 77; as Inspector General for Azerbaijan and East Caucasus, 79; and seizure of Tabriz, 79; see also Azerbaijan, Persian
Nakashidze, V.I., Prince, Governor of Baku, 40–1, 43
Nakhichevan khanate, 2, 6, 7, 10, 11, 41, 159
Naqshbandi order, 8
Nargin Island, 83, 188
Narimanov, Nariman, N., 52, 55, 87, 88, 149; in the Baku Sovnarkom, 118; in the Commissariat for Foreign Affairs, 168–9; and Constituent Assembly, 109; as head of Azrevkom, 181; as head of Azerbaijani Sovnarkom, 183; and letter to Ussubaköv, 194; in the "March Days," 116–17; as organizer of Ijtima-i amiyyun, 66
Nicholas I, tsar of Russia, 6, 7, 10, 13
Nicholas II, tsar of Russia, 38, 43, 84
Nicholas Nicholaevich, Grand Duke, 82, 84
Nobel brothers, 20, 200 n62
North Caucasus, 120, 126, 127, 130, 177
North Caucasus Mountaineers Republic, 125, 152
Nukha, 5, 18, 19, 22
Nuri Pasha, 140, 161, 189; commander of the Army of Islam, 130; in Azerbaijani politics, 131; as fighter in Daghestan, 161

Oghuz Khan, 70
Oghuzianism, 71, 78
Oil industry, 20–3, 143–4, 149–50, 200 n62, 63; nationalization of, 135; see also Baku
Ordubad, 6, 19, 22

Ordubadi, M.S., Azerbaijani writer, 69
Ordzhonikidze, Grigorii, 177, 180, 184, 186
Ottoman State, 3, 7, 59, 60, 70; and Azerbaijani Republic, 129–41; and Transcaucasia, 119–28; Turkic revival in, 70; World War and Caucasus front, 76–81; see also Caucasus front; Turkey
Ottomanization of Azerbaijani literary language, 29, 31–2, 61–2
Ozakom (Osobyi Zakavkazskii Komitet) 84–5, 90

"Pan-Azerbaijanism," 67–8, 121, 193; sentiments of solidarity in, 157–8; see also Azerbaijan, Persian; Tabriz province
Pan-Islamism, 33–4, 35, 44, 77, 85, 88, 90, 91, 111, 122, 172; see also al-Afghani, Ittihad
Pan-Slavism, 31, 33
Pan-Turkism, 31, 70–1, 90, 93, 146, 172, 192, 193; as a cultural doctrine, 132; and Huseynzadä, 33, 59; and Ziya Gökalp, 70–1; see also Gasprinski; Turkism; Ziya Gökalp
Parliament, Azerbaijani, 144–5; agrarian reform in, 147; Azrevkom's ultimatum to, 181–2; groups in, 145
Paskevich, I.F., General, 6
Pepinov, Ahmäd, 88, 165, 167, 173; see also Himmät-Mensheviks
Persia, 10, 11, 26, 28, 130; Akhundzadä and, 25; and Anglo-Persian Treaty of 1919, 158; and Azerbaijani-Persian treaty, 158; challenge to the Russian conquest, 5–7; proposals for the union of, 157–8; and revolution of 1905–1911, 64–69; suzerainty over Azerbaijan, 2, 3; territorial claims on Azerbaijani Republic in Versailles, 155; in World War, 79–80; see also Azerbaijan, Persian; Qajars; Tabriz
Persian Revolution, 1905–1911, 64–9; see also Aghayev; Azerbaijan Persian; Molla Näsr al-din; Räsulzadä; Tabriz
Persian workers in Baku, 64–5; see also Ädalät; Ijtima-i Amiyyun

Peter the Great, 3, 43
Petrovsk, 96, 113, 116, 137, 176
Provisional Government, 84, 90, 92; Muslim military units in, 112; and the nationality question, 96–7; overthrow of and Musavat, 100; see also Kerenski regime

Qajar, Mirza, Colonel, 188; see also Ganja uprising
Qajars, 5, 65
qavm, 31, 60, 171; qavmiyyet, 191
Quluzadä, Mammäd Jälal, Azerbaijani writer, 61; see also Molla Näsr al-din

RCP(B) (All-Russian Communist Party [Bolsheviks]), 166–7, 170; Politburo's resolution on Himmät and Azerbaijan, 169; resolution on national party organizations, 171; see also Himmät
Ramishvili, Noi, 117, 125
Räsulzadä, Mammäd Amin, 82, 93, 100, 104, 132, 134, 185; in All-Russian Muslim Congress 91–2; on Azrevkom's ultimatum, 181–2; in Himmät, 52–5; and Musavat, 74; in the Parliament, 146; in Persian revolution, 69; on *umma* and *millät*, 75; see also Musavat
Ratgauzer, Ia., 73
Red Army, 133, 137–8, 188–9; see also Eleventh Army
RSDWP (Russian Social Democratic Workers Party), 35, 37, 54–5; April Conference on national self-determination, 97–8; Baku Committee of, 51, 53; Himmät's relation to, 53–4; and split into Bolshevik and Menshevik organizations, 88; see also Bolsheviks
Rusheni, Hasan, 119–20
Russia, Soviet: attack on Georgia by, 186; and Baku problem, summer 1918, 133–4; and diplomatic offensive against Azerbaijan, 174–5; proclamations on nationalities' rights by, 100–1; sovietization of Azerbaijan by, 183–4; see also Lenin, RCP(B); Sovnarkom
Russia, tsarist: and administrative reforms, 10–17; and annexation of Transcaucasia, 3–7; and Azerbaijani cultural–literary revival, 26; economic policies of, 17–20; and Muslim-Armenian strife, 40–1, 42–3; and Persian revolution, 67, 69; in World War, 74–83
Russian National Council, Baku, 142
Russian settlers, 16, 113, 149, 200 n51; see also Mugan Steppe
Russification, 12, 15, 16, 148
Russo-Persian wars, 5–6, 198 n13, 198 n15, 198 n16, 198 n17; see also Qajars
Russo-Ottoman war, 1828–9, 7
Russo-Tatar schools, 24
Rustambäkov, Shafi bäy: in Adäm-i Märkaziyyät, 86; and calls for dictatorship, 180; as Minister of Interior, 176; in Musavat, 93; and opposition to ceding Batum to Turkey, 123

Sabir, Mirza Alakpar, 67, 70
Sabit, Fuad, 161, 178
Sadeq, Mamalek, 66
Safavids, 1, 2, 3
Safikiurdski, Aslan, 108, 117, 140, 185
Sardarov, M., 55, 168
Sarikamish, battle of, 78, 79, 80, 81
Sattar Khan, 67–8, 187
Savage Division, 76, 94, 112–13, 115, 130
Seim, 50, 98, 117; declares war on Turkey, 124; Georgian Mensheviks' proposals for, 109; Musavat's support for, 109; and peace talks, 121–3; proclaims Transcaucasian Federation, 125
Serebrovski, A.P., 184
Shaikh ul-Islamzadä, 122, 132, 165, 178
Shakhtakhtinski, M.A., 50, 61; see also Azärijilär
Shälälä, literary magazine, 57, 62; see also *Yeni lisan*
Shamil, 8–9, 12, 199 n25, 26, 27, 29; see also Daghestan; Murids
Shamkhor massacre, 113
Shari'a, 11, 16, 88, 190
Sharq-i rus, Azerbaijani newspaper,

29, 40, 48, 61; see also Shakhtakhtinski, M.A.
Shaumian, Stepan, 114–15, 135, 137; as Chairman of Baku Soviet, 85, 95, 101–2; as Commissar for the Caucasus, 104; in the "March Days," 116–18; and execution, 139
Shchendrikov brothers, 37
Sheki, khanate, 2, 4, 5, 6, 9, 10
Shemakha, 19, 113, 115; *guberniia*, 14
Shikhlinski, Ali Agha, General, 76, 113, 148, 176, 181
Shirvan, khanate, 2, 4, 5, 6, 9, 10, 11
Shirvani, Haji Sayyid 'Azim, 25, 30
Shiʿa (Shiʿites), 2, 9, 27, 83; anti-Ottoman feelings of, 7, 72; Persian orientation of, 31
Shiʿa–Sunni strife, 7, 8, 25, 191; Aghayev on, 71–2; Pan-Islamism and reconciliation, 34; Shirvani on, 25
Shusha, 5, 41–2, 189; see also Muslim-Armenian clashes
Social Revolutionaries, Party of (SRs), 85; and Left SRs, 102, 104, 135; and Muslim Left SRs; and Right SRs, 102, 104, 105, 135, 138; split in, 102; see also Akinchi
Solomon I, king of Imeretia, 4
Sovnarkom (Soviet Narodnykh Kommissarov), 100, 101, 105, 108–10, 115, 118, 127; see also Lenin; Russia, Soviet
Stalin, Joseph, 54; as Commissar for Nationalities' Affairs, 100–1, 133, 169
State Duma, 84; Azerbaijanis in, 44, 50, 50–1, 81; see also Jafarov, M.; Ziyatkhanov, I.
Sultanov, Hamid, N., 87, 168, 170, 181, 183, 188
Sultanov, Khosrow, 143
Sunnis, 8–9, 27–29, 145, 199 n23; see also Shamil; Shiʿa–Sunni strife

Tabriz, 2, 6, 121, 132, 157, 158; and capture by the Ottomans, 79; and foray by Halil, 80; Khiabani uprising in, 186; Ottoman occupation of 1918, 130; in Persian revolution, 64–9; and uprising of 1908, 68–9

Tabriz province, 64, 68, 80, 130; see also Azerbaijan, Persian
Taghiyev, Ismail, 50
Taghiyev, Zeynal, Abd-ul, 23, 27, 31, 35, 52, 76, 90
Talaat Pasha, Ottoman Grand Vizier, 146
Talysh, khanate, 2, 5, 7, 9, 10, 11
Tanzimat, 27, 59
Täräqqi, Azerbaijani newspaper, 57
Tarjuman, Crimean Tatar newspaper, 31, 47; see also Gasprinski
Teshkilat-i Mahsusa, 80
Theatre in Azerbaijan, rise of, 27
Thomson, W.M., General, 141, 154; on Khoiski and his government, 142, 144; and the problem of Mountainous Karabagh and Zangezur, 143, 159
Tiflis, 24, 43, 80, 88, 105–6, 109, 112, 149, 167, 185–6
Tiflis *guberniia*, 14, 15
Topchibashev (Topchibashi), ʿAli Mardan bäy, 35, 46, 48, 49, 86, 162; as chairman of Second All-Russian Muslim Congress (1906), 49; as head of Azerbaijani delegation in Versailles, 154; as president of Parliament, 146; and proposals for union with Persia, 157, 204 n111; in State Duma, 50
Transcaucasia, 7, 9, 84, 91, 101, 153, 159, 161, 167, 186; administrative reforms in, 10, 12, 14–15; and declaration of independence, 124; and Mudros Armistice, 140; and peace with Turkey, 119–28; and programs for autonomy and unity, 45, 50; Russian economic policies in, 17; Russo-Ottoman rivalry in, 3; secessionism and regional government of, 106–11; in Versailles, 154–7; in World War, 78, 81; see also Seim
Transcaucasian conferences, 158–9
Transcaucasian Federation, 124–8; see also Seim
Transcaucasian Muslims, 32, 51, 76, 82, 89, 129; see also Azerbaijanis
Trebizond peace talks, 121–4
Tsalikov, Ahmed, 91
Tsentrokaspiy dictatorship, 137–8

Index

Tsereteli, Irakli, 105, 123, 128
Tsitsianov, P., General, 4
Turan, 70–1, 76, 140; see also Pan-Turkism, Ziya Gökalp
Türk yurdu, Turkish literary magazine, 71–2, 75
Turkestan, 91–2, 99
Turkey, 3, 5, 7, 29, 33, 40, 42–3, 68, 72, 130, 140, 142; Kemalist Turkey and Azerbaijan, 160–4; see also Ottoman State
Turkic Revolutionary Committee of Social Federalists, 45
Turkism, 35, 88; rise of, 31–2; in Azerbaijan after February 1917, 85; and the 1908 revolution in Turkey, 70–2; promotion by Huseynzadä in Istanbul, 33; rejection of by Ittihad, 88; see also Pan-Turkism; Turan; Ziya Gökalp
Turkish Communist Party in Baku, 178–9
Turkmanchai Treaty, 10, 198 n18
Turkmens, 1, 7, 71

ʿUmma, 34, 73, 88, 91, 191, 193
Ussubäkov (Yusufbäyli), Nasib bäy: assassination of, 185; as Azerbaijani Prime Minister, 146; in Difai, 44; and emigration to Turkey, 70; as founder of Adäm-i Märkaziyyät, 86; and left Musavatists, 173; as Minister of Education of Transcaucasian Federation, 125; resignation of, 178; and second cabinet, 173; as spokesman for goals of Musavat, 121

Väzirov, Hasan, 118, 136, 139; see also Akinchi (organization)
Väzirov, Näjäf bäy, Azerbaijani playwright, 27–8
Vehib Pasha, Ottoman general; and Brest-Litovsk conference, 120; and Erzincan armistice, 119; and evacuation of Batum, Kars, and Ardahan, 122; and peace talks, 124; and violation of armistice, 120
Versailles Peace Conference, 153–6
Volga Tatars, 30, 39, 47, 49, 92, 99; and the Ittifaq, 49; and leadership of the Russian Muslims, 47
Volunteer Army, 152; see also Denikin
Vorontsov, Mikhail S., Prince, 13–14, 24, 26, 199 n43; and December Rescript of 1846, 13, 199 n44
Vorontsov-Dashkov, I.I., Count: on political attitudes of the Muslims, 72; and rapprochement with the Armenians, 42–3; retirement of, 81–2; as Viceroy of the Caucasus, 38; and the zemstvo campaign, 47

Wardrop, Oliver, British High Commissioner, 157
Wilson, Woodrow, U.S. President, 154

Yeni lisan movement, 62, 207 n78
Young Turks, 68, 70, 79, 140, 160–1, 164; see also Committee of Union and Progress

Zakataly, 147, 189
Zakavkom (Zakavkazskii Kommissariat), 106–7, 117, 119–20, 121
Zand dynasty, 2
Zangezur, 143, 155
Zärdabi, Hasan bäy, 29, 30, 32, 202 n88; and Azerbaijani language, 28; and Azerbaijani press; and Azerbaijani theatre, 27; see also Äkinchi
Zemstvos, 16; campaign for, 47, 205 n33
Zeynalov, Zeynal, 50
Zhordania, Noi, 105; declaration in the Seim, 110–11
Ziya Gökalp: on expansionist policy, 120; influence of Huseynzadä on, 33, 59, 203 n103; and Turkism in the Ottoman State, 70–1; see also, Oghuzianism; Pan-Turkism; Turan; Turkism
Ziya-i Kafkasiyyä, Azerbaijani newspaper, 29
Ziyatkhanov, Adil, 157; see also Azerbaijani-Persian treaty; Persia
Ziyatkhanov, Ismail: in Difai, 44; and liberals' petition, 46; see also Muslim–Armenian clashes

Printed in the United Kingdom
by Lightning Source UK Ltd.
101035UKS00001B/103-135

9 780521 522458